DAVID
CROCKETT

Published by J. Reid. New York.

DAVID CROCKETT

· THE LION OF THE WEST ·

MICHAEL WALLIS

W. W. NORTON & COMPANY
New York · London

Frontispiece: Portrait of David Crockett painted by John Gadsby Chapman, Washington, D.C., 1834. (Harry Ransom Humanities Research Center, University of Texas at Austin)

For information about permission to reproduce selections from this book, write to Permissions, W. W. Norton & Company, Inc., 500 Fifth Avenue, New York, NY 10110

For information about special discounts for bulk purchases, please contact W. W. Norton Special Sales at specialsales@wwnorton.com or 800-233-4830

Manufacturing by RR Donnelley, Harrisonburg
Book design by Judith Stagnitto Abbate / Abbate Design
Production manager: Anna Oler

Library of Congress Cataloging-in-Publication Data

Wallis, Michael, 1945–
David Crockett : the Lion of the West / Michael Wallis. — 1st ed.
p. cm.
Includes bibliographical references and index.
ISBN 978-0-393-06758-3 (hardcover)
1. Crockett, Davy, 1786–1836. 2. Pioneers—Tennessee—Biography.
3. Legislators—United States—Biography. 4. United States. Congress. House—Biography.
5. Alamo (San Antonio, Tex.)—Siege, 1836. I. Title.
F436.C95W35 2011
976.8'04092—dc22
[B]
2011000216

W. W. Norton & Company, Inc.
500 Fifth Avenue, New York, N.Y. 10110
www.wwnorton.com

W. W. Norton & Company Ltd.
Castle House, 75/76 Wells Street, London W1T 3QT

1 2 3 4 5 6 7 8 9 0

FOR SUZANNE FITZGERALD WALLIS

FOR NEVER LOSING FAITH IN ME

AND

JOE SWANN, A TRUE SON OF TENNESSEE

CONTENTS

PERSONAL INTRODUCTION

It's hard for anyone born, say, after 1958 to recall the "Davy Crockett" frenzy that swept America in the 1950s. So profound was the cultural inundation that no baby boomer can fail to recall this charismatic American hero's name. Such recognition, to my way of thinking, is a good thing, but the veritable flood of misinformation about Crockett's life that resulted—which I became aware of only later in life, and which in part has motivated me to write this book—created a mythology that continues to this day.

My first exposure to this inimitable American icon came, and I can vividly recall the date, on the frosty night of December 15, 1954, in my hometown of St. Louis. The ABC television network had just aired *Davy Crockett, Indian Fighter*, the first of three episodes produced by Walt Disney for his studio's then new series, which had premiered two months earlier. Called simply *Disneyland* during its first four years, this anthology series, under a variety of other names, including, most commonly, *The Wonderful World of Disney*, was to become one of the longest-running prime-time programs on American television.

I was just nine years old that December evening, but I could have predicted the show's success. I was hooked moments after hearing the theme music, "When You Wish upon a Star," sung by cartoon insect Jiminy Cricket from the soundtrack of the movie *Pinocchio*. Longtime Disney announcer Dick Wesson introduced host Walt Disney and, with some visual assistance from a flittering Tinkerbell, Uncle Walt unleashed the legendary frontier character Davy Crockett from the twelve-inch screen of our 1950 table model RCA Victor television set into our living room, as if from a runaway train.

I was a goner. Within only minutes the larger-than-life Crockett, clad in buckskin and wearing a coonskin cap, had won me over. My fickle nine-year-old heart pounded. The previous summer, at two separate events in a department store parking lot, I had shaken the hand of Hopalong Cassidy and the Cisco Kid, but now they were instantly demoted to lesser status on my list of heroes. Even Stan Musial—"swinging Stan the Man," the legendary St. Louis Cardinal All-Star slugger, whose name was etched in granite at the top of that list—was in jeopardy of being topped.

By the time that first episode ended, the image of Crockett, as portrayed by twenty-nine-year-old Fess Parker, was firmly ensconced in my psyche. I did not even consider staying up for *Strike It Rich* and *I Got a Secret*. I forgot about the promise of fresh snow and the good sledding sure to follow. Instead I headed straight to my room, where I pored over the *World Book Encyclopedia* entry for Crockett, dreaming of the swashbuckler with a proclivity for dangerous behavior, a most commendable quality for any red-blooded American kid.

As I would quickly learn, I was not alone. More than forty million others tuned in to *Disneyland* that Wednesday night. By the time the next episode, *Davy Crockett Goes to Congress*, aired (on January 16, 1955), followed, on February 23, by *Davy Crockett at the Alamo*, I, along with much of the nation—especially the growing ranks of what would later be called the baby boom generation—was swept up by the Crockett frenzy. We wanted more.

And more came in the form of an unprecedented merchandising whirlwind, in which Crockett was commercialized in ways that would have been unthinkable to the man himself. Every kid had to have a coonskin cap like Davy's, and almost overnight the wholesale prices of raccoon pelts soared from twenty-five cents a pound to six dollars, with the sale of at least ten million furry caps. Within only months of the series premiere, more than $100 million was spent on at least three thousand different Crockett items, including pajamas, lunch boxes, underwear, comics, books, moccasins, toothbrushes, games, clothing, toy rifles, sleds, and curtains. The catchy theme song "The Ballad of

Davy Crockett" sold more than four million copies and remained No. 1 on the Top Ten list for thirteen weeks. On May 7, 1955, I proudly wore my coonskin hat when Gisèle MacKenzie sang the top tune of the week on *Your Hit Parade*. Like every one of my pals, I knew the words were true. We sang Crockett's ballad at the top of our lungs as we built forts from old Christmas trees and cardboard boxes, transforming the neighborhood into our own version of Crockett country.

Davy Crockett quickly became our obsession. Until he came into our lives, we had mostly played cowboys and Indians; other times, we went to war as pretend soldiers, using the helmets and canteens our fathers and uncles brought home from the war. The nearby woods where we skinny-dipped in the creek turned into our hunting ground for imaginary ferocious bears like the ones Davy stalked. The dusty hill topped by a stand of oaks on the edge of the playground became our Alamo, and every day we pretended that we were in pitched battle against the forces of Santa Anna. We became Davy Crockett, William Travis, and Jim Bowie, the trio of legendary Alamo heroes. No one wanted to be with the Mexican side, so our enemy, as if borrowing a page from the cold war, was largely invisible. In the end we died anyway, just as our heroes did so long ago, but we knew we would miraculously be resurrected and come back the next day for another round of combat.

The following year, in the summer of 1955, Walt Disney unveiled his fantasy world, Disneyland, in southern California. But our family, eager to introduce me to the historical origins of Davy Crockett, opted not to go west on Route 66 and visit the Magic Kingdom. Instead we headed due south out of St. Louis to the state of Tennessee. Proudly wearing my new coonskin hat, with Mom riding shotgun and Dad at the helm of our dark green 1952 Plymouth—dubbed the Green Dragon—we cruised into real Crockett country.

After crossing the Mississippi River and entering Tennessee, we skirted Reelfoot Lake, studded with cypress trees, not far from the last place that Crockett called home. In Nashville, we saw the regal Capitol and the cavernous Ryman Auditorium, at that time home of the Grand Ole Opry. We paused at the Hermitage, the residence and final resting place of President Andrew Jackson—a Crockett political mentor who was to become his student's chief nemesis.

During those dozen or so days spent traversing my new hero's old stomping grounds, we experienced southern culture—the South that carries on with its own state of mind. We dined on crunchy southern fried chicken, catfish and hush puppies, country ham, biscuits and gravy, and pecan pie. I even recall that we sampled those creamy grits that came on every breakfast plate whether ordered or not. When we tangled with succulent Delta barbecue I pretended it was bear steak. At Chattanooga, near the Tennessee–Georgia line, we obeyed the commands of the signs that seemed to be painted on every barn rooftop—SEE BEAUTIFUL ROCK CITY and SEVEN STATES—from atop Lookout Mountain.

Everywhere we went we also saw flags and decals bearing the Confederacy's stars and bars, as if the Civil War had not ended ninety years before. And, in every town we drove through, life-size stone likenesses of Confederate soldiers stood at ease in the tidy courthouse squares where old men in open-collar white shirts and straw hats sat cross-legged and traded yarns about the past. The tableau seemed endless.

From the car windows I watched harvest hands stooped in the fields, tending cotton that once was king when great plantations flourished. In Memphis, where Elvis was on the verge of stardom, we ate a picnic lunch in a city park near a huge bronze statue of Nathan Bedford Forrest, the planter and slave dealer who became a Confederate general and first imperial wizard of the Ku Klux Klan. To those who recall the South of the midtwentieth century, these icons were both all too familiar and hardly considered invidious.

In that distant summer of 1955, not only throughout the South but well beyond, we saw signs designating which toilets and drinking fountains people could use depending on their skin color. These were images that were likewise familiar and staunchly accepted. Six months after our trip, a bus boycott in Montgomery, Alabama, began after a resolute black seamstress refused to give her bus seat to a white man. But the summer of 1955 was before we knew of Rosa Parks and Martin Luther King Jr., or Medgar Evers and James Meredith.

In fact, nothing could distract me from my infatuation with Davy Crockett. I knew that a vaccine had been found to stem the polio epidemic that panicked every mother in the land, including mine. Although the tirades of a paranoid Joe McCarthy and frequent "duck and cover" drills at school kept much of the nation fearful, life was pretty good for a nine-year-old boy gliding through Davy Crockett's stomping grounds in the Green Dragon.

The highlight of that summer vacation came when we neared the Davy Crockett birthplace, in eastern Tennessee, and the days that followed, in the nearby Smoky Mountains. We checked into a mom-and-pop motel in Gatlinburg, the resort town that billed itself as the "gateway to the Great Smoky Mountains." We hit the pottery and souvenir shops in the nearby town of Pigeon Forge, and I ate my share of taffy and fudge from the sweetshops along Gatlinburg's main drag. In a few years these mountain towns would mushroom in size, thanks to a commercial boom, as Gatlinburg and the Great Smoky Mountains National Park became important tourist destinations. But back then there was no Dollywood, nor were there discount shopping malls, theme parks, and hordes of tourists.

I dipped my bare feet in icy cold Little Pigeon River, rode with my dad on the new ski lift to the top of Crockett Mountain, and saw the first black bears I had ever glimpsed in the wild. I slept in my coonskin hat.

The woman who ran the motel where we stayed told my dad about a good place to gather blackberries, and one morning we walked up the road and found the patch just as she described. In no time we filled a big coffee can to the top and my coonskin hat overflowed with fat juicy berries. Back at the motel the woman generously made a batch of blackberry cobbler that was the best I ever put to my lips. I called it "Crockett Cobbler" and imagined it was just like the kind that my hero ate when he was nine years old. We went to the berry patch again, and when we left to drive back to Missouri, my dad put a couple of empty milk cartons of berries in the ice chest.

All the way home, I gazed out the windows of the Green Dragon and thought about what it must have been like to be Davy Crockett. Now, all these many years later, I still cherish the memories of that trip. I think of it whenever I take out a photograph of my father and me sitting on the living room sofa. He is clowning around and has me hold a napkin to my chin while spoon-feeding me Crockett Cobbler. On my head is my coonskin hat. For the life of me, I cannot remember whatever happened to it.

MICHAEL WALLIS
Tulsa, Oklahoma
May 6, 2010

Author Michael Wallis (in coonskin cap)
eating "Crockett Cobbler" with his father,
Herbert Wallis, St. Louis, Missouri, 1956.
(Wallis Collection)

PREFACE

THIS IS NOT ANOTHER straightforward chronological biography of Davy Crockett, nor is it a regurgitation of the many myths and lies perpetuated about Crockett over the years. Instead this book is for those people interested in learning the truth—or at least as much as can be uncovered—about the historical and fictional Crockett, and how the two often became one. I hope that readers will gain some new historical insight into the man and how he captured the imagination of his generation and later ones as well.

In the course of researching and writing this book, I came to know David Crockett. I scoured all the places he lived and journeyed—from throughout the breadth of his native Tennessee to Washington, D.C., and cities of the northeast and, finally, to Texas, where he spent but a few months before his much mythologized death at the Alamo. I learned about the man's accomplishments and shortcomings, discovering that the Davy Crockett created by Walt Disney in 1954 was definitely not the David Crockett who actually lived, and that much of the distortion of truth about Crockett began in his own lifetime and only increased after his death.

The authentic David Crockett was first and foremost a three-dimensional human being—a person with somewhat exaggerated hopes and well-checked fears, a man who had, as we all do, both good points and bad points. He was somewhat idiosyncratic, possessed of often unusual views, prejudices, and opinions that governed how he chose to live his life. Crockett could be calculating and self-aggrandizing, but also as valiant and, indeed, as resourceful as anyone who roamed the American frontier. As a man, he was both authentic and contrived. He was wise in the ways of the wilderness and most comfortable when deep in the woods on a hunt, yet he also could hold his own in the halls of Congress, a fact that distinguished him from so many other frontiersmen. Remarkably, he enjoyed fraternizing with men of power and prestige in the fancy parlors of Philadelphia and New York. Crockett was, like none other, a nineteenth-century enigma. He fought under Andrew Jackson in the ruinous Indian Wars, only later to become Jackson's bitter foe on the issue of removal of Indian tribes from their homelands. Crockett's contradictions extended beyond politics. He had only a few months of formal education, yet he read Ovid and the Bard. He was neither a buffoon nor a great intellect but a man who was always evolving on the stage of a nation in its adolescence, a pioneer whose inchoate dreams aptly reflected a restless nation with a gaze firmly pointed toward the West.

Perhaps more than anyone of his time, David Crockett was arguably our first celebrity hero, inspiring people of his own time as well as a twentieth-century generation. The man David Crockett may have perished on March 6, 1836, in the final assault on the Alamo, but the mythical Davy Crockett, now an integral part of the American psyche, perhaps more so than any other frontiersman, lives powerfully on. In this way his story then becomes far more than a one-note Walt Disney legend, while his life continues to shed light on the meaning of America's national character.

DAVID CROCKETT

Almanac cover, 1848.
(Photograph by Dorothy Sloan, Dorothy Sloan Rare Books)

PART I

"Kilt Him a B'ar"

AVID CROCKETT BELIEVED in the wind and in the stars. This son of Tennessee could read the sun, the shadows, and the wild clouds full of thunder. He was comfortable amid the thickets and canebrakes, the quagmires, and the mountain balds. He hunted the oak, hickory, maple, and sweet gum forests that had never felt an axe blade. He was familiar with all the smells—the odor of decaying animal flesh, the aroma of the air after a rain, and the pungent smell of the forest. He knew the rivers lined with sycamore, poplar, and willow that breached the mountains through steep-sided gorges with strange-sounding names, many with Indian influences like the Nolichucky, the French Broad, the Pigeon, the Tellico, the Hiwassee, the South Holston, the Watauga, the Coosa, the Obey's, the Wolf, the Elk, and the Obion. He stalked the dimensions of lakes and streams studded with ancient cypress. He learned that dog days arrive not with the heat of August but in early July, when the Dog Star rises and sets with the sun. He carried his compass and maps in his head. He traversed the land when it was lush in the warm times and when it was covered with the frost that Cherokees described as "clouds frozen on the trees."

The wilderness was, indeed, Crockett's cathedral, and as the stress of his political and home life began to wear him down, it was the forest where he took refuge. Even with the debates that continue to rage today about who the real David Crockett was, no one disputes that this was a man who approached nature as a science and hunting as an art and who found excitement in combining the two. Crockett had a calling and was a hunter by trade, relying on black bears just as much to clothe and feed his family as for the rich fodder they provided for stories told around the campfires and when campaigning for political office.

Yet, contrary to "The Ballad of Davy Crockett," the popular tune from the mid-1950s, Crockett did not "kilt him a b'ar when he was only three."[1] For that matter, Crockett was not even "Born on a mountaintop in Tennessee." Indeed, he most likely never signed his name Davy but always David, and only took to wearing the ubiquitous coonskin cap so much identified with him when he thought it would help boost his public image. To uncover the truth about Crockett, one must travel to the land he knew and loved most—the Tennessee that was America's frontier. That was his training ground and the school in which he was to become a legendary student. For the authentic Crockett—the man with only a smattering of formal education—possessed uncanny woods wisdom. From his boyhood in eastern Tennessee to his adult years in the middle of the state and, finally, in western Tennessee, Crockett honed his outdoor skills and applied them to his everyday life.

Over the years, he came to understand his quarry and its ways in almost an existential way. He knew adult male bears, or boars, weighed as much as six hundred pounds and females, or sows, usually weighed no more than four hundred pounds. He learned that black bears could live twenty-five years or more and were solitary except during mating time, and that a cub weighed only about as much as an apple when born but quickly grew on its mother's fat-rich milk. He understood, as his fellow pioneers did, that an angry sow with cubs, just like a "he-bear" when cornered, was a formidable adversary. He never forgot that the only thing predictable about black bears is that they are unpredictable.

Crockett's remarkable woodsmanship saved his life many times. On a moonless January night in the rough country near Reelfoot Lake, in far western Tennessee, Crockett, thirty-nine, soaked to the bone and freezing, found himself locked in combat with a fully grown black bear. "I made a lounge [sic] with my long knife, and fortunately stuck him right through the heart," he later explained in his autobiography.[2] Exhausted from the struggle, he calmed his pack of panting hounds and managed to pull the bear from the crevice in the frozen ground where they had fought. After butchering the animal, he tried to kindle a fire but could find nothing dry enough to burn. His moccasins, buckskin breeches, and hunting shirt were frozen to his numb body and he knew that unless he kept moving he would die.

"So I got up, and hollered a while, and then I would jump up and down with all my might and throw myself into all sorts of motions," Crockett wrote. "But all this wouldn't do; for my blood was now getting cold, and the chills coming all over me. I was so tired, too, that I could hardly walk; but I thought I would do the best I could to save my life, and then, if I died, nobody would be to blame."[3]

He found a stout tree about two feet in diameter without any limbs on it for thirty feet. Crockett locked his arms and legs around the trunk and shinned up the tree until he reached the limbs, and then he slid back down to the ground. "This would make the insides of my legs and arms mighty warm and good," he wrote. "I continued this till daylight in the morning, and how often I clomb [sic] up my tree and slid down I don't know, but I reckon at least a hundred times."[4]

— As the sun rose, Crockett set out to find his camp, where one of his sons and another hunting companion waited. After breakfast they salted all the dressed bear meat and secured it atop a high scaffold. Then they followed the dogs into the thick canebrake on the trail of more bear. By his own count, during that seven-month hunting season spanning 1825–1826, Crockett had killed 105 bears, including 47 in just one month.[5]

Crockett, like the other good hunters of the day, stalked bears by finding tracks fresh enough for dogs to follow and by reading signs. He looked for claw marks or hair on tree bark and checked the freshness of scat to see how long ago the bear had passed through the area. If the scat was dried out and colonized with insects it meant the bear was long gone. Scat also revealed what the bears had eaten. That diet included almost anything: carrion, animal matter, insects, wild honey, snakes, and plenty of vegetation, like squawroot in the spring, berries in the summer, and nuts and acorns in autumn. If the droppings were dark and runny it indicated the bear had eaten meat and might still be around for several days to feed off the carcass.

Savvy hunters were aware of the bears' nonretractable curved claws that allowed them to bring down a deer or a hound with one powerful blow. Bears also used the claws to scramble up trees, especially when they spied wild grapevines or if snarling dogs were in close pursuit. For Crockett, bear hunting with dogs was like no other hunting. He loved the adrenaline rush as he fought for breath and tried to keep up behind a pack of baying hounds on the trail of a bear crashing through the brush. For a seasoned and passionate hunter like Crockett, the chorus of dog howls was sweet music.

Much like the human company he kept, Crockett preferred the company of mongrel hounds to purebred dogs with fancy pedigrees. A few of the names that Crockett supposedly bestowed on his dogs include Soundwell, Old Rattler, Tiger, and Sport. One account suggests that Crockett named his favorite hound Jolar, said to be an ancient Gaelic-Scots word for eagle-eyed.[6] No matter their names, Crockett was known to use stocky crossbred dogs that lived solely to run bears. But while running his hounds and stalking bears remained a constant passion, Crockett also found that his reputation as a fearless hunter brought other dividends. Over the course of his life, Crockett's bear hunting ability became a key ingredient in the manufacture of the populist hypermasculine persona he often used to bolster his public image and political career.

The real Crockett successfully combined his expertise with a rifle and passion for hunting with his trademark homespun humor and masterful storytelling technique. In so doing he was able to rise from the canebrakes to the halls of Congress. The stories he gathered from his adventures as a woodsman became entertainment from the backwoods that made his campaigns original and successful. In thus putting them to use, he became one of the first notable political figures to emerge from the ranks of common men and not the landed gentry.

TWO

BORN ON A
RIVERBANK IN FRANKLIN

ONTRARY TO WHAT has often been implied, mostly by Texans themselves, David Crockett was not a Texan. Crockett remained a Tennessean until his dying day. While he did meet his end during an exploratory trip in the then-Mexican state of Texas, he spent most of his life in Tennessee and more than half of those forty-nine years in the east Tennessee of his birth. Writers frequently have skimmed over Crockett's early life in a rush to get to the period when he achieved celebrity and became well known as a colorful frontier hunter, political figure, and prominent participant in the legendary battle at the Alamo. All too often, Crockett's two months spent in Texas at the end of his life garner more attention than the decades he spent living in Tennessee.

By all appearances, Crockett was well aware of the importance geography played in his life. He never forgot that his east Tennessee frontier roots ran deep and shaped much of his character. An examination of Crockett and his many incarnations, starting with his birth and boyhood, reveals a man who never fully completed his own biographical metamorphoses. He died as a work still very much in progress.

Yet from his first breath, Crockett was a characteristically American product. He squalled into the world on August 17, 1786.[1] It was a

Thursday, and, true to the old rhyme, he was indeed a Thursday's child who had far to go, much like the newly conceived nation in which he grew up. The Revolutionary War had been over for only three years, and a growing number of citizens on life's periphery, especially on the frontier, felt the new American government was mistreating them. Soon after Crockett's birth, insurgent farmers in western Massachusetts, led by Daniel Shays, revolted against local authorities because of high debt and tax burdens.

What we do know reliably is that Crockett was born in a snug frontier log house on the banks of the Nolichucky River, near its confluence with Limestone Creek. The Crocketts resided in the backwoods of what was then known as the State of Franklin, a part of North Carolina that later became Tennessee. John and Rebecca named their newest son David, after the infant's paternal grandfather, massacred nine years earlier, along with his wife and others, by a band of marauding Indian warriors.

One of nine Crockett children, David was the fifth of six sons. His elder brothers were Nathan, William, Aaron, and James Patterson. Brother John was a year younger than David, followed by two sisters, Elizabeth (mostly known as Betsy) and Rebecca.[2]

The identity of the eldest Crockett sibling, always believed to have been a daughter, remained unknown for many years. This mystery was resolved only in July 2008, at a three-day gathering of the Direct Descendants and Kin of David Crockett (DDDC) at Crockett's birthplace on the Nolichucky River. For the first time, indisputable evidence was presented that David's elder sister was Margaret Catharine Crockett. She was born to John and Rebecca Crockett at Womack's Fort, built by Jacob Womack as a refuge from Indian war parties in the northeast corner of what eventually became Tennessee.

Identification of Crockett's long "unknown" sister surprised the organization's members, including Joy Bland, DDDC historian and a fourth great-granddaughter of David Crockett. "I don't have a doubt," Bland replied, when asked if enough evidence existed to authenticate the discovery. "Great descendants are coming from her [Margaret Catharine] and contributing to our history. There is a bible record that proves this."[3] This record was found in the family Bible of Louisa Taylor Lemmons, granddaughter of Margaret Catharine, and was brought to light by Timothy E. Massey, a great-grandson of Margaret Catharine.[4]

In the Bible, a letter written by Louisa Taylor Lemmons spells out the family lineage: "This is what your momma always tole of your mammaw. Your mammaw was Margaret Catharine Crockett then oldest younon of old John Crockett of Limestone Creek. She was borned at a place called Womack's Fort. Her brother was Col. David that all the stories are about."[5]

According to the handwritten letter, the girl was only twelve years old when she was "served out" by her father, John Crockett, to a prominent family residing at Jonesborough—a town established in 1779, only seventeen years before Tennessee was granted statehood. Soon after going to work as a household servant, the girl "got in the motherly way," presumably through the amorous advances of her master. Margaret Catharine was dismissed by her employer's wife, only to be turned away at her own family home by John Crockett, the pregnant girl's uncaring father, who, more than likely, was angry that a convenient source of income had dried up.

It is difficult to imagine the feelings a pregnant girl, still a child herself, must have experienced. Pregnancy and childbirth were life-threatening events, and the infant death rate was high. Without proper care and attention, women and older girls frequently died from traumatic deliveries or a variety of complications. But, beyond the physical and psychological pain, a bound-out servant who turned up pregnant usually was branded as a cunning and seductive Jezebel and was blamed for the dalliance that led to her condition.

A compassionate preacher and his family, living on Limestone Creek, took in the abandoned girl. A short time later, a daughter was born whom Margaret Catharine named Catharine. However, the rigors of childbirth weakened the young mother, and later that same day she died. Her "earthly body was laid to rest . . . at the big oak tree at the

stone fort buring [*sic*] ground." The man who had impregnated Margaret Catharine sent her surviving daughter dolls and candy at Christmas
but never publicly acknowledged that she was his child.[6] It is no surprise
that the Crockett family buried her story.

The practice of parents binding out their children for wages was
nothing new on the Tennessee frontier of the late 1700s. Neither was
the indenturing of neglected or orphaned children, even in larger cities
such as New York, where a four-year-old and a toddler eighteen months
old were bound out to grow up as servants.[7] Legally speaking, children
were the property of parents and had no more standing than livestock.
Fathers not only were considered the titular head of every household but
also ruled both their wives and their offspring. This power was absolute,
and punishment, which followed the stern disciplinary measures spelled
out in the Bible, was severe. As even a well-to-do wife of an antebellum
plantation owner put it, "All married women, all children and girls who
live in their fathers' house are slaves."[8]

Although there is no evidence that David ever knew Margaret Catharine, the boy, too, eventually fell prey to his father's callousness. Before
he reached his adolescence, David was bound out to a stock herder in
order to pay off one of John Crockett's many debts.

In his autobiography, Crockett addresses his humble beginning
in the self-effacing manner he often used when he wrote: "I stood no
chance to become great in any other way than by accident. As my father
was very poor, and living as he did *far back in the back woods*, he had
neither the means nor the opportunity to give me, or any of the rest of
his children, any learning."[9] Crockett failed to mention that, despite his
family's monetary deficits, and unlike many people living on the frontier
of America in the late eighteenth century, his parents were not illiterate.
While they had only a rudimentary education, both John and Rebecca
signed documents with their full names and not their marks.[10]

David's parents always signed their surname as Crockett, but other
people spelled it in a variety of ways, as happened with many family
names in early America. Common variations were *Crocket, Croket,*

Crocit, and *Crokit.* David never spelled his name any other way than Crockett, although at least on one occasion he did admit that the middle *c* and the extra *t* were unnecessary.[11]

Variations of Crockett were not uncommon in Scotland, and by far the greatest number of Crockett families hailed from Coupar Angus, north of the mouth of the Tay River, on the eastern coast of central Scotland, one of the oldest settled areas of the British Isles.[12] For hundreds of years, Moot Hill, not far from Scone Palace, was the site of the coronations of many Scottish kings, including Robert the Bruce. Coupar Angus also was the home of the Picts, an ancient tribe of fierce warriors whose name in Latin translates as "Painted Ones," in reference to the elaborate tattoos that the Picts proudly displayed on their naked bodies. Pict men and women fought side by side in battle, and the Picts were known as the only tribe the Romans could not subdue.[13]

The characteristics of these mysterious people are interesting in light of what is known about David Crockett. For the Picts had a great love of horses and hounds and were known to ride effortlessly in groups of three with only a saddle blanket and snaffle bit. It was said that Picts would whisper commands to their horses, riding as one with the steed as they vanished without a trace into the rugged Highlands. The men were powerfully built, with short legs and barrel chests, and were renowned as extraordinary fighters possessing great physical strength and stamina. It was suggested that the Arthurian knight Lancelot was a Pictish king from Angus, the land of the Crockett clan. According to local tradition, Guinevere, quasi-legendary queen to King Arthur, was a Pictish princess from Sterling Castle who was buried north of Coupar Angus at the town of Meigle.[14]

"Arthurian history is not unlike Crockett history in many respects," explains Crockett historian Joseph Swann. "The size of the legend engulfs its historical subject. It is often a tedious process to extract history from legends that grow up around historical icons like Arthur and Davy. Still these two legends may both have roots in the same small area of land in east-central Scotland."[15]

The Crockett roots eventually spread to Ireland during the early

1600s. That was when members of the clan joined the ranks of the Ulster Scots, or Scots-Irish. This group of Scots and North Britons were encouraged by the ruling English government to migrate on a large scale to Ulster, in Northern Ireland, to help hold lands confiscated from malcontent Irish lords. Although predominantly Celtic Scots, including a lesser number of the Pictish or Gaelic Highland Scots, they differed from the Highland Scots and the native Irish in almost every respect, from religion to language, politics, and customs.[16]

Transplanted to these confiscated lands in the area of Northern Ireland known as Ulster, the predominantly Presbyterian Scots, including members of the Crockett family, brought with them a bitter dislike for the pope and the Roman Catholic Church, a dislike that turned to hatred after a few generations had occupied lands in Ulster. Irish attempts to isolate and eradicate the Scots caused them out of necessity to become more rigid and self-reliant. This created an intense animosity between the transplanted Protestant Scots and the disposed Irish Catholics, which led to the resentment and strife that continued for many years to come.[17]

Finally, the Scots-Irish had their fill of social, religious, political, and especially economic oppression. They boarded ships and moved to America in a mass migration of more than a quarter of a million people during the years 1718 to 1775. They settled in the backcountry of Pennsylvania, since the best land there had long been taken. Among the ranks of the stalwart Scots-Irish who left the North Tyrone–East Donegal area in the early eighteenth century and migrated to America were David Crockett's grandparents.[18] The Crockett family's adventure had only just begun.

THREE

THE CROCKETTS ARRIVE

ESPITE THE BEST EFFORTS of legions of diligent researchers and historians, David Crockett's genealogy has always been confusing. Even identifying which members of Crockett's immediate family were the first to leave Ireland with other Scots-Irish and sail to America is an uncertain proposition.

In his autobiography, David Crockett writes: "My father's name was John Crockett, and he was of Irish descent. He was either born in Ireland or on a passage from that country to America across the Atlantic. He was by profession a farmer, and spent the early part of his life in the state of Pennsylvania."[1]

While many authors have accepted this statement as fact, some respected Crockett scholars disagree and contend that Crockett erred. It was actually David's grandfather, also named David, and sometimes referred to as David the elder to distinguish him from his famous grandson, who was born about 1725 in Ireland, or aboard ship at the time of the migration across the Atlantic.[2] The fact remains that the Crocketts came to America just as other Ulster Scots did, aboard a heaving and crowded immigrant ship.

Some Ulstermen and their families, weary of warfare and religious persecution, were so desperate for free and fertile land that they paid their way by signing on as indentured servants. But first they had to survive the dangerous Atlantic crossing, which, depending on the winds, could take anywhere from three weeks to three months. Not only were the ships overloaded, but rations were short, the food vermin-ridden, and the water stagnant. The entire vessel, especially lower decks, reeked from the stench of dysentery, vomit, sweat, and rot. Every soul aboard suffered from lice infestations and a multitude of other maladies. Hunger and thirst were constant, and some passengers died by drinking salt water or their own urine. Burial at sea was particularly difficult; survivors had to watch the shrouded corpses of loved ones cast into the sea. The despair and tension often erupted into brawls, even between family members.

Yet, even with all the horrors that had to be endured aboard ship, the weary and bedraggled passengers believed they had arrived in the Promised Land when the journey to American shores finally ended. Immigrant ships docked at various ports of entry, where enticing advertisements urged the new arrivals to help settle the lands opening up in the west. Philadelphia became the Scots-Irish favored port of entry, since the Pennsylvania colony, established by Quakers, appeared to welcome them. The puritanical New England colonies were less tolerant of the newcomers and had no use for either Scots or Irish.[3] The first of the Ulster settlements appeared at Donegal, Pennsylvania, not far from the larger town of Lancaster. Others sprang up beyond, in the rich Cumberland Valley. The Ulster Scots, mostly tenant farmers, were motivated to find a place of their own where land was cheap and they could achieve a reasonable measure of economic freedom and opportunity. The primary pattern of their western migration took them out of Pennsylvania along the Shenandoah Valley of Virginia, continuing south and west into what would become Tennessee, or, as the Crocketts did, into North Carolina and then to Tennessee.[4]

Many of the Scots-Irish migrated as whole congregations, or family groups, just as they had done with their Presbyterian ministers from Scotland to Ireland to America. The extended family unit was extremely tight-knit, and it was common for entire communities of these pioneers to migrate along the same route, stopping at the same places along the way.

"The word clannish was used to describe these Scots for good reason," explains Joseph Swann, himself a descendant of Scots-Irish pioneers who knew the Crockett family. The Scots-Irish were more concerned with establishing new settlements than with integration. They were intolerant by nature and preferred self-sufficient isolationism to integrated social and vocational progress.[5]

The Scots-Irish, or Scotch-Irish, as they were erroneously called in America, soon became known as a distinct frontier breed.[6] They were accustomed to isolation in a hostile environment. The hard experiences they had endured fighting each other in their homeland and the native Irish in Ulster had tempered their spirits and stiffened their resolve. This made them especially well suited to life on the new western frontier. When not fighting among themselves, they fell upon the American Indians they encountered with the same kind of murderous zeal.

Crockett's paternal grandfather may have scouted the area or made the move to Virginia as early as 1743. The signature "David Crockatt" appears as a witness to a lease dated January 1743 in Frederick County, Virginia, between Morgan Bryan—grandfather of Rebecca Boone, wife of Daniel Boone—and Roger Turner.[7] Bryan had come to the area in about 1730 and brought settlers from Pennsylvania with him. This document is not only the first known written record of David the elder, but his association with Bryan becomes a direct link between the families of two of America's most mythologized frontier heroes.

By 1748, David the elder had established a home in the Shenandoah Valley, just over the border in the northernmost part of Frederick County, Virginia, "4 miles from Watkins Ferry lying on both sides of the Wagon Road."[8] These settlers would soon find out that county sheriffs were entitled to a percentage of the annual taxes levied on residents by the House of Burgesses for the support of civil government in the colony. David Crockett's name is listed among the tithables of Frederick County in 1748.[9]

Of considerable importance at about this time was the fact that David the elder wed the teenaged Elizabeth, whose year of birth is estimated to be 1730, and who would remain a devoted frontier wife and mother for almost thirty years. Elizabeth's maiden name is unknown, but there is much speculation that she was the daughter of Jonas and Elizabeth Hedge. This is based on a recorded deed signed by David the elder and bearing the mark of Elizabeth. The document shows that the couple sold 352 acres of land that had been granted to Hedges, indicating that he may have given the property to the Crocketts.[10]

It is unclear exactly how many children Elizabeth bore. Crockett family genealogists have pieced together a possible birth order for as many as seven sons: William, David Jr., John, Robert, Joseph, Alexander, and James. Of these sons, little is known of David Jr. and Alexander, although the signatures of both David Crockett Sr. and David Crockett Jr. have been found on recorded documents. It is likely that there also would have been daughters in this family, but despite a few vague references, no supporting records have ever surfaced. John Crockett, who would father the famous David Crockett, was born about 1753 in Frederick County, Virginia.[11]

The Crocketts were some of the earliest settlers in the area around Frederick Town, Virginia, which in 1752 would be renamed Winchester, the seat of Frederick County. Once the camping grounds of Shawnee Indians, this area of Virginia was settled in the early 1730s by Pennsylvania Quakers who traveled what had been known as the Warriors' Path before becoming the Great Wagon Road. This also was the route taken by Crockett family members and their fellow Scots-Irishmen when they settled on the eastern flank of North Mountain in Nollville, Virginia, and, later, Berryville, a Frederick County settlement near Winchester.

At the same time that David the elder moved from Pennsylvania to Virginia, a sixteen-year-old George Washington also arrived in Frederick County. He started work as a surveyor and, with his earnings, soon began purchasing land. By 1755 he kept a small office in a Winchester log cabin while he supervised the construction of Fort Loudon at the north end of town, bringing in blacksmiths from his family's Mount

Vernon estate to do the ironwork. Washington also held his first elective office in the county, serving in the House of Burgesses, and, during the French and Indian War, he commanded a regiment headquartered in Winchester. No records have been found that indicate whether Washington had contact with the Crocketts; it is doubtful. However, before the close of the century, the nation's new capital, less than seventy miles northwest of Winchester, would be named for Washington, and some years after that, the Crockett clan would have one of their own serving in the U.S. Congress.

The family of David and Elizabeth Crockett left Frederick County, Virginia, by June 13, 1768, the date on their last deed, and wended their way to the newly created Tryon County (renamed Lincoln County ten years later), west of the Catawba River in southwest North Carolina.[12] Their final land transaction was the sale of 352 acres of land to Robert Watt, the parcel of land once owned by Jonas Hedge that led to speculation that Elizabeth was a Hedge daughter.

Besides civic chores, such as serving as jurors and witnessing legal documents, the Crocketts stayed busy facing the demands and hardships of daily life on the frontier wilderness. The forests of Tryon County offered plenty of game for sharp-eyed marksmen toting their long rifles crafted by skilled German gunsmiths in Pennsylvania. Hunters also spent considerable time shooting and trapping varmints. In Tryon County, the bounty for the scalp of an adult wolf earned a pound sterling, while a young wolf scalp brought ten shillings and a wild cat scalp five shillings. Like other frontier boys, the Crockett sons learned how to handle firearms and how to track animals. They were taught that a rifle was an essential tool and that, indeed, there was truth to the adage that a man must choose his rifle with as much care as he chose his wife.[13] Several Crockett sons were soon to marry.

It is probable that sometime in 1775—the year the American Revolution broke out in northeast New England—one of the sons, John Crockett, married Rebecca (or Rebekah) Hawkins, whose family was said by some early Crockett researchers to have come from Joppa, Maryland, founded on the Gunpowder River in the early 1700s. According to the official genealogy of the Crockett family, Rebecca was the daughter of Nathan, born in 1722, and Ruth Cole Hawkins, born in 1724. Both of them were born in Baltimore County, Maryland, where they also married, on February 14, 1744. This family later moved to the same area in Virginia where the Crocketts lived. Rebecca's known siblings were brothers Aaron, Joseph, Matthew, Wilson, John, Nicholas, and Nathan Jr., and sisters Mary Elizabeth and Ruth.[14]

The early life of Rebecca Hawkins Crockett has been obscured, and many inaccuracies have been handed down. Some accounts list her birthplace as Baltimore and the year of birth as 1764. One source declares that she and John Crockett married in 1780. Much of the confusion resulted from *Notable Southern Families*, a work published in 1928 in which authors Janie French and Zella Armstrong claimed that the Crockett family was the offspring of French Huguenots who had migrated to Ireland and then to America. However, many more reliable researchers, including Crockett descendants, have questioned those findings and pointed out inaccuracies and glaring errors in the French and Armstrong work. Although the Huguenot information frequently resurfaces as well-documented fact, it is not. No link has been established between the Huguenot Crocketts and the family of David Crockett. Nor does any reliable information support the claims by French and Armstrong that Rebecca Hawkins Crockett was in any way related to Sarah Hawkins Sevier, the wife of John Sevier, a future governor of Tennessee and a U.S. congressman.[15]

In his 1834 autobiography, Crockett wrote what he knew of his mother: "She was an American woman, born in the state [colony] of Maryland, between York and Baltimore. It is likely I may have heard where they were married, but if so, I have forgotten. It is, however, certain that they were, or else the public would never have been troubled with the history of David Crockett, their son."[16]

For Crockett, who never demonstrated a longing to learn more about his family's past, that bit of information seemed to be enough.

---- **FOUR** ----

OVER THE MOUNTAIN

IN 1776—THE YEAR AMERICA declared its independence and the war against Great Britain produced a growing cohesion among the former colonies—the determined Crockett tribe, including John; his bride, Elizabeth; and led by David the elder—packed up its belongings and made its way over the formidable Appalachian barrier into what eventually became the northeastern tip of Tennessee.[1]

Like the waves of other settlers, land speculators, and squatters pouring into this territory, the Crocketts knowingly defied a royal decree that closed off the western frontier to colonial expansion. King George III had issued his Royal Proclamation of 1763 following Britain's acquisition of French territory in North America at the end of the French and Indian War.[2] This measure was intended to stabilize relations of various Indian tribes by making all lands west of the heads of rivers flowing into the Atlantic Ocean from the west or northwest off-limits to any white settlement. Instead of abiding by the proclamation—once described as "a triumph of naïveté, geographical ignorance, and wishful thinking"— restless colonists, eager to increase their holdings and gain new ground, simply ignored it.[3] They were angered by the ban on expansion and followed the trails blazed before them by the Longhunters and other

Overmountain Men, mostly Scots-Irish settlers who had come west over the Appalachians, or the Allegheny Mountains, as they were then called.

Longhunters—so named because of the duration of their wilderness hunts—came from Pennsylvania and the Carolinas, but most started in the Holston River Valley of Virginia or the adjacent valley of the Clinch River. They were the first American frontiersmen to go beyond the Blue Ridge Mountains, making their living as hunters, trappers, and scouts for land surveyors. Throughout the 1760s and 1770s, Longhunters provided invaluable information for the settlers streaming into the future states of Tennessee and Kentucky.[4] Although they often adopted the Indian way of life, including some of the dress, most Longhunters considered Indians as competition and, defying the government and more liberal East Coast sentiment, were known to shoot them on sight. They also poached game on Indian lands, disregarded treaties, and randomly broke laws.

A particularly well known Longhunter was Daniel Boone, who explored the upper Holston River valley for a land speculator, later playing a key role in the early settlement of Tennessee. One of Boone's camps on Boon's Creek, a tributary of the Watauga River, become the home of his friend and hunting companion Captain William Bean, Tennessee's first known permanent white settler, who built his log cabin at the site in 1769.[5] That same year, Robert Crockett, a rugged Longhunter and kinsman of David Crockett the elder, was ambushed and killed by Indians near his camp on the headwaters of Roaring River on the old war trail leading from Cherokee territory to Shawnee land.[6] It was an act that would be deeply ingrained in the consciousness of the Crockett clan.

An ethnic mélange of settlers followed the Great Wagon Road and the well-trodden routes of the Longhunters, including English, Welsh, Irish, German, Swiss, French Huguenot, and some African slaves. Most of the newcomers, however, were Scots-Irish, such as the Crocketts. Reflecting early class division in the fledgling Republic, all of them had long detested the autocratic power of the British king and resented what they considered a conspiracy to take away their God-given freedom.

"If abused, they fight; if their rights are infringed they rebel; if forced, they strike; and if their liberties are threatened, they murder," wrote Tennessee historian John Trotwood Moore. "They eat meat and always their bread is hot."[7] It was frequently said that the Scots-Irish in Tennessee feared only God himself. And yet another adage about these early pioneers suggested that they kept the Sabbath, as well as anything else they could get their hands on. For the Crocketts, that meant getting their hands on the new lands that waited over the mountains.

The principal communities that were being established in the region of what became east Tennessee were on the North Holston, Watauga, and Nolichucky rivers, and in Carter's Valley, a settlement named for merchant John Carter. In fact, the Crockett family chose Carter's Valley as their new home.[8] They found thick forests and distant mountains— the oldest east of the Mississippi—sitting "like dethroned kings," as poet Sidney Lanier put it. The Crocketts and other settlers built one-room log cabins with dirt floors and mud and stick fireplaces close to the swift-flowing streams threading from the highlands. They found hidden springs, cleared land for planting, and, working together, carved settlements out of the land with their own hands.

David Crockett, his sons, and the other newly arrived white settlers believed they had moved to within the boundary of the Virginia Colony, but a survey revealed that almost all of the settlements were south of North Carolina's western claims in land that had been guaranteed to the Cherokee Nation. In 1772, when ordered to disband and relocate to north of the boundary, the settlers, who were living beyond the bounds of any organized government, formed an alliance they called the Watauga Association, with John Carter being made one of the commissioners. At the same time, the audacious Wataugans, as they called themselves, schemed to get around the sanctions for purchasing land imposed on them by the British.[9] In 1775, they dispatched a delegation, loaded down with gifts and trade goods, to a parley with the Cherokee leader Attakullakulla to see about leasing Indian land. Despite pleas from the aging Indian leader's son, Dragging Canoe, who eloquently but forcefully protested that tribal land was melting away "like balls of snow in the sun," a deal was struck that eventually led to whites purchasing Cherokee land. "You have bought a fair land, but there is a cloud hanging over it," Dragging Canoe told the Wataugans. "You will find its settlement dark and bloody."[10] Dragging Canoe's prediction would prove true, and eventually there would be serious repercussions for the white settlers, including the Crocketts.

The estimated two thousand white émigrés soon transformed much of the Cherokee land by clearing forests and planting crops and orchards. More log cabins popped up across the landscape, and, despite bringing in livestock that encroached upon much of the grasses and tall cane along the streams, the white families killed great numbers of deer, bear, and other game. It became clear to the Cherokees that, unlike the Long-hunters, who came and went, this new wave of whites were going to remain. The Cherokees had never expected such a great number of new-comers, and many tribal elders who had never agreed to the transactions in the first place were deeply troubled by what they witnessed. Serious dissension developed within the tribe, and the more militant Cherokees grew emboldened and understandably formed an alliance with the Brit-ish during the American Revolution.

After several skirmishes with the Cherokees, the settlers sought out-side assistance to stem further hostilities. On July 5, 1776, the day after the signing of the Declaration of Independence in Philadelphia, David Crockett and his eldest son, William, were two of the more than one hundred thirteen Wataugans who signed (or, as two men did, made their mark on) a petition asking North Carolina to annex their land and provide protection from the British and Cherokee warriors. Because North Carolina and Virginia had not agreed on boundary lines, similar petitions were sent to the Virginia government in 1776 and 1777 from Carter's Valley—including the signatures of David the elder and those of David Jr., William, and John Crockett.[11] The Watauga Association con-tinued until 1778 and was finally annexed to North Carolina. By then it was too late for David the elder and some members of his family who had built a split-log cabin and established growing fields. In his *Narra-tive* of 1834, Crockett recounted his father's early life in east Tennessee when he wrote: "He settled there under dangerous circumstances, both to himself and his family, as the country was full of Indians, who were at that time very troublesome."[12]

Those "troublesome" times struck the family with a fury in the spring of 1777. John Crockett was away, on duty as a frontier ranger, one of the volunteers who were authorized bounties of land in return for combating hostile Indian raiding parties.[13] During much of 1776 and 1777, John's elder brother Robert also was gone, serving with the militia as a draftsman and helping build fortifications on the North Carolina frontier. While these Crockett men were off protecting other settlers, a party of Creek Indians and renegade Cherokees, known as Chickamaugas, emerged from the forest and descended on the homestead of David and Elizabeth Crockett. "By the Creeks, my grandfather and grandmother Crockett were both murdered, in their own house, and on the very spot where Rogersville, in Hawkins county, now stands. At the same time, the Indians wounded Joseph Crockett, a brother to my father, by a ball which broke his arm; and took James a prisoner, who was still a younger brother than Joseph, and who, from natural defects was less able to make his escape, as he was both deaf and dumb."[14]

If a son named David Crockett Jr. in fact existed, then perhaps he also perished in the Indian raid along with his parents. Some sources also believe that an unnamed Crockett daughter was present and was brutally scalped but survived. No records have been found to substantiate such a story. A reference to the massacre is found in an April 27, 1777, letter from Colonel Charles Robertson to Richard Caswell, the governor of North Carolina, in which a dozen unnamed victims are mentioned.[15]

William and Robert Crockett were named executors of the estate of their slain father and legally represented the interests of Joseph and James, their minor orphaned brothers. Joseph, who had his arm broken by a rifle ball in the attack that killed his parents, lost the use of his hand and fashioned an imitation hand so that he could eat. Joseph later was appointed straymaster for Sullivan County, Tennessee, by Governor William Blout and helped gather stray livestock and return them to their rightful owners.[16] James, the youngest Crockett son, was the only family member held captive by the Indian raiders. "He remained with them for seventeen years and nine months," David wrote in the *Narrative*, "when he was discovered and recollected by my father and his eldest brother, William Crockett; and was purchased by them from an Indian trader, at a price which I do not remember; but so it was, that he was delivered up to them and they returned him to his relatives."[17] For the rest of his life, those who knew him, including family, referred to James as "Dumb Jimmie." In Fentress County, Tennessee, where he eventually lived, he was once lost in a hollow on the waters of White Oak that became known as Dumb Jimmie's Hollow.[18] James spent most of his remaining years searching in vain for lost silver and gold mines he had been taken to blindfolded while being held captive.

The murderous attacks profoundly affected the Crockett family. In the aftermath of his parents' violent deaths, John Crockett was concerned about the safety of surviving family members, especially his wife, Rebecca, but he continued his service in the militia for the duration of the war against Great Britain. John, along with his brothers William, Robert, and Alexander, faithfully served under Colonel Isaac Shelby in the summer of 1780 at the pivotal Battle of King's Mountain in northwest South Carolina. Credited by many historians as the engagement that turned the tide of the American Revolution's southern campaign, this fierce battle forever dashed any hope that Britain had of attracting American colonists to their cause.

After gathering at Fort Watauga in what is now Elizabethton, Tennessee, the Crocketts and their fellow Overmountain Men, made up about a half of the colonial force that met the British Loyalists at King's Mountain. Using Indian-style guerrilla tactics and taking deadly aim with their long rifles, the American patriots either killed or took prisoner large numbers of their enemy, including the British commander, who tried to escape through the battle lines. The entire engagement lasted one hour and five minutes.[19]

"The next morning, which was Sunday, the scene became really distressing; the wives and children of the poor Tories came in, in great numbers," wrote James Collins, one of the backcountry patriots who took part in the battle.

Their husbands, fathers, and brothers. Lay dead in heaps, while others lay wounded or dying; a melancholy sight indeed! We proceeded to bury the dead, but it was badly done; they were thrown into convenient piles and covered with old logs, the bark of trees, and rocks; yet not so as to secure them from becoming a prey to the beasts of the forest, or the vultures of the air; and the wolves became so plenty that it was dangerous for anyone to be out at night, for several miles around; also, the hogs in the neighborhood gathered into the place to devour the flesh of men.[20]

The plunder of battle, including horses, guns, powder, and lead, was distributed to the victors. Articles of clothing also were taken from the dead Tories. The combat-hardened patriots had not forgotten British atrocities and their refusal to grant quarter to prisoners. As a result, at King's Mountain, many captive enemy survivors were tortured, bayoneted, or hacked to death with sabers. Some were given cursory trials and several were hanged.

"The overmountain men had proved their worth and had settled a long awaited score," Joseph A. Swann said of King's Mountain. "The battle was a testimony to the tough resourcefulness of the proud Ulster-Scots and the deadly accuracy of their long rifles. The superior range and accuracy of the rifles of the overmountain men had proved far superior to the heavier, smooth bored muskets used by the Tories."

Those frontier Scot pioneers were establishing a name for themselves as effective fighters and excellent marksmen—a reputation that David Crockett, as the son of one of the heroes of that battle, would take to a legendary level. On a larger level, this kind of brutal fighting, which often culminated in massacres, helped establish a martial precedent, one that challenged the traditional methods of warfare, and for which the nineteenth-century West would become known.

—— FIVE ——

ON THE NOLICHUCKY

FTER TAKING PART in the annihilation of the British and Tory forces at King's Mountain, John Crockett and his brothers, fervently believing that God had ordained their victory, came home to Carter's Valley, with the Overmountain Men's war cry, "The sword of the Lord and of Gideon," still echoing in their ears.[1] It was time to tend to family matters that had been put on hold while the war raged around them. It was time to begin the search for a deaf and mute brother being held captive by the Cherokees, as well as dispose of their murdered and scalped parents' property.

The Crockett brothers understood that they were not the only ones called upon to serve. "Every able bodied man in the county was required to go," recalled Samuel Hill, a ranger whose family moved to the Nolichucky settlements at the outbreak of the Revolution.[2] Militia duty meant serving multiple tours of anywhere from three to nine months at a time, which placed tremendous strains on relationships and left frontier families unprotected. Much like the Crocketts, another member of the militia came home to find his brother killed and his mother and two sisters taken captive by Indian raiders. After setting out with a pursuit party of neighbors, the man found his mother's corpse "stripped naked, her head skinned." He still managed to catch up with the war party and free his sisters.[3]

Atrocities involving not only men, but also the victimizing of women and children were common and committed by both sides in the long series of Indian wars that continued after the American Revolution. Death at the hands of warring Indians was so common that when one was told a man or woman had died, one did not ask the cause but only how the person was killed. Undoubtedly the same question was raised in Cherokee villages when a death was announced. Retaliation and fear drove the brutality and violence. During the War for Independence, white militia sought to eliminate the Cherokee as a British ally and punish them for attacking white settlements. These punitive actions continued after the Revolutionary War and well into the 1800s, as more whites moved into Indian lands. Whites were killed and brutalized, as were Indian men, women, and children. Dozens of Cherokee villages were left in ruins, hundreds of acres of crops destroyed, and livestock killed or seized. Many of the white soldiers shouted the Indian scalp cry in battle and took as many scalps for trophies as the Indian warriors they fought.[4] Indian captives were sold as slaves and white prisoners were held for ransom. It became a deadly cycle of vengeance. Tales of scalpings and atrocities were told and retold, feeding the fires of intolerance and cultural division. Yet some veterans of these outrages, among them John Crockett, preferred silence to bragging. For the remainder of his life, he spoke very little of his experiences as a frontier ranger, even with young sons anxious to hear every gory detail of combat against both the British and the Indians.

"I have an imperfect recollection of the part which I have understood my father took in the revolutionary war," David Crockett wrote in his autobiography of his father's role in the War for Independence.

I personally know nothing about it, for it happened to be a little before my day; but from himself, and many others who were well acquainted with its troubles and afflictions, I have learned that he was a soldier in the revolutionary war, and took part in that bloody struggle. He fought at Kings Mountain against the British and tories, and in some other engagements of which my remembrance is too imperfect to enable me to speak with any certainty.[5]

John was spared a trip to the Washington County Courthouse in Abingdon, Virginia, when it came time for the disposition of his deceased parents' estate. That task was left to his brothers William and Robert, who had been named administrators of their father's last will and testament.[6] Both of them acted as the legal guardians of their younger brothers when it came to putting four hundred acres of land in the names of "Alexander and James Crockett Orphans of David Crockett Decesd on the waters of the Holston on the head Waters of Black Creek including said Crockett Decesd Improvement."[7] The older brothers also arranged for the sale of their father's other holdings in Carter's Valley. In the inventory and appraisal of the estate were several horses, a small herd of yearling cattle and bulls, saddles and bridles, a wagon, a musket, plows and sickles, a spinning wheel, bedding and furniture, clothing including a man's great coat, a bell, and kitchen utensils.[8] It had to have been difficult for the Crockett siblings to sell off their slain parents' personal belongings and the everyday objects that they had used as children, such as the saddles they learned to ride on and the muskets they fired when their father taught them how to shoot.

Amid an assortment of tools and implements was found a hackle, a comblike tool through which raw hair was passed in preparation for the weaving that Elizabeth Crockett had done for many years. Like some of the other precious items, it was given to a family member in remembrance of the woman who helped raise all of them. There also was an unknown quantity of brimstone, or sulfur, one of the key ingredients, along with saltpeter and charcoal, used in the making of black powder.[9] Most gunpowder came from England, and even though the 1777 ban on importation by the British Parliament was eventually lifted, it remained one of the most precious commodities on the frontier. Almost forty-five years later, the then adult David Crockett would try his hand at manufacturing gunpowder, an ill-fated venture.

Yet despite the celebrated failures and mishaps that David Crockett may have had to endure during his life, he fared far better than did his father. Try as he might, it seemed that John Crockett was never quite able to improve his own life and livelihood. Some folks said that John was snake-bit, an old expression in the Shenandoah Valley and elsewhere for a person plagued with hard luck. "Poverty, as well as danger, was the birthright of the pioneer; and John Crockett inherited his full share of it," observed historian James Shackford.[10]

Still, by the spring of 1783, after the surrender at Saratoga and when Congress officially declared an end to the Revolutionary War, John and Rebecca Crockett, along with their growing brood of children, had already moved on. They pulled up stakes in Carter's Valley and relocated to Washington County, soon to become Greene County, North Carolina.[11]

Traversed by a series of valleys and ridges, Greene County was situated between the Unaka Mountains on the south and Bays Mountains on the north. Rising as the confluence of the North Toe River and the Cane River in western North Carolina, the Nolichucky River—principal stream of Greene County—trended westward. Called the "Chucky River" by early settlers, the Nolichucky flanked ranges and cut between mountains as it flowed in a curving course, fed by tributaries such as Lick Creek, Horse Creek, and Camp Creek. At the border of Greene County, one of the larger tributaries, Big Limestone Creek, joined the river. It was here that the Crockett property was located, and it was here that David, the sixth of Rebecca and John Crockett's nine children, was born, on August 17, 1786.[12]

In the years just prior to David's birth, it appeared that John's fortunes had changed. In April 1783, he was appointed a constable in the newly formed county, establishing a family political tradition. He was to be reappointed in 1785 and 1789.[13] Even though, as David put it in his autobiography, John was "by profession a farmer," it seems he tried his hand at many tasks, and was a respected, moderately influential man in Greene County.

John also took a stab at speculating in land when David was just ten months old, learning to walk in his family's log house on the Nolichucky. On June 4, 1787, John sold the two hundred acres he had purchased four years earlier in Sullivan County for one hundred shillings for fifty pounds.[14] At the time of the transaction, both John and Rebecca signed the bill of sale, which brought them virtually no profit, since one pound sterling was worth about twenty shillings.

By the late 1780s, John was appointed a magistrate of Greene County. As a justice of the court, he was presiding on August 5, 1788, when the young and sinewy Andrew Jackson received his license to practice law in Greene County.[15] John Crockett was also active politically, as a staunch Franklinite, one of the supporters of the State of Franklin, the independent state (1785–1789) established by frontier settlers.[16]

After seceding from North Carolina, the rebellious settlers wrote their own constitution and elected as their governor the popular Revolutionary War hero and "Indian fighter" John Sevier, nicknamed Nolichucky Jack or Chucky Jack for his exploits along the Nolichucky River.[17] Sometimes called "Frankland," meaning "land of free men," the new state was named after Benjamin Franklin, the aging patriot who told the Franklinites, only a few years before his death in what was then the nation's capital, that he was honored to have a state named for him but politely explained that he was too old and sickly to be of much help in their cause.[18] In a letter to Governor Sevier sent from Philadelphia in 1787, however, Franklin did offer a suggestion:

> There are two things which humanity induces me to wish you may succeed in: the accommodating your misunderstanding with the government of North-Carolina, and the avoiding an Indian war by preventing encroachments on their lands. Such encroachments are the more unjustifiable, as these people, in the fair way of purchase, usually give very good bargains.[19]

Doctor Franklin's sage advice was not taken.

In August 1788, around the time of David's second birthday, John and about eight hundred other area men embarked with Brigadier General Joseph Martin on an ill-fated campaign against Dragging Canoe, leader of the same Chickamaugas who massacred John's parents and others back in Carter's Valley.[20] Martin was a Revolutionary War hero married to Betsy Ward, daughter of Nancy Ward, a prominent Cherokee leader, and her English trader husband. In 1777, Virginia Governor Patrick Henry, a signer of the Declaration of Independence, appointed Martin the Indian agent for the Cherokee Nation. This particular action led by Martin was sparked by the recent massacres of more white families and cries for revenge that echoed throughout the land. The campaign was but one of many that took place during the almost twenty years of raids, ambushes, and sometimes full-scale battles between the Cherokees and the ever-growing number of American frontiersmen who illegally encroached into Indian lands.

The various militias gathered at White's Fort, where Knoxville now stands, and then crossed the Hiwassee River and moved overland to the point where the Tennessee River broke through the Cumberland Mountains.[21] Scattered fighting ensued, but when the Chickamaugas offered unexpected resistance and Brig. Gen. Martin gave the order to pursue them, most of his men rebelled. They refused to follow because he had allied himself with the state of North Carolina during the contentious struggle over the failed State of Franklin, and hard feelings had developed between Martin and John Sevier, also a much-admired hero. Martin had no other choice but to go home.[22]

A weary Martin resigned as Indian agent following the inglorious murder of several Cherokee leaders, including pacifist chief Old Tassel, killed while meeting under a flag of truce. The charismatic John Sevier, however, rode on to more glory even as all hope vanished for Franklin's gaining admission to the United States. As Franklin and North Carolina competed for the loyalties of the people, Sevier stayed popular and beloved in many circles, based on his past exploits with the Watauga Association, the Battle of King's Mountain, and his constant offensive against the Cherokee people. He managed to hang on even when the Cherokee, Chickamauga, and Chickasaw nations collectively began to fight back and attack the settlements in Franklin, causing an outcry for Franklinites to settle their differences with North Carolina so the state militia could come to their rescue.

As Franklin began to collapse, Sevier became involved with some last-ditch intrigues to gain control of Indian lands and even considered an alliance with Spain. Eventually, some of his property was seized for back taxes, and Sevier was arrested on a charge of treason under North Carolina state law. In 1789 he received a pardon and won election to the North Carolina Senate. The following year, the State of Franklin was declared dead, and the land that soon became Tennessee was again ceded by North Carolina to the federal government. During the territorial period, Sevier went to the First U.S. Congress from North Carolina, and on June 1, 1796, when Tennessee joined the Union as the sixteenth state, Sevier was elected the first governor, an office he held for several terms.[23]

By that date, the family of John Crockett had been gone from their cabin on the Nolichucky for almost four years. David was about nine years old when this move took place, and in writing in his *Narrative* later in life, he could vividly remember but one traumatic experience. After the passage of more than forty-five years, Crockett described what he witnessed as if it had just happened.

> My four elder brothers, and a well-grown boy of about fifteen years old, by the name of Campbell, and myself, were all playing on the river's side; when all of the rest of them got into my father's canoe, and put out to amuse themselves on the water, leaving me on the shore alone. Just a little distance below them, there was a fall in the river, which went slap-right straight down. My brothers, though they were little fellows, had been used to paddling the canoe, and could have carried it safely anywhere about there; but this fellow Campbell wouldn't let them have the paddle, but, fool like, undertook to manage it himself.

I reckon he had never seen a water craft before; and it went just any way but the way he wanted it. There he paddled, and paddled, and paddled—all the while going wrong,—until, in a short time, here they were going, straight forward, stern foremost, right plump to the falls; and if they had only a fair shake, they would have gone over as slick as a whistle. It was'ent this, thought, that scared me; for I was so infernal mad that they had left me on the shore, that I had as soon seen them all go over the falls a bit, as any other way. But their danger was seen by a man the name of Kendall, but I'll be shot if it was Amos; for I believe I would know him yet if I was to see him. This man Kendall was working in a field on the bank, and knowing there was no time to lose, he started full tilt, and he come like a cane brake afire; and as he ran, he threw off his coat, and then his jacket, and then his shirt, for I know when he got to the water he had nothing on but his breeches. But seeing him in such a hurry, and tearing off his clothes as he went, I had no doubt but that the devil or something else was after him—and close on him, too— as he was running within an inch of his life. This alarmed me, and I screamed out like a young painter [panther]. But Kendall didn't stop for this. He went ahead all might, and as full bent on saving the boys. . . . When he came to the water he plunged in, and where it was too deep to wade he would swim, and where it was shallow enough he went bolting on; and by such exertion as I never saw at any other time in my life, he reached the canoe, when it was within twenty or thirty feet of the falls; and so great was the suck, and so swift the current, that poor Kendall had a hard time of it to stop them at last, as Amos will to stop the mouths of the people about his stockjobbing. But he hung on to the canoe, till he got it stop'd, and then draw'd it out of danger. When they got out, I found the boys were more scared than I had been, and the only thing that comforted me was, the belief that it was a punishment on them for leaving me on shore.[24]

It is believed by the most conscientious Crockett researchers that this incident on the Nolichucky took place much as described by Crockett in his autobiography. The waterfall is documented in old deeds, and the Crockett account seems plausible. However, it is even more probable that, in this particular instance, Crockett purposely took some liberties with the name of the man who rescued the boys from certain death in the river. Amos Kendall was, in truth, not a Tennessee farmer but the close confidant and intellectual force behind the administration of President Andrew Jackson, who was dramatically elected president in November of 1828 and whose decidedly expansionist westward gaze anticipated the government's Manifest Destiny policy by numerous decades. In the late 1820s and early 1830s, Kendall and Jackson were Crockett's most bitter enemies and political rivals. Kendall not only served as U.S. Postmaster General under both Jackson and later Martin Van Buren but also wrote some of Jackson's most important speeches.[25]

In the 1830s, when Crockett was dredging up his past with fellow author Thomas Chilton as they crafted his life story, the opportunity to take a dig at an old enemy and portray him as a common farmer was too good to pass up. By the same token, there is credible evidence that a George Kindle lived in the vicinity of the Crockett home about the time of the river incident. His name appears on two deeds for property on Little Limestone Creek.[26] The case for this man as the rescuer is strong.

To this day, those who visit the Crockett birth site can still see the sandy shoal where the swift waters of the Nolichucky suddenly plunge in a turbulent sheer drop of at least five feet and the river makes a sharp bend against a massive limestone wall. It is not hard to visualize a canoe filled with panic-stricken boys hurtling through the water and a man pulling off his clothes as he races to their rescue, while on the bank a little boy with no breeches watches the scene unfold.

SIX

A BOY'S LEARNING

DAVID CROCKETT'S FAMILY left his ancestral birth-place near the mouth of Big Limestone Creek on the Nolichucky in 1792, and relocated just five miles to the northwest on a 197-acre tract of land purchased by John Crockett close to the headwaters of Lick Creek.[1] The primary reason for this move was for the Crocketts to live closer to Rebecca's brother Joseph Hawkins and his wife, Esther, who had already established their family homestead on a nearby 200-acre land grant.

The spacious abodes that now dot the Greene County area are a far cry from the cramped one-room utilitarian cabins that accommodated large frontier families. These dwellings were often built with packed dirt floors and were windowless except for tiny square openings near the chimney called "granny holes" (because they allowed an extra bit of light for a grandmother while she sewed on the hearth and tended the fireplace).[2] The mountain views were just as scenic then, but there was not much time to enjoy them.

Soon after his family settled in a new log house, young David once again experienced an event "which made a lasting impression on my memory."[3] This episode, later described by Crockett in his autobiography, began on a September morning in 1793, when Absalom Stone-cipher, a handsome twenty-five-year-old from one of the first pioneer families in the community, donned his favorite red flannel shirt, picked up a basket, and went out in search of succulent wild grapes that were ripe and in abundance by early autumn.[4] Clusters of fat purple grapes hung from vines as big around as a man's arm. The time was right for making sweet wine and jelly that would last all winter. Settlers also had learned from the Cherokees that grapes boiled with geranium root made a potent rinse to wash the mouths of infants suffering from thrush, a common infection that left painful lesions.

Stonecipher waded into a thicket of heavy brush and gathered low-hanging fruit, unaware that only fifty yards away Joseph Hawkins, David's uncle and Stonecipher's neighbor and friend, had his Kentucky rifle at the ready while on the hunt for whitetail deer. Hawkins, too, was on a hunt of his own. Deer love nothing more than a meal of juicy grapes, and Hawkins figured he was in the right place to find some quarry for supper. Hawkins was a good shot, seldom known to miss. As Stonecipher pulled at the grapes, Hawkins picked up the motion and saw a reddish hue that he thought looked much like a feeding deer.[5]

"It was a likely place for deer; and my uncle, having no suspicion that it was any human being, but supposing the raising of the hand to be the occasional twitch of a deer's ear, fired at the lump, and as the devil would have it, unfortunately shot the man through the body," Crockett related in the Narrative.[6]

At the same time that Stonecipher heard the sharp report of the rifle, he felt a searing burn as the hot lead struck him just above the beltline and tore into his stomach. He screamed and fell hard to the ground. Hawkins—realizing his mistake—raced to his aid and managed to load the wounded man on a horse and take him to the nearby cabin of Samuel Humbert, in the glen at the head of Horse Camp Creek. As soon as Stonecipher was carried into the cabin, Hawkins sent for his brother-in-law, John Crockett, who lived in the vicinity and was respected and looked up to in the community for his woods wisdom and frontier skills.[7]

When John learned of the accidental shooting, he told David, 7, to help saddle horses and come along in case he was needed. On the way out of the Crockett cabin, John grabbed his own Kentucky rifle, and they rode off to tend to the gravely wounded man. After arriving and making a quick examination of Stonecipher's wound, John determined that the rifle ball had passed through Stonecipher and had apparently not damaged any major organs. Still, Crockett knew that infection was always a possibility. If the young man was to survive being shot in the gut, bold action was needed at once.

Stonecipher was laid on a table before the cabin's large hearth. The fire blazing in the fireplace was always tended and never allowed to go out. Samuel Humbert had brought the fiery embers to this place in 1777 from the old family home in Virginia when he followed his friends the Stoneciphers to the new frontier. Humbert believed that home fires were important to the family and clan because they were cleansing fires and connected one generation to the next.[8]

The fire in Humbert's cabin had burned continuously for sixteen years, and by its light John Crockett pulled the ramrod from the barrel of his rifle and wrapped a silk handkerchief around the rod. With Joseph Hawkins, members of the Humbert family, and young David all gathered around the prone man on the table, John inserted the ramrod into the gunshot wound and pushed it through and out the exit hole on the other side. Then he took both ends of the silk handkerchief that remained in the wound and pulled it back and forth through the opening.[9] The procedure, which John probably learned while serving in the militia, cleansed all debris from the wound and helped prevent infection.

Watching his father save a man's life impressed David, who, over time, lost track of Stonecipher. "What became of him, or whether he is dead or alive, I don't know; but I reckon he did'ent fancy the business of gathering grapes in an out-of-the-way thicket soon again," Crockett wrote. When Crockett's autobiography appeared in 1834, Absalom Stonecipher was very much alive. Humbert's sixteen-year-old daughter, Sarah, whom Stonecipher married in 1796, had nursed him back to full health in front of the eternal fire.[10]

Eighteenth-century rural life anywhere in the new United States was challenging, but on the frontier of Tennessee it was especially perilous. Tending to gunshot wounds was but one of many skills one had to learn in order to survive. Just the basics of everyday life, such as felling timber and raising barns, often ended in tragic injuries. As Absalom Stoneci-pher learned, an innocent morning hunt for a basket of grapes could prove fatal. Bear maulings, rabid skunks, and poisonous snakebites were ever-present threats, as was travel by horseback or on foot through fields and woods where Indian warriors seeking revenge as well as the scalps of white intruders might lie in wait.

Doctors were few and far between on the frontier, and many times they were no more capable of dealing with illness or an emergency than the people they treated. They relied on an arsenal of barbaric and primitive cures that included bloodletting, purging, leeching, blister-ing, and dosings of arsenic and mercury.[11] Most physicians, like lawyers of the time, were self-taught and had little, if any, scientific knowledge, often using home remedies based on superstition and the belief that the stronger a medicinal brew tasted and smelled, the more effective it would be. Yet frequently the folk medicine practiced by rural moth-ers, healers, and midwives had real value. Much of their knowledge of herbs, roots, bark, and berries to use for extracts and potions came from the Cherokees, Creeks, Choctaws, and other Indian tribes, and proved less harmful and more effective than the advice of medical professionals.[12]

For the Crockett family, and many others like them, a knowledge of basic medicine and medical techniques, the procurement of food and fresh water, and the maintenance of adequate shelter had to be foremost in their minds at all times. That meant interminable hard work. Anyone who did not work was not worth his or her keep. That was certainly the philosophy of John Crockett, who constantly struggled to support a growing family and stay out of financial trouble. All of his adult life, John faced debt due to his inability to handle money and a penchant for trying out various schemes to get ahead. When times got tough and debt collectors started showing up, John Crockett usually followed the same pattern—he uprooted his family, left for greener pastures, and started another venture.

That was the case in May 1794, when he sold his acreage on Lick Creek for one hundred pounds and moved to another tract of land at the mouth of Cove Creek, a tributary of the Nolichucky River in southeast Greene County.[13] Stretched thin financially, John gambled and entered into a business partnership with Thomas Galbraith (or Galbreath), a native of Bucks County, Pennsylvania, and a veteran of the Revolutionary War. Together the two men undertook the building of a gristmill on the creek after Galbraith secured a permit.

The conversion of grain to flour or meal was an ancient process dating back thousands of years. In Tennessee during the 1790s, the most important crops were grains, such as wheat, oats, barley, and rye, that provided forage as well as the staff of life—bread. But the main crop was corn, and that is what most farmers grew. The ground meal used for cornbread, hoecakes, mush, and spoon bread was the backbone of the pioneer diet. A family supper might consist of nothing more than slabs of hot cornbread and some sweet cow's milk. Everyone ate cornbread, usually at all three meals.[14]

Widows seldom if ever were charged full price for milled grain, but all others paid full price and usually never questioned it. Barter was an important and accepted currency when cash or goods were short, and services such as sewing and manual labor were traded for sacks of precious meal and flour.[15] Saturdays were mill days, and customers would crowd around, exchanging not only their services but also news and gossip. In the winter, when doing business outside was all but impossible, people filed into a warming hut and huddled around a fire.

Not a soul ever got the chance to sit by a fire or buy a sack of meal at the gristmill being built by Crockett and Galbraith. Just as the mill neared completion, a tremendous storm caused the creek to flood, washing away both the mill and the Crocketts' home.[16] Reflecting the family's keen belief in the Bible, David, years later, called the disaster "the second epistle to Noah's fresh[et]," a reference to the Old Testament deluge. "I remember the water rose so high, that it got up into the house we lived in, and my father moved us out of it, to keep us from being drowned."[17]

The flood at Cove's Creek devastated John Crockett and proved to be a crushing blow from which he never fully recovered. He and his family were left homeless and without any immediate income. Following the disaster, Thomas Galbraith and his wife, Elizabeth, took pity on the Crocketts, providing them with food and shelter until they could get back on their feet and find new quarters.[18]

John surely appreciated the hospitality of his partner, but he also had to feel somewhat ashamed that he and his family were forced to survive on the goodwill of others. In only a few weeks John dreamed up a new plan of action, and the Crocketts took their leave from the Galbraith residence and departed Greene County. They were bound for a three-hundred-acre tract on Mossy Creek, in neighboring Jefferson County, that John had purchased in 1792, shortly before he forged the partnership to build the ill-fated gristmill.[19]

The move brought the Crocketts no immediate relief. Soon after relocating to Jefferson County, John was forced to start selling parcels of the property he owned there. In November of 1795, the county sheriff auctioned off most of the rest of the land to settle an outstanding Crockett debt of $400. After losing title to the property in the bankruptcy sale, the Crocketts, by special arrangement, were able to relocate on a tract of land owned by John Canaday, a Quaker settler who lived in the Panther Springs area.[20] At this site, John Crockett and his family operated a tavern to accommodate travelers on the old stage road connecting Knoxville, Tennessee, to Abingdon, Virginia, and other points east. The exact location of the Crockett tavern has long remained a confused and debated issue. At least three east Tennessee sites have been identified over the years, but more than likely it was built in Morristown, where a replica of it was constructed in 1959. "His tavern was on a small scale, as he was poor; and the principal accommodations which he kept, were for the waggoners [sic] who traveled the road,"[21] David later wrote of his father and the roadside inn that also served as the Crockett family home.

At this tavern David learned his father's true measure. The youngster already knew that John was capable of dire acts when it came to fending off creditors; he never forgot that his father was once so deep in debt that he bound out his eldest daughter. Over the years, John's indebtedness only increased. A small amount of money owed Gideon Morris for thirteen bushels of Indian corn—the debt was incurred back in 1783—still had not been paid at the time of Morris's death in 1798. A one-word comment from the account of the deceased man's estate listed Crockett's situation as "Desperate."[22]

SEVEN

COMING OF AGE

F JOHN CROCKETT HAD ANY TRUE sense of right and wrong, he allowed room for rationalization to justify his behavior when it came to his callous treatment of family. He was one of the Scots-Irish with a "Presbyterian conscience," a term used by Sam Ervin, the native North Carolinian and folksy U.S. senator, who charmed national audiences when he became a national figure during the early 1970s Watergate investigation. Ervin, a self-described "old country lawyer" of Scots-Irish descent, said that such a conscience "won't keep you from sinning, but it'll keep you from enjoying your sin, and it will smite you unmercifully if you don't do what it tells you is right."[1]

No call for swift biblical justice, however, can be found in any of David's writings about his father. Instead he paints a rather sympathetic portrait of a distraught man in need of luck—a beleaguered soul constantly faced with grinding out a sparse living but with only himself to blame for his misery. "His hardships were deepened by misadventures that brought debts and creditors rather than fortune,"[2] is how one historian summed up John Crockett.

The rough-and-tumble country tavern that John and Elizabeth Crockett maintained for so many years never completely freed the family from debt but eventually brought in enough income to keep at least a few creditors at bay. A steady stream of herders and teamsters traveling the "Big Road" stopped at the tavern to refresh themselves with dippers of icy water from the cedar-lined well. Travelers tromped inside for hot meals and drank newly made woods whiskey served in hollowed-out cow horns, then found a night's rest beneath quilts and bearskins on bedding and mattresses stuffed with dried corn shucks and goose feathers.

All of the Crocketts, no matter their age, had duties to perform, and for David and his brothers that included hunting game for the tavern table. David learned the basics of handling firearms from his father and uncles. The need to make every shot count to conserve expensive ammunition was instilled in him. In the present-day community of Morristown, the reconstructed Crockett Tavern lies a few miles southeast of a long hill known as Crockett's Ridge. Local tradition holds that this was where David most enjoyed hunting, eventually honing his marksmanship skills.[3]

In spite of his sharp hunter's eye and contributions to the tavern's larder, David was briefly bound out after his twelfth birthday. As he succinctly put it, "I began to make my acquaintance with hard times, and a plenty of them."[4] John Crockett, in need of quick revenue, traded seven weeks of labor from two of his eldest sons in exchange for credit for goods and supplies, including whiskey, at a local store.[5] Just two years later, in 1798, John decided the time had come for twelve-year-old David to be used as a financial asset to whittle down the family's mounting debts.

"An old Dutchman, by the name of Jacob Siler, who was moving from Knox county to Rockbridge, in the state of Virginia, in passing, made a stop at my father's house," David wrote. "He had a large stock of cattle, that he was carrying on with him; and I suppose made some proposition to my father to hire some one to assist him." The boy was shocked when he learned that his father had bound him out to Siler but had made no arrangements for David's eventual return home. "Young as I was, and as little as I knew about travelling, or being away from home, he hired me to the old Dutchman, to go four hundred miles on foot, with a perfect stranger that I had never seen until the evening before."[6]

David offered no explanation of how his mother must have felt to see her young son walk out of her life and not know when, or if, she would ever see him again. There is a conspicuous absence of much mention at all of Elizabeth Crockett throughout her son's *Narrative*. She apparently did not figure in any of the major decisions affecting the family and seems to have made little impression on David. As strong and tenacious as most frontier wives and mothers had to be, the reality was that they still resided in a world ruled by dominant males.

As David set out with Siler and the herd of cattle, Elizabeth and the rest of the family had no inkling that it would be several months before he would return to them. "The old Dutchman" was thirty-five, born Jacob Sëyler Jr. in Virginia in 1763, the youngest son of immigrants from northern Alsace-Lorraine, then a part of Germany.[7]

As David helped water and feed the cattle and keep them moving on the Abingdon Road, he found Siler a pleasant and thoughtful man who saw to the boy's needs and treated him well. When they finally reached their destination, just three miles from the Natural Bridge, a landmark geological formation created when Cedar Creek carved out a gorge in the mountainous limestone, David was even provided lodging at the home of Siler's in-laws, Peter and Elizabeth Hartley, and made to feel welcome.[8]

"My Dutch master was very kind to me, and gave me five or six dollars, being, pleased, as he said, with my services," David wrote of Siler. "This, however, I think was bait for me, as he persuaded me to stay with him, and not return any more to my father. I had been taught so many lessons of obedience by my father, that I at first supposed I was bound to obey this man, or at least I was afraid to openly disobey him; and I therefore staid with him, and tried to put on a look of contentment until I got the [Siler-Hartley] family all to believe I was fully satisfied."[9]

After four or five weeks of living at the Hartley place and continuing to work for Siler, David found his chance to leave and return home to

Tennessee. One day, as he played alongside the road with two local boys, three wagons passed, one driven by a man named Dunn and the others by his two sons. David recognized the Dunns from their frequent rest stops at the Crockett Tavern.[10] When they told the boy they were taking their loads of goods to Knoxville, David explained that he, too, wanted to go home. The Dunns invited him to join, with the promise to protect David if they were pursued. With that, he returned to his quarters, gathered his clothing and the little bit of money he had, and waited for morning, when he planned to sneak away and join the Dunns at the tavern, where they spent the night. "I went to bed early that night, but sleep seemed to be a stranger to me," David recalled. "For though I was a wild boy, yet I dearly loved my father and mother, and their images appeared to be so deeply fixed in my mind, that I could not sleep for thinking of them."[11]

Several hours before daybreak, fearful of being discovered but driven by his "childish love of home," he rose to face a blinding snowstorm and at least eight inches of fresh snow already on the ground. By the time the boy plodded the seven miles to the inn, the snow, according to Crockett, was "about as deep as my knees." A warm breakfast by the fire revived the chilled boy for the journey ahead. "The thoughts of home now began to take the entire possession of my mind, and I almost numbered the sluggish turns of the wheels, and much more certainly the miles of travel, which appeared to me to count mighty slow."[12]

By the time the Dunn wagons pulled up for the night at the home of John Dunn on the Roanoke River, David had grown so impatient with the slow pace that he announced he was going to continue his homeward trek alone on foot. Dunn tried to reason with him, but he would have none of it. "Mr. Dunn seemed very sorry to part with me, and used many arguments to prevent me from leaving him," related Crockett. "But home, poor as it was, again rushed on my memory, and it seemed ten times as dear to me as it ever had before. The reason was, that my parents were there, and all that I had been accustomed to in the hours of my childhood and infancy was there; and my anxious little hart panted also to be."[13]

A determined David set out by himself the next morning, but, near the first ford of the Roanoke River, a man returning from market with a drove of horses overtook him. The man led a saddled horse, which he kindly allowed David to mount and ride, thus sparing the youngster the river's frigid waters. David rode with the man until they reached a fork in the road and parted. The man and his horses took off for Kentucky, and David trudged the remaining miles to his family, who were over-joyed to see him walk through the tavern door that evening.

Life went reasonably well for David as he returned to his daily chores and frequent hunts for fresh meat. But during the autumn of 1799, John Crockett "took it into his head" to send thirteen-year-old David and his four older brothers to a subscription school at nearby Barton Springs, where Benjamin Kitchen attempted to teach book learning to the few area youngsters desirous of a rudimentary education.[14]

David's tenure at Kitchen's country school, however, was short-lived. Students of all ages, some nearly as old as their teacher, crowded into an airless room and tried to master the three Rs. David had only attended four days of classes and was just beginning to learn his letters when he had a falling-out with "one of the scholars" who was much older and larger than himself. Not wanting to draw his big brothers into his personal business, David determined to waylay the bully after school. He lay in wait along the roadside, and when the other boy wandered by, David sprang from the bushes and "set on him like a wild cat." He scratched the boy's face "to a flitter jig, and soon made him cry out for quarter in good earnest."[15]

The next morning, fearful of the repercussions sure to follow when word of his ambush reached the schoolmaster, David only pretended he was going to school. Instead, he went out into the woods, only emerg-ing at evening to walk home with his brothers, all of who were sworn to secrecy. This ruse went on for several more days until a curious Kitchen sent a note to John Crockett inquiring about his hooky-playing son. John demanded an explanation. "I knew very well that I was in a devil of a hobble," Crockett related, "for my father had been taking a few *horns*, and was in a good condition to make the fur fly."[16] Vowing to whip David harder than Kitchen ever could, John cut a stout hickory switch and the chase was on. "I put out with all my might, and soon we were both up to the top of speed," wrote David. He was thoroughly convinced that if his father or the schoolmaster got his hands on him he "would have used me up." After being pursued by his father for more than a mile, David managed to escape by topping a hill and hiding in a clump of brush until his "huffing and puffing" father passed and gave up the hunt.

To avoid the wrath and hickory rods of either his father or his teacher ever again, David "cut out," and went to the home of Jesse Cheek, only a few miles from the Crockett Tavern.[17] In 1795, Cheek built a general merchandise store and stock pens at what was known as Cheeks Crossroads. The store sold a wide range of dry goods, supplies, foodstuffs, and as many as sixty different books, including Bibles, hymnals, almanacs, and primers. Locals and travelers purchased gun flints, axes, tobacco, chocolate, bulk tea and coffee, scythes, rat traps, saddlery, pewter candlesticks, fiddles and Jew's harps, and a variety of spirits and liquors.[18]

At the store, David found one of his older brothers already there with Cheek, who was about to depart on a cattle drive. David was cheered by the presence of his brother, and, for his part, Cheek was only too happy to hire on both Crockett boys as drovers. They set out immediately, bound for Virginia to deliver Cheek's herd of a cattle. For David it was the beginning of a two-and-a-half-year adventure that would introduce the teenager to new and distant places and expose him to people and experiences that would shape the rest of his life. In many ways, this interlude provided David with a more useful education than any he would have received in Benjamin Kitchen's school. It was a journey to test the young man's mettle and temper his courage.

EIGHT

THE ODYSSEY

VEN FOR THE LATE EIGHTEENTH century, David Crockett did not have a typical adolescence. His journey into manhood commenced in the autumn of 1799, when he set out with Cheek, again bound for the state of Virginia. This trip was intended as a cooling-off period to give the angry John Crockett time to calm down and forgive David's trespasses, in particular his dropping out of school after less than a week of attending classes. David originally had no intention of being gone so long. Before he finally did come home, in the spring of 1802, John Crockett, unsure if his prodigal son was even still alive, had forgiven David.

The party left on a crisp fall morning. Jesse Cheek's small band of drovers included one of David's brothers as well as one of Cheek's brothers. They took the well-used route east out of Tennessee into northern Virginia, with stops along the way at Abingdon, Lynchburg, and Charlottesville.[1] After flanking the Blue Ridge Mountains, they passed through Chester Gap, obscured by hanging clouds of morning fog as thick as wood smoke. They then moved on to the heart of the Shenandoah Valley. Their final stop was Front Royal, chartered in 1788 and often called "Hell Town" due to the glut of strong drink and comely women readily available for rough mountaineers and travelers off the Shenandoah River.[2] It is not known if David or any of his fellow drovers partook of either the liquor or the women, as randy cowhands were known to do seventy-five years later in the cattle towns of Kansas.

David had no plans to tarry long in the same country where his grandfather David Crockett and other family had once lived before crossing over the mountains to what became Tennessee. After Cheek sold the herd to a local buyer, David and the other Cheek brother started back home in advance of the others, including David's brother. With but one horse available for their return trip, David and his traveling companion agreed that they would share the steed equally so one of them would not have to walk more than the other. It was a failed plan. After three days on the road, David found that the Cheek brother hardly ever gave up his perch on the saddle.[3] Unwilling to continue with someone so contrary, the footsore Crockett felt he would be better off looking for alternative transportation and, with four dollars of pay in his pocket, struck out on his own.

Crockett purchased a few provisions and had resumed his journey back to Tennessee when he encountered Adam Myers, a teamster hauling a wagonload of goods. Myers, from Greene County, Tennessee, where David was born, seemed "a jolly good fellow."[4] He proposed that Crockett reverse directions and go with him to his delivery destination in Gerrardstown, Virginia, now West Virginia, and then immediately return to Tennessee.

"On a little reflection, I determined to go back with him, which I did; and we journeyed on slowly as wagons commonly do, but merrily enough." As the wagon slowly bumped down the road, Crockett concluded that he had made the right decision. "I often thought of home, and, indeed, wished bad enough to be there; but when I thought of the school-house and Kitchen, my master, and the race with my father, and the big hickory he carried, and of the fierceness of the storm of wrath that I had left him in, I was afraid to venture back; for I knew my father's nature so well, that I was certain his anger would hang on him like a turkle [sic, turtle] does to a fisherman's toe, and, if I went back in a hurry, he would give me the devil in three or four ways."[5]

Just two days out on the eastbound trip, Crockett and Myers encountered the rest of the original Jesse Cheek drovers on their way home. The other Crockett son tried his best to talk David into going back to their family. Crockett's brother "pressed him hard" and came up with several persuasive arguments, such as "the pleasure of meeting my mother, and my sisters, who all loved me dearly."[6] David came close to yielding and even shed tears, an uncharacteristic behavior for such an adventurous young man, but when the thought of that "promised whipping" came to mind, he finally "determined that make or break, hit or miss, I would just hang on to my journey, and go ahead with the waggoner."

Crockett and Myers accordingly pressed on to Gerrardstown. After unloading the shipment, Myers tried to find some cargo to take back to Tennessee and learned that the closest goods available were to the southeast in Alexandria, near the new city of Washington. Crockett opted to stay in Gerrardstown and find temporary work until Myers returned with the back load.

Crockett hired on as a laborer with John Gray, a local farmer who in 1787 had helped lay out Gerrardstown with David Gerrard, whose father, John Gerrard, not only gave the village its name but also served as pastor of the first Baptist church west of the Blue Ridge Mountains. John Gray was Scottish to his fingertips, but he was willing to shell out twenty-five cents a day in wages to the young Scots-Irish hireling who plowed the grain fields as well as any man. "I continued working for him until the waggoner got back, and for a good time afterwards, as he continued to run his team back and forward, hauling to and from Baltimore."[7]

In the spring of 1800, Crockett had put aside enough money to purchase some decent clothing and decided to take time off and sport his new wardrobe. Myers was bringing a wagonload of flour to Baltimore, so Crockett joined him and gave the teamster his remaining savings of about seven dollars to tuck away for safekeeping. The leisurely wagon

ride from Virginia into Maryland was uneventful until they reached Elli-
cott's Mills, just outside Baltimore. Founded by Quakers, this bustling
town built on seven hills on the banks of the Patapsco River had one of
the largest merchant mills in the nation—the place where Myers was to
deliver the barrels of flour that filled his wagon.

"Here I got into the wagon for the purpose of changing my clothing, not thinking that I was in any danger; but while I was in there
we were met by some wheel-barrow men, who were working on the
road, and the horses took a scare and away they went, like they had seen
a ghost,"[8] Crockett later wrote. When the spooked horses bolted, the
wagon tongue and both axletrees snapped, tossing Crockett and several
heavy wooden barrels out in the road. David was shaken up but somehow avoided being "ground up fine as ginger." He spoke of the incident
years later in his autobiography as a member of Congress when he wrote,
"[But] this proved to me, that if a fellow is born to be hung, he will never
drown; and, further, that if he is born for a seat in Congress, even flour
barrels can't make a mash of him."

His determination and body intact, Crockett helped Myers with the
flour unloading, and the broken runaway wagon was hauled to a Baltimore shop for repairs. Over the couple of days they had to wait, Crockett
sported his new clothes and explored the city, and that included going to
the busy wharf to see the big sailing ships. The curious youngster stepped
aboard one of the vessels, and the ship's captain told him that he was in
need of another crewman and inquired of Crockett if he would be interested in a voyage to London. Crockett jumped at the chance, and when
he was asked about his parents, he explained that they lived hundreds of
miles away in Tennessee and that he was on his own. Crockett admitted
that by then "I had become pretty well weaned away from home, and I
cared but little where I was, or where I went, or what become of me."[9]

After reaching an agreement with the captain, Crockett hurried back
to tell Myers and get both his clothes and the stash of money. Myers
refused to give Crockett either and vowed that he would confine the
young man and take him back to Tennessee. Unable to board the ship

without his most precious belongings, David continued on with Myers. Over the next several days, as they traveled once again down the road, Myers kept a constant watch on the boy and several times threatened him with his wagon whip.[10] At last, Crockett saw an opening and being "resolved to leave him at all hazards," he managed to get his clothing and sneak away but "without a farthing of money to bear my expenses."

As usual, Crockett's luck held, and after going just a few miles, he came upon yet another teamster, "as resolute as a tiger." They struck up a conversation, and when Crockett began crying and spoke of his plight and the treatment he had received, the new acquaintance became angry and pronounced Myers "a scoundrel, and many other hard names."[11] Coincidentally, this man was named Henry Myers, but he was from Pennsylvania, not related in any way to the Tennessee Myers. David and the man backtracked and found Adam Myers. "You damn'd rascal, you have treated this boy badly," Henry Myers bellowed.[12] The trembling Adam Meyers confessed that he had already spent David's seven dollars and promised to pay it back to him when he got to Tennessee. That satisfied Crockett. He persuaded his champion to leave the other Meyers alone and they departed.

The new duo traveled together for several days. When they reached a point where they had to part ways, the older man took up a collection from some other "waggoners" at a roadhouse and handed Crockett three dollars to help tide him over until he found more work.[13] That grubstake got Crockett as far Christiansburg, Virginia. The seat of government for Montgomery County, this town had been established in 1776 and named for William Christian, a famed Indian fighter and brother-in-law of Patrick Henry. When Crockett first came to town, the legend was already being told of Daniel Boone coming to the area for an extended visit and getting in trouble with the law for failing to pay a loan he took out to purchase supplies for his axemen blazing the Wilderness Trail.[14]

Shortly after arriving in Christiansburg, Crockett hired on for a month of hard farmwork with James Caldwell for one shilling a day. After that, he bounded himself to Elijah Griffith, a Christiansburg hatter.[15] In exchange for his room and board and a chance to learn the hatter's trade, Crockett agreed to work for Griffith for a four-year term of service. He joined the other journeymen and apprentices at the shop, hopeful that he may have found a trade that would earn him the decent living he yearned for. Hatmaking had become a viable business on the frontier, with wagonloads of hats leaving Virginia for Tennessee and returning with furs and pelts, maple syrup, feathers, and peach brandy.

Unfortunately for David, not every hatter succeeded. After only eighteen months of learning the trade, Crockett rose one morning to learn that he was once more out of work. His employer had become so far behind with his debts that he packed up in the middle of the night and left the country.[16] Broke and without gainful employment, Crockett for a time hired on at John Snider's Hattery Shop, which enabled him to pull together the money needed to return to Tennessee. Life on the open road had been a useful teacher, but home and hearth beckoned. In the late winter of 1802, Crockett "cut out for home."[17]

He had barely started the journey when he faced the frigid crossing of the white-capped New River at the point where it connects with the Little River, ten miles south of Christiansburg.[18] Try as he might, Crockett was not able to convince any of the ferryboat operators to take him across. They all told him that it was far too dangerous for anyone to attempt a crossing until the stormy weather abated and the winds died down. He eventually found someone who reluctantly agreed to lend him a canoe. Using rope to secure his bundle of clothes and belongings in the canoe, he pushed off into the choppy water.

"When I got out fairly on the river, I would have given the world, if it had belonged to me, to have been back on shore,"[19] Crockett recalled of that treacherous crossing. "But there was no time to lose now, so I just determined to do the best I could, and the devil take the hindside." After much struggle, he was able to turn the canoe into the swift waters and then paddled with all his might upstream for about two miles until the current carried him across. "When I struck land, my canoe was about half full of water, and I was as wet as a drowned rat. But I was so much rejoiced, that I scarcely felt the cold, though my clothes were frozen on me."

Desperate to get warm, Crockett had to hike at least three miles before coming to a house where he could find comfort and dry his frozen clothing by the fire. The youngster also accepted a quaff of spirits, or, as he explained, "I took 'a leetle of the creator [critter],'—that warmer of the cold, and cooler of the hot—and it made me feel so good that I concluded it was like the negro's rabbit, 'good any way.' "[20] After the river crossing, Crockett proceeded home to Tennessee. While passing through Sullivan County, he was surprised to find his brother, who had gone with him so long before, at the start of the Cheek cattle drive. After a good visit and rest, Crockett left on the final leg of his journey.

He arrived at the Crockett Tavern late one evening. There were several wagons pulled up and what appeared to be a considerable company of guests inside. Instead of bursting through the door, David simply inquired if there was an empty bed for him. It was assumed that he was another paying guest, and he was told that he could stay the night. He found a place on a bench and spoke as little as possible. "I had been gone so long, and had grown so much, that the family did not at first know me," Crockett wrote. "And another, and perhaps a stronger reason was, they had no thought or expectation of me, for they all long had given me up for lost."[21]

At last everyone was called to supper. David joined the family and other guests at the long table. In only an instant the new tavern guest was identified. David's sister Betsy had been staring at him ever since his arrival. Suddenly she sprang to her feet and ran to his side. The ecstatic girl seized David around the neck and exclaimed, "Here is my lost brother!"[22] Almost thirty-four years later, when working with Thomas Chilton on the *Narrative*, Crockett had trouble describing his exact feelings at that moment.

"The joy of my sisters and my mother, and indeed of all the family, was such that it humbled me, and made me sorry that I hadn't submitted to a hundred whippings, sooner than cause so much affliction as they had suffered on my account." Crockett also noted, probably with a sly grin, that due to his increased age and enhanced size at the time of his homecoming, "together with the joy of my father, occasioned by my unexpected return," there would not be any more dreaded whippings. He was right.

NINE

RISE ABOVE

LIKE A PRODIGAL SON finally forgiven, Crockett entertained his family with many tales of the high and low adventure he had experienced during his long sojourn. He spoke of the people he encountered and places he saw. He told about being broke and being flush, nights spent sleeping in barn lofts, runaway horses, great sailing ships that beckoned, and of times bitter and times sweet. He talked of the kindness of strangers and the cruelty of those he thought were friends. As the stories unfolded, everyone clearly saw that at almost sixteen years of age, the young man had grown in stature and muscle, and strengthened his resolve and character. Crockett had proven his manhood, an unwritten but understood obligation for frontier males.

David was barely thirteen years old when he left his home in east Tennessee. Two and a half years on his own had exposed the young man to different people and places. Important life lessons had inevitably been learned. "He left his home a novice in the ways of the world but returned a person who understood considerably more about himself— what he wanted and what he valued," writes Joseph Swann. "He was beginning to rise above his circumstances against great odds."[1]

The same could not be said for David's father. Each time John Crockett attempted to rise above his lot in life, the odds overwhelmed him. Debt remained the Crockett family's cornerstone and hounded its patriarch like a cur dog pack pursuing a bear. The Crockett Tavern offered only meager accommodations, suitable for wagoners and wanderers but a cut below the more comfortable inns and roadhouses of the day. No doubt Elizabeth and her girls prepared tasty meals, kept the place neat and clean, and made sure the bed ticking stuffed with dried leaves was free of lice and other vermin. Still, the charges for food, drink, and lodging were low in east Tennessee due to a legal ruling in 1800 that froze most fees that taverns were allowed to charge. With the price of meals set at no more than ten cents, a night's lodging six cents, fodder and good pasture for wagon teams six cents, and half-pints of brandy, whiskey, and rum also just six cents, it was difficult to turn a profit.[2] Glad as he was to be back in the fold, David had to have known what was apparent to others—that while he may have changed, his family's fortunes had not.

In the spring of 1802, not long after David returned home, his father came to him seeking help. Prone to drink, John told his teenaged son that once more he found himself in a financial bind that even an ocean of hard cider could not wash away. During David's absence, his father continued to buy on credit and had run up more debts, including one that was long past due for thirty-six dollars to Abraham Wilson, a resident of the Panther Springs community.[3] With the industrious David back on the scene, John saw an opportunity. He proposed that David hire out to Wilson and work off the outstanding debt. In return, David would be released from ever having to turn any of his future earnings over to his father, as was the custom of the day for all minors. The proposition appealed to David and he quickly agreed.

Wasting no time, David immediately went to Panther Springs to meet with Wilson. The arrangement between them called for six months of labor; in exchange, John Crockett's note would be fully forgiven. David would be working at a range of tasks for approximately six dollars a month, which broke down to twenty cents a day in wages, or the cost for a full pint of tavern wine. The thought of being free of his father's strict parental control was a powerful incentive.

"I set in, and worked with all my might, not losing a single day in six months," Crockett reported in his autobiography. "When my time was out, I got my father's note, and then declined working with the man [Abraham Wilson] any longer, though he wanted to hire me badly. The reason was, it was a place where a heap of bad company met to drink and gamble, and I wanted to get away from them, for I know'd very well if I staid there, I should get a bad name, as nobody could be respectable that would live there."[4]

When his son delivered the paid-off note, John Crockett was genuinely pleased. As David later reflected, "Though he was poor, he was an honest man, and always tried mighty hard to pay off his debts." What he failed to mention, however, was that often John had his own children do the heavy lifting for him.

As soon as his work for Abraham Wilson ended, David found employment with John Canaday, a man who would come to have a major impact on Crockett but who for 150 years went unnamed in all published works, or was inaccurately identified as John Kennedy.[5] The problem with the Canaday surname mostly stemmed from Crockett's own *Narrative*, in which he phonetically spelled the name Kennedy, based on the pronunciation: accented on the first syllable, with the second *a* silent. It was likely that David's Ulster ear caused him to hear the name as Kennedy, a common variation of Canaday. Of interest, but puzzling, are Tennessee land records that posted the name as John Kennedy, while tax lists used the correct spelling. The Canaday clan—having spelled their name in a variety of ways, including Canady, Cannaday, and Kennedy—answered to any of them.[6]

The Canadays were a Quaker family, all members in good standing of the Society of Friends. John Canaday, born in Prince George County, Maryland, in 1741, and his wife, Margaret Thornbrough Canaday, born in 1744 and a native of Lancaster County, Pennsylvania, met and married in 1764 in Rowan County, North Carolina, where both their families had settled.[7] In 1796, the Canadays migrated to the new state of Tennessee accompanied by three of their grown sons, joined later by their daughter and three other sons. All of them settled in Jefferson County and affiliated with the recently formed Lost Creek Monthly Meeting, only the second Friends meetinghouse in Tennessee.[8] Lost Creek became a thriving center of Quaker life and worship and had a profound influence in East Tennessee history and culture during the antebellum years. Quakers recognized the evils of slave ownership and by the late 1780s had freed their slaves. If a Quaker farmer needed work done he relied on his family or else employed laborers.

After hearing that the many Quakers residing in the area "were remarkable for their kindness," the notion of working on the tidy Canaday farm appealed to Crockett.[9] At their first meeting Canaday hired the strapping lad for two shillings a day, provided that after a week's trial the young man's work proved satisfactory. At week's end, Canaday, or the "honest old Quaker," as Crockett referred to him, announced that he was pleased with Crockett's work ethic. Then the shrewd farmer informed David that he held a note on John Crockett in the sum of forty dollars. Canaday further explained that the note would be surrendered if David paid it off by working for him for six months. It has been surmised that Canaday owned the property where the Crockett Tavern operated and that the outstanding debt resulted from back rent that John owed.[10]

"I was certain enough that I should never get any part of the note," Crockett wrote. "But then I remembered it was my father that owed it, and I concluded it was my duty as a child to help him along, and ease his lot as much as I could. I told the Quaker I would take him up on his offer, and immediately went to work."[11]

For six months, he labored as hard as any field hand in Tennessee for Canaday, who, in turn, provided David with quarters and meals at the Canaday home. The Canadays treated David like one of their own. "I never visited my father's house during the whole time of this engagement, though he lived only fifteen miles off. But when it was finished, and I had got the note, I borrowed one of my employer's horses, and, on a Sunday evening, went to pay my parents a visit."

Presently, David took the newly redeemed note from inside his shirt and handed it to his father, who, upon seeing it, straightaway thought

Canaday had sent it for collection. John "looked mighty sorry" and told his son that he did not have the money to pay off the note and was not sure what he should do. "I then told him I had paid it for him, and it was then his own; that it was not presented for collection, but as a present from me. At this, he shed a heap of tears; and as soon as he got over it, he said he was sorry he couldn't give me any thing. But he was not able, he was too poor."[12]

Seeing his father sob, receiving finally some heartfelt gratitude for what he had done without being asked, proved payback in itself for David. For two backbreaking terms of servitude over the course of a year, David had voluntarily worked without any personal income to clear his father's due notes. Now the ledger between them was finally wiped clean, and David had some options to weigh. Just after the emotional scene with his grateful father, David made up his mind about how to proceed. "The next day, I went back to my old friend, the Quaker, and set in to work for him."[13]

For the next four years, until David was twenty years old and about to wed Polly Finley, he lived and worked for the Quakers on land they bought at the headwaters of Panther Creek, near the community of Panther Springs.[14] David's time with the Canadays was time very well spent. During those years he became literate and received the only formal schooling he ever had, excluding the few hectic days spent in Kitchen's subscription school years earlier. David also found a true role model and enduring friend in John Canaday, who proved a counterbalance to his father. "The influence of John Canaday on David was profound," according to Crockett historian Joseph Swann. "Although David continued to do many things of which Canaday did not approve, they both evidently thought enough of each other to be sensitive and tolerant. John Canaday was a father figure for David—one quite different from his natural father. John Canaday's influence on David's character development, in those formative years, should not be underestimated."[15]

On the surface it appeared that the aging Quaker farmer and the upstart young man had little in common. Unlike the Canadays, the Crocketts seemed to avoid taking part in organized religion, even though it is likely that David's mother was the "Rebecca Crocit" who, with eight others, was baptized at the Bent Creek Baptist Church on a cold February morning in 1803.[16] It also could be assumed that, given their strong Scots-Irish bloodlines, both sides of the Crockett family had, at one time, ties with the Presbyterians. There was a marked difference between the culture and lifestyle of the Quakers and the Ulster Scots. Beyond the wide cultural gap between David and his mentor, there was also a generational gap of forty-five years that had to be overcome.

Canaday had to have seen qualities in Crockett that made the effort to befriend and help the young man worthwhile. One can only assume that John Crockett's dire straits acted as a countervailing influence on his son, who had no wish to emulate his father. David's irrepressible passion for life and yearning to better his state continually drove him in the right direction. Instead of taking the path of least resistance, however, he almost always chose the difficult route. He firmly believed that in the long run it was the wisest course to follow.

────── T E N ──────

LOVESICK

AS THE NINETEENTH CENTURY emerged into being, an astute Virginian took the helm of a fledgling nation that had been born of revolution and now was eager to expand. Many eyes were fast turning westward toward a vast and uncharted continent, not least of those the new president, Thomas Jefferson. Restless frontiersmen set out to clear the wilderness, conquer native tribes, and exploit the land's wealth of resources. They also unknowingly supplied ample infusions of romance into the American myth. At the vanguard were Scots-Irish descended from Ulster forefathers. They became the first settlers to call themselves Americans.

David Crockett was steadily evolving into one of those high-spirited Americans. Like the developing nation, he, too, continually grew stronger and more self-confident. Much of his positive attitude came from being gainfully employed from age sixteen to twenty by John Canaday. After going to work on the Canaday farm, one of David's immediate goals was to purchase a new wardrobe to replace his few clothes, which, as he described them, were "nearly all worn out," and "mighty indifferent."[1]

A logical reason for Crockett's desire to improve his appearance resulted from his growing interest in the opposite sex. Whether or not Crockett enjoyed any amorous adventures when he trekked around the countryside is unknown. Back home, the young man's dark good looks and muscular frame had to have appealed to the young women living in the area. Likewise, those same women most certainly caught the eye of Crockett.

The possibility of romance came David's way in the summer of 1803, two months into his long term of service for the Canaday clan. David was love-struck by the arrival of Amy Summer, a nineteen-year-old visiting the Canadays from her home in Surry County, North Carolina. Amy's father was a half-brother to John Canaday, making her his half-niece. She also was a Quaker and, back in North Carolina, part of the Westfield Monthly Meeting of Friends.[2] Even with all his self-assurance, David became tongue-tied whenever he thought about sharing his true feelings with Amy.

> For though I have heard people talk about hard loving, yet I reckon no poor devil in this world was ever cursed with such hard luck as mine has always been, when it came over me. I soon found myself head over heels in love with this girl . . . and I thought that if all the hills about there were pure chink, and all belonged to me, I would give them if I could just talk to her as I wanted to; but I was afraid to begin, for when I think of saying anything to her, my heart would begin to flutter like a duck in a puddle; and if I tried to outdo it and speak, it would get right smack up in my throat, and choak me like a cold potatoe.[3]

After a few false starts, Crockett finally mustered the gumption to approach Amy. "I told her how well I loved her; that she was the darling object of my soul and body; and I must have her, or else I should pine down to nothing, and just die away with the consumption."[4]

Apparently, the young woman was not taken aback by David's sudden admission of love. However, she was "an honest girl, and didn't want to deceive anybody," and her response was not what Crockett sought or expected: she explained that she was already spoken for and was engaged to marry her first cousin, Robert Canaday, the youngest son of Crockett's employer. David was shattered. "This news was worse to me than war, pestilence, or famine; but still I knowed I could not help myself. I saw quick enough my cake was dough, and I tried to cool off as fast as possible; but I had hardly safety pipes enough, as my love was so hot as mighty nigh to burst my boilers. But I didn't press my claims any more, seeing there was no chance to do any thing."[5]

Fortunately, those vanquished expressions did no lasting harm to the anguished seventeen-year-old. Having mastered the woods, he was both resilient and insightful. He analytically pondered his failure to win Amy's heart, and concluded that it was going to take more than fresh trousers and shirts to achieve any success in love or, for that matter, in life. "I began now to think, that all my misfortunes growed out of my want of learning," mused Crockett. "I had never been to school but four days . . . and did not yet know a letter."[6]

One of the married Canadays lived a mile away and had opened a school in his home. Crockett was able to strike an arrangement with the Canadays allowing him to attend school for four days and then work on the family farm for two days to pay for his learning and board.[7] On the seventh day, David, like everyone else, followed God's lead and rested.

The work-study regimen worked well. David applied himself and became both a diligent student and a devoted farmworker. He kept up this routine for six months and learned enough to read his primer, write out his own name, and "cipher some in the first three rules of figures." For the rest of his life Crockett was to continue to make improvements in his reading and writing skills. Several signed documents and letters in his hand attest to this. He also read various periodicals and books, including selections from Shakespeare; Benjamin Franklin's autobiography; and, as it was later known, a rudimentary translation of Ovid's *Metamorphoses*, which must have provided ample, if not even salty, entertainment, with its amorous tales of spurned and passionate love.[8]

"And this was all the schooling I ever had in my life, up to this day," Crockett wrote of his time in the Quaker school. "I should have continued longer, if it hadn't been that I concluded I couldn't do any longer without a wife; and so I cut out to hunt me one."

In no time, Crockett found a young woman who could not have seemed more appropriate. She was living about ten miles from John Canaday's farm, at the Dumplin community, not far from Dandridge in Jefferson County. Named Margaret Elder, she was from "a family of pretty little girls" whom David had known for many years. "They [the Elders] had lived in the same neighborhood with me, and I thought very well of them."[9] Margaret, described later as "a tall, buxom lass, with cherry bitten cheeks and luscious lips, mischievous eyes, and hands doubly accustomed to handling the spinning wheel or rifle trigger,"[10] appeared to be everything David wanted in a frontier wife. He steadily courted her "until I got to love her as bad as I had the Quaker's niece; and I would have agreed to fight a whole regiment of wild cats if she would only have said she would have me." The increasingly frustrated Crockett, however, was unable to extract commitment from the always loving but also coy and elusive Margaret. Maybe she saw the inevitable in her future—a lifetime of waiting at home with a passel of kids while her husband stalked game, entered shooting matches, and caroused with the other menfolk.

In the late summer of 1805, David and Margaret were asked to serve as attendants at the marriage of Robert Canaday and Amy Summer, the beguiling Quaker girl Crockett had once desired.[11] After he and his "little queen," as he referred to Margaret, performed their duties, Crockett was inspired to press his case for them to wed. Margaret remained evasive, but Crockett persisted and "gave her mighty little peace," until at last she caved in and agreed to marry him. He was ecstatic and later noted that marrying Margaret would make him "the happiest man in the created world."

By this time, Crockett had become friendly with a young man from Kentucky who had been bound out to work for John Canaday. This fellow was about the same age as David and, like him, had also discovered the bevy of eligible Elder girls and became smitten with one of Margaret's sisters. Aware that Canaday frowned on "courting frolics," the pair of young bucks devised a scheme that enabled them to woo the Elder sisters without their employer knowing about it.[12] "We commonly slept up-stairs, and at the gable end of the house there was a window. So one Sunday, when the old man and his family were all gone to meeting, we went out and cut a long pole, and, taking it to the house, we set it up on end in the corner. . . . After this we would go upstairs to bed, and then putting on our Sunday clothes, would go out the window, and climb down the pole, take a horse apiece, and ride about ten miles to where his sweetheart lived, and the girl I claimed as my wife."

The young men—always careful to sneak back into the Canaday house before daybreak—continued their night courting and romancing right up until the time of David and Margaret's wedding. The couple had set an autumn date, and on October 21, 1805, Crockett donned his best—and no doubt only—suit of clothes and rode to the Jefferson County courthouse at Dandridge to procure the marriage license.[13] Just nineteen, he was more than ready to quit being a bachelor and create a home of his own.

The marriage plans dissolved unexpectedly a few days later when David caught wind of a shooting match and frolic. The crack marksman saw a good chance to make some money. He told Canaday that he was off to hunt deer but, instead, picked up his rifle and rode directly to the match. After all, it was being held on the way to the Elder home, where he planned to end his day by finally asking for their daughter's hand, something that he had long put off.

At the shooting match, Crockett's aim with his long rifle was as true as ever, and, when it ended, he and a companion had won the prize—a whole beef. He sold his portion for a hefty five dollars in "real grit," gold and silver coins. With "a light heart and my five dollars jingling in my pocket," he rode off to see his fiancée and her parents.[14] A couple of miles from the Elder home, Crockett stopped on an impulse for a brief chat with one of Margaret's uncles. At the cabin he found that her younger sister was visiting, and when David greeted her, the girl burst into tears.

She blurted out that Margaret was jilting David. She had no intention of marrying him but instead, the very next day, was going to wed another man, who had also procured a wedding license.

"This was as sudden to me as a clap of thunder of a bright sunshiny day," Crockett recalled. "It was the cap-stone of all the afflictions I had ever met with; and it seemed to me, that it was more than any human creature could endure. It struck me perfectly speechless for some time, and made me feel so weak, that I thought I should sink down."[15]

After a while, David recovered enough to pull himself upright and take his leave. Through her sobs, the girl urged him to continue on to her home and reason with Margaret. She said her parents preferred David to the other suitor, and there was a chance he could break up the match. "But I found I could go no further," he noted long after, ". . . concluding I was only born for hardships, misery, and disappointment."[16]

Crockett was not guiltless in this matter. More than likely his propensity for shooting matches and social frolics contributed to the demise of the couple's relationship. Furthermore, his blustery, dominating personality may have failed to recognize the emotional needs of a prospective spouse. There was clearly room on both sides for blame.

ELEVEN

POLLY

FTER MARGARET ELDER CAST HIM aside for another, Crockett laid low for a time, licking his wounds and regretting his lot in life. He had come to the conclusion that he was snake-bit when it came to finding love, just as his father was when it came to staying out of debt. Crockett described himself as someone who had been "born odd, and should always remain so, and nobody would have me."[1] For several weeks he was restless day and night. He hardly slept and practically stopped eating. Canaday and other friends worried about David and tried to boost his spirits.

"They all thought I was sick," wrote Crockett, "and so I was. And it was the worst kind of sickness—a sickness of the heart, and all the tender parts, produced by disappointed love."[2]

As had been the case with other trials and tribulations Crockett had already faced, the passage of time seemed to be the best healing balm. Also, time simply was far too precious to waste on self-pity. "With men of the backwoods, heartache was a luxury,"[3] was how James Shackford summed up Crockett's situation. "The backwoodsman had to arrive at journey's end restored and prepared for the next stage. The whole of a twenty-year sorrow had to be crammed into a fistful of heart's-ease gathered along the way of a day's journeying through the forest."

Crockett threw himself back into his labors for Canaday and, whenever there was some spare time in the evenings or on the Sabbath, nothing was more restorative than a mind-clearing jaunt in the woods with his rifle in hand. Hunting always proved to be Crockett's salvation, sanctuary, and escape. Still, like a young god in Ovid's classic work, he believed that the only way to complete his metamorphosis into manhood was to find a wife.

While out on one of his hunts, Crockett stopped in a forest clearing at the cabin of a woman he described as a "Dutch widow."[4] The woman had a single daughter, but Crockett had no interest in her as a spouse, for although she was smart enough and certainly a skilled conversationalist, she was "as ugly as a stone fence." Seeing she had little chance of snaring David, the girl told him that "there was as good fish in the sea that had never been caught out of it." Crockett doubted her, but whether she was right or not, "I was certain that she was not one of them. For she was so homely that it almost give me a pain in the eyes to look at her."[5]

In spite of the rejection, the girl invited Crockett to her family's upcoming reaping, where she promised to introduce him to "one of the prettiest little girls" in attendance.[6] David had misgivings, but he enjoyed reapings, the community harvest gatherings that mainly were social events and included plenty of food, drink, dancing, competitions, and opportunities for bragging and storytelling—all pursuits that he savored.

The reaping was fast approaching when David told Canaday that he would give him two days of work if he allowed the bound boy to go along to the festivities. The old Quaker refused and "reproved me pretty considerable roughly for my proposition." Canaday further advised Crockett to stay away since there would be "a great deal of bad company there" and it might hurt the young man's good name.[7] But Crockett had made a promise to the Dutch girl, so he shouldered his rifle and went to the summer harvest celebration.

Frontier frolics, reapings, corn huskings, and quilting parties meant hard work for those in attendance, but everyone, especially young men like Crockett, looked forward to the good times that followed. Likewise, the house and barn raisings also brought people together. After the work was completed, brush and branches were gathered to feed a fire that blazed all night long. The flames attracted settlers from miles around to come listen to lively fiddles, sip some whiskey, and dance up a storm.[8]

By the day of the reaping, Crockett had concluded that "the little varment," as he now called Margaret Elder, had treated him so badly that it was time to put her totally out of his mind and find himself a wife.[9] True to her word, the Dutch girl introduced Crockett to the mother of the girl she had told him of earlier. This "old Irish woman," as Crockett first identified her in his autobiography, was Jean Kennedy Finley, the wife of William Finley, widely known as Billy. Although family records are scarce, it is believed both of the Finleys were born around 1765 in Lincoln County, North Carolina, and wed in 1786, the year of Crockett's birth. The couple had eight known children—sons John, James, William, Samuel, and David, and daughters Mary Polly, Jean, and Susannah.[10]

Jean Finley—a loquacious and willful woman—was in no way bashful. She praised Crockett's rosy red cheeks and told him she had just the sweetheart for him—the eldest of her three daughters, who only used her middle name, Polly. "In the evening I was introduced to her daughter, and I must confess, I was plaguy well pleased with her from the word go. She had a good countenance, and was very pretty, and I was full bent on making up an acquaintance with her."[11]

As soon as the fiddlers showed up and dancing commenced, David asked Polly to join him in a reel, a lively dance that originated in the Scottish highlands. The young woman graciously took his calloused hand, and after they finished the dance, she and David found seats together and visited. "I found her very interesting; while I was setting by her, making as good a use of my time as I could, her mother came to us, and very jocularly called me her son-in-law." Puzzled by this comment, Crockett decided the woman was joking. Nonetheless, he paid as much attention to the mother as to the pretty daughter for the rest of the evening. Even at his young age, Crockett had learned the importance of winning over the mother if he wanted to land the daughter. "I went on the old saying, of salting the cow to catch the calf. I soon became so pleased with this little girl, that I began to think the Dutch girl had told me the truth, when she said there was still good fish in the sea."[12]

The frolic lasted until almost sunrise, and when David finally parted from Polly, he "found my mind had become much better reconciled than it had been for a long time." He went home and made a bargain with the Canaday son who had been his teacher. Crockett promised him six months of work for a "low-priced horse" needed right away so he could properly court Miss Polly Finley. When he mounted his horse— the first one he had ever owned—and rode to the Finley home, David met Polly's father, Billy, whom he found very affable. Jean Finley was just as talkative as ever.[13]

The feisty mother bombarded the young man with all sorts of questions to find out if he was the right man for her daughter. Crockett soon discovered that the "old Irish woman" did not like what she heard. Despite the gushing reception he received from Polly's mother at the reaping where they first met, she was not in favor of a Crockett union with her daughter. Probably Crockett's financial standing in the community had a lot to do with Jean's attitude toward him.

Later, when Polly returned home from a meeting escorted by another attentive young man, David began to think "I was barking up the wrong tree again," but he was determined to make his stand.[14] The sun had long disappeared behind the mountains, and when darkness closed in, Polly suggested that, because David had a lengthy ride home ahead of him, he stay for supper and spend the night at the Finley home. "Her mother was deeply enlisted for my rival, and I had to fight against her influence as well as his," Crockett related. "But the girl was the prize I was fighting for; and as she welcomed me, I was determined to lay siege to her." His persistence worked and he simply outlasted the other suitor that night. In disgust, the other young man gritted his teeth and skulked off as Crockett shot him hard looks "as fierce as a wild-cat."[15]

About two weeks after this confrontation, Crockett was out on a wolf hunt with several of his friends and their pack of hounds. They hunted in an area that was new and unfamiliar and Crockett somehow became separated from the others. Not only did he find himself alone, but nightfall was fast approaching, and storm clouds brewed in the darkening sky. Crockett had wandered at least six or seven miles when suddenly he caught a flash of movement in the trees and saw "a little woman streaking it along through the woods like all wrath."[16] Crockett gave chase. "For I was determined I wouldn't lose sight of her that night anymore. I run on till she saw me, and she stopped." He caught up with the woman and found, to his surprise and delight, that it was none other than Polly Finley. She had been out searching for her father's horses and had also lost her way and had no notion of how far she was from home. Crockett was overjoyed with his unexpected bounty.

"For I thought she looked sweeter than sugar; and by this time I loved her almost well enough to eat her." Instead he restrained himself, and together they followed a footpath that led them to a dwelling where they were given food and shelter. "Here we staid all night," wrote Crockett. "I set up all night courting; and in the morning we parted. She went to her home, from which we were distant about seven miles, and I to mine, which was ten miles off."[17]

Crockett was determined not to allow yet another prospective wife slip away from him. He pressed his wooing of Polly, and tried his level best to win over her headstrong mother. An indication of Crockett's serious intent to make Polly his bride was revealed when he sold his cherished rifle—the first gun he ever owned—to the Canaday son in order to cut the work time to pay off the debt for his horse.[18] Any frontiersman had to be crazily infatuated if he was willing to sell a classic Kentucky rifle of the finest quality to help secure a girl's hand in marriage.

At last the young couple discussed a wedding date, and David donned his best clothes and rode to the Finley place to ask for Polly's hand. Billy Finley was cordial, but his wife clearly did not welcome Crockett to her home. "When I got there, the old lady appeared to be mighty wrathy; and when I broached the subject, she looked at me as savage as a meat ax."[19] Crockett tried to use his charm, but nothing seemed to work or soften Jean Finley, whose "Irish was up too high to do any thing with her." Crockett made sure the Finleys knew that he intended to marry Polly one way or another; if the wedding could not take place at their home, the couple would go elsewhere. Before riding off, David told Polly he would be back in several days with a saddled horse for her to use and that she should be prepared to leave. On his way home, David stopped at the house of a justice of the peace, who agreed to perform the ceremony.

On August 12, 1806, Crockett once again rode to the county seat of Dandridge and went to the courthouse to apply for another marriage license.[20] His friend Thomas Doggett, of Morristown, accompanied Crockett. County Clerk Joseph Hamilton issued the marriage bond after both men cosigned, pledging $1,250, an immense sum at the time, on the condition there be "no cause to obstruct the marriage of the said David Crockett with Polly Findley [sic]."[21]

Nothing would prevent this union. On Saturday, August 16, 1806, David, following the custom of the day, gathered an escort that included two of his brothers, a sister-in-law, an unmarried sister, Thomas Doggett, and another friend. With David in the lead, the entourage rode off to fetch Polly. A larger company of friends and neighbors who had heard of the wedding and wished to attend met them about two miles from the Finley place. One of Crockett's brothers, his sister, and Doggett were sent ahead to the Finley cabin bearing empty flasks, or flagons. Custom called for the vessels to be filled with strong drink to signal that a cordial greeting and hospitality could be expected.[22] Jean Finely shunned the riders, but Billy Finley, in turn, ignored his wife. He filled the flasks to overflowing, and the delegation returned to the main group with the tokens of welcome and passed them around for those gathered to quaff before proceeding on to the waiting Polly.

Upon arriving, David remained mounted and asked Polly if she was ready to ride away with him to their marriage. She said she was, and jumped up on the spare horse Crockett led. Then Billy Finley intervened. He stopped the riders at the gate and implored David to stay and have the wedding at his home. David had always respected Polly's father and replied that he would remain if Jean herself would ask him and also apologize for her rude behavior. Finley summoned his wife, and after an intense private visit, she finally acquiesced. "She came to me and looked at me mighty good, and asked my pardon for what she had said, and invited me to stay," wrote Crockett about his soon to be mother-in-law. "She said it was the first child she ever had to marry; and she couldn't bear to see her off in that way; that if I would light, she would do the best she could for us."

David accepted the offer and immediately sent off for Henry Bradford, the justice of the peace, to perform the ceremony.[23] The anxious bridegroom "was afraid to wait long, for fear of another defeat." That evening at the Finleys' cabin, with a slew of witnesses looking on, David and Polly were wed. At long last, Crockett's dream of having a wife had been realized. He was just one day shy of his twentieth birthday, a typical age then for a young man to marry.

FINLEY'S GAP

FOLLOWING THEIR WELL-ATTENDED wedding cere-mony and the ensuing frolic, David and Polly Crockett spent their first night together as husband and wife beneath the roof of the Finleys' snug cabin, hardly a honeymoon love nest with several family members sleep-ing in close proximity. Early the next morning the newlyweds departed for the Crockett Tavern at Morristown, where another large company of family and friends waited to celebrate the nuptials and mark David's twentieth birthday.

"We passed the time quite merrily," Crockett recalled, "until the company broke up; and having gotten my wife, I thought I was com-pletely made up, and needed nothing more in the whole world. But I soon found this was all a mistake—for now having a wife, I wanted every thing else; and, worse than all, I had nothing to give for it."[1]

That was not quite true, for upon the couple's return to the Finley place, Crockett was pleasantly surprised to find his mother-in-law in the "finest humor in the world." The Finleys gave David and Polly the gift of "two likely cows and calves," which Crockett thought a modest dowry. Still, it was better than what he had expected to receive from them. The livestock was certainly more than what his father, John Crockett, apparently provided, beyond some food and horns of whiskey at the tavern party.

John Canaday, Crockett's longtime employer and friend, who had not attended any of the festivities because of his strong Quaker beliefs, proved the most generous of anyone. He gave David and Polly an order for fifteen dollars' worth of goods at a local store, a great deal of money at that time and a true indication of the depth of affection Canaday had for David.[2] "With this [the Canaday gift], we fixed up pretty grand, as we thought, and allowed to get on very well," wrote Crockett.

Like so many young frontier couples, David and Polly started out with only the barest necessities. They possessed no property and had no money. As the best land in the area had already been claimed and the game was quickly being thinned out, Crockett now faced a lifetime of growing a few crops on rented land and working for other people, just as he had done all of his life.

They set up housekeeping in a small rented cabin within sight of his in-laws' place. The Finleys had established their home years before near where the headwaters of Long Creek and Dumplin Creek rise on either side of Bays Mountain, at a point that soon became known as Finley's Gap. Nearby ran the Great Indian War Trail, the path used in 1776 by 1,800 frontier militiamen led by Colonel William Christian in the campaign against the Cherokees who had allied with the British.[3] After seeing the rolling terrain and loamy soil during their march, many of those veterans came back with their families, resulting in heavy settlement activity.

By the early 1780s, communities were being established around Bays Mountain and along the Holston and French Broad rivers in what was soon to become Jefferson County. Some of those first white settlers included Thomas Jarnagin, owner of large tracts of rich bottomland on the north side of the Nolichucky River, who specialized in making corn whiskey and in 1784 had built the first mill in the county on Long Creek.[4] By the following year, with the coming of more settlers, large tracts of land were cleared that had been covered with dense forest and canebrakes.

The Finleys may have been there before any of the others. Around 1786, when Thomas Rankin, of Cumberland County, Pennsylvania, arrived at the upper end of Dumplin Creek, he found Billy Finley was already there, living in a comfortable log house in Finley's Gap at Bays Mountain.[5]

The first domicile that David Crockett and his eighteen-year-old bride called home was not nearly as comfortable as Billy Finley's two-story log house on a rock foundation. Situated in the hollow near the Finley house, the simple dwelling that the young Crocketts rented from a neighbor was described as "not much more than a shanty."[6] It was constructed of pine logs that were not hewn or even stripped of bark. The cracks between the logs were daubed with mud and the chimney made from mud and sticks, a common technique in 1806. The cabin was topped with a clapboard roof, probably of heart pine or white oak. There were two small rooms, two outside doors, and a door through the middle partition wall. There were no windows.[7] A nearby spring gurgled up plenty of water cold enough to make teeth hurt, and the woods provided fresh meat. The Crocketts would live here for six years, and this is where their first two children would be born.

Some aspects of the couple's early married years seemed pleasant enough. There is no evidence of further disagreements between David and his mother-in-law, even though it would not have taken too long for Jean Finley to realize that her early assessment of Crockett's lack of financial stability was proving painfully correct. It is unclear just how Polly faired during those first few years, other than David's descriptions of her domestic life, which left little time for anything but work. "My wife had a good wheel, and knowed exactly how to use it," observed Crockett. "She was also a good weaver, as most of the Irish are, whether men or women; and being very industrious with her wheel, she had, in little or no time, a fine web of cloth, ready to make up; and she was good at that too, and almost any thing else that a woman could do."[8]

Meanwhile, Crockett proved that he was good at proverbially everything a man could do too, or, at least a free white man living in the foothills of Tennessee in the early nineteenth century. Crockett frequently showed up at competitive shooting matches and other events and activities, and hunted for game in the surrounding forests and hills. He frequently paid calls on friends such as James Blackburn, a Virginia native who lived two miles from Finley's Gap on the waters of Long Creek and the headwaters of Carson's Branch. Crockett enjoyed Blackburn's company and stayed in touch with him for the rest of his life. Crockett also spent time on Long Creek with James McCuistion, a long-time neighbor of the Finleys, who had purchased Crockett's prized first .48-caliber flintlock rifle from the Canaday son shortly after the Quaker schoolteacher took it in barter from David in exchange for a horse. The weapon was still in McCuistion's possession when he died in 1836 and has remained in his family ever since.[9] Today, it is owned by Joseph Swann, the Crockett historian and a McCuistion descendant, and is on public display at the Museum of East Tennessee History in Knoxville.

Crockett would have been pleased that his first Kentucky rifle—a symbol of his most passionate pursuit—remains for all to see. When he lived at Finley's Gap, long before he had achieved any acclaim, Crockett looked for ways to leave some sort of sign so he would be remembered after he was gone. Stories circulate about a certain tree at Colliers Crossroads, not far from the Crockett home. In the early 1900s it was said people still came there to see the beech tree that Crockett topped and the unknown words he cut with his hunting blade in the tree's thick hide. Another local story is told of one of Crockett's neighbors coming upon David chopping two distinct marks high up on the trunk of a cucumber tree. The man asked what he was doing. Crockett went right on hacking away and answered, "I am doing this for the memory of Davy when Davy is dead and gone."[10]

The Crocketts' first two children were John Wesley Crockett, born on July 10, 1807, and William F. Crockett, born on November 25, 1808. It is likely that David and Polly named the boys for their own fathers. "In this time we had two sons, and I found I was better at increasing my family than my fortune,"[11] Crockett mused.

David scratched out a bit of a living by tenant farming his small crop patch, and picked up a little more income hiring out to others in the area. "Crockett was a poor man when I first saw him," recalled John L. Jacobs, a neighbor of the Finleys. "He was then a married man, lived three-fourths of a mile from my Father in Findley's [*sic*] Gap. He was then making rails for my father. I went to him where he had cut a very large yellow pine tree. He frequently called on me to hand him the wedge or glut, whichever he needed."[12]

By far, Crockett's best method of getting food was ancestral. His ability with a rifle constantly improved, and whenever possible he took to the woods and hills to track and kill both small and large game. Toting home a deer or turkey meant David, Polly, and their two little boys would eat well for a while, but bagging a black bear provided them with an abundance of edible flesh as well as valuable fat and fur. Both bear meat and oil from the layers of fat were in great demand across the American frontier and well beyond. Bear pelts were fabricated into a variety of goods, including rugs, bed robes, coats, and tall dressy fur caps—fashioned from the prized thick, glossy fur of a mother bear with cubs and proudly worn by various army regiments.[13] As early as the mid-1700s, colonial America exported thousands of bear pelts. By the time Crockett took to the woods with his hounds and long gun, great quantities of bear fat and oil—stowed in barrels or sewn up in deerskins—were being shipped by barges down the Mississippi River to New Orleans, eastern seaboard cities, and European markets.[14] In the field following a kill, hunters wrapped the butchered meat in the bear's own skin and carried the oil home in the bear's bladder. The oil was clarified by boiling it with shaved slippery elm bark, then stored for later use. The bladder could be used as an oilcloth for wrapping packages, and the fat served as cooking oil, lamp fuel, various home remedies, and insect repellent.[15] Smart hunters such as Crockett sometimes followed the example of many Indian tribes and slathered on bear fat to protect their bodies from the cold.

Along with jerked venison, wild turkey, rabbit, squirrel, cured hams, and slabs of bacon, generous cuts of bear meat hung from the rafters of Crockett's smokehouse and were staples in his family's diet. Supposedly, the choicest cuts from bear came from the paws and thighs, although cured side meat and the spareribs of young bears also were favored.[16] Generally, no matter which part of the bear was consumed, those who partook agreed that the taste was dependent on the diet and age of the animal. Before he left Finley's Gap, Crockett was said to own "seven of the most vicious bear dogs in the South."[17] The only problem for hunters such as David was that the bear population was beginning to dwindle due to all the settlers moving into the region. He needed new hunting grounds and fewer folks around him.

"We worked on for some years, renting ground, and paying high rent, until I found [hunting] wasn't the thing it was cracked up to be; and that I couldn't make a fortune at it just at all," wrote Crockett. "So I concluded to quit it, and cut out for some new country . . . as I knowed I would have to move at some time, I thought it better to do it before my family got too large, that I might have less to carry."[18]

Before Crockett could make a move, a crisis erupted on Polly's side of the family that required urgent attention. One of Polly's five brothers, John Finley, who had wed Nancy Barnes, a local girl, on June 18, 1811, found himself at the center of an embarrassing legal action that threatened his reputation, livelihood, and perhaps even his life. His dilemma stemmed from gossip circulating the settlements and crossroads of Jefferson County that, in October of 1810, Finley had sexual intercourse with a mare, owned by William Bradshaw.[19]

Such a "crime against nature" was considered to be as detestable as any offense, and in many places if judged guilty the resulting punishment could mean execution. Respect for law and order demanded harsh consequences. As early as 1792, the first criminal indictment was recorded in Jefferson County, when a man named Reuben Roach was found guilty of stealing three yards of linen and three yards of royal ribbon. He received ten lashes on his bare back at the public whipping post.[20] A few years later, Jesse Jeffrey was convicted of horse theft, a crime that often ended on a gallows. Instead, the sentence handed down ruled that the man "should stand in the pillory one hour, receive thirty-nine lashes upon his bareback well laid on, have his ears nailed to the pillory and cut off, and that he should be branded upon one cheek with the letter H and on the other with the letter T, in a plain and visible manner."[21] Some citizens thought that hanging would have been a more humane punishment. If stealing a horse could get a person strung up, or whipped and mutilated, the Finley family shuddered to think what the punishment would be for "buggery of a horse."

Adam Peck was hired to defend John Finley against the charges of bestiality. A respected lawyer and veteran of the Revolutionary War, Peck also was an early pioneer of the Mossy Creek settlement and one of the county's first state representatives. Peck and his client went on the offensive and in 1811 filed a case of slander against Finley's three accusers—David Givens, Richard Grace, and William Bradshaw, owner of the horse allegedly made "victim" by Finley. Legal proceedings continued for quite sometime as both sides made their case before Judge James Trimble.[22]

Several persons were called to give testimony. Crockett was among those summoned by the sheriff to appear in court to speak on behalf of Finley, his brother-in-law and the plaintiff in the slander suit filed against the three men. Several other neighbors and friends of the Finley family were called to give their support, including James McCuistion. According to court records, Crockett had to be served his court summons in distant Franklin County, well to the west in south-central Tennessee.[23] Crockett, it seems, was in Franklin County scouting for a new home for his family and did not make it back in time to testify.

The sordid Finley proceedings finally concluded with Judge Trimble finding for the plaintiff. John Finley never received what he considered his just due after the trial. He died in 1814, and it was not until the following year that two hundred bushels of corn were paid as retribution to his heirs, William and James Finley.[24] By then David Crockett was long gone from the mountains of east Tennessee. For in the autumn of 1811, after making further inquiries and scouting a few more sites, Crockett determined the time had come to pack up his household and take his leave.

The frontier was moving on and David, at age twenty-five, wanted to move right along with it. As was always his way, he had a desire to know what waited for him on the other side of every river and mountain he encountered. His curiosity and restlessness never wavered. And so the Crocketts loaded up their few possessions on packhorses and, accompanied by his father-in-law, Billy Finley, they set out to start afresh. They left behind the rickety cabin on rented land and their friends and loved ones. They crossed over the mountains and headed west.

Almanac cover, 1837.
(Photograph by Dorothy Sloan, Dorothy Sloan Rare Books)

PART II

THIRTEEN

KENTUCK

ALTHOUGH BY EARLY OCTOBER of 1811 Crockett had left his original home and stomping grounds far behind, he never forgot the people and land of eastern Tennessee, and it was this early indoctrination that contributed mightily to his lore. His life was more than half over when he left, but for the rest of his years he corresponded with many old friends and associates who stayed along the streams and hills where he grew up.

One of the best examples of Crockett's strong attachment to his roots also reveals how obsessive he became about staying out of debt. This was undoubtedly a result of witnessing his father's constant struggle with creditors. When David departed Jefferson County in 1811, he also left behind an outstanding debt of one dollar borrowed from John Jacobs, the farmer he had once worked for, splitting rails.[1] Knowing that the debt had not been forgiven nagged at Crockett for a decade. In his mind, a debt, no matter how small, had to be paid off. It was a matter of personal honor and reputation.

John L. Jacobs, the son of the man to whom Crockett owed that single dollar, clearly recalled the day that debt was paid off. It was in

1821, and Crockett was back in east Tennessee, leading a herd of horses he intended to sell in North Carolina.

"One morning I was standing in the door next to the main road," said Jacobs in 1884, reminiscing about early times in the hills of Jefferson County. "I looked down the road toward Mossy Creek and saw a fine looking man riding in front of a large drove of horses. He rode opposite me and stopped and asked me if my mother was in the house. I answered she was. 'Tell her to come to the door.' I did so, and when she appeared he said, 'How do you do, Mrs. Jacobs?' My mother said, 'Sir, you have the advantage of me.' 'I am Davy Crockett,' responded he. 'Is that you Davy?' said my mother. 'Yes,' said he, 'this is Davy Crockett.' "[2]

Once he was recognized, there followed a general shaking of hands and an exchange of small talk about family members' health and other news from the past ten years. At that moment, explained Jacobs, "his horses came rushing by and nearly got ahead of him." David quickly thrust his hand into his pocket, pulled out a silver dollar, and handed it to the startled woman. "Here, Madam, is a dollar I owed your husband, John Jacobs, when I left this country," Crockett told her.

"My father had died in the meantime," his son later wrote. "My mother said, 'Davy, I don't want it.' " Crockett could not accept her response. "I owed it," he said, "and you have to take it." The woman complied and took the coin, and with no further ado Crockett rode off to sell his horses.[3]

Much had transpired in Crockett's life during the years after leaving east Tennessee, in what became an endless search for the right place to settle. He found himself caught up in the great westward migration just like thousands of others—mostly poor and, often, desperate people searching for a fresh start. In October of 1811, the desire to settle in newly opened land brought Crockett to Lincoln County, Tennessee. Named for Revolutionary War General Benjamin Lincoln, the county had been formed in 1809 and was said to have much fertile soil. "The Duck and Elk river country was just beginning to settle, and I was determined to try that,"[4] wrote Crockett.

He was issued a warrant for five acres of land south of the headwaters of Mulberry Creek, a branch of the Elk River that divided Lincoln County into two nearly equal parts. With the assistance of Billy Finley, he cleared sassafras and brush on a rise that he dubbed "Hungry Hill" and hastily built a makeshift cabin to shelter Polly and the two boys. They dug a well and built a fence corral for Crockett's old horse and pair of two-year-old colts. As he had done before at Finley's Gap, Crockett carved his initials, "D.C.," in a soaring beech tree on the property line.[5]

"I found this a very rich country, and so new, that game, of different sorts, was very plenty," Crockett wrote of the family's latest home. "It was here that I began to distinguish myself as a hunter, and, to lay the foundation for all my future greatness; but mighty little did I know of what sort it was going to be."[6]

Shortly after helping his daughter and son-in-law get settled, Billy Finley bid them farewell and retraced his journey back to his home at Finley's Gap. It may have been the last time Polly saw her father.

One of Crockett's first acquaintances in the new territory was the feisty James Burns Gowen, who was born in Virginia in 1785. An insane man, wielding an axe, had murdered his father, and Gowen's mother was said to be a cousin of the Scottish poet Robert Burns.[7] Two years Crocket's senior, Gowen also was bound out, along with a brother, after their father's slaying. Gowen and Crockett often were seen with their packs of dogs headed into the trees and loaded for bear. After an evening hunt, they pulled bones together from roasted bear ribs, and slept beneath a covering of tree branches with their rifles and hounds as their only companions.

"It was here, wrestling with the sassafras that adorned the summit of Hungry Hill[,] that the brawn and bravery was developed that afterward made [Davy] famous as a soldier as well as a hunter and backwoods statesman," Gowen related to relatives before his death in 1880. "So here in the jungles of the forest living with his first wife, the faithful one who crossed the mountains of East Tennessee with him . . . this old pioneer no doubt spent his happiest days. He says himself that his reputation as a hunter was made on Mulberry."[8]

This reputation eventually proved quite useful to Crockett, as it helped propel him into the limelight. His hunting expeditions, either alone or in the company of colorful backwoods characters, supplied the material for many of Crockett's best stories, which he honed and polished for strategic use at public and private occasions.

"The forest and the mountain stream had great charms for him," wrote John S. C. Abbott in his 1875 biography of Crockett. "He loved to wander in busy idleness all the day, with fishing-rod and rifle; and he would often return at night with a very ample supply of game. He would then lounge about his hut, tanning deerskins for moccasins and breeches, performing other little jobs, and entirely neglecting all endeavors to improve his farm, or to add to the appearance or comfort of the miserable shanty which he called his home."[9] In spite of his rather harsh critique of Crockett's domestic habits, Abbot—the author of many popular nineteenth-century historical works and biographies—also pointed out some of what he considered to be Crockett's strengths. "He had an active mind, and a very singular command of the language of low, illiterate life, and especially of backwoodsman's slang," wrote Abbot. "Though not exactly a vain man, his self-confidence was imperturbable, and there was perhaps not an individual in the world . . . whom he looked up to as in any sense his superior. In hunting, his skill became very remarkable, and few, even of the best marksmen, could throw the bullet with more unerring aim."[10] There was an abundance of deer, and much smaller game, in the area close to his homestead, but Crockett noticed that black bears had been hunted heavily and "were not so plenty as I could have wished."[11]

Even when Crockett stalked game in those forests, the face of the land was changing due to the growing tide of settlers moving westward with the frontier. The earliest of these settlers claimed the lush valley land, so those who came later were forced to stake out less desirable sites on sides of mountains. As they cleared the land, the steep slopes eroded and became too poor to farm. The solution was to move on to yet another location. Crockett did not see the old-growth forests that flourished long before his family ever came to the shores of America. That was back in the time when it was said that a squirrel could travel the canopy of the woodlands from the Atlantic to the Mississippi without once touching the ground. Frontier settlers sliced down great mixes of hardwoods that spilled over the rolling old mountains in a multilayered carpet. The first people to enter the yet unbroken wilderness followed bison trails, the only breaks in the thick undergrowth. These trails were cut deep and wide by the hooves of the big lumbering animals seeking clear spring water, salt licks, and grassy meadows, much like the Indians and white men who hunted them. Old trails became well-used paths for restless pioneers such as Crockett and his kin. They were soon followed by land speculators and developers anxious to wrest the land from the Indians who dwelled there long before any whites even knew of the existence of the mountains blanketed with chestnuts, hemlocks, and fir. To the newcomers the wilderness was an adversary that had to be conquered and tamed. The land had to be dismembered and parceled out to families and town builders.

On November 25, 1812, Polly Crockett gave birth to her third child. This time it was a daughter. She was named Margaret, after David's oldest sister. Crockett cherished the baby girl, who went by the nickname Polly, but he also had to wonder how he was going to feed yet another mouth. Although it was important for frontier families to be large so there were plenty of helping hands, there also was a price to pay before a child was old enough to earn its keep.

After less than two years in Lincoln County, Crockett was beginning to feel the itch to move once more. Besides the decline in the bear population, Crockett, not agriculturally inclined, was having problems making a go of it as a farmer. He spent much of his time out hunting, and not nearly enough behind the plow. Taking a chance by adding to his holdings to provide more crop fields, he put in a claim for an additional fifteen acres. The plan did not work. He soon fell behind on his taxes and in the end lost all of his land, including his original five-acre plot.[12]

By the time the delinquent tax payment resulted in foreclosure, Crockett had already moved the family away from Hungry Hill. In late 1812 or perhaps early 1813, the Crocketts established residency in adjacent Franklin County, formed in 1807 and named in honor of Benjamin

Franklin. Lying in a portion of the valley of the Elk River, the county contained an abundance of streams, springs, and caves. David cleared land and built a cabin home on the Rattlesnake Spring Branch of Bean's Creek, about ten miles southwest of the county seat of Winchester and a few miles north of the Alabama border.[13] It is not clear if Crockett purchased part of a two-hundred-acre tract of land in late 1812 or leased it, as would have been the case for those without any money. Another common alternative would have been to settle on the land as squatters.

Whatever arrangement Crockett worked out in order to get his property, it is known that he named the new home Kentuck. The choice of this name, sometimes spelled Kaintuck, may have signaled a future move to the land of Daniel Boone, whom Crockett knew of only by reputation. By 1812, however, Boone was seventy-eight years old and long gone from Kentucky: he had been happily residing in Missouri for thirteen years.[14]

Crockett built a log cabin with just enough room for a family of five, while Polly stayed busy with her chores and tended two growing sons and an infant daughter. David cleared and cultivated some of the land, and put in corn and row crops, but he took to the woods as much as he could. Crockett, as we have seen, was a hunter first and farmer a distant second. He continued to go hunting with James Burns Gowen, and also stalked game with a new neighbor, Archard Hatchett. A Virginian by birth who settled in Tennessee in 1806, Hatchett farmed and raised livestock, as well as fourteen children fathered with two wives. The pair roamed far on long hunts, and along the way Crockett continued his practice of tattooing his initials with his hunting knife on the trunks of trees. Before dying on his family farm in 1852, Hatchett told stories of herding cattle with Crockett and of their hunting trips, and the old man made sure his son James knew the locations of some of the trees that Crockett had marked. More than thirty years later in the 1880s, a logging crew inspecting timber came across a beech tree on the highest point of Round Mountain with Crockett's initials carved deep in the bark. James Hatchett was there that day to tell the story, but also to make sure that the tree was spared from their saws and axes.[15] Such accounts of Crockett are still told throughout Tennessee.

Crockett's own considerable storytelling skill was sharpened in Franklin County as he became acquainted with the old-timers and wisdom keepers who dwelled there. Some of the more memorable storytellers—including William Russell and Jesse Bean, two figures of note from prominent Tennessee families, who were touted as the first white men to settle the land that became Franklin County—had been long acquainted with the Crocketts. The Russell and Bean families had intermarried and spread their kin all across the frontier. Russell's sister, Lydia, was the wife of Bean's father, the intrepid William Bean, a rugged adventurer who had hunted with Daniel Boone. In 1769, the elder Bean, after leaving Virginia, became the first permanent white settler in what eventually became Tennessee.[16]

The Russells also provided plenty of story fodder. William Russell, a native North Carolinian and another early arrival in Tennessee, had fought in several engagements during the Revolutionary War, including the Battle of King's Mountain. Russell's house on Boiling Fork became the place for holding court, musters, and other legal proceedings in Franklin County until the town of Winchester was laid out in 1810, and a proper courthouse was built.[17] One of Crockett's good friends was old Major Russell's son, George, the namesake of his uncle Captain George Russell, who followed his brother-in-law, William Bean, to Tennessee in 1770 and was promptly killed by Indians while on a hunting trip near his home at German Creek.

Jesse Bean, one of old William's sons, was born in Virginia and came to Tennessee with the rest of his family. That is where his younger brother, Russell, was born in 1769, making him the first white child born to a permanent settler in Tennessee. Jesse had become a highly sought-after gunsmith well before he established a home and business in Franklin County. Russell was also an expert gun maker and often the subject of some of the wildest stories told on the Tennessee frontier. Crockett feasted on tales about the colorful Bean family, especially an infamous one based on an incident in 1802, when Russell returned to his Jonesboro, Tennessee, home after a long absence.

The story, as Crockett heard it, was that Bean had delivered a cargo of his handcrafted guns to buyers in New Orleans, where he then remained for two years, engaging in cock fighting, horse racing, foot races, and other pleasures.[18] When he got back to Jonesboro and walked into his cabin, Bean was shocked to find his wife, Rosamond, nursing an infant. Outraged at this blatant act of infidelity, the swaggering Bean swigged down some fresh whiskey and decided to mark the baby so he could then distinguish it from the eight children that he had fathered. Bean yanked out his hunting knife and sliced off the baby's ears. For such a horrific deed, Bean was fined, imprisoned, and branded on the palm of his hand, as was the custom. To show his distain for such treatment, Bean bit out the brand from his hand and spit the flesh on the floor.[19]

Though divorce was an infrequent occurrence in those days, the stricken Rosamond soon divorced Bean, who managed to escape prison and, because the authorities feared him, remained at large. While free, Bean let it be known that he would get revenge on the seducer responsible for getting his wife pregnant. He assaulted the man's brother and beat him unmercifully, but was still free when the matter came to the attention of a young judge who demanded that the sheriff serve the arrest warrant and bring the culprit to him. The sheriff tried and failed, even attempting to assemble a posse to help apprehend Bean, but he could not enlist any volunteers.

A drunken and menacing Bean bellowed that he would shoot "the first skunk that came within ten feet of him."[20] The judge had heard and seen enough. "By the Eternal, I'll bring him," vowed the judge. He adjourned his court and went straight to Bean, who was cursing and waving a pistol. The judge never flinched. With a pistol in each hand, he walked right up to the big fellow, stared into his red eyes, and roared, "Now, surrender you infernal villain, this very instant, or I'll blow you through!"[21] Bean looked into the judge's eyes, laid down his weapon, and gave up with no further fuss. The judge marched him to the courtroom, where he was tried and heavily fined.

Tall and lanky, with reddish hair and blazing blue eyes, the young judge was in fact future U.S. president Andrew Jackson. Later, when Bean was asked why he gave up so easily, he explained that when he looked into Andy Jackson's eyes he could see the fire, and he knew that he had best give up or die.[22] One day—under far different circumstances—those same fiery eyes would glare at David Crockett.

Jackson, in his early career as a circuit court judge, not only presided over matters such as the Bean trial but also had occasion to travel through Franklin County. In 1808, Jackson received a patent from the State of Tennessee for 1,000 acres located on the Boiling Fork, just below Winchester. The following year he acquired an additional 640 acres on the Elk River.[23] Jackson also enjoyed a long relationship with the Bean and Russell families. Only ten years after the encounter with Russell Bean, many members of both families faithfully served under then General Jackson when duty called. Among the volunteers was Russell Bean, who, it was said, eventually got back with his wife when Jackson brokered reconciliation.[24] Crockett, too, would be in that number fighting under Jackson's command, as would Jesse Bean, the master craftsman who supplied so many fine hunting rifles.

Jesse lived by the creek that was named for him, and in a nearby cave he set up the gun shop that brought him fame and a bit of fortune well beyond the county and state. Known for their precision, Bean rifles became the standard for all other weapons on the frontier. Rifles crafted by various Beans had been put to good use at the Battle of King's Mountain during the last days of the Revolutionary War, and were coveted by militia and outback white settlers as their weapons of choice for killing Indians or large game.

As the autumn of 1813 approached, the gunsmith shop and powder mills tucked into the stone grottoes on Bean's Creek would be pressed into service once again. So would most of the able-bodied men from Franklin County, including the crack shot David Crockett.

FOURTEEN

"REMEMBER FORT MIMS"

THE UNITED STATES STUNNED the diplomatic world on June 19, 1812, when President James Madison declared war on the imperial power of Great Britain.[1] Growing resentment over the seizure of U.S. ships primarily caused the conflict, which lasted until 1815, although Eric Jay Dolin notes in *Fur, Fortune, and Empire* that competing claims over fur territory in the Northwest were compelling factors. Britain, already at war in Europe, was desperate to find fresh sailors, and so began the press-ganging of American crews into the British navy and confiscating of all cargo bound for Napoleonic France. These appropriations caused the United States to cut off all trade with the continent.[2] At the same time, some members of Congress began beating the drums of war when they saw an opportunity to claim the rest of the North American continent still in the hands of the King of England.

Nowhere was the cry for war louder than in certain political circles in landlocked Tennessee and surrounding states. These warmongers were not as worried about halting the impressments of American seamen as they were about finding a solution to what was called "the Indian problem." Mostly southern congressmen—such as Henry Clay of Kentucky and John C. Calhoun of South Carolina—the "War Hawks," as they were known—firmly believed that taking more Indian property would appease the gnawing hunger for territorial expansion.³ Many Indian tribes, encouraged by the British, resisted giving up any more of their land. Forcibly evicting Indians who refused to comply promised to spark economic opportunities and open new lands for white settlement.

While most of the major engagements between America and Britain occurred in the Northeast, along the Canadian border, or at sea, in Tennessee war was being waged against the bands of Creek Indians who allied with Britain. It was a war that thrust the state into the national spotlight, for when Madison called on Tennessee to help defend their land, thousands of Tennesseans anxious to get into the melee came forward as volunteers, helping to establish the moniker the "Volunteer State."⁴ The nickname caught on but was not commonly used until after the Mexican War in the 1840s when, once again, tens of thousands of Tennessee men and boys rode off to battle.

There was no lack of volunteers from jingoistic Franklin County when the Creek Indian War broke out in 1813 and became intertwined with the War of 1812. One of the first local men to step forward was David Crockett. "I was living ten miles below Winchester when the Creek War commenced,"⁵ Crockett remembered. The call to arms that the twenty-seven-year-old Crockett answered in those last days of the summer of 1813 resulted from news that flashed across the frontier of the killing and scalping of more than four hundred settlers at Fort Mims, a stockade in what was then southern Mississippi Territory, about thirty miles north of the coastal town of Mobile.

The tragic Creek War that resulted was in reality a Creek civil war between opposing factions of the tribe. On one side were the Creeks from the lower towns of eastern Alabama and Georgia, who, as a means of survival, had turned away from most of their traditional beliefs and assimilated into the white culture. Many of them were of mixed blood and over time had adopted the white settlers' religion, language, manner of dress, and lifestyle. They farmed and raised livestock like the whites, and some Creeks acquired their own black slaves to work the land, much as other southeastern tribes, particularly the Cherokees, also were doing.

The Creeks from the upper towns in south-central Alabama, how-ever, were not about to give up the ways of their ancestors. They under-went a religious revitalization that inspired them to retain their culture and identity. These staunchly traditional Creeks despised their tribes-men in the lower towns. About the time that Crockett and his family moved westward out of east Tennessee, the hatred between the Creek factions intensified when the famous Shawnee leader, Tecumseh, a sym-bol of courage respected and revered by his followers and many of his enemies, traveled from the Great Lakes to the Gulf of Mexico. Tecumseh was seeking support for his vision of a vast Indian coalition that would fight to recover the many lands stolen from the tribes through the dubi-ous treaties white men had crafted and broken ever since their arrival in North America.

The imposing Tecumseh had no success convincing the Choctaws and Chickasaws to join his confederacy against further white expan-sion, so he turned to the Creeks.[6] In October 1811, he attended a Creek council meeting along with members of other southeastern tribes. The charismatic Tecumseh implored the gathering to unite and resist any further American aggression. His eloquence touched many there, espe-cially younger warriors with a deep sense of pride for their people and land.

"Let the white race perish!" he bluntly told them, espousing the kind of bellicose language that spawned similar invective from the frontiers-men. "They seize your land; they corrupt your women; they trample on the bones of your dead! Back whence they came, upon a trail of blood, they must be driven! Back—aye, back to the great water whose accursed waves brought them to our shores! Burn their dwellings—destroy their stock—slay their wives and children, that the very breed may perish. War now! War always! War on the living! War on the dead!"[7]

When one of the powerful chiefs in attendance resisted and chal-lenged the call to action, an angry Tecumseh made an ominous promise: "Your blood is white. . . . You do not believe the Great Spirit sent me. You shall believe it. I will leave directly and go straight to Detroit. When

I get there I will stamp my foot upon the ground and shake down every house in Tookabatcha."[8]

Just as Tecumseh had vowed, two months later there was a tremendous rumble from deep within the earth that toppled every dwelling in the village of Tookabatcha. This put all the people into a complete state of shock, and they cried, "Tecumseh has got to Detroit! We can feel the shake of his foot!"[9]

The powerful Tecumseh may have been stamping the ground at Detroit, but he had some help from a coincidental and catastrophic natural occurrence. Between December 16, 1811, and late April 1812, a series of devastating earthquakes shook the Mississippi Valley and beyond when more than two thousand tremors, some of Old Testament proportions, rocked the land.[10] Eventually the quakes were called the New Madrid Earthquakes because tiny New Madrid, in the boot-heel region of what was to be named Missouri, was the village closest to the epicenter. It was estimated that the tremors affected more than a million and a half square miles, making whole towns disappear, swallowing up untold numbers of people, and even causing the Mississippi to reverse course and flow backward for several hours.[11] Between the shocks, people heard the moans of the dying, the bleating of animals, and the screeching of birds. The air was clogged with a thick vapor that smelled like sulfur. Dazed survivors of the initial tremors believed the end of the earth had come and the gates of hell were opening.

The earthquakes were so powerful that they were felt by people in all directions—in New York, New Orleans, Canada, and on the western fringes of the Missouri River. President James Madison claimed that he was tossed from his bed in Washington by the initial shock. It was said that the catastrophic quakes stopped clocks in Boston and set bells ringing in Virginia.[12]

If people from so many locales experienced the shocks, Crockett certainly had to have felt them at his home near the border of Tennessee and Mississippi Territory (Alabama). But he never made mention of it, even though this natural disaster would come to have quite an impact on

Crockett. Besides helping to spur on traditional Creeks to war (because they perceived that Tecumseh's prediction had come true), the earthquakes created a remarkable lake, twenty-five miles long and from one-half to eight miles in width on the Tennessee side of the Mississippi River.[13] Later named Reelfoot Lake, this body of water sat untouched for many years after Chickasaw Indians and the few white settlers living there vanished due to the many quakes. During that time the area became a paradise for hunters and fishermen; it would later become known as "the land of the shakes."[14]

Throughout 1812 raids and reprisals for massacres took place between militant Creeks and the "Friendly" Creeks siding with the Americans, thus widening the divide within the tribe. The Upper Creeks, called Red Sticks because of the bright red war clubs they carried, were determined to halt further white encroachment. While these Red Sticks were proud of these wooden clubs, which had come to symbolize the traditional Creek warriors, they also knew that more powerful arms were needed in order for them to triumph over their enemies.[15] In July 1813, Peter McQueen, a mixed-blood Creek leader, and a party of his Red Sticks journeyed to Pensacola, in Spanish-controlled Florida, to purchase guns and gunpowder from the Spanish governor.[16] On July 27, during their return trip to the upper villages in Alabama, at the time Mississippi Territory, they paused at some springs near a small settlement called Burnt Corn, on the Old Wolf Trail. After a meal, the Red Sticks were resting on the creekbank when 180 militiamen hiding in the surrounding forest ambushed them. The force of white and mixed bloods swept down on the camp, scattering the horses and sending the startled Red Sticks fleeing into the canebrakes. The attackers became so carried away with looting the camp that they dropped their guard, allowing the Red Sticks to regroup and launch a counterattack, which scattered the Americans and sent them running in full retreat.[17] Known as the Battle of Burnt Corn, it was a victory for the outnumbered Creeks. The outraged Red Sticks considered this encounter to be a declaration of war by the American settlers.

Seeking revenge, the Red Sticks turned their attention to Fort

Mims, located at the junction of the Tombigbee and Alabama rivers, just north of Mobile. This was the stockade where the militia who had been humiliated at Burnt Corn took refuge, along with many other white and mixed blood families fearful of Red Stick retaliatory strikes sure to follow. Their fear was well founded. The Red Stick attack on the flimsy fortification built around the home of wealthy mixed-blood merchant Samuel Mims came August 30, 1813.[18]

The assault was led by the son of a Scot trader and Creek mother, who had been born William Weatherford but took the name Red Eagle. He had been greatly influenced by the inspiring message of Tecumseh when the Shawnee chieftain said:

> The Muscogee [the name for the Creek tribe] was once a mighty people. . . . Now your blood is white; your tomahawks have no edge; your bows and arrows were buried with your fathers. Oh, Muscogees, brush from your eyelids the sleep of slavery. Once more strike for vengeance, once more for your country. The spirits of the mighty dead complain. The tears drop from the weeping skies.[19]

Tecumseh proved unsuccessful in his effort to form a united Indian coalition. He died in Canada on October 5, 1813, fighting on the British side against his old adversary William Henry Harrison in the Battle of the Thames. Tecumseh did, however, die knowing of the events that transpired at Fort Mims.

On that sweltering August day, Red Eagle carried the words of Tecumseh in his heart as a war party of a thousand Red Sticks descended on Fort Mims. After easily gaining entry into the ramshackle stockade, the Red Sticks systematically slaughtered as many as five hundred men, women, and children. "Every Indian was provided with a gun, war club, and a bow and arrow pointed with iron spikes," recalled Dr. Thomas Holmes, who was able to escape by chopping a hole through the stockade wall from inside a cabin during a lull in the slaughter. "With few exceptions they were naked; around the waist was drawn a girdle from which was tied a cow's tail running down the back and almost dragging the ground. It is impossible to imagine people so horribly painted. Some were painted half red and half black. Some were adorned with feathers. Their faces were painted so as to show their terrible contortions."[20]

So horrific was the carnage that even Red Eagle tried to rein in the massacre, but to no avail. The avenging Red Sticks were overwhelmed by too many memories of mistreatment at the hands of the white Americans. This meant that no quarter could be given to anyone except for some of the black slaves taken as part of the spoils of war.

An American army officer who led the detachment dispatched to bury the dead was sickened by what they found. "Indians, negroes, white men, women and children lay in one promiscuous ruin. All were scalped, and the females of every age were butchered in a manner which neither decency nor language will permit me to describe. The main building was burned to ashes, which were filled with bones. The plains and woods were covered with dead bodies."[21]

The premeditated Fort Mims massacre spread fear and panic across the frontier and left the entire nation in shock. Yet for the hawkish Tennesseans and their white neighbors in Mississippi Territory, particularly the land speculators, this horrific event was seen as just the impetus needed to escalate an all-out war of attrition against the Creeks. The vivid accounts from Fort Mims survivors, some of which described pregnant women who had "their unborn infants cut from the womb" and laid by their sides, so inflamed the passions of the white population that soon a war cry thundered across the frontier—"Remember Fort Mims!"[22]

In that sanguinary autumn of 1813, a young man with so much still ahead of him heard only the cry for Fort Mims, and he answered accordingly. War fever was upon the land and Crockett had caught it.

FIFTEEN

"WE SHOT THEM LIKE DOGS"

ELEVEN DAYS AFTER THE MASSACRE at Fort Mims, David Crockett saddled his horse and rode the ten miles from his home, Kentuck, to the town of Winchester.[1] Men from throughout the county gathered in the village square to join the campaign against the hostile Creeks.

Only the day before, far to the north of Tennessee, American Captain Oliver Hazard Perry had led his fleet of ten warships to victory over a British squadron in the three-hour Battle of Lake Erie. As the smoke began to clear, Perry sent General William Henry Harrison a hastily scribbled message: "We have met the enemy and they are ours."[2] On the Tennessee frontier, no such boast could be made.

"There had been no war among us for so long, that but few, who were not too old to bear arms, knew anything about the business," Crockett wrote of that day.

I, for one, had often thought about war, and had often heard it described; and I did verily believe in my own mind, that I couldn't fight in that way at all; but after my experience convinced me that this was all a notion. For when I heard of the mischief which was done at the fort [Fort Mims], I instantly felt like going, and I had none of the dread of dying that I expected to feel. [3]

Polly Crockett did not share her husband's feelings or his point of view about the prospects of combat. Like any dutiful wife, even one somewhat hardened by frontier life, she feared for David's safety but also fretted about the prospects of being left alone with three small children. Before he rode off for the muster in Winchester, Polly, perhaps not fully aware of her husband's determination, begged him not to go to war.

"I reasoned the case with her as well as I could, and told her, that if every man would wait till his wife got willing for him to go to war, there would be no fighting done, until we would all be killed in our own houses; that I was able to go as any man in the world; and that I believed it was a duty I owed to my country."

Crockett was not certain if his rationalization for going off to war satisfied Polly or not. But she could tell that he "was bent on it," so she cried some more and then went back to her work. "The truth is," Crockett admitted, "my dander was up, and nothing but war could bring it right again."

At the muster in Winchester Square, vivid descriptions of the atrocities at Fort Mims circulated the crowd, and a young local lawyer, Francis Jones, addressed the men with a speech that thoroughly aroused Crockett and his friends. Afterward, Jones announced he was forming a company of volunteers and asked anyone willing to take up arms and go after the Red Sticks to step forward. "I believe I was about the second or third man that step'd out; but on marching up and down the regiment a few times we found we had a large company."[4]

It appears that a celebration following the first muster got out of hand, and the recently built log jailhouse was burned to the ground during the night.[5] Nevertheless, the blaze did not stop the business of war from moving forward. Jones was elected captain of the company—called Francis Jones's Company of Mounted Riflemen—and Crockett was listed on the muster roll with the rank of private.[6] Captain Jones appreciated Private Crockett's ability with a rifle, and apparently the respect between them was mutual.

Jones was one of fourteen captains from nine Tennessee counties, including Franklin, assigned to the Second Regiment of Volunteer Mounted Riflemen. Under the command of Colonel Newton Cannon, along with Colonel John Alcorn's regiment, the unit was part of General John Coffee's brigade.[7] When it soon became clear that most of the young men would be marching off to battle, those men who were more than forty-five years old, many of them veterans of the Revolutionary War, formed a home guard company and called themselves the Revolutionary Volunteers of Franklin County. They pledged to look after the families and property of the younger men and to protect the honor of the state and nation against any disaffected persons, "if any such there should be amongst us."[8]

At the summit of the state's military chain of command stood the resolute Andrew Jackson. Immediately after the Fort Mims massacre, Jackson was appointed to lead the 2,500-member Army of West Tennessee, while Major General John Cocke commanded the Army of East Tennessee—making a statewide force of 5,000 troops authorized by the state legislature.[9] Jackson would assume control of the entire force when the two groups converged in northern Mississippi Territory before proceeding due south to cut a wide and bloody swath through the heart of the Creeks' land. Jackson welcomed the orders.

After serving as a delegate to the state's first constitutional convention and as Tennessee's first congressman in 1796, Jackson was elected to the U.S. Senate, only to later find a job more to his liking as a superior court judge back home in Tennessee. He spent six years on the bench and was mostly remembered as a good judge who rendered swift rulings, never allowed a backlog of cases, and liked wearing a judicial gown in his courtroom, a sign of respect for his position. He enjoyed traveling the state, staying in boardinghouses and taverns, holding court, and punishing felons of all stripes. In 1802 shortly after his famous confrontation with Russell Bean, the thirty-five-year-old Jackson—already a scarred combat veteran—was elected major general of the Tennessee militia.[10]

Now a flinty forty-six-year old, Jackson was recovering from bullet wounds recently received during a sword and gun fight on a Nashville street. The fracas resulted from a running disagreement between Jackson and his own aide-de-camp, protégé, and future U.S. Senator Thomas Hart Benton, and the latter's brother, Jesse.[11] Despite a serious infection in his left shoulder and doctors threatening to take one of his arms, Jackson persevered. When word of the debacle at Fort Mims first reached Jackson, by then convalescing at his home, the Hermitage, he responded vehemently. "Brave Tennesseans!" he intoned. "Your frontier is threatened with invasion by the savage foe. Already they advance towards your frontier with their scalping knives unsheathed, to butcher your wives, your children, and your helpless babes. Time is not to be lost."[12]

Such exhortations were not lost on Private David Crockett, who could not have agreed more—time was not to be lost. Crockett bid farewell to Polly and his children on September 20 and rode off to join his company and begin what he had been promised would be only a ninety-day enlistment. "Expecting to be gone only a short time, I took no more clothing with me than I supposed would be necessary, so that if I got into an Indian battle, I might not be pestered with any unnecessary plunder, to prevent my having a fair shake with them."

From Winchester, the mounted volunteers, led by Captain Jones, crossed the border into Mississippi Territory. They rode to the town of Beaty's Spring, just south of Huntsville, camping there for several days, waiting for other troops to form up and join them. On October 6, Major John H. Gibson asked Captain Jones to provide two men to take part in a scouting mission into the Creek territory on the other side of the Tennessee River. Gibson told Jones that he wanted good woodsmen who were "best with a rifle."[13] Although the other men would complain about losing such a good provider, Jones knew the ideal candidate was Crockett. He told Major Gibson that Crockett was his man.

"I willingly engaged to go with him, and asked him to let me choose my own mate to go with me, which he said I might do," Crockett related. David picked George Russell, the son of Major William Russell, the veteran settler Crockett knew from back home on Boiling Fork.[14] When Crockett called eighteen-year-old George Russell forward, however, Gibson seemed displeased with the choice and said that he was looking for a man, not a boy. "I must confess I was a little nettled at this," wrote Crockett, "for I know'd George Russell, and I know'd there was no mistake in him; and I didn't think that courage ought to be measured by the beard, for fear a goat would have the preference over a man. I told the major he was on the wrong scent; that Russell could go as far as he could, and I must have him along." Gibson reluctantly went along with Crockett's choice.

The next morning the scouting party, made up of Major Gibson, Crockett, Russell, and ten others, left camp and crossed the Tennessee River at Ditto's Landing. They went deep into unfamiliar country and after a day or so divided into two separate parties. Crockett and the five others riding with him encountered mixed-blood settlers and friendly Creeks wearing white plumes or deer tails in their hair, a scheme devised by General Jackson to let his men know which Indians were friendly and which were the enemy Red Sticks.[15]

When the scouts came across a lone Indian runner, he told them that he had seen a large war party crossing the Coosa River headed toward General Jackson and his troops. Crockett and his men raced by the light of the moon to Colonel Coffee's new camp back at Ditto's Landing on the south side of the Tennessee River. A breathless Crockett reported to the colonel with news of the enemy war party, but Coffee did not seem to give it much credence. Coffee's reaction did not sit well with Crockett, but the next day, when Major Gibson finally showed up with his party, Crockett again told Coffee the story he had related the night before. This time Coffee accepted the junior officer's report about the enemy party and quickly issued orders for countermeasures to be taken. "When I made my report, it wasn't believed, because I was no officer," lamented Crockett. "I was no great man, but just a poor soldier."[16] This incident in the field influenced the way he viewed commissioned military officers from that time on.

An account of life at Camp Coffee in mid-October 1813, which was written just prior to the Civil War, presents an interesting description of Crockett:

> There they were, twenty-five hundred of them, in the pleasant autumn weather, upon a high bluff overlooking the beautiful Tennessee, all in high spirits, eager to be led against the enemy. There were jovial souls among them. David Crockett, then the peerless bear-hunter of the West . . . was there with his rifle and hunting shirt, the merriest of the merry, keeping the camp alive with his quaint conceits and marvelous narratives. He had a hereditary right to be there, for both his grandparents had been murdered by the Creeks, and other relatives carried into long captivity by them. . . . No man ever enjoyed a greater degree of personal popularity than did David Crockett while with the army; and his success in political life is mainly attributable to that fact. David met with many messmates, who spoke of him with the affection of a brother, and from them I have heard many anecdotes, which convince me how much goodness of heart he really possessed. He not infrequently would lay out his own money to buy a blanket for a suffering soldier; and never did he own a dollar which was not at the service of the first friend who called for it. Blessed with a memory, which never forgot any thing, he seemed merely a depository of anecdote; while at the same time, to invent, when at a loss, was as easy as to narrate those, which he had already heard. These qualities made him the rallying point for fun with his messmates, and served to give him the notoriety which he now possesses.[17]

Those times spent "overlooking the beautiful Tennessee, all in high spirits" were brief for Crockett and his comrades. Most of the time they stayed in the field, snooping for Red Sticks, pillaging Indian dwellings, and building temporary stockades. While on mounted patrol, countless times they forded the Tennessee and the Coosa, as well as many other rivers and creeks. The volunteers traversed ancient Indian tra᾽ the Black Warriors' Path, beginning at Melton's Bluff not fa᾽ that Jackson owned.

With Colonel Coffee, soon to be made a brigadier general, in the lead, Crockett and the hundreds of other Tennessee Volunteers followed the trail to the confluence of the Mulberry and Sipsey forks of the Black Warrior River, where they burned down Black Warrior Town after first looting the Creeks' stores of corn, beans, and dried beef. The food did not last them long, and the men did not seem to forage well, so again Colonel Coffee gave Crockett permission to find some game.

"I turned aside to hunt, and had not gone far when I found a deer that had just been killed and skinned, and his flesh was still warm and smoking," Crockett wrote of that hunting trip. "From this I was sure that the Indian who killed it had been gone only a few minutes; and though I was never much in favour of one hunter stealing from another, yet meat was so scarce in camp, that I thought I must go in for it. So I took up the deer on my horse before me, and carried it on till night. I could have sold it for almost any price I would have asked; but this wasn't my rule, neither in peace nor war. Whenever I had any thing, and saw a fellow being suffering, I was more anxious to relieve him than to benefit myself. And this is one of the true secrets of my being a poor man to this day."

Crockett distributed the deer meat to his grateful friends, who had long grown tired of eating mostly parched corn. A short time later, he flushed a gang of feral hogs from a canebrake and quickly shot one in its tracks. Some other militiamen were close by and heard the commotion. "In a few minutes, the guns began to roar, as bad as if the whole army had been in an Indian battle," Crockett recalled. He shouldered his dead hog back to camp and when he got there found many other hogs and "a fine fat cow."[18] That evening, and for several more to come, no one went to sleep hungry.

By November 1, 1813, Brig. Gen. Coffee and his brigade of cavalry and mounted riflemen established a new camp on the Coosa River. The following day, Coffee ordered nine hundred mounted dragoons and some seventy Cherokee warrior allies to attack and destroy the nearby Creek village of Tallushatchee, where a large number of Red Sticks were known to be living. Crockett rode in the ranks of the attack force.[19] On the morning of November 3, the sleeping village was completely encircled by troops, and, at one hour after sunrise, the attack was launched. Coffee's surprise attack worked. Although the Creeks fought with great valor, the American force overpowered and viciously killed as many as possible, including men, women, and children. It was a sight that Crockett never forgot. His descriptions of the horrific scene at Tallushatchee are some of the most harrowing in his entire *Narrative*. Crockett wrote of seeing as many as forty-six Creek warriors seek cover in a house.

> We pursued them until we got near the house, when we saw a squaw sitting in the door, and she placed her feet against the bow she had in her hand, and then took an arrow, and raising her feet, she drew with all her might, and let fly at us, and she killed a man. . . . his death so enraged us all, that she was fired on, and had at least twenty balls blown through her. This was the first man I ever saw killed with a bow and arrow. We now shot them like dogs; and then set the house on fire, and burned it up with the forty-six warriors in it. I recollect seeing a boy who was shot down near the house. His arm and thigh were broken, and he was so near the burning house that the grease was stewing out of him. In this situation he was still trying to crawl along; but not a murmur escaped him, though he was only about twelve years old. So sullen is the Indian, when his dander is up, that he had sooner die than make a noise, or ask for quarters.

From the start of the assault until the last Red Stick was slaughtered, at least 186 Creeks were killed and about 84 more taken prisoner, mostly women and children. The total losses from Brig. Gen. Coffee's brigade were 5 men killed and 41 wounded.[20]

After burning down the town, Coffee's brigade returned to the camp at Ten Islands, where General Jackson had arrived and was there to greet them. Besides words of praise for their victory, Jackson had little else to offer the weary men. The contractors hired to feed the army failed to deliver fresh provisions, and the troops had eaten only half rations for several days. Hoping to find some overlooked food caches, the tired and famished troopers returned to the destroyed Creek village the next day. The scene sickened Crockett.

> Many of the carcasses of the Indians were still to be seen. They looked very awful, for the burning had not entirely consumed them, but gave them a terrible appearance, at least what remained of them. It was, somehow or other, found out that the house had a potato cellar under it, and an immediate examination was made, for we were all hungry as wolves. We found a fine chance of potatoes in it, and hunger compelled us to eat them, though I had rather not, if I could have helped it, for the oil of the Indians we had burned up on the day before had run down on them and they looked like they had been stewed with fat meat.

Crockett's descriptions of the scene at Tallushatchee show him repulsed by the slaughter. The story, as he told it, unfolds without sentiment or hyperbole. The details and facts speak for themselves but are far from colorless. And that is what would be expected from any good storyteller, even one horrified by what he had witnessed.

SIXTEEN

Riding with
Sharp Knife

ONLY A FEW MONTHS after enlisting as a Tennessee Volunteer, Crockett had to have realized that he was a hunter, not a soldier. That is not to say he failed to carry out his soldierly duties or refused to participate in assaults on Indian villages. He held his own in any skirmish or full-blown battle with Creek Red Sticks.

If confronted or challenged, Crockett never cowered or backed down from man or beast. Anyone armed only with a knife willing to fight a fully-grown bear to the death may have exhibited a great deal of recklessness but certainly had no coward in him. And that was just the point. Crockett was much more comfortable hunting and killing wild game than he was hunting and killing human beings. The role Crockett liked best during his military stint was the same one he preferred as a civilian, that of hunter-gatherer. And if Andrew Jackson or his underlings had just figured that out, a major morale problem could have been avoided when, by the winter of 1813, soldiers were so hungry and tired they were on the brink of all-out mutiny.

Throughout the entire campaign against the Creeks, Jackson's greatest threat did not come from the outmanned and poorly armed Indians but from critical supply shortages and desertions by troops unhappy with both the lack of decent rations and the terms of their enlistments. Napoleon, who was simultaneously fighting and losing his own war in Europe, famously once said that an army marches on its stomach, meaning any army's success depends not on courage or logistics but on adequate food. When preparing to invade Russia, the biggest obstacle Napoleon faced was not firepower and fortifications but food: it was difficult to find, and the winter was particularly cruel. Andrew Jackson was no Napoleon Bonaparte. Yet he managed to avoid ultimate defeat, like the one that awaited Napoleon in 1815.

In early November 1813, Jackson, trying to keep morale high, praised his troops' resounding victory at Tallushatchee. Upset that his victorious soldiers had been forced to eat potatoes soaked with human flesh, he finally recognized that nourishing rations and forage were as important as powder and lead. But until contractors, hampered by low water in the Tennessee River, could find a way to provide fresh provisions, there still was a war to wage. To keep their minds off food, Jackson busied the troops with establishing another camp close to Ten Islands on the Coosa River.[1] It was named Camp Strother, after Maj. John Strother, the chief topographer and surveyor for General Jackson.[2]

At Camp Strother on November 7, a lone Indian runner emerged from the night shadows to tell Jackson of a large number of allied Creeks besieged by at least 1,100 Red Sticks in full war paint at Talladega, thirty miles to the south.[3] The messenger had made a daring escape by covering himself with a hog's skin and, in the darkness of night, got down on his hands and knees, grunting and rooting, and crawled through the hostile camp past guards who thought he was a hog looking for food.[4] Fortunately, he shed his clever disguise before he got to Camp Strother, or he would have been taken for a tasty pig and picked off by Crockett or another hungry sharpshooter.

Armed with this fresh intelligence about the enemy, Jackson—his arm still in a sling from the slug that smashed through his shoulder while he caned Thomas Hart Benton—called for his senior officers and drew up a battle plan. Just after midnight, a force of 1,200 infantry and 800 cavalry forded the Coosa River and started for Talladega.[5] Crockett,

cradling his rifle and astride his horse, was among them. By the following evening the long column drew near the sleeping village.

As morning broke, Jackson and his officers positioned the troops
and started the attack, using tactics employed a few days earlier at Tallushatchee. The results were the same, with even more Creeks killed.
Crockett was right in the middle of the action and later remembered the
Red Stick warriors "rushing forth like a cloud of Egyptian locusts, and
screaming like all the young devils had been turned loose, with the old
devil of all at their head."[6]

War cries quickly turned to screams of agony as the warriors fell under
withering fire from all sides. "We fired and killed a considerable number
of them," wrote Crockett. "They then broke like a gang of steers, and ran
across to our other line, where they were fired on again; and so we kept
them running from one line to the other; constantly under a heavy fire,
until we had killed upwards of four hundred of them."[7] American losses
amounted to 15 killed outright and 86 wounded. Among the dead were
a few commissioned officers and a young man named James Patton,
who had a wife and two small children and lived less than a mile from
Crockett's Kentuck home. "We buried them all in one grave, and started
back to our fort; but before we got there, two more of our men died of
wounds they had received; making our total loss seventeen good fellows
in that battle."[8]

Early on in the campaign against the Creeks, Jackson acquired a
reputation for toughness among his soldiers. Some of them said that he
was "as tough as hickory," and it took no time for the name "Old Hickory" to stick.[9] After the fight at Talladega and for many years to follow,
another sobriquet seemed even more appropriate for Jackson. This new
nickname came from the Creeks and also was used by the Cherokees
and other tribes to describe him. The called him "Sharp Knife," or sometimes "Pointed Arrow," because of his keenness for killing their people.
A few years after the Creek campaign, when Jackson invaded Florida,
the terrified Spanish called him "the Napoleon of the woods."[10] All of
the monikers fit Jackson as perfectly as his snug regulation moon-shaped
officer's hat, or *chapeau de bras*.

Back at Camp Strother after his latest victory at Talladega, "Sharp Knife" and his exhausted and half-famished troops found that additional provisions still had not been delivered. While contractors in Knoxville continued to search for a route to reach the troops, starvation threatened, and there were murmurs of growing discontent from suffering soldiers throughout the camp.

"I have been compelled to return here for the want of supplies, when I could have completed the destruction of the enemy in ten days," a frustrated Jackson complained in a letter to one of the contractors. "I find those I had left behind in the same starving condition with those who accompanied me. For God's sake send me with all dispatch, plentiful supplies of bread and meat. We have been starving for several days and it will not do to continue so much longer. Hire wagons and purchase supplies at any price rather than defeat the expedition."[11]

To stay occupied, the soldiers fortified their camp with protective palisades and blockhouses, and by mid-November Camp Strother was upgraded a notch and became Fort Strother. Facing almost certain famine, with still no real relief in sight, the men mostly stayed in their huts and tents when not on a guard or work detail. The large hog pen remained empty. For some sustenance, soldiers chewed on old boiled beef hides and supped on bitter broths of stewed acorns and mashed hickory nuts.[12] Any scraps of dried meat they managed to finagle were so salty it only made their constant thirst that much worse. Whiskey rations were long gone, and tobacco was difficult to come by. To add to their misery, the temperatures were dropping by the day.

"The weather also began to get very cold," wrote Crockett, "and our clothes were nearly worn out, and horses were getting very feeble and poor. Our officers proposed to Gen'L Jackson to let us return home and get fresh horses, and fresh clothing, so as to be better prepared for another campaign."[13]

Jackson refused to let the men go home, which resulted in a near mutiny. Many years later, Crockett—no longer a lowly private—took a few liberties with the facts when relating the story of "Old Hickory Face," as Crockett later called his former commanding general.[14] Crockett claimed to have been a participant in the mutinous activity against Jackson, but it is doubtful he was. He described the mutiny as a success. In fact, Jackson actually triumphed after he called the mutineers' bluff and rode out before them, brandishing a musket and personally threatening to shoot the first soldier who dared desert the ranks and go home. He stared down the whole brigade just as he done years before with Russell Bean.

"In the end Jackson was compelled to accede," Jackson biographer H. W. Brands wrote of the aborted mutiny.

> The general could threaten to blow mutineers to kingdom come, but neither his threats nor his cannons could put food in the men's mouths or clothes on their backs. In the weeks after the showdown he quietly discharged the most malcontented, judging their departure good riddance, and he allowed the others, including Crockett, to take a few weeks to refresh, restock, and get ready for the final offensive against the Red Sticks.[15]

Despite documented evidence to the contrary, some researchers believe Crockett remained with Jackson's army for several more weeks and did not return home until late January 1814. That was not the case. Crockett's first term of enlistment officially ended on Christmas Eve 1813. Records show that he served three months and six days at eight dollars per month pay, plus allowance for use of his horse, and travelling expenses.[16] The total due Crockett came to $65.59.

With his pay tucked away in his woolen hunting shirt, Crockett mounted up and turned northward to Tennessee and to his home. Polly and the boys, Wesley and William, were waiting, and so was his daughter, Margaret, or "Little Polly," just a year old. All the way back on that long ride, Crockett had to wonder if the girl would even remember him.

SEVENTEEN

"ROOT HOG OR DIE"

CROCKETT CLEARLY REALIZED that the war against Great Britain and their Indian allies was far from over. Despite a joyous reunion with family at Kentuck, in January 1814, he knew he could not stay long. In only nine months he would be off again for another round of fighting. Still, this interlude gave him time to get reacquainted with Polly and their three children. He also put in some crops, laid in a stack of firewood, and tended to repairs on the family's cabin. And, of utmost importance, with no officers around barking orders, he also was allowed the luxury of hunting anytime he pleased.

Crockett had to have been happy to sleep with Polly in his arms, teach his boys how to hunt, and play with his little girl. He wore clean clothes, ate three meals a day, and enjoyed the occasional horn of whiskey while sharing accounts of fighting Red Stick warriors with General Jackson. Almost twenty-eight, he already possessed a storehouse of memories and a growing repertoire of story material. In his accounts, he sometimes interjected his homespun, self-effacing humor.

While Crockett enjoyed his respite at home away from the death and destruction of war, Jackson and his troops continued to pursue and battle the Creeks until their deathblow, on March 27, 1814. Consequently, Crockett missed taking part in the most decisive engagement of the entire Creek campaign. On that date, Jackson and his Tennessee militia, augmented with regular infantry and a contingent of Cherokees and allied Creeks, crushed the hostile Red Sticks at Tohopeka, a fortified stronghold at Horseshoe Bend on the Tallapoosa River in the heart of Creek country.[1] The battle raged all day, but the Creeks, behind the breastworks, could not stem Jackson's forces.

One of the first soldiers to scramble over the wall into the village was a bold lieutenant from Tennessee named Sam Houston. He was an adventurous young man who had run away from home at sixteen and was adopted into a Cherokee chief's family. Houston spent a year living with the Cherokees, who gave him the name Colonneh—"the Raven."[2] In 1813, Houston was teaching in a log schoolhouse not far from the Tennessee town of Maryville, where he was known to have purchased powder and shot for his Indian friends. Badly in debt and pleased his beloved Cherokees had allied with the United States in the fight against the British and the Creeks, Houston received his mother's blessing and joined the army. He left with the gold ring and musket she gave him and a silver dollar enlistment bonus in his pocket.[3]

At Horseshoe Bend, Houston was shot in the groin with an arrow, which he asked a fellow lieutenant to remove. When the man tried but failed, Houston brandished his sword and bellowed out a threat, causing the perplexed officer to rip out the barbed arrow and along with it a hunk of flesh and a torrent of blood. Ordered by Jackson to remove himself from the battle, Houston soon took up a musket and returned to the fray, only to be struck twice by bullets to his shoulder and arm. Despite the loss of blood, Houston somehow survived, but the wound from the arrow never completely healed and bothered Houston for the rest of a long and illustrious life.[4]

As doctors worked on Houston at Horseshoe Bend, the volunteers and regulars fought on until they had slaughtered almost the entire enemy force. No quarter was asked for and no quarter was given. The Red Sticks fought on in desperation. Finally, the killing stopped at nightfall, with more than nine hundred Creeks dead on the ground or floating in the river. Jackson's victorious combined force, including friendly Creek and Cherokee allies, amounted to about seventy dead and two hundred wounded.[5] Jackson ordered his slain soldiers to be sunk in the river so they could not be scalped. In the meantime, some of the victorious troops sliced off the tip of each dead Creek's nose to keep an accurate body count, while others cut long strips of skin from the backs of the corpses to be dried and made into bridle reins.[6]

The Battle of Horseshoe Bend earned the dubious distinction as the most devastating defeat of native people in the history of North America. "The carnage was dreadful," Jackson, not known for his sympathy for Indians, wrote on April 14 to his wife, Rachel, at the Hermitage. He went on to describe the engagement as "this day that has been the hot bed of the war, and has regained all the Scalps, taken from Fort Mims."[7] Jackson and his soldiers had not forgotten the cry "Remember Fort Mims!" Likewise, the Creek people never forgot Horseshoe Bend, where they had felt the brutal blade of "Sharp Knife."

Over a month later, on May 28, as a reward for his success against the Creeks, Jackson was commissioned a major general in the regular army of the United States and made commander of the Seventh Military District, which included Tennessee, Louisiana, and the Mississippi Territory.[8] Meanwhile, many of the surviving Red Sticks found sanctuary in Spanish Florida or blended into the rest of the Creek population. Bands of starving Creeks surrendered throughout the spring and summer of 1814. One of those who personally surrendered to Jackson was the Creek leader Chief Red Eagle. Surprisingly, Jackson was so impressed with his courage and acceptance of defeat that he pardoned him and turned him free. Red Eagle, living by his Christian name William Weatherford, became a respected gentleman planter in what soon became Alabama, and in his later years occasionally visited Jackson at the Hermitage, where they discussed racehorses and their former days as opposing warriors.[9]

Most Creeks, however, did not fare as well as Red Eagle. On August 9, 1814, Jackson forced the Creeks to sign a treaty at Fort Jackson. In punishment for daring to oppose the invasion of their ancestral lands,

Jackson ordered the Creeks to cede half of their tribal domain—23 million acres in all—in southern Georgia and the eastern Mississippi Territory to the United States.[10] In this same pact the Creeks also agreed to vacate the southern and western regions of what became Alabama, where, within five years after the treaty was signed, white settlers had taken over the entire region. This extreme act of retribution applied not only to Red Sticks but also to the entire Creek Nation, even those Indians who had fought on Jackson's side. "What Jackson had done had the touch of genius," noted the historian Robert Remini. "He had ended the war by signing a peace treaty with his allies! Jackson converted the Creek civil war into an enormous land grab that insured the ultimate destruction of the entire Creek Nation."[11]

The Treaty of Fort Jackson was the end not just of the Creek Nation but of all other southeastern Indian tribes. For although the Cherokees, Chickasaws, and Choctaws also fought for the United States against the renegade Creeks, these tribes, too, were soon pressured to give up their lands. Within twenty-five years they would be gone from their ancestral homes. A long-established way of life for these tribes ended as white newcomers steadily settled the rural lands of the South.

"Jackson's demands were extortionate and a shameful betrayal of his former Creek allies,"[12] wrote John Finger in his chronicle of Tennessee. "Of the thirty-five chiefs who finally signed the infamous Treaty of Fort Jackson, only one was a former Red Stick. Millions of acres of prime agricultural land—cotton land—now became available to white settlers and speculators. Frontiersman everywhere cheered Old Hickory for his feats on both the battlefield and the council ground."

Jackson's victory ceased hostilities in only one theater of the War of 1812. Land and sea battles continued elsewhere, and in late August, a British expeditionary force brazenly marched unopposed into Washington, D.C. President James Madison and his apparently imperturbable wife, Dolley, had to flee the White House, which the invaders set ablaze along with the Capitol, the Library of Congress, and most other public buildings, as well as a number of private residences.[13]

Andrew Jackson had hated Great Britain ever since he was a boy during the Revolutionary War and was slashed on his head and hand by a Red Coat sword after refusing to clean a British officer's muddy boots.[14] While Washington, D.C., smoldered, Jackson put out a call for new Tennessee volunteers to help drive the British from Florida, where they planned to incite and equip surviving Red Sticks and other Creeks who refused to accept the punitive treaty Jackson had concocted. "I owe to Britain a debt of retaliatory vengeance," Jackson wrote to his wife. "Should our forces meet I trust I shall pay the debt—she is in conjunction with Spain arming the hostile Indians to butcher our women & children."[15]

At Kentuck, Crockett caught wind of the latest call to arms. "Soon after this, an army was to be raised to go to Pensacola, and I determined to go again with them," Crockett later wrote, "for I wanted a small taste of British fighting, and I supposed they would be there."[16]

Repeating the scenario when he first enlisted, Crockett had to deal once again with Polly and fend off her tearful pleas for him to stay. "Here again the entreaties of my wife were thrown in the way of my going, but all in vain; for I always had a way of just going ahead, at whatever I had a mind to." A neighbor who had been drafted came to Crockett and offered $100 if Crockett would go in his place, but in a show of noble cause, Crockett turned the man down.[17] "I told him I was better raised than to hire myself out to be shot at; but that I would go, and he should go too, and in that way the government would have the services of us both."

Once again, Crockett said his sad good-byes to Polly and the children, and rode off for his second hitch as a soldier. Brig. Gen. John Coffee asked all volunteers from West Tennessee to assemble at Camp Blout near Fayetteville, the seat of Lincoln County, where the Crocketts had briefly lived. On September 28, 1814, Crockett reported to the first muster and signed up for a six-month enlistment in Capt. John Cowan's company of Tennessee Mounted Gunmen. This time, Crockett entered as a noncommissioned officer with the rank of third sergeant.[18]

In about a week, Gen. Coffee had gathered a thousand volunteers and was ready to move south to join Gen. Jackson and face the British at Pensacola. But there was one problem—no food. As happened continually through the Creek campaigns, Coffee was forced to report to Jackson, "I have been detained by the contractors for want of traveling rations."[19] Finally, in early October, the brigade was supplied and followed the trail south. They crossed the Muscle Shoals on the Tennessee River near Melton's Bluff and then passed through the Choctaw and Chickasaw country.

Crockett's outfit tried to catch up with the main army but remained at least two days behind. In early November, the troops reached a place known as Cut Off, near the juncture of the Tombigbee River with the Alabama River, only to find out that there was no forage available for their mounts.[20] They left their horses and some guards and covered the last of the journey on foot. "It was about eighty miles off," noted Crockett, "but in good heart we shouldered our guns, blankets, and provisions, and trudged merrily on. About twelve o'clock the second day [November 8], we reached the encampment of the main army, which was situated on a hill, overlooking the city of Pensacola."[21] Because Crockett's commanding officer, Maj. Russell, was well liked by Gen. Jackson, the tardy troops' arrival "was hailed with great applause, though we were a little after the feast, for they had taken the town and fort before we got there." Without permission from federal authorities, Jackson had invaded and temporarily seized Pensacola. His soldiers faced feeble Spanish resistance and the British detachment beat a retreat to the warships moored offshore in Pensacola Bay. In one stroke, and with just a few men lost, Jackson had eliminated the threat of British intrigue in Florida and scattered the remnants of the Red Sticks. After sloshing through palmetto-studded wetlands swarming with mosquitoes and snakes, the Tennesseans were ready to explore Pensacola, its narrow streets filled with mulattoes, runaway slaves, and Creoles. Brothels and drinking houses offered rum, smoked mullet, turtle, and oyster suppers.

"That evening we went down into the town," recounted Crockett, "and could see the British fleet lying in sight of the place. We got some liquor, and took a 'horn' or so, and went back to camp. We remained there that night, and in the morning we marched back towards the Cut-off. We pursued this direction till we reached old Fort Mimms, where we remained two or three days."[22]

Jackson had scattered a large number of his troops at garrisons throughout the Mississippi Territory. By mid-November, he issued new orders, while en route to Mobile, placing Maj. Uriah Blue, of the Thirty-ninth Infantry, in command of the West Tennessee Mounted Gunmen.[23] This included William Russell's outfit in which Crockett served as one of the sergeants. Meanwhile, Maj. Gen. Jackson was off for Mobile, and from there he would head west to Louisiana and victory on January 8, 1815, when he pummeled a force of 5,300 crack British soldiers commanded by Maj. Gen. Sir Edward Pakenham at the Battle of New Orleans. The battle left massive British casualties including Pakenham, while just thirteen Americans died in the fighting. Jackson had already built a substantial reputation with his big win at Horseshoe Bend. However, the victory at New Orleans—a battle ironically fought almost two weeks after a peace treaty ending the war had been signed—meteorically elevated Old Hickory to national prominence, his election as president coming thirteen years later. Even the newspapers of the northeastern cities gave Jackson high marks for his stunning performance in Louisiana.

There would be no glory for Crockett and his comrades-in-arms, relegated to mopping-up actions in the backwash of the war. The remainder of Crockett's service in the war mostly entailed scouting for any lingering Red Sticks and foraging for food. Supply shortages continued to be the biggest problem facing the field commanders, and that most certainly included Maj. Blue and his new regiment of 1,000 mounted gunmen, who became stuck at Fort Montgomery waiting for provisions. Finally, the frustrated Blue ordered the regiment to march in spite of having only insufficient rations of flour and beef. The troops soon came upon cattle left to roam after their owners were massacred. Crockett and some other soldiers killed several beeves and provided enough meat to keep the regiment on the move. At the camp they set up on the Escambia River almost twenty-five miles north of Pensacola in the outback of the Florida Panhandle, boats brought them what Crockett described as "many articles that were both good and necessary; such as sugar and coffee, and liquors of all kinds."[24]

Maj. Russell took his company northeast along the Escambia and Conecuh rivers. From there he sent out sixteen scouts, including Crockett, along with some Chickasaw and Choctaw warriors to hunt down hostiles hiding in the dense mangroves and swamps. Crockett wrote that they "came to a place where the whole country was covered with water, and looked like a sea."[25] Surrounding the band of men were millions of acres of wetlands and cypress swamps teeming with alligators and snakes. The scouts did not hesitate but plunged into the brackish water "like so many spaniels, and waded on, sometimes up to our armpits, until we reached the pine hills. . . . Here we struck up a fire to warm ourselves, for it was cold, and we were chilled through by being so long in the water." Later that same night, their Indian spies reported they had found a Creek camp. The Choctaws and Chickasaws painted their bodies and faces in preparation for battle, as was their custom. "They then brought the paint to old Major Russell," related Crockett, "and said to him, that as he was an officer, he must be painted too. He agreed, and they painted him just as they had done themselves."

Along the way, the Indian spies came across two Creeks and killed them. When Crockett and the others got to the scene, the Choctaw scouts had already cut off the dead Creeks' heads and were "counting coups," by striking the severed heads with war clubs. "This was done by everyone of them; and when they had got done, I took one of the clubs, and walked up as they had done, and struck it on the head also. At this they all gathered round me, and patting me on the shoulder, would call me 'Warrior—warrior.'" After they scalped the heads they pushed on to the Creek camp in a thick cane brake where they "took two squaws, and ten children, but killed none of them, of course."[26]

Besides a few minor skirmishes and taking a few prisoners, who were promptly scalped by the Choctaws and Chickasaws, the main activity, as always, was finding something decent to eat. "At the start we had taken only twenty days ration of flour, and eight days rations of beef,"[27] wrote

Crockett. "We were, therefore, in extreme suffering for want of something to eat, and exhausted from our exposure and the fatigues of our journey. I remember well, that I had not myself tasted bread but twice in nineteen days." Several men accompanied by their Indian allies rode point to find provisions while the army kept on the move. Crockett did his part to fend off starvation. "As the army marched, I hunted every day, and would kill every hawk, bird, and squirrel that I could find. Others did the same; and it was a rule with us, that when we stop'd at night, the hunters would throw all they killed in a pile, and then we would make a general division among all the men."

Crockett was convinced that he had to take control of the dire situation when, one day while searching the camp for food for a sick soldier, he came across two of his officers eating broiled gizzards after they had divided the turkey flesh among their men. "And now seeing that every fellow must shift for himself, I determined that in the morning I would come up missing; so I took my mess and cut out to go ahead of the army. We know'd that nothing more could happen to us if we went than if we staid, for it looked like it was to be starvation any way; we therefore determined to go on the old saying, *root hog or die*."[28] This adage went back to early settlement days, when hogs were commonly turned loose to forage for themselves rather than being fed. It came to stand for frontiersmen who were often in dire straits and also had to root around for whatever they could find to survive. For a man like Crockett, it was a phrase that stood for self-reliance.

After several days of finding no quarry, Crockett began to weaken. "We all began to get nearly ready to give up the ghost, and lie down and die." He brought back some small game, and two turkeys. They also found a bee tree loaded with good honey and used their tomahawks to open the tree. Crockett found a bear, but without dogs he could only watch it disappear in the trees. Soon after that he shot a large buck deer and got the dressed venison back to camp just in time. William Russell was just about to shoot his own horse to feed the men when Crockett appeared with fresh meat. Crockett and his friend handed out all the meat and the honey.[29] Later Crockett swapped some of his powder and bullets with an Indian in exchange for two hatfuls of parched corn, which he brought back to the other soldiers.

By late December 1814, several weeks before Jackson's appointment in New Orleans, Crockett and his fellow troops were headed home. Their time was up and the war was close to ending for them and everyone else. When they reached the Coosa River near Fort Strother, they met troops from east Tennessee on their way to Mobile. In the ranks Crockett found his younger brother, John, as well as some old neighbors and friends he had not seen in years.[30] It was, in fact, a sweet reunion. They gave Crockett plenty of provisions for himself and his horse and he stayed with them for a night before they continued on to Mobile.

"Here I had enough to go on, and after remaining a few days, cut out for home." And with that, David Crockett's time as a soldier came to an end, and not a day too soon.

EIGHTEEN

CABIN FEVER

WHAT SOME PEOPLE called America's "Second War of Independence" ended in a blaze of glory, and soon led to a surge in national pride that swept the country. The peace agreement with Britain signed at Ghent in Belgium in 1814, followed early the following year by General Jackson's anticlimatic but stunning victory at New Orleans, lifted American's spirits and marked a time of significant change as the nation came of age. "Never did a country occupy more lofty ground," noted U.S. Supreme Court Justice Joseph Story in 1815. "We have stood the contest, single-handed, against the conqueror of Europe; and we are at peace, with all our blushing victories thick crowding on us."

In the last days of January 1815, as David Crockett returned from the war, he had no thoughts of "blushing victories." He could not have known that the nation had been set on a course of transformation from an undeveloped country of frontiersmen and small farmers, like him, into an economic power. Crockett's vision of the nation and beyond was limited to his own domain. Like the other soldiers he had served with, he only cared about getting home to Tennessee. The sight of a curl of wood smoke rising from the chimney at his cabin on Bean Creek in Franklin County had to have been a sight to behold for war-weary Crockett. He was anxious to be back with Polly and his children and he was determined not to leave his family again.

"I found them all well and doing well," Crockett recounted of his homecoming, "and though I was only a rough sort of a backwoodsman, they seemed mighty glad to see me, however little the quality folks might suppose it. For I do reckon we love as hard in the backwood country, as any people in the whole creation."[1]

Crockett had been home for a few days and was only beginning to tell stories of his latest experiences when he received official orders to report back for duty. His enlistment had not been completed, and he was still subject to military recall until March 27. The new orders directed Crockett's outfit to return to Mississippi Territory and proceed to the country between the Black Warrior and Cahaba rivers to scout for any remaining hostile Indians. Crockett had no intention of obeying. "I know'd well enough there was none, and I wasn't willing to trust my craw any more where there was neither any fighting to do, nor any thing to go on."[2]

Instead of dutifully packing up and heading out for yet a third time, Crockett solved the problem by using a common legal procedure—paying someone to serve as a substitute. Crockett offered the balance of his army wages to a young man who was eager to go and fight Indians. In the past, a neighbor wanted to pay Crockett to go to war in his stead, and Crockett flatly refused, but it seems he had had a change of heart. The substitute went off to serve out the rest of Crockett's enlistment, and when he returned Crockett noted that "sure enough they hadn't seen an Indian any more than if they had been all the time chopping woods in my clearing."[3]

Later, Crockett received a discharge certificate signed by Brig. Gen. John Coffee in Nashville on March 27, 1815. It read: "I certify that David Crockett a 4th Sergt. in my brigade of Tennessee Volunteer Mounted Gun-men, has performed a tour of duty of six months service of the United States—that his good conduct, subordination, and valor, under the most trying hardships, entitle him to the gratitude of his country, and that he is hereby honorably discharge [*sic*] by his general."[4] For his six months and two days of service, Crockett received $66.70, from which he paid off the young man who served out the final weeks of the enlistment. It is unknown if listing his rank as Fourth Sergeant when he started at the higher rank of Third Sergeant was a clerical error, or if a demotion was light punishment for Crockett's inclination to do as he pleased.

"This closed out my career as a warrior, and I am glad of it," Crockett wrote about that time of transition, "for I like life now a heap better than I did then; and I am glad all over that I lived to see these times, which I should not have done if I had kept fooling along in war, and got used to it. . . . The battle at New Orleans had already been fought, and treaties were made with the Indians which put a stop to their hostilities."[5]

Yet the peace that Crockett was just beginning to enjoy was short-lived. Death—his constant companion during his time as a soldier— had followed him home and, in the early spring of 1815, arrived at his cabin door. That March, Polly Crockett took to her bed gravely ill. Her health rapidly declined, and, after a painful struggle, Polly died. She was only twenty-six years old. No records have been found indicating the cause of death or the exact date that Polly passed away at the Bean Creek cabin. Medical care was limited and life expectancy short on the frontier. For many years, complications from childbirth were said to have brought about Polly's death, based on the erroneous belief that daughter Margaret was not born until after David came home from the Indian Wars in 1815. But Margaret's birth date was November 25, 1812, which meant the little girl was twenty-eight months old at the time her mother died, thus eliminating childbirth as her cause of death. Others have theorized that it could have been one of several maladies that plagued the frontier, including typhoid fever, dysentery, small-pox, streptococcal infections, pneumonia, or malaria, which also beset Crockett in the years to come.[6]

Another possibility for Polly's death was a mysterious torment known as milk sickness. Also called "sick stomach," "puking illness," and "the slows," milk sickness followed frontier migration patterns and for a time was rampant in Tennessee.[7] It was only many years later, through the advancement of modern medicine, that it was determined that milk sickness was a vegetable poisoning caused by tremetol, an alcohol found in the white snakeroot plant.[8] Grazing cattle or deer feeding in the woods ate the plant, and humans acquired the disease by drinking the milk or eating the flesh of affected animals. In a matter of days the victims showed symptoms—abdominal pain, vomiting, extreme constipation, and fatigue. Soon those stricken fell into a stupor, quickly followed by coma and death.

Polly's death devastated Crockett. He had seen death up close many times during his service in the recent war, but he could not have been prepared to witness the passing of the woman he so dearly loved. "I met with the hardest trial which ever falls to the lot of man," he later wrote of that sad time. "Death, that cruel leveler of all distinctions . . . entered my humble cottage, and tore from my children an affectionate good mother, and from me a tender and loving wife."[9]

Crockett, never a particularly religious person, did, on occasion, make reference to a higher power. Polly's death was one of those times. "It was the doing of the Almighty, whose ways are always right, though we sometimes think they fall heavily on us; and as painful as it is even yet the remembrance of her sufferings, and the loss sustained by my little children and myself, yet I have no wish to lift up the voice of complaint."[10]

Polly's corpse was washed and dressed in the best frock she had. David fashioned a coffin, and he dug a grave on a hillside near their homestead at Kentuck. He piled some fieldstones to mark the place. For about 140 years only the remnants of that stone cairn indicated the site of Polly's grave. In 1956, in the wake of the revival of interest in all things Davy Crockett caused by the Walt Disney television shows, the Tennessee Historical Commission, with public donations, erected a granite monument with the inscription:

Polly Finlay [*sic*] Crockett
Born 1788 in Hamblen County
Married to
David Crockett
Aug. 12, 1806
Mother of
John Wesley Crockett—1807
William Crockett—1809
Margaret Finley Crockett—1812
Died 1815

Almost twenty-nine years old and trying to scratch out a living on a badly neglected farm, Crockett found himself alone with three small children, John Wesley, seven; William, six; and Polly, going on three. It was far from an enviable position, or, as Crockett put it, "my situation was the worst in the world." He turned to his brother, John, the younger brother David had met near the end of the war when he was on his way home. John had married the former Sally Thomas in Jefferson County in 1812, and by the time Polly died they had moved to Franklin County.[11] It is likely that Sally helped nurse and tend to Polly in her final days.

"I couldn't bear the thought of scattering my children," wrote Crockett, "and I got my youngest brother, who was also married, and his family to live with me. They took good care of my children as they well could, but yet it wasn't like the care of a mother. And though their company was to me in every respect like that of a brother and sister, yet it fell far short of being that of a wife. So I came to the conclusion it wouldn't do, but that I must have another wife."[12]

Crockett had no time for long courtships or wooing coy damsels. He was driven by a practical need to find a dependable helpmate so he could earn a living and, most importantly, feed his family. Crockett did not wait long to look for a new wife, and he did not have to go very far to find one. He was well aware that his neighbor, the war widow Elizabeth Patton, was as likely a candidate as any women in Franklin County.

She and her son, George, and daughter, Margaret Ann—close to the age of Crockett's two eldest children—lived on what Crockett described as "a snug little farm" just west of his Kentuck on Bean Creek.[13]

Born in Swannanoa, North Carolina, on May 22, 1788, Elizabeth was one of the eight children—two sons and six daughters—of Robert Patton, a native of Ireland, and his wife, Rebecca. The Pattons were prominent Presbyterians and donated land for the Patton Meeting House, one of the earliest churches established west of the Blue Ridge Mountains. As the owner of a thriving plantation with more than a thousand acres of prime farmland on both sides of the Swannanoa River, the Pattons were considered well-to-do and of considerable wealth. It was also well known around the county that Elizabeth had $800 in gold, a considerable sum in those times.[14]

Elizabeth married her cousin James Patton, son of her father's brother, and they moved to Tennessee, where George and Margaret Ann, nicknamed Peggy Ann, were born. Crockett was acquainted with James Patton, a Tennessee Volunteer killed at the Battle of Talladega in 1813, where Crockett had also fought against the Red Sticks.

Elizabeth needed a husband and Crockett needed a wife. "I began to think, that as we were both in the same situation, it might be that we could do something for each other," Crockett explained.[15]

Nothing at all like Polly Crockett, Elizabeth was described as large, sensible, and practical. It was said she had a good business mind and was someone with regular habits. It seemed little, if any, great passion would mark David and Elizabeth's relationship, but it also seemed that the Pattons' 250-acre farm and gold coin sweetened the idea of marriage for Crockett. "I soon began to pay my respects to her in real good earnest; but I was as sly about it as a fox when he is going to rob a hen-roost," Crockett noted. "I found that my company wasn't at all disagreeable to her; and I thought I could treat her children with so much friendship as to make her a good stepmother to mine, and in this I wasn't mistaken, as we soon bargained, and got married, and then went ahead."[16]

On May 21, 1815, Crockett was elected a lieutenant in the local county militia, and his marriage with Elizabeth took place sometime that summer, just a few months after Polly's death.[17] Decades after the nuptials, an amusing story surfaced about the wedding ceremony. It had been passed down through the family of Richard Calloway, a Franklin County magistrate and a Crockett friend who was called upon to perform the wedding ceremony in the Patton home, filled with neighbors, friends, and kinfolk of the bride and groom, including their children. Just as the bride was due to make her entrance, a grunting pig that had slipped through an open door burst into the room, causing much laughter and commotion. Crockett rose to the occasion and, with his foot, ushered the porcine intruder out the door while exclaiming, "Old hook, from now on, *I'll* do the grunting around here."[18]

True to his promise, Crockett did do the grunting. Only months after the wedding, while the combined family of five small children was just getting comfortable with their new living situation, Crockett was stricken with an illness. It was not milk sickness or cholera or smallpox. It was something altogether different. Crockett showed all the symptoms— restlessness, irritability, and an uncontrollable need to open the cabin door and run. Elizabeth and the brood of children were about to learn that there was no real cure for what took hold of the man: cabin fever.

Crockett had caught it and he could not shake it.

NINETEEN

A TINCTURE OF LUCK

HE INK SIGNATURES scrawled on their marriage contract had barely dried when David surprised his new bride with news of a honeymoon. The only problem was that Elizabeth was not invited to come along. This was to be a hunting expedition, a purely male endeavor, and Crockett would have three of his male neighbors for companions. Besides, the time had come to seek new land for settlement.

It was not as though Crockett had worn out his welcome in Franklin County. On the contrary, he had become a significant figure in his own community as well as in all the surrounding districts. At the camp meetings—popular and boisterous outdoor religious revival events—he was often one of the main attractions because of his engaging personality and ability as a storyteller. Camp meetings were as much social gatherings as spiritual events, and they usually lasted several days, bringing together people from far and wide. Crockett would stand under the shelter of a brush arbor, belt out a few hymns, and endure the fiery sermons of roving circuit preachers exhorting the faithful to either get right with the Holy Ghost or face the wrath of a furious God. That still left plenty of time for him to entertain the attendees with colorful stories of fighting

Indians and hunting bears in the deep woods, while perhaps sneaking in a few horns of stump liquor when no one was looking.

David found that he was a natural-born crowd pleaser so well liked that his former comrades had made him Lieutenant Crockett in the militia of Franklin County, the first of several elections Crockett would eventually win over the course of the next eighteen years.

One of his supporters in the militia election was Jacob Van Zandt Jr., the same age as Crockett and one of his frequent companions on foraging hunts during the Creek War, when they supplied fresh meat for their fellow soldiers.[1] Jacob came from a well-known and admired Franklin County family, headed by his father, Jacob Van Zandt Sr., a native of Holland who came to America and served as captain with the North Carolina militia in the Revolutionary War. The elder Van Zandt took part in the Battle of Cowpens and by 1800 had settled with his wife, Catherine Moon Van Zandt, in Tennessee.[2] The Crockett family was held in such high esteem by the Van Zandt clan that when Jacob Sr., made out his last will and testament, he requested David and his younger brother John to act as two of the witnesses at the signing of the document. Van Zandt's generous gifts of slaves and land to his kin did not become public until 1818, when the old man died, a few years after the Crockett family had left Franklin County. However, the signing of the will occurred on October 9, 1815,[3] a significant date because not long afterward Crockett kissed his wife and five children good-bye—an act he had repeated many times before and would continue to perform until his own death—and headed south out of Tennessee into country that would become central Alabama. Crockett had seen plenty of what seemed like good land during his travels in the war, and since much of this land was opening to public domain it seemed a good idea to have a look.

In his *Narrative*, Crockett identifies his trio of fellow hunters only as neighbors named Robinson, Frazier, and Rich, probably because when Crockett wrote the book he had forgotten their first names.[4] He did not forget the journey, however, which provided plenty of excitement and more chances for Crockett to prove his mettle.

"We set out for the Creek country, crossing the Tennessee river; and after having made a day's travel, we stop'd at the house of one of my old acquaintances, who had settled there after the war. Resting here a day, Frazier turned out to hunt, being a great hunter; but he got badly bit by a very poisonous snake, and so we left him and went on. We passed through a large rich valley, called Jones's valley, where several families had settled, and continued our course till we came near to the place where Tuscaloosa now stands."[5]

Black Warrior's Town, located on what the white settlers called the Black Warrior River, would not become Tuscaloosa until 1819, taking its name from *tushka*, meaning warrior, and *lusa*, meaning black, the name of the old Choctaw Chief Tuskalusa, who was defeated in battle by Hernando de Soto in 1540.[6] Crockett had been to this place before, when he was a soldier and his outfit had looted stores of corn and beans from the deserted Creek settlement before burning it to ash.

Crockett and the two remaining hunters hobbled their horses for the night and stretched out for a rest. During the night, Crockett heard the bells on the horses as they freed themselves from the loose ties and took off, probably headed back to where they had started. At first light, Crockett started in pursuit of the horses on foot, carrying his rifle. For hours he looked everywhere, wading creeks, sloshing through swamps, and pushing through thick brush. At each cabin he came to along the way, Crockett was told the horses had been seen passing by, but at the end of the day there was no further sign of them. He doubled back to the last cabin he had passed and spent the night.

"From the best calculation we could make, I had walked over fifty miles that day; and the next morning I was so sore, and fatigued, that I felt like I couldn't walk any more,"[7] Crockett wrote in his *Narrative*. "But I was anxious to get back to where I had left my company, and so I started and went on, but mighty slowly, till after the middle of the day. I now began to feel mighty sick, and had a dreadful head-ache. My rifle was so heavy, and I felt so weak, that I lay down by the side of the trace, in a perfect wilderness too, to see if I wouldn't get better."

Although Crockett did not say so in his autobiography, he had been stricken with malaria, and would suffer from its effects for the rest of his life. Malaria did not exist in the Americas until the 1500s, but that changed with the coming of Spaniards and their African slaves; soon the disease spread throughout the hemisphere. The bite of infected female mosquitoes transmitted the infectious disease, which made it especially dangerous in the American South, where consistently warm temperatures allowed mosquitoes to breed year-round. Throughout the 1700s malaria struck many settlers in the southeast, causing a Scots-Irish pioneer to say that Virginia had so much malaria it was "only good for doctors and ministers," while a German immigrant noted, "They who want to die quickly go to Carolina."[8] Malaria moved westward with the white settlers into Tennessee and all across the Mississippi Valley. Twice the capital of Alabama had to be relocated because of outbreaks of malarial fevers in the early 1820s.

Luckily for Crockett, a pair of Indians—probably friendly Choctaws—came across him as he lay sweating and trembling from chills and fever on the side of the trail. They offered Crockett some ripe melon, but he was far too ill to eat. The Indians knew what the white man was facing, and they told him the hard truth. "They then signed to me, that I would die, and be buried; a thing I was confoundedly afraid of myself."[9] Crockett asked them to take him to the nearest house, and by signing they agreed. "I got up to go; but when I rose, I reeled about like a cow with the blind staggers, or a fellow who had taken too many 'horns.'"

He paid one of the Indians a half-dollar to carry his rifle and go with him. After they had traversed about a mile and a half, they came to a cabin. Crockett felt that he "was pretty far gone." The people there were kind and put the stricken man to bed. "The woman did all she could for me with her warm teas, but I still continued bad enough, with a high fever, and generally out of my senses." The next day two neighbors that Crockett knew from back home happened by, and they managed to get the sick man on a horse and take him back to the campsite where he had left the other two hunters, Robinson and Rich. The ride only worsened Crockett's condition, and by the time he was returned to his camp he could not sit up.[10] "I thought the jig was mighty nigh up with me, but I determined to keep a stiff upper lip," Crockett wrote. "They carried me to a house, and each of my comrades bought him a horse, and they all set out together, leaving me behind."

Crockett had been left at the home of a man named Jesse Jones, who, along with his wife, cared for the stricken man as if he was their own son. About the Jones family, Crockett later wrote that they "treated me with every possible kindness in their power, and I shall always feel thankful to them."[11] Without the attention he received at this modest frontier cabin, Crockett surely would have perished. For five days he was unconscious, and for at least two weeks he remained in a state of delirium. Finally, out of sheer desperation, Mrs. Jones poured an entire six-ounce bottle of Bateman's Drops down Crockett's throat. This was a drastic step. This patent medicine—it had been around since the 1720s—usually was taken in small doses of only a few drops at a time. The main ingredients were opium, aniseed, and camphor, and if swigged indiscriminately Bateman's Drops could be toxic, if not lethal. The desperate Mrs. Jones had no other choice. She reasoned that Crockett was bound to die anyway, so why not take a gamble.[12]

"She gave me the whole bottle, which throwed me into a sweat that continued on me all night," recalled Crockett, "when at last I seemed to make up, and spoke, and asked her for a drink of water. This almost alarmed her, for she was looking every minute for me to die. She gave me the water, and, from that time, I began slowly to mend, and so kept on till I was able at last to walk about a little."

Gradually, Crockett's health returned, and even though he was not fully recovered, he reached a point where the malaria did not seem debilitating. He had to get moving, so when a waggoner happened by the Jones cabin, he asked if he could hitch a ride as far as the man's house, which Crockett found out was just twenty miles from his own place. "I still mended as we went along, and when we got to his stopping place, I hired one of his horses, and went on home. I was so pale, and so much reduced, that my face looked like it had been half soled with brown paper."[13]

At the Crockett home, Elizabeth and the children grew more worried with each passing day. There had been no word at all from Crockett, and they were prepared for the worst. Robinson and Rich, her husband's two friends, had returned weeks before, trailing three horses they found on the way; they were the same ones Crockett had been searching for when he was stricken with malaria. Perhaps out of embarrassment for leaving Crockett behind, when the two men brought Crockett's horse to Elizabeth they said that her husband had met his death during the expedition.[14] They told the stricken woman that they had come upon some men who watched Crockett draw his last breath and then buried him.

Elizabeth had already been widowed by war and understood the realities of life and death on the frontier. Yet she was not fully convinced that her highly resourceful husband was really dead. The practical Elizabeth wanted proof, so she hired a man to retrace Crockett's journey. She directed the man to look for her husband and find out the truth of the matter. If David had left any money or personal effects behind, Elizabeth told the man to fetch them home to her and the children. The hired man was still on the trail and missed meeting up with Crockett before he slipped back into Franklin County.

Likely Elizabeth thought she was looking at an emaciated ghost when she discovered David standing in the doorway of the cabin. Her astonishment had to have been overwhelming. That all changed in an instant when David smiled, and her lost husband walked back into her life.

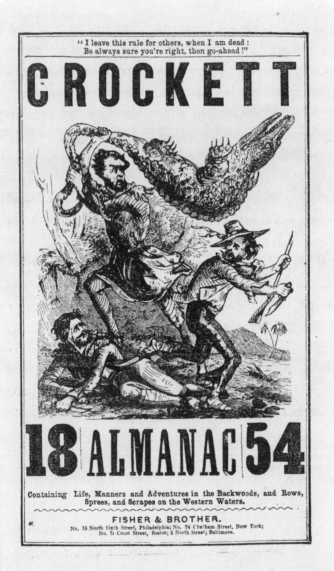

Almanac cover, 1854.
(Photograph by Dorothy Sloan, Dorothy Sloan Rare Books)

PART III

"ITCHY FOOTED"

CROCKETT HAD SURVIVED yet another brush with death. Finding himself "still in the land of the living and a-kicking," he wisely recuperated at his cabin on the Rattle Snake Spring Branch of Bean's Creek. Like other denizens of the frontier, Crockett had little knowledge of what was going on in the rest of the nation at the time. The only news that interested him was anything that had a direct impact on his own family's daily life. For most of the winter of 1815 and well into the summer of 1816, as his recovery from the bout with malaria progressed, he tended to family and farm. The youngsters were glad to have their father back with them, and Elizabeth kept him healthy and happy while she put up with a hot summertime pregnancy.

On September 16, 1816, Elizabeth gave birth to a healthy son, whom they named Robert Patton Crockett—the first in a new "crop" (Crockett's word) born to her and David.[1]

The same week of Robert's birth, while David and his neighbors quaffed celebratory horns of liquor, others were at work acquiring more Indian land for white settlement. Andrew Jackson and fellow federal treaty commissioners David Meriwether and Jesse Franklin used threats, coercion, and bribery to grab up more enormous land grants from the

Cherokee and Chickasaw tribes.[2] During negotiations, the Cherokee leaders implored Jackson to reduce the size of the land cession but he refused to budge and overcame all resistance. Jackson told them that the price the Cherokees paid by giving up land had to be great if their tribe wanted a lasting relationship with the United States. The treaty with the Cherokees, who surrendered millions of acres in return for a series of monetary payments, was signed on September 14, 1816, at Turkey Town.[3] The treaty also promised peace and friendship between the Cherokee Nation and the United States forever. Jackson's memory must have soon failed him, for in a letter to newly elected President James Monroe written just a year later, he noted: "I have long viewed treaties with the Indians an absurdity not to be reconciled to the principles of our government."[4] Jackson's outspoken contempt for Indian treaty rights was not motivated only by an insatiable hunger for more land. It would be too simplistic to conclude that Jackson was simply a greedy "Indian hater." His attitude toward Indians was patronizing and paternalistic. Jackson believed that, like the scores of slaves laboring on his plantation, Indians were childlike creatures in need of guidance from a father figure. He rationalized that he had their humanitarian interests in mind and that the treaties he negotiated and policies he later enforced were beneficial to Indians and protected them from the white population.

Jackson's treatment of Indians was not exclusive to any one tribe but to all Indians, as the Chickasaw tribe soon learned. They fared no better than the Cherokees. On September 20, in signing the treaty at the Chickasaw council house in northern Mississippi, Jackson promised the tribe less than $200,000 in exchange for millions of acres of Chickasaw lands, or almost a quarter of the amount taken from the Creeks at Fort Jackson a few years earlier. As a Jackson biographer succinctly noted, "It was a formidable purchase."[5]

Jackson was not finished. On October 24, 1816, the Choctaws ceded their land east of the Tombigbee River in return for an annual payment of $16,000 for twenty years and $10,000 in merchandise.[6] All of this pleased Jackson, but still he wanted more Indian lands open to white settlement, and he would not stop until that desire was fulfilled. But before he put together another army, including many Tennessee volunteers, to sweep into Florida to punish the Seminole tribe hiding there and wrest the territory away from the Spanish, Jackson looked to some personal interests.

During 1817 and 1818, while pulling together his Florida invasion force to burn Seminole villages, Jackson, his friend John Coffee, and several Tennessee cronies joined land speculators snapping up newly opened parcels of property, including former Creek lands in the future state of Alabama.[7] Although he was widely considered by most white citizens as a national hero after his spectacular defeat of the British at the Battle of New Orleans, Jackson had no wish to provide any fodder for his political foes. To avoid even the slightest criticism for buying land at government auctions, Jackson emphasized that he was not motivated by personal gain but only wished to encourage settlement to protect the frontier. Few people ever questioned Jackson on this point, but instead held him in even higher esteem for defeating the Indian menace and making valuable land available for settlement.

One of the Tennesseans most pleased with the promise of new land was Crockett. Growing aware that so-called civilization was creeping in around him, Crockett was primed and ready to explore new territory, and the recent treaties gave him ample reason to do so. That autumn of 1816, news of the various Indian treaties was better medicine than an entire case of Bateman's Drops. No tribal claims remained to delay expansion, leaving the door to the West wide open.

By late autumn, Crockett—despite flare-ups of malaria—was dead-set on moving his family out of Franklin County. "The place on which I lived was sickly, and I was determined to leave it," Crockett wrote. "I therefore set out the next fall to look at the country which had been purchased of the Chickasaw tribe of Indians. I went on to a place called Shoal Creek, about eighty miles from where I lived, and here again I got sick. I took the ague and fever, which I supposed was brought on me by camping out. I remained here for some time, as I was unable to go farther; and in that time, I became so well pleased with the country about there, that I resolved to settle in it."[8]

After he fought off another bout of the recurrent malaria, Crockett rode far to the northeast to spend the winter of 1816–1817 with some of his kinfolk just three miles below the Kentucky border.[9] David's uncles William, Robert, Joseph, and James Crockett had lived for many years in the Wolf River area on the Cumberland Plateau of what eventually became Fentress County, Tennessee. The brothers had moved there not long after the deaf and mute James, affectionately called "Deaf and Dumb Jimmie," was ransomed from a Cherokee trader after being held captive for seventeen years. Uncle Robert later moved north to Cumberland County, Kentucky, where he died an old man and left his land and several slaves to his children, including a son also named David Crockett.[10] Robert's last will and testament was read March 2, 1836, only four days before his famous nephew was killed in battle at the Alamo.

Uncle Jimmy resided only a few miles north of the settlement of Sand Springs—which later became the county seat of Jamestown—in a house owned by the illustrious Conrad "Coonrod" Pile.[11] A salty old Longhunter who settled in the area in 1791, Pile had a dozen children, including a daughter, Delila, married to William Crockett, another of David's uncles, who lived in the small settlement of Boatland on the Obey River.[12] A center for boat building, Boatland was where flatboats came up the Obey, also called the Obed by later mapmakers, to take on loads of turpentine and tar bound for Nashville and other markets. David spent the winter in a beach flat near Boatland, getting reacquainted with relatives and picking up boat-making skills that he later would put to use.

He also hunted with Coonrod Pile, a man twenty years Crockett's senior who long before had found a location to his liking at the Three Forks of Wolf River. Coonrod chose the site because of the cool, clear spring water flowing near his camp, where he cooked game on a hot stone, drank from a turtle shell, and slept inside a cave on a bed of dry leaves and grass. He kept a fire burning at the cave entrance day and night to discourage wild critters from visiting. It was said that he feared neither man nor beast but was deathly afraid of lightning; if a big storm approached, he ran to his cave as quickly as he could. By the time Crockett met the old man, Coonrod had amassed a sizable fortune manufacturing guns, maintaining tollgates on a turnpike road, and overseeing his sizable farmlands. Coonrod lived in a large log house with no windows and only one door that opened by his bedside. Next to the bed, he kept a rifle at the ready and a pitchfork with sharpened prongs.[13]

Almost a century after Crockett and Coonrod hunted the river bottoms and hollows, another famous Tennessee marksman emerged from the Pall Mall Valley—Alvin C. York.[14] York became the most famous American solider in World War I after he won the Medal of Honor for leading an attack on a German position, killing 28 German soldiers and capturing 132 others. Best known as Sergeant York, this farm boy from the Valley of the Three Forks was Conrad Pile's great-great-grandson. He grew up hearing tales of both his illustrious ancestor and David Crockett. "I think we had just about the best shots that ever squinted down a barrel," York wrote in his war diary. "Daniel Boone and Davy Crockett used to shoot at these matches long ago. And Andrew Jackson used to recruit his Tennessee sharpshooters from among our mountain shooters."[15]

As would be revealed many years later, Crockett's brief stay at Boatland had a far-reaching impact on other impressionable young men. Yet in early spring of 1817, Crockett's focus returned to the new lands that waited to the west. He bid good-bye to family and friends on the Wolf River and at Boatland and made the long ride home to begin preparing his family for another move.

Before leaving Franklin County, Crockett went to the hillside not far from Kentuck for one more visit at Polly's grave, marked by the cairn of rocks. He pulled some weeds, doffed his hunter's hat, and mumbled a few words. Then he and his family—on horseback and piled into wagons—went to Shoal Creek.

Many years later, James Burns Gowen, a hunting companion and neighbor when David, Polly, and their babies made their first move west, described Crockett as "an itchy footed sort of fellow who went bear hunting with a knife, bagged a covey of wild turkey with a single shot, went Indian hunting with Andrew Jackson and finally got himself elected to Congress."[16]

By 1817 Crockett had hunted Indians with Jackson, but he probably had not yet killed a bear with a knife, and he never did bag a bunch of turkeys with just one shot. Crockett would go to Congress some years away. However, Gowen's finest description of Crockett was as "itchy footed," as true as anything that had ever been said about the man.

"NATURAL BORN SENSE"

DAVID CROCKETT GOT OFF to a good start on his 160 acres of newly opened Choctaw Purchase land at the head of Shoal Creek, in what was soon to become Lawrence County, Tennessee. But he was not the first white man to settle there. For several years prior to the Choctaws' ceding their land, mostly Scots-Irish squatters from North Carolina had illegally moved into the area.[1] By 1815, the first settlement appeared on Big Buffalo River; a gristmill and distillery followed, and then some Primitive Baptists arrived and built a church. The soil was fertile and yielded fine crops of corn, wheat, cotton, and tobacco, with much game to be found in the hardwood forests and along the many spring-fed streams.

During the less than five years he lived in these parts, Crockett launched his public career. This was where he developed his own style of rhetoric and sharpened his oratory skills. It was here that he first entered mainstream politics. And it was in Lawrence County that history began to take notice of him.

Nearing his thirty-first birthday, Crockett and his boys quickly built a cabin along Shoal Creek, the first of three homes the family would have while living in this region. They had sold a large portion of their land back in Franklin County and leased out the rest of what had been the Patton farm. This income, along with Elizabeth's family money, bought them a little time to adjust to their new surroundings and get to know their neighbors.

Even before the family had completely moved to Lawrence County, Crockett was quickly emerging as a community leader. He had already been named one of five commissioners of the Shoal Creek Corporation, a panel of local men charged with laying out county boundaries.[2] Coming up with a name for the proposed county proved to be easy. There was unanimous approval when the commissioners proposed to name it after Captain James Lawrence, the popular naval hero of the War of 1812 who, when mortally wounded, shouted to his crew, "Don't give up the ship."[3] As far as a name for the county seat, it was simple enough to continue the pattern and call the place Lawrenceburgh, soon changed to Lawrenceburg without the "h." All that remained was finding a place to build a courthouse. As smoothly as establishing county boundaries and the naming chores had progressed, site selection for the Lawrence County seat of government proved to be fraught with controversy.

Crockett and four other county residents were charged with choosing the site. The other selection commissioners were Maximilian H. Buchanan, a major landowner in the area; Josephus Irvine, who enjoyed fisticuffs and was often fined for fighting; Enoch Tucker, one of Crockett's close friends and business associates; and Henry Phenix, operator of a "house of public entertainment."[4]

At their first meeting, the five members sharply divided into two camps, each with a specific location and his own special interests. On one side were Crockett and Tucker, championing land at a point where Shoal Creek straightened out and flowed south to the Tennessee River. This site was very near the property Crockett and Tucker owned on Shoal Creek. They claimed it was the ideal spot since it was the "exact geographic location of the county," as recommended by the Tennessee General Assembly.[5] Crockett pointed out that such a location would be more easily accessible to all county residents. The other faction demanded that the county seat be built near property they owned on the new Military Road, under construction by some of Andrew Jackson's soldiers. It would soon become an alternative to the historic Natchez Trace, an important road for several Indian tribes and by the late 1700s a vital link between outposts of civilization for white settlers.[6]

The two sides locked in heated arguments and neither would budge. Crockett was incensed because Irvine, who had been authorized to build the courthouse, started to erect the building on the site his team had picked before state officials had made a final decision. Accusations, citizen petitions, and a flood of other documents from the two factions bombarded the Tennessee General Assembly in Murfreesboro, where in 1818 the state capital was moved because, unlike Knoxville, Murfreesboro was located in the exact geographic center of Tennessee.[7]

Ultimately, Crockett lost the battle over location, although the dispute raged on and was not fully resolved until 1823, a year after Crockett had moved from Lawrence County farther west to the Obion River country.[8] In fact, Lawrenceburg was built just where Crockett's opponents had chosen—a 400-acre tract of land that had been granted to John Thompson by the State of North Carolina in 1792 for services rendered as a soldier in the Revolutionary War. Private Thompson never claimed the land, probably because he considered it worthless since it was located in the heart of Chickasaw territory.[9]

The squabble over where Lawrenceburg should be located made Crockett a few enemies, but it also broadened his appeal and heightened his public image. Soon after he came to the area, Crockett was called upon to help bring some order to an emerging county "without any law at all," where, according to Crockett, "so many bad characters began to flock in upon us."[10] His neighbors formed a backwoods confederation and asked Crockett to be an unofficial magistrate. He took the appointment quite seriously but kept his sense of humor. "When a man owed a debt, and wouldn't pay it, I and my constable ordered our warrant, and then he would take the man, and bring him before me for trial," Crockett later explained. "I would give judgment against him, and then an order of execution would easily scare the debt out of him." There also were times when Crockett had to be stern and use corporal punishment. "If any one was charged with marking his neighbour's hogs, or with stealing any thing, which happened pretty often in those days—I would have him taken, and if there was tolerable grounds for the charge, I would have him well whip'd and cleared."[11]

Crockett must have done a satisfactory job. The confidence his neighbors placed in him was proven when on November 25, 1817, the state legislature—based on citizens' recommendations—named Crockett as one of twelve magistrates, or justices of the peace, in the emerging county.[12] "This was a hard business for me, for I could just barely write my own name; but to do this, and write the warrants too, was at least a huckleberry over my persimmon," wrote Crockett, using one of his pet phrases for "a cut above." In describing his work as a justice of the peace in his autobiography, Crockett once again presented himself as a simple, semiliterate country man without much education but with an ample load of horse sense. "My judgments were never appealed from," Crockett continued, "and if they had been they would have stuck like wax, as I gave my decisions on the principles of common justice and honesty between man and man, and relied on natural born sense, and not on law, learning to guide me; for I had never read a page in a law book in my life."[13]

Crockett's "natural born sense" proved to be more valuable to his future political career than anything he could have learned in school. His selection as town commissioner and justice of the peace gave him a taste of government as well as the desire to dig deeper into the political stew pot for a bigger spoonful. The governmental posts he held in Lawrence County, combined with his sizable reputation as a war veteran and skilled hunter, ignited a busy career of public service.

Crockett was flattered when Capt. Daniel Matthews, an officer in the local militia, asked for his support in an upcoming election to choose a regimental colonel. Matthews was a prosperous farmer who consistently raised more corn than anyone else in the entire county.[14] Crockett had no trouble giving his endorsement. However, he was hesitant when Matthews suggested that Crockett join his ticket and run for the post of regimental major. "I objected to this, telling him that I thought I had done my share of fighting, and that I wanted nothing to do with military appointments."[15] Matthews was as stubborn as Crockett. He spoke of Crockett's record as a soldier in the Indian Wars and reminded him that his constituents in Franklin County had elected him to the rank of lieutenant before he moved away. At Matthews's insistence, Crockett—confident that he and Matthews would support each other—gave in and agreed to run.

To launch their joint campaign, Matthews hosted a huge corn-husking frolic on his farm and invited every citizen eligible to vote in the county. The plan was for Matthews and Crockett to come forward at the end of the frolic and make their formal joint announcement for colonel and major in the militia. A swarm of people descended on the Matthews place, including the entire Crockett clan. However, just before the speeches were to be given, one of Crockett's friends tipped him off that the whole thing was a ruse cooked up by Matthews, whose own son was also going to be a candidate for major. Crockett had been duped and set up as a patsy candidate.[16]

"I cared nothing about the office," Crockett later admitted, "but it put my dander up high enough to see, that after he had pressed me so hard to offer, he was countenancing, if not encouraging a secret plan to beat me." Crockett confronted Captain Matthews, who admitted to the double-cross but offered his apology and said that his son "hated worse to run against me than any man in the county." That was when Crockett delivered a surprise of his own. "I told him his son need give himself no uneasiness about that; that I shouldn't run against him for major, but against his daddy for colonel."[17] A stunned Matthews graciously shook Crockett's hand and then addressed the crowd. He announced his candidacy and added that he would be running against David Crockett.

There was polite applause and then Crockett came forward with his speech. He liked giving the final speech of the day and would employ this tactic of getting in the last word in all of his future runs for elected political office. He kept his remarks brief and with a smile and a few winks explained his reasons for taking on Captain Matthews, "remarking that as I had the whole family to run against any way, I was determined to levy on the head of the mess." The people gathered around him burst into cheers. Crockett's self-effacing and humorous speech became the template for every one of his future political campaigns.

Crockett always went directly to the people, an action that would characterize his entire political career. He stumped every nook and cranny of the county, as if he were hunting only for votes. At each stop, he delivered his humorous speeches, shook hands, and swigged a little whiskey. It all paid off, for when the final votes were tallied, Crockett was declared the winner by a hefty margin and took great delight in the fact that, not only did he beat the father, but the son also lost badly to another candidate running for major.

On March 27, 1818, David Crockett was commissioned lieutenant colonel commandant of the Fifty-seventh Regiment of Militia.[18] The rank he earned was not a gratuitous tile of "Colonel" that came to be handed out to so-called southern gentlemen of means. Crockett was not a plantation colonel but a high-ranking militia officer duly elected by the citizens to head up a regiment. Yet he also was a new breed of frontier populist who had challenged the plantation hierarchy and prevailed. The title of colonel stuck and remained with him for the rest of his years. Colonel David Crockett of Tennessee—it had a definite ring.

Crockett wasted no time in making his mark in Lawrence County. In rapid succession he was appointed justice of the peace and town commissioner, and then was elected lieutenant colonel of the local militia. The family was healthy and for the most part David's flare-ups of malaria stayed in check. As a new year approached, a special gift arrived in the Crockett's newest home built on the Military Road, just south of the public square. On Christmas Day 1818, Elizabeth gave birth to daughter Rebecca Elvira—bringing to seven the number of Crockett's blood children and Patton stepchildren.[19]

GENTLEMAN FROM THE CANE

DURING HIS BRIEF TENURE as both magistrate and commissioner in Lawrence County, David Crockett was exposed to the rudiments of law and learned all he could right on the job. He oversaw property disputes, took depositions, issued warrants and licenses, paid out bounties for wolf scalps, supervised county road improvements, and assisted with the census. On one occasion Crockett was made custodian of funds to be collected from a county resident "for the support of a bastard child."[1]

As the commander of the local militia, Crockett's main duty was to make sure the small units scattered around the county held periodic musters and that the entire regiment gather at least once a year. This regimental muster was "the grand event of the year and brought together more of all sorts of people than any meeting or 'gathering' that occurred."[2] Militiamen were not issued uniforms but wore their best hunting shirts and marched with their own flintlock rifles. The highlight of the big musters were the shooting matches that featured best shots from rival units in fierce competition for, if nothing else, bragging rights until the next muster. When the smoke cleared and the boasting commenced, plenty of food, drink, and fiddles appeared and a long frolic followed, lasting through the night and into the next morning. If commissioned officers took part in the shooting matches, most likely one of those taking aim was Colonel Crockett.

The assortment of civic duties and community obligations thrust upon Crockett broadened his general knowledge and gave him a sense of fulfillment but brought him little income. These activities also took a great deal of time away from the farming he found so tedious and the hunting treks he so adored. The added pressures of a concerned wife and inadequate finances led to Crockett's resignation as justice of the peace on November 1, 1819. A short time later he resigned his commission as lieutenant colonel in the militia and was replaced by his former first major, Josephus Irvine, from the faction opposing Crockett in the Lawrenceburg site selection.[3]

Since moving to the area, Crockett had acquired several hundred acres of land. He also co-owned a large tract of property with his fellow town commissioner and ally, Enoch Tucker, that eventually became an iron mining operation after the Crockett family moved away.[4] But it was on another parcel of land, on the middle fork of Shoal Creek at Lawrenceburg, that Crockett launched his latest strategy for making money. On that site in late 1819, Crockett established a substantial complex that included a gristmill, a gunpowder factory, and a whiskey distillery. Crockett reported in his autobiography that he paid $3,000 for construction, "more than I was worth in the world."[5] Without hesitation, Elizabeth put money into the venture in an effort to force her wandering husband to settle down in one place. For a while her strategy worked. David stayed put, devoting long hours to his diversified business interests on the creekbanks near the family home.

Yet even with Elizabeth's financial contribution, the Crocketts fell short and had to borrow money just to complete the buildings and give them a cushion until everything was operational and producing an income. Crockett's solid reputation for honesty and fairness helped procure the badly needed loans, but soon he was falling far behind on other loans taken out earlier to buy land, including a 60-acre plot and a sizable 320-acre parcel. In late October 1820, he sent an urgent letter to John

Christmas McLemore, one of his creditors, in which he explained that he had been "detained longer than expected my powder factory have not been pushed as it ought and I will not be able to meet my contract with you. . . . I will pay you interest for the money until paid. I do not wish to disappoint you—I don't expect I can pay you the hole [*sic*] amount until next spring."[6]

McLemore was a major land speculator with sharp business acumen who invested heavily in West Tennessee's development and was one of the founders of the city of Memphis. Through his marriage to Rachel Jackson's niece, McLemore had the ear of Andrew Jackson and other power brokers in the state.[7] Lending money to a man of Crockett's position at that time was not one of McLemore's major deals. Besides, he liked speculating in risky ventures, and in this instance he knew that Crockett was good for the loan, which apparently was the case. Crockett sold a bit of land, paid off some outstanding debts, and by New Year's Day 1821 reached another milestone.[8] He resigned as town commissioner on that date and over the next month pondered a run for higher political office.

Crockett's decision to run for political office marked a dramatic new period in his life. In February 1821, he announced his candidacy for state representative for Lawrence and Hickman counties in the Tennessee State Legislature. "I just now began to take a rise,"[9] Crockett later mused about his decision.

Some of Crockett's associates—mostly neighbors, hunting companions, and local merchants—were taken aback by the announcement. Running for state elective office seemed to be in direct conflict with the kind of man they knew Crockett to be. He loved being in the outdoors and alone in the wilderness, and yet he was seeking the votes of citizens to send him to the state capital in Murfreesboro, the place that stood for everything he wished to escape. On the other hand, many other friends thought his chances of victory were excellent. Like Crockett, they also knew he could use the income from being in office, and they urged him to offer his name as a candidate. These supporters had to have been as surprised as Elizabeth and the children when, shortly after making his public announcement, Crockett inexplicably left, not just the area he wanted to represent but also the entire state of Tennessee. In March 1821, he assembled a herd of horses and drove them across the state to Buncombe County, North Carolina, where his wife's parents and other Patton kinfolk lived.[10] This was the same journey during which Crockett passed through his old home country near Finley's Gap and stopped at the John Jacobs place to give Mrs. Jacobs the dollar he owed her deceased husband.

Perhaps Crockett figured the money he made from the sale of the horses would help finance his campaign. The only problem was that he was gone more than three months and did not return to his home until early June, leaving little time to make the rounds of the two county legislative districts before the election, set for August. Crockett was barely back from his North Carolina romp when he kissed Elizabeth—due to deliver yet another baby in less than two months—and rode off on the campaign trail. Fortunately, the older Crockett children and neighbors pitched in to help Elizabeth while her husband searched for votes.

The political campaign evoked in Crockett a folksiness and frontier flair that displayed his expansive personality in full force. One of the first events he attended was a big squirrel hunt down on the Duck River in Hickman County. He soon found that politicking in the canebrakes mostly was a good excuse for a no-holds-barred party. "They were to hunt two days; then to meet and count the scalps, and have a big barbecue, and what might be called a tip-top country frolic," explained Crockett. "The dinner, and a general treat, was all to be paid for by the party having taken the fewest [squirrel] scalps. I joined one side, taking the place of one of the hunters, and got a gun ready for the hunt. I killed a great many squirrels, and when we counted scalps, my party was victorious."[11]

Before the dancing got under way, the various political candidates were called on to make a speech. Instead of using his talent as a storyteller, Crockett became self-conscious, figuring he had to make some sort of formal address. He approached the event organizers and tried to get out of speaking, since, as he put it, making a speech as a candidate "was a business I was as ignorant of as an outlandish negro," his language reflecting a racist sentiment typical of the day.[12] Crockett's opponent was confident and not at all concerned about running against someone he considered to be "an ignorant back-woods bear hunter." Seeing he had no choice, Crockett tried to speak to the crowd but "choaked [*sic*] up as bad as if my mouth had been jam'd and cram'd chock full of dry mush." Then, as the crowd stood staring at the befuddled Crockett, he had a brainstorm—tell one of the humorous stories he knew so well.

The instantaneous decision would change the course of regional Tennessee political history of the early nineteenth century.

At last I told them I was like a fellow I had heard of not long before. He was beating on the head of an empty barrel near the road-side, when a traveler, who was passing along, asked him what he was a doing that for? The fellow replied that there was some cider in that barrel a few days before, and he was trying to see if there was any then, but if there was he couldn't get at it. I told them that there had been a little bit of a speech in me a while ago, but I believed I couldn't get it out. They all roared out in a mighty laugh, and I told them other anecdotes, equally amusing to them, and believing I had them in a first-rate way, I quit and got down, thanking the people for their attention. But I took care to remark that I was as dry as a powder horn, and that I thought it was time for us all to wet our whistles a little; and so I put off to the liquor stand, and was followed by the greater part of the crowd.[13]

Crockett's confidence as a stump speaker increased at every event he attended. Whenever he was in doubt, he just "relied on natural born sense," an endless repertoire of anecdotes and jokes, and those "treats of liquor" for the potential voters with a thirst. The people who came to the barbecues, shooting matches, frolics, and rallies did not seem to care if Crockett avoided speaking about political issues but instead told them outrageously funny yarns that most of the time featured himself as the brunt of the joke. Crockett never put on airs. He was trying to represent the common men and women, just like himself, and not the landed gentry, creating an ethic for this western portion of Tennessee that challenged the hierarchical structure of the plantation culture. Crockett's constituents had heavily calloused hands, sunburnt necks, and contrary dispositions if anybody—including the government—pushed them too hard.

During the busy campaign, on the second day of August, Elizabeth gave birth to her last child—a baby girl whom she and David named Matilda.[14] That brought the number of children living under the cabin roof to eight. Two weeks after Matilda's birth, her father turned thirty-five, the halfway mark to the biblical "threescore years and ten." Later that month, a stream of voters rode or walked to the polls from first light until it got dark. When all the ballots were counted, Crockett was declared the winner. He had beaten his opponent by a two-to-one margin, or, as he more precisely put it: "I was elected, doubling my competitor, and nine votes over."[15]

Not long after the election, Crockett visited with James Knox Polk, future president of the United States, at a political gathering in the town of Pulaski. Polk, just twenty-six, was an ardent admirer and lifelong supporter of Andrew Jackson, and served as the clerk of the State senate during Crockett's first term in the legislature. Polk offered Crockett his congratulations—he was already well acquainted with him from appearances as a lawyer in Lawrence County—and then conjectured, "Well, colonel, I suppose we shall have a radical change of the judiciary at the next session of the Legislature."[16] According to Crockett, this rhetorical question from Polk caught him totally off guard. "Very likely, sir," replied Crockett, who then quickly took his leave. "For I was afraid some one would ask me what the judiciary was; and if I knowed I wish I may be shot. I don't indeed believe I had ever before heard that there was any such thing in all nature; but still I was not willing that the people there should know how ignorant I was about it." It seems likely that this was yet another instance when Crockett exaggerated his supposed ignorance, the ploy that so pleased his supporters, who, of course, he hoped would read his autobiography.

Crockett was present and accounted for at the state capital in Murfressborough (as Murfreesboro was spelled at that time) when the first session of the Fourteenth General Assembly convened, on September 17, 1821.[17] His first term as a state lawmaker—representing Hickman and Lawrence Counties—was relatively quiet. Crockett was appointed to only one committee, the rather inconsequential Standing Committee of Propositions and Grievances.

The opening days of the session were uneventful except for an incident on the floor of the chamber that proved to be a valuable lesson for Crockett and the other legislators. During debate, a nervous Crockett, still trying to get his bearings and unfamiliar with legislative procedure and protocol, rose with some nervousness to speak on behalf of a measure under consideration. When he finished and took his seat, James C. Mitchell, a leading criminal lawyer of the day and the representative for three Tennessee counties, rose to speak in opposition. In the course of rebutting Crockett's remarks, Mitchell referred to Crockett as "the gentleman from the cane," a term that many believed denoted a common person from the backwoods.[18] Some of the other members chuckled at Mitchell's remark. Crockett took immediate offense. He leapt to his feet and demanded an apology. None was forthcoming, and, later, during the recess outside the chambers, Crockett accosted Mitchell and restated his demands and promised a good country whipping for Mitchell if he refused. The impeccable Mitchell, dressed in the fine suit of clothes worn by gentlemen of distinction, tried to reason with Crockett and assured him that he meant no insult but had used the expression merely to describe the canebrake country where Crockett resided. The explanation did not satisfy Crockett or soothe his wounded pride.[19]

As luck would have it, that evening Crockett came upon a cambric ruffle lying on the dirt road just like the one worn at the neck by Mitchell. The following morning, Crockett pinned the fancy ruffle to his own coarse shirt and strode into the chamber. Waiting until the eloquent Mitchell finished speaking once again, Crockett arose to offer his comments on the matter under discussion. As a pontificating Crockett walked back and forth, the frilly ruffle caught the eye of other members of the body and soon titters and giggles turned into uproarious and prolonged laughter at the stark contrast between the foppish neck scarf and Crockett's country garb. A humiliated Mitchell, who later served with Crockett in the U.S. Congress, quickly fled the chamber, as if he had been effeminized by the swashbuckling frontiersman. Crockett took his bows as the others cheered. Crockett won his spurs that day and he did so without shedding blood in a duel. From that moment on, the title "gentleman from the cane" was no longer considered derogatory. It was a badge of honor for Crockett and for the people he represented.

TWENTY-THREE

LAND OF THE SHAKES

LTHOUGH CROCKETT WAS ENSCONCED as a lawmaker in Murfreesboro, it became quickly evident that he was not able to detach himself from the hardships of the frontier. Only twelve days into his first session as a state lawmaker, "the gentleman from the cane" was dealt a devastating blow. On September 29, 1821, an urgent message from Elizabeth reached Crockett in Murfreesboro with the news that a torrential summer storm had caused the Tennessee River and all its tributaries, including Shoal Creek, to flood. The Crockett family's gristmill and gunpowder factory on the swollen creek were completely demolished and washed away by the flash flood. All that remained of the complex was a portion of the dam, the millrace, and the distillery. Floodwater filled the log house where the Crocketts lived, but, thankfully, none of the family was lost or injured.

News of the catastrophe stunned Crockett. An accidental explosion of the gunpowder mill was of utmost concern to him; the usually calm waters of Shoal Creek seemed far less menacing. Obviously thankful that his loved ones were not injured, Crockett nonetheless realized that, in one swift blow, a promising business venture had vanished. Crockett later wrote, "the misfortune just made a complete mash of me."[1]

He immediately requested and was granted a leave of absence to go home and survey the damage. Before he departed, the dutiful rookie legislator took time to cast his vote for General William Carroll for governor of Tennessee. In those years, governors and U.S. senators were elected by the state legislature, and Crockett wanted to perform this important duty and support Carroll, a Pennsylvania native and well-known and admired liberal who had fought as one of Andrew Jackson's colonels in the Creek War.[2] After voting for Carroll—who was victorious in the election and would serve as governor for all but two years between 1821 and 1835—Crockett rode back to Lawrence County as fast as his horse would go. When he arrived, he discovered the disaster was every bit as bad as Elizabeth had described in her message. As someone later observed, Crockett came home expecting the worst, and that was exactly what he found.[3] Only splinters remained of the buildings. Without a gristmill to grind corn, the badly damaged distillery was useless. David, Elizabeth, and their children had to seek shelter in the homes of other Crockett and Patton family members living in the area.

For David, the sight of his own mill in ruins surely triggered a flashback to his childhood in east Tennessee when his father, John Crockett, was driven to ruin by a horrendous flood that swept away his gristmill. Determined to avoid the debt that overwhelmed his father, David wisely listened to Elizabeth's counsel. She knew more about the operation of the mill and the family finances than Crockett, who was usually away either hunting or politicking. In the 1880s, William Simonton, from a respected family of Lawrenceburgians that stretched back to early settlement times, recalled that as a boy he often saw Elizabeth running the mill in her husband's absence. Simonton spoke of Elizabeth's great strength and said that she always was grinding or lugging sacks of grain with ease.[4] Of course, she did all of that work while nursing an infant, overseeing a couple of toddlers, and trying to keep her older children out of trouble.

Elizabeth advised her husband not to pack up and run away from the dilemma but to face the adversity head-on, just as they always had done in times of trouble. She told David to practice what he preached—

to be always sure he was right and then go ahead. "She didn't advise me, as is too fashionable, to smuggle up this, and that, and t'other, to go on at home; but she told me, says she, 'Just pay up, as long as you have a bit's worth in the world; and then every body will be satisfied, and we will scuffle for more.'"[5]

Much of the milling operation had been financed by Elizabeth's funds, but there also were several loans that had to be satisfied. "I determined not to break full handed, but thought it better to keep a good conscience with an empty purse, than to get a bad opinion of myself, with a full one. I therefore gave up all I had, and took a bran-fire new start."[6] The best course of action for the Crocketts was to clear up as many of their debts as possible and then start over.

"I had some likely negroes, and a good stock of almost every thing about me, best of all I had an honest wife,"[7] a reflective Crockett wrote almost twelve years later. This was his first mention of slaves in his autobiography. Slavery was a part of everyday life in Tennessee, particularly in the middle and western sections of the state, where tobacco and cotton were the favored crops. Back in Crockett's homeland of eastern Tennessee, small farmers who had no need for a large slave workforce largely dominated the hilly land. Also, even early in the state's history, eastern Tennessee harbored a great deal of antislavery sentiment. Since Crockett never farmed on the scale of the larger farms and plantations, he would have had no need for many slaves or hired hands to help with the work. Although it is not known if those "negroes," as Crockett calls them, were his slaves or on loan from a family member or friend, the 1820 Lawrence County census records listed one slave, gender not given, living in the Crockett household.

Three months later, on October 9, 1821, Crockett returned to Murfreesboro and his work as a state legislator. Despite the troubles he faced, he also seemed steadfast and genuinely concerned about the welfare of his two-county legislative district and other matters of state importance. He not only introduced bills to help Hickman and Lawrence counties, where small farms produced such staple crops as cotton, corn, wheat, and oats but also supported the call for a revised state constitution that would adjust property taxes and place more of the burden on the wealthy class, providing some long overdue relief to citizens of modest means. Bearing in mind his fondness for all sorts of wagering, it was odd that Crockett voted to prohibit gambling. He may have taken such a stance on behalf of his constituents, the small landholders and squatters who had to work hard just to subsist. Yet given his own experiences as a bound-out boy, it was no surprise when he voted against a measure that would have allowed the state to hire out debtors as laborers. For many of the more seasoned politicians of the time, Crockett was a novelty of sorts, but still someone who had to be taken seriously.

"He was one of the earliest specimens to emerge of that nineteenth-century type, the Backwoodsman, a type that was often more given to noise and a kind of shrewdness than to solidity,"[8] wrote a scholar in 1956, near the peak of the revival of interest in Crockett. Others agreed but narrowed their assessment of the man as a political force and pinpointed his primary objective—helping people just like himself, who had been unable to acquire property of their own. In Crockett, backwoods citizens witnessed a new sort of politician emerge, one quite different from the patrician Jackson, who, despite his attempts to come off as a man of the people, in fact was a large landowner and shrewd businessman who did quite well in the marketing of cotton, tobacco, and slaves.

The differences between the two men became clear when one examined Crockett's record not only as a state lawmaker but as a congressman. Virtually every vote that Crockett spoke up for and cast, in some way or another, was of a populist nature, generally directed against the established landholding gentry and meant to help the large number of settlers moving into the recently opened western lands.

The potential those lands promised also greatly appealed to Crockett. As soon as the first session of the Fourteenth General Assembly concluded its business and adjourned on November 17, he packed his trunk and bags and headed home to prepare for an expedition to the western frontier of Tennessee. Although he enjoyed seeing his wife and children, he saw no good purpose spending the winter in a crowded cabin as the guests of kindly relatives. Crockett knew there was land to be scouted in Carroll County, named for Governor Carroll, and newly established on November 7, only ten days before the legislative session ended.[9] The vast expanse stretched all the way from the Tennessee River to the Mississippi.

Crockett had never been to the area before, but he was well aware of its existence; on July 10, 1788, his father-in-law, Robert Patton, had received from the state of North Carolina a 1,000-acre land grant for his service in the Revolutionary War.[10] In October 1821, when Patton learned of the tremendous property loss suffered by the Crocketts due to the flood, he deeded 800 of the acres to Elizabeth and David. The deed was executed in Buncombe County, North Carolina, where Patton resided after Crockett agreed to pay $1,600 for the acreage.[11] Elizabeth's brothers-in-law, Abner Burgin and James Edmonson, witnessed the transfer of the deed, and at least one of them brought the document to Tennessee for Crockett's signature.

Crockett was eager to have a look at the newly purchased tract and pick a new site to which his family could move after his debts were cleared up in Lawrence County. He recruited his eldest son, John Wesley, an already physically impressive fourteen-year-old, and another young man, Abram Henry, and they cut out for the Obion River, 150 miles to the northwest.[12]

For the first time in his life, Crockett rode into what had become known as "the land of the shakes," ever since the thundering series of earthquakes of 1811–1812 that were felt hundreds of miles away. It had been more than a decade since the earthquakes shook the region, but from time to time tremors could still be felt. The ground was scarred by deep fissures and cracks, some extending for miles through the canebrakes and woods already thick again with stands of hickory, oak, and gum. A focal point of the region was Reelfoot Lake, a large body of water created by the earthquakes and studded with cypress trees, some hundreds of years old.

In 1891—some seventy years after Crockett arrived there—a *New York Times* correspondent, who toured the land of the shakes and visited Reelfoot Lake, described the place as a "peculiarly weird and uncanny" place.[13] The *Times* article, entitled "A Sportsmen's Paradise," published with no byline, went on to report: "No where perhaps in the United States, at least east of the Rocky Mountains, is to be found another such perfect sporting ground for gunners and fishermen. Bears, deer, wolves, panthers, wildcats, wild turkeys, and all sorts of lesser game abound in the forest on the borders of the lake. . . . Far out in the lake, beyond the sight of shore, one gets the impression of being in a vast ruined temple. On every side rise endless spires of decaying cypresses, branchless, leafless, shorn of their beauty, gleaming in the still air like gaunt, mysterious monuments of destruction and death."[14]

Tangles of dead tree trunks and logs lay submerged just below the lake's surface. The knees of ancient cypresses flanking the edges of the water stood as timeless sentinels. In the upper branches eagles preened in their great nests. Animals of all sorts roamed the canebrakes and thickets, and the shimmering waters of the lake seemed alive with fish and fowl. On quick inspection, this place seemed tailor-made for Crockett. He knew that as soon as he and his two young companions arrived on winded horses, trailing their packhorse loaded with enough provisions for a month. As far as Crockett was concerned, the land lacked for nothing. "It was a complete wilderness, and full of Indians who were hunting. Game was plenty of almost every kind, which suited me exactly, as I was always fond of hunting."

The men accordingly staked off some land and selected a site for the family home close to Rutherford's Fork, the southernmost branch of the Obion River. Crockett liked the lay of the land and the proximity to water and wood—two frontier basics. There were not many settlers living in the vicinity, but as soon as the Crockett party had hobbled their horses in a grazing meadow, they took off on foot to visit a family named Owens at their cabin more than seven miles away. It was early winter, and the Obion was running full and icy cold. All three of them waded into the river "like so many beavers" and sloshed through water that sometimes came up to their necks, forcing John Wesley to swim.[15] Crockett led the way, using a long pole to feel his way along and cutting back fallen brush and overhanging branches with his tomahawk. Finally they reached land and found the cabin, where a team of boatmen had gathered. Owens and his wife were congenial and dished out hot food and comforted the shivering John Wesley. "The old gentleman set out his bottle to us, and I concluded that if a horn wasn't good then, there was no use for its invention," Crockett observed. "So I swig'd off about a half pint, and the young man [Abram Henry] was by no means bashful in such a case; he took a strong pull at it too, I then gave my boy some, and in a little time we felt pretty well."[16]

After warming by the fire, Crockett left the other two at the cabin and tagged along with the men to see about a boat loaded with whiskey, flour, sugar, coffee, and salt. The men had been hired for $500 to take the goods to a place called McLemore's Bluff, named for the same person who had lent Crockett money back in Lawrence County. The river level was too low for the boat to travel, so while they all waited for rains, Crockett used his charm to persuade the boat owner and crew to go with him to his new claim of land, where they "slap'd up a cabin in no time."[17] Crockett also managed to get four barrels of meal, a barrel of salt, and ten gallons of whiskey. In return he agreed to pay them back by supplying fresh meat for the 100-mile journey up the Obion to unload their cargo. Once the river rose, Crockett went with the crew, leaving John Wesley and Abram Henry behind at the new cabin.

Crockett ranged out on the riverbanks and into the trees. He hunted all day and by nightfall had a buck deer and five elk dressed out and hanging in trees along the Obion. In the course of his wandering, he eventually became separated from the boat. He hollered as loud as he could and fired his gun, and finally the crew responded with gunfire, but by then they were at least two miles beyond Crockett. Relying on his vast reservoir of woods wisdom, he did not panic but made a plan and pushed on. "It was now dark, and I had to crawl through the fallen timber the best way I could. . . . For the vines and briers [sic] had grown all through it, and so thick, that a good fat coon couldn't much more than get along." After more hooting and hollering and rifle shots, Crockett got to the boat. The cold numbed his aching body. "I took a pretty stiff horn, which soon made me feel much better; but I was so tired that I could hardly work my jaws to eat."[18] They fetched most of the game he had killed and moved on. Finally, after eleven days on the Obion, the boat landed at McLemore's Bluff.

The captain gave Crockett a skiff to get back to his starting point, and a young crewman named Flavius Harris, weary of the water, hired on to work at the new homestead.[19] The two of them paddled downstream and returned to John Wesley and Abram Henry at the cabin. Crockett and his three helpers cleared a field and planted corn, but since there was no livestock on the land they did not take time to cut rails and build a proper fence. The cabin was stout enough and had a stone fireplace and even a porch. It would do until the next autumn when Crockett returned with the whole family in time to harvest the corn. Flavius Harris agreed to stay on with Abram Henry. They would look after the place. Crockett took to the woods and killed ten bears, and a great abundance of deer to dry and store away and also keep his two hired men fed and content.

Then Crockett and his boy saddled their horses and rode away. He hated to leave the land of the shakes, but Betsy, or Bet, as he often called Elizabeth, was waiting with their children.[20] The problem was, others were waiting for him as well. They were lawyers and bill collectors and Crockett had no names of endearment for them. All the way home, he practiced what he would tell them and hoped his words would be enough.

TWENTY-FOUR

IN THE EYE OF A "HARRICANE"

WITH MISSOURI'S ENTRY into the union in 1821, the United States continued stretching farther west under the leadership of second-term president James Monroe. That same year not only did the Santa Fe Trail open to merchants bound for the ancient city, but large parties of fur trappers and traders departed St. Louis bound for the West, while Stephen F. Austin began moving immigrant Americans into the Mexican state of Texas.

Crockett, content for the moment to remain in Tennessee, also was on the move. He and his son John Wesley arrived back in Lawrenceburg in late April 1822. They had been gone far longer than anticipated and, among other things, had missed another Christmas with the family, all still residing with various relatives since the Shoal Creek flood. Crockett mustered his children and Elizabeth and told them all about the new land waiting for them in the Northwest. He also spoke of the adventures with the boatmen, the land scarred by earthquakes, and of the plentiful game in "the land of the shakes."

When there was a lull in the telling of tales, Elizabeth interrupted and gave her husband an update of all that had transpired on the home front while he was off scouting her father's old land grant. Not surpris-

ingly, none of the news was good. In his absence a number of lawsuits
had been brought against Crockett, mostly for debts that had accumulated since the loss of the mill. Some of the claims had been challenged,
but for the most part the court sided with the creditors.[1]

On April 5, just a few weeks before he returned home, Crockett's
power of attorney was awarded to Mansil Crisp, a respected citizen who
had also served as justice of the peace.[2] Crisp was given the authorization
to satisfy any remaining creditors as best as he could. Crockett, who had
once owned hundreds of acres in Lawrence County, was by July 1822
left with nothing but the goodwill of others. He must have been relieved
when Governor Carroll issued a proclamation calling the Fourteenth
General Assembly back into special session, as he could draw his legislature's pay and give Squire Crisp some time to settle the outstanding
judgments.

Crockett rode to Murfreesboro, stabled his horse, and secured lodging for himself at an inn that catered to legislators. The Rutherford
County Courthouse on the town square was where the General Assembly had gathered in the past, but, during the recess, the building had
burned down, so the special session convened in the nearby First Presbyterian Church, where the customary spittoons were forbidden.[3] After
the opening gavel fell, one of the first orders of business for legislators
was to grant premiums for a levy of taxes to build a new courthouse of
brick construction.

Crockett was actively involved in the brief session, which mainly
had been called for lawmakers to deal with various pressing land issues.
Still, he was very much a political novice, and as such kept a low profile
and learned as he went along. The adjudication and disposal of vacant
and unappropriated lands remained at the forefront of political activity
throughout Crockett's career both in Tennessee and later in the U.S.
Congress. In light of the ongoing economic depression sparked by the
financial panic of 1819, Crockett introduced several bills on behalf of
the poor and needy, whose requests he nearly always championed especially when he very much felt that he had joined their ranks.

Although from time to time Crockett owned a few slaves, one of

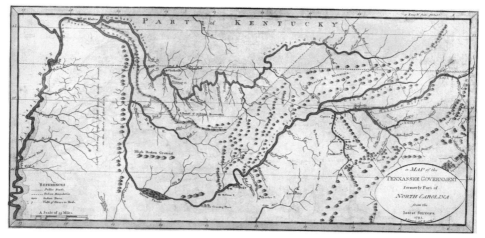

Map of Tennessee when it was part of North Carolina, 1795. (Courtesy of Birmingham Public Library Cartographic Collection)

(FAR LEFT) Tennessee's first governor John Sevier (1745–1815), portrait circa 1790. (Courtesy of the C. M. McClung Historical Collection of the Knox County Public Library)

Tsi'yu-gunsini ("Dragging Canoe"), Cherokee war chief. (Mike Smith, artist)

Nine hundred "overmountain men" from Virginia and Tennessee assemble at Sycamore Shoals for the King's Mountain campaign, September 1780. *The Overmountain Men* by Lloyd Branson. (Courtesy of the Tennessee State Museum, Nashville)

(ABOVE) *Battle of King's Mountain, October 7, 1780* by Alonzo Chappel. (Courtesy of the C. M. McClung Historical Collection of the Knox County Public Library)

Treaty of the Holston, July 2, 1791. (Courtesy of the C. M. McClung Historical Collection of the Knox County Public Library)

Replica of David Crockett's 1786 birthplace by the Nolichucky River. (Photograph by Michael Wallis)

The Crockett Tavern Museum, Morristown, Tennessee. (Photograph by Michael Wallis)

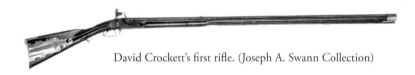

David Crockett's first rifle. (Joseph A. Swann Collection)

Marriage bond, David Crockett and Polly Finley, August 12, 1806. (Recorded in the office of the County Court Clerk of Jefferson County, Tennessee)

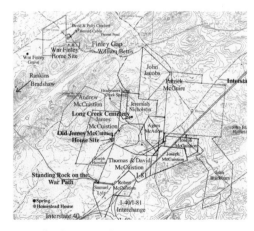

Long Creek map, Jefferson County, Tennessee. (Courtesy of Robert Jarnagin)

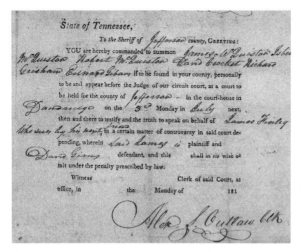

Crockett's summons to appear as a witness on behalf of his brother-in-law James Finley, Jefferson County, Tennessee, 1811. (Jefferson County, Tennessee, Archives, Lu Hinchey, director)

Anonymous portrait of Jean Laffite, pirate, ally of Andrew Jackson at the Battle of New Orleans, and slave smuggler. (Courtesy of the Rosenberg Library, Galveston, Texas)

Major General Andrew "Old Hickory" Jackson. (*Major General Andrew Jackson, President of the United States, 1829–1837,* painted by Thomas Sully [1783–1872]; James Burton Longacre [1794–1869], engraver; engraving published by Wm. H. Morgan, Philadelphia, circa 1820; Library of Congress, Prints and Photographs Division)

Early portrait of Sam Houston. (San Jacinto Museum, Houston, Texas)

Hand-colored lithograph of Creek Chief McIntosh, circa 1836, printed and colored by J. T. Bowen and published originally by D. Rice and A. N. Hart, Philadelphia. (On loan from Oklahoma State Senate Historical Preservation Fund, Inc.)

Burial site of Polly Crockett, first wife of David Crockett, near Rattlesnake Branch, Franklin County, Tennessee. (Joseph A. Swann Collection)

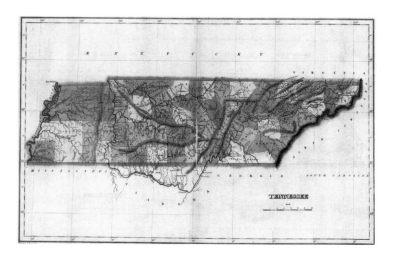

(ABOVE) Map of Tennessee, 1822. (Courtesy of Birmingham Public Library Cartographic Collection)

David Crockett delivers a stump speech during his congressional campaign. (From an 1869 edition of the autobiography *A Narrative of the Life of David Crockett of the State of Tennessee* by David Crockett, published by John E. Potter and Company, Philadelphia)

Replica of Crockett's last home in Rutherford, Tennessee. (Photograph by Michael Wallis, Michael Wallis Collection)

Final resting place of Crockett's mother, Rebecca, in Rutherford County, Tennessee. (Photograph by Michael Wallis, Michael Wallis Collection)

Reelfoot Lake, formed during the New Madrid earthquakes of 1811–12. (Photograph by Michael Wallis, Michael Wallis Collection)

Obion River, Gibson County, Tennessee. (Photograph by Michael Wallis, Michael Wallis Collection)

The Trail of Tears, painting by Robert Lindneux, 1942. (Courtesy of Woolaroc Museum, Bartlesville, Oklahoma)

Sam Houston, a Crockett associate and the first president of the Republic of Texas. (Prints and Photographs Collection, Dolph Briscoe Center for American History, University of Texas at Austin)

Portrait of Crockett on stone by Samuel Stillman Osgood, circa 1834. (Photograph by Dorothy Sloan, Dorothy Sloan Rare Books)

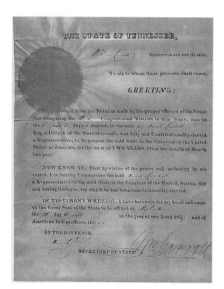

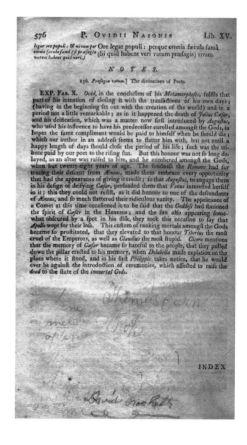

Congressional credentials issued to David Crockett. (National Archives and Records Administration)

(RIGHT) Page 576 of a 1774 edition of Ovid's *Metamorphoses* with Crockett's 1832 signature. (Special Collections Library, University of Tennessee, Knoxville)

Engraving by artist Asher B. Durand based on an 1834 watercolor portrait of Crockett on paper, painted by Anthony Lewis De Rose. (Print Collection, Miriam and Ira D. Wallach Division of Art, Prints and Photographs, New York Public Library, Astor, Lenox and Tilden Foundation)

Lithograph depicting President Jackson seated on a collapsing chair, with the "Altar of Reform" toppling next to him, 1831. The scurrying rats are (left to right): Secretary of War John H. Eaton, Secretary of the Navy John Branch, Secretary of State Martin Van Buren, and Secretary of the Treasury Samuel D. Ingham. (Lithograph by Edward W. Clay)

U.S. President James Knox Polk, a fellow Tennesseean and political adversary of Crockett. Daguerrotype by Mathew B. Brady, February 14, 1849. (Mathew B. Brady, photographer)

Map of the Mexican state of Texas, 1835, compiled by Stephen F. Austin. (James P. Bryant Collection, Dolph Briscoe Center for American History, University of Texas at Austin)

William Barret Travis, the ambitious and quick-tempered Alamo commander. (Courtesy of Texas State Library and Archives Commission)

The site of David Crockett's death on March 6, 1836. (Michael Wallis Collection)

The only known oil-painting portrait of the notorious James Bowie, painted from life, circa 1820. Frontiersman, land speculator, and slave trader, Bowie died at the Alamo on March 6, 1836. (Alleged portrait of Bowie attributed to various artists, including William Edward West [1788–1857])

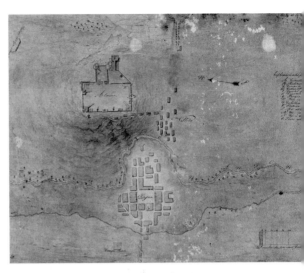

Mexican military map of San Antonio de Bexar and the Alamo fortifications, compiled by Colonel Ygnacio de Labastida, March 1836. (Map Collection, Dolph Briscoe Center for American History, University of Texas at Austin)

This rare image—an 1849 daguerrotype of the Alamo chapel by an unknown photographer—is the earliest known extant photograph taken in Texas. It is also the only known photograph of the Alamo taken before it was repaired and rebuilt by the U.S. Army in 1850. (Dolph and Janey Briscoe Collection, Dolph Briscoe Center for American History, University of Texas at Austin)

Equestrian portrait of Antonio López de Santa Anna, president of Mexico, general in chief of the Army of Operations, and commander of Mexican forces at the siege of the Alamo. (Prints and Photographs Collection, Dolph Briscoe Center for American History, University of Texas at Austin)

This fanciful wood engraving from 1836 is thought to be the first published illustration of Crockett's death at the Alamo. It appeared in *Davy Crockett's Almanac of Wild Sports in the West*. (Dolph Briscoe Center for American History, University of Texas at Austin)

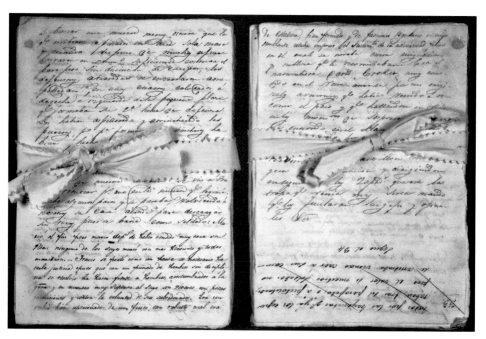

The Personal Narrative of Lt. Col. José de la Peña, which includes his detailed description of Crockett's execution immediately following the fall of the Alamo. (José de la Peña Papers, Dolph Briscoe Center for American History, University of Texas at Austin)

James Kirke Paulding, author of the 1831 play *The Lion of the West*, which featured a frontier character named Nimrod Wildfire who was loosely based on David Crockett. Paulding also served as secretary of the navy from 1838 to 1841. (Naval History and Heritage Command)

Carte de visite of Frank Mayo in the title role of *Davy Crockett; or, Be Sure You're Right, Then Go Ahead* by Frank Murdoch, 1872. Mayo, who coauthored the play, starred in the drama from 1872 until his death in 1896. (Billy Rose Theatre Division, New York Public Library for the Performing Arts, Astor, Lenox and Tilden Foundations)

This famous clipper ship, named for Crockett, was constructed on the Mystic River in Connecticut and launched in 1853. A profitable ship for forty years, it sailed primarily from New York to San Francisco and New York to Liverpool. (Courtesy of G. W. Blunt White Library at Mystic Seaport Museum, Mystic, Connecticut)

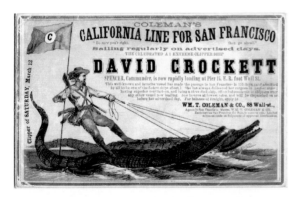

"Col. Crockett's Desperate Fight with the Great Bear," *Almanac* illustration, 1835. (Photograph by Dorothy Sloan, Dorothy Sloan Rare Books)

Almanac cover, 1836. (Photograph
by Dorothy Sloan, Dorothy Sloan
Rare Books)

Almanac cover, 1836. (Photograph
by Dorothy Sloan, Dorothy Sloan
Rare Books)

Almanac illustration, 1836. (Photograph by Dorothy Sloan, Dorothy Sloan Rare Books)

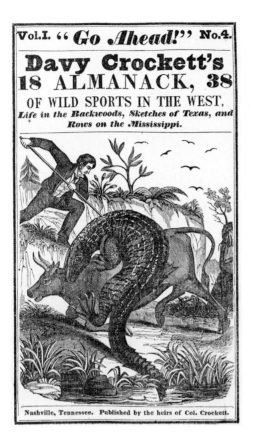

Almanac cover, 1838. (Photograph by Dorothy Sloan, Dorothy Sloan Rare Books)

(BOTTOM LEFT) *Almanac* cover, 1839. (Photograph by Dorothy Sloan, Dorothy Sloan Rare Books)

(BOTTOM RIGHT) *Almanac* cover, 1841. (Photograph by Dorothy Sloan, Dorothy Sloan Rare Books)

his bills sought relief for "Mathias, a free man of color."[4] This action supports the belief that, although Crockett on a small scale supported the horrendous institution, he was capable of showing some compassion. Crockett also introduced other relief measures to help one of his attorney's relatives and several friends and associates from his legislative district. He was dead-set against a proposal to repeal redemption laws, or manumission, a process for a party to purchase and free slaves, and he also opposed repeal of a law to provide for widows and orphans and stop fraud in the execution of last wills and testaments.

Near the close of the special session, Crockett vehemently opposed a bill that called for the restoration of certain fees to justices of the peace and constables. Under this corrupt system, duplicitous peace officers urged citizens to file civil suits, from which the officials would collect a percentage of any settlement. This practice of "fee-grabbing" was an issue that directly involved Crockett, for not only had he served as a justice of the peace, but he also was on the receiving end of many civil actions.[5] When the proposed repeal legislation came up for a vote, Crockett took to the floor of the assembly and spoke against it.

"There is no evil so great in society—among the poor people—as the management and intrigue of meddling justices and dirty constables," Crockett said, based on his own observations of such indignities. "I have seen more peace and harmony among my constituents since the repeal of the fees, than I have for several years before. I do most earnestly hope that the house will be unanimous in putting the bill to instant death."[6] The proposed bill was rejected and Crockett's speech was quoted in the *Nashville Whig*, published by John P. Erwin, a lawyer who served two terms as Nashville's mayor.[7] Crockett's financial picture was dismal, but his political future was taking shape.

On August 24, just one week after Crockett's thirty-fifth birthday, the special session was adjourned and David immediately returned to Lawrenceburg. After he consulted with his wife and Mansil Crisp, the decision was made to retain just a small parcel of land in distant Carroll County and sell off almost all of the 800 acres that had been conveyed to him the year before by his father-in-law, Robert Patton. Crockett simply did not have the $1,600 he owed Patton for the acreage. On August 25, a deed of sale was drafted and Crockett sold the Carroll County land to John McLemore, the powerful land speculator, and one of his associates, James Vaulse, from Davidson County, for exactly the $1,600 due Patton.[8] It was a difficult transaction but Crockett's only option if he wanted to become debt-free.

The Crocketts began packing up the little bit of furniture and goods they still had in preparation for the journey to Carroll County. It likely required two wagons for such a move, considering there were two adults and eight children, ranging in age from Matilda, only a year old, to John Wesley, just turned fifteen and as capable as a fully grown man. Other family members and friends also decided to make the move and either accompanied the Crocketts or came a short time later. In his autobiography Crockett made no mention of any slaves going with them. He probably sold or signed over ownership of the slave he once owned in order to satisfy one of the debts.

As was his style, Crockett quickly rebounded from having to sell off land to satisfy a debt. Besides, he was excited about the new land that awaited him. He summed up the move in a few words when he wrote that he took his family and "what little plunder I had, and moved to where I had built my cabin, and made my crap."[9] (Crockett meant "crop," referring to the corn he had planted the past spring.)

The newest Crockett family cabin was near freshwater springs and unbroken forests of hickory, poplar, gum, and beech. A common saying from that time described the region as having "fifty bushels of frogs to the acre, and snakes enough to fence the land." Not surprisingly, even as he and the entourage traversed the 150 miles to Carroll County, Crockett managed to fit in some hunting. He not only provided fresh meat for campfire meals but also made a little bit of money, something that in those times was hard to come by and even harder to hold. While moving westward in early September, he shot and killed two wolves. He skinned them out and on September 9 brought their scalps to Huntingdon, the seat of government of the newly formed county. There he sought out the home of R. E. C. Dougherty, where court was held and county business disposed of until the log courthouse, then under construction, was completed in early December.[10] According to the court minutes for that day: "David Crockett came into open court and made oathe [*sic*] to the killing of one wolf over the age of four months in the bounds of this county."[11] The other wolf he shot was just a pup under four months old and not eligible for any reward. Nonetheless, Crockett was pleased to rejoin his family on the trail with a three-dollar bounty in his purse.

When the Crocketts finally reached their new homestead on the east side of the Rutherford Fork of the Obion River, Abram Henry and Flavius Harris greeted them. The two young hired hands had continued to make improvements on the cabin and land and were relieved to have more company. The Crockett children staked out their secret places in the thickets and forests and busied themselves with the many daily chores required of everyone, regardless of age. Elizabeth was pleased when three of her sisters and their families soon joined them— Margaret Patton and husband Abner Burgin, Sarah Patton and husband William Edmundson, and Ann Catherine Patton and husband Hance McWhorter.[12] They established homes within rifleshot of the Crocketts. Eventually five of Elizabeth's sisters, along with their families, moved to the new settlement, as did Elizabeth's father, Robert Patton, after the death of his wife. He still owned 200 acres in his original land grant and purchased another 1,200 acres, which he distributed among his daughters and sons-in-law.[13] George Tinkle and his son, Lindsey Kavendar Tinkle, two of Crockett's close friends and companions, also made the move to the Obion River country with their families.

Crockett was pleased that loved ones surrounded Betsy, and by late autumn, with the corn harvested, he ventured into the canebrakes bordering streams and creeks. The thick stands of the bamboolike plant provided cover and forage for all sorts of wildlife and game. Crockett ate the tender new shoots and let his livestock graze in the cane that grew near his cabin. Indian tribes made arrow shafts, knives, and scrappers from cane, and it could be carved into flutes and pipes and burned in ceremonial fires. Some tribes used shaped cane blades to remove body hair or lance wounds. Thickets of giant cane—some of it fifteen feet tall—

sprang up in the dense tangles of broken trees, vines, and brush that had been devastated by the earthquakes and fierce windstorms. Crockett called these places "harricanes," and he recognized their value.[14]

For weeks he roamed far and wide and periodically returned home with field-dressed game to be put up for consumption during the winter, although by Crockett's own accounts his offspring and hired men devoured the fresh meat as fast as he packed it back to the cabin. By mid-December, Crockett was still gathering "wild meat" when he discovered that he was running out of gunpowder. "I had none either to fire Christmass [sic] guns, which is very common in that country, or to hunt with."[15] He remembered that one of brothers-in-law had agreed to store an extra keg of powder for him and was holding it at his cabin, only about six miles west on the opposite side of Rutherford's Fork of the Obion.

"There had just been another of Noah's freshes, and the low-grounds were flooded all over with water," Crockett recalled. "I know'd the stream was at least a mile wide which I would have to cross, as the water was from hill to hill, and yet I determined to go over in some way or other, so as to get my powder. I told this to my wife, and she immediately opposed it with all her might. I still insisted, telling her we had no powder from Christmass [sic], and, worse than all, we were out of meat. She said, we had as well starve as for me to freeze to death or get drowned, and one or the other was certain if I attempted to go."[16]

Crockett politely listened to Betsy and then, as always, went ahead. He put on his moccasins and woolen wrappers, tied up a bundle of extra clothes and extra pair of shoes, and started out for his powder. The snow was about four inches deep when he left, and by the time he reached the river, only about a quarter of a mile from the cabin, it looked like an ocean. Crockett waded into the swollen river and started to make his way, using logs whenever possible to cross deep spots. At times he was in waist-deep water, and it did not take long before he had little feeling in his legs and feet. When he attempted to cross another slough on a log he fell into icy water up to his head but somehow managed to keep his dry clothes and rifle above the surface. He got to the other side, put on his dry clothing, and eventually made his way to his brother-in-law's cabin.

> I got there late in the evening, and he was much astonished at seeing me at such a time. I staid all night, and the next morning was most piercing cold, and so they persuaded me not to go home that day. I agreed, and turned out and killed him two deer; but the weather still got worse and colder, instead of better. I staid that night, and in the morning they still insisted I couldn't get home. I knowed the water would be frozen over, but not hard enough to bear me, and so I agreed to stay that day. I went out hunting again, and pursued a big *he-bear* all day, but didn't kill him. The next morning was bitter cold, but I knowed my family was without meat, and I determined to get home to them, or die a-trying.

Crockett picked up his powder keg and hunting tools and left. When he reached the water, it was a sheet of ice as far as he could see. He carefully stepped into the freezing river. The combination of frigid air and icy water took his breath away, but he plodded ahead, perhaps wondering if he had made the right decision. Just as he started walking, the thinner ice along the bank broke through. Although shivering and numbed, Crockett plodded forward, using his tomahawk to break up the ice in his path until he reached a place where the ice was thick enough to hold him. He pulled himself out of the stream and his soaked buckskins immediately turned to ice. After walking a short way, the ice broke again, and the swiftness of the current was so fast no more ice would form. Summoning every bit of strength left in his ice-covered body, Crockett kept moving forward. Frostbitten and bordering on delirium, he somehow managed to keep the powder keg and his rifle out of the water. "By this time I was nearly frozen to death, but I saw all along before me where the ice had been fresh broke, and I thought it must be a bear struggling about in the water," Crockett recalled. "I, therefore, primed my gun, and, cold as I was, I was determined to make war on him, if we met."[17]

Invigorated by the notion that a bear might be nearby, Crockett staggered on through the freshly broken snow. "I followed the trail till it led me home, and I then found it had been made by my young man that lived with me, who had been sent by my distressed wife to see, if he could, what had become of me, for they all believed that I was dead." As soon as Crockett stumbled through the cabin door, Elizabeth and their children swarmed around him, sobbing tears of joy and rejoicing that he was alive and had once again bested death. "When I got home I wasn't quite dead, but mighty nigh it; but I had my powder, and that was what I went for."[18]

Crockett took a few horns and collapsed into bed. During the night a heavy rain came and turned to sleet, but "in the morning all hands turned out hunting," he recalled. Some of the hunters left Crockett's cabin determined to find turkeys along the river, but Crockett wanted larger game. "I told them, I had dreamed the night before of having a hard fight with a big black nigger, and I knowed it was a sign that I was to have a battle with a bear; for in a bear country, I never know'd such a dream to fail."[19]

Crockett set out with his hounds looking for bear. This time he found much more than he expected, and this January 1823 hunt became one of Crockett's favorite stories. The episode was described with great relish and flair in the *Narrative*.

According to Crockett, he set out along the Rutherford Fork of the Obion River near Reelfoot Lake and quickly bagged a pair of fat turkeys. Lugging the birds over his shoulder, he pushed on but was "infernal mad," with his hounds continually "barking up the wrong tree" when he encountered "about the biggest bear that was ever seen in America."[20] The bear looked "like a large black bull" and was so intimidating that at first even his dogs were afraid to attack. Eventually they took off after the bear. They chased him into a thicket and up a large black oak tree. Crockett took the turkeys from his back, hung them on a sapling, and "broke like a quarterhorse after my bear." Cradling his rifle, he climbed through brambles and vines to within about eighty yards of the tree.

With the bear facing him, Crockett primed his gun and fired. The bear raised a paw and snorted as Crockett reloaded and fired once more. The big animal tumbled from the tree and immediately one of Crockett's best hounds cried out in pain. Without hesitating, Crockett charged with his tomahawk in one and butcher knife in the other. When he drew near, the bear released the dog and focused his attention on the approaching man. Crockett, seeing his wounded dog had crawled off, raced back to his rifle. He loaded the weapon a third time, turned, and fired, this time killing the bear.[21]

Crockett blazed a trail to his cabin with his tomahawk and recruited one of his brothers-in-law, probably Abner Burgin, and Flavius Harris to help him retrieve the meat. They returned to the kill site with the four horses necessary to carry the dressed meat home.

"We got there just before dark, and struck up a fire, and commenced butchering my bear," recalled Crockett. "It was some time in the night before we finished it; and I can assert, on my honour, that I believe he would have weighed six hundred pounds. It was the second largest I ever saw. I killed one, a few years after, that weighed six hundred and seventeen pounds. . . . We got our meat home, and I had the pleasure to know that we now had plenty, and that of the best; and I continued through the winter to supply my family abundantly with bear-meat and venison from the woods."[22]

The hunts continued all winter. Crockett had gunpowder to spare. With the coming of the New Year, volleys of celebratory rifleshots fired into the darkness echoed through the harricanes and canebrakes and never sounded better.

TWENTY-FIVE

A FOOL FOR LUCK

THE WINTER HUNTS were so successful that by early 1823 Crockett had accumulated enough animal skins from all the game killed out in the harricanes to warrant a trip to Jackson, situated along the Forked Deer River. On a clear day in February, he and John Wesley secured the pelts and furs on a packhorse and began the forty-mile trek to the town, originally named Alexandria, that had been renamed in honor of Old Hickory, and served as the county seat of Madison County, after the former president.[1]

Once they arrived, the Crocketts sold the pelts and then bought sugar, coffee, salt, lead, gunpowder, and other staples. They found supper and lodging for the night. Before departing for home, Crockett bumped into some old friends from the Creek War and made time to "take a horn" with them in a nearby tavern.[2] While engaged in storytelling, Crockett was introduced to Dr. William Edward Butler, on whose land the new county courthouse now sat, and early settlers Major Joseph Lynn and Duncan McIver. Crockett found them "all first rate men" and was told that all three were under consideration as candidates for the next legislative session. When one of them suggested, perhaps with tongue firmly planted in cheek, that Crockett think about running for another term in the General Assembly, he guffawed and pointed out that he now lived "at least forty miles from any white settlement" and had no thought of continuing in politics.[3] The conversation turned to other matters, probably bear hunting, and presently Crockett said his good-byes and he and his son returned home.

Only a week or two later, Crockett was surprised when a passing hunter stopped at his dogtrot cabin and offered congratulations on his decision to run for office. Crockett figured the fellow was joking, but then the hunter pulled out a creased copy of the *Jackson Pioneer*, which carried the paid announcement of Crockett's candidacy for the Tennessee state legislature. Crockett immediately thought of his tavern meeting with the three men and figured the bogus story was all their doing. "I said to my wife that this was all a burlesque on me, but I was determined to make it cost the man who had pout [*sic*] it there [,] at least the value of the printing, and of the fun he wanted at my expense."[4]

Crockett did not ask the newspaper to retract the announcement but instead found another hired man to help Betsy and, as he later wrote, "turned out myself electioneering." He quickly found that his reputation preceded him. Wherever he went, people knew about the great bear hunter and the "gentleman from the cane." His growing popularity convinced the trio of Butler, Lynn, and McIver not to dilute their strength by running against each other as well as Crockett. During a strategy meeting, they determined that of the three of them, Butler, considered the founder of Jackson and a well-connected town commissioner, had the best chance of defeating Crockett. When he was told that his lone opponent was Butler and that the other two had dropped out of the running, Crockett admitted that he faced a worthy adversary. Butler was wealthy, articulate, educated, and, most importantly, was married to one of Andrew and Rachel Jackson's nieces.[5]

"The doctor was a clever fellow, and I have often said he was the most talented man I ever run against for any office,"[6] admitted Crockett. Indeed, Butler had graduated from medical school at the University of Pennsylvania and served as a distinguished officer with General Jackson during the War of 1812.

The campaign strategy Crockett came up with played on what were perceived as his weaknesses and Butler's strengths. Crockett capitalized on his reputation as a hunter and self-effacing backwoods character who had much more in common with the hearty pioneer stock that made up much of the electorate than did the aristocratic and refined Butler.

One of Crockett's favorite ploys, developed early on in his political career, was to campaign in a buckskin-hunting shirt with two large pockets. In one pocket he kept a big twist of tobacco and in the other a bottle of liquor. "When I met a man and offered him a dram, he would throw out his quid of tobacco to take on, and after he had taken his horn, I would out with my twist and give him another chaw," explained Crockett. "And in this way he would not be worse off than when I found him; and I would be sure to leave him in a first-rate good humor."[7]

Throughout the campaign, Crockett and Butler remained cordial and respectful. When Crockett was on the stump in Jackson, he received an invitation to dine at the Butler residence, a much larger and elegant home than the Crockett cabin. When he arrived for dinner, Crockett was so impressed with a luxurious carpet covering most of the floor that he refused to tread on it and spent the evening stepping around it and keeping his feet on the rungs of the chair. Later, at one of the rallies, Crockett drew on this episode and talked of Butler's lavish home and a carpet that was nothing like the bearskins that adorned most cabin floors. "Fellow citizens, my aristocratic competitor has a fine carpet, and every day he walks on finer truck than any gowns your wife or your daughters, in all their lives, ever wore."[8]

As the campaign progressed, two more candidates—Messrs. Shaw and Brown—entered the race, but Crockett and Butler remained the front-runners. During months of traveling from one small settlement to the next and making joint appearances, the candidates became well acquainted with each other's standard speech. Crockett cleverly seized on this at one of the many stops and instead of giving his talk last as he always preferred, he agreed to speak first and allow Butler to have the last word. Crockett rose and proceeded to deliver Butler's stock speech almost verbatim, which, of course, left the flustered doctor scrambling for something else to say when his turn came to speak.[9]

All of the shenanigans and outlandish speeches paid off for Crockett. When the votes cast in the two-day-long August 1823 election were tallied, the two minor candidates managed to get only a few votes, but Crockett was at the top and beat Butler by a 247-vote majority.[10]

"This reminded me of the old saying—'A fool for luck, and a poor man for children,' "[11] Crockett observed. The hackneyed adage may have had a ring of truth, but luck rarely comes to fools. Crockett was no fool. He was a risk taker who never let his rifle get out of reach. He became the epitome of a man who could lick any problem with his own two hands and his wits. Crockett was one of the first politicians to perfect the tactic of "branding" opponents as being "too elite" to connect with and represent the general populace. That was why he appealed to the hardscrabble folks living on the frontier in the nineteenth century.

Crockett certainly did not know it at the time, but with his victory in 1823 he was well on his way to becoming a folk hero in a nation that had heroes, such as George Washington, but no genuine folk heroes. There were plenty of mythologized heroes from the past, and the Founding Fathers, including some who were still alive, were admired and respected but not, other than Washington, the stuff of legend. Even the admirable Daniel Boone, who had died an old man just a few years before in Missouri, seemed distant and removed, particularly since he much preferred solitude to the legend that overshadowed him. Andrew Jackson and other notable political leaders of the were the objects of hero worship in many circles, but people—especially the so-called common man—saw something else in the brash yet unpretentious David Crockett of Tennessee. The common man was on the rise, as Jackson's political success revealed, and Crockett also had all the makings to become one of America's first heroes for the masses.

Although he clearly grasped how his homespun demeanor appealed to people, hero worship was not Crockett's immediate agenda in September 1823 when he made his return to Murfreesboro for the Fifteenth

General Assembly. He took his seat as the duly elected state legislator now representing the five counties of Carroll, Humphreys, Perry, Henderson, and Madison. The entire western region was expanding quickly, and by the close of the second session Crockett's own legislative district would swell to a total of eleven new counties with the addition of Gibson, Fayette, Dyer, Tipton, Haywood, and Hardeman.[12] Throughout the first session, which concluded in late November 1823, as well as during the second session, lasting only a month in September–October 1824, Crockett continued his "squatter's rights" crusade. His primary focus remained helping West Tennessee settlers buy land at a reasonable cost.

During both sessions, he took an active role in various committee assignments and on many issues, including a vote against using prisoners as laborers. Many of the convicts were debtors, a group that obviously had Crockett's sympathy. Although he stood in opposition to a proposal to prohibit "tippling houses," he endorsed another measure banning the retail sale of spirits on election day, an odd stance given Crockett's generous use of whiskey as a vote-getting device. In the second session, he introduced a measure to improve the navigation of the rivers·of the Western District and sponsored other bills promoting marriage with widows, opposing divorce in general, and banning the archaic custom of dueling, an activity not foreign to Crockett's former commander, Andrew Jackson.[13]

Jackson had steadily become the most powerful political force in Tennessee, and it was during the initial legislative session in the fall of 1823 that Crockett had his first public sparring match with some of Jackson's most ardent supporters over the election of the next U.S. senator from Tennessee.[14]

Incumbent U.S. senator John Williams was intent on running for a second six-year term. Jackson, however, a longtime political foe of Williams dating back to the Creek War, when Colonel Williams served with Sharp Knife, wanted Williams gone. So did the political machine grooming Jackson for a run for the presidency of the nation in 1824. Another election victory for the most vocal of Jackson's critics would seriously harm his image and prospects nationally. As time for the election neared and no strong candidate to stand against Williams had emerged, Jackson reluctantly agreed to become the spoiler and run for the Senate. Jackson won the October 1 election and then promptly resigned, having managed to keep Williams from returning to Washington.[15] It did not go unnoticed that one of Williams's vocal supporters had been State Assemblyman David Crockett, who had recently beaten one of Jackson's relatives in an election.

"I thought the colonel [Williams] had honestly discharged his duty, and even the mighty name of Jackson couldn't make me vote against him," Crockett wrote several years later when he and Jackson, by then president, were at loggerheads and bitter enemies. "I never would, nor never did, acknowledge I had voted wrong; and I am more certain now that I was right than ever. I told the people it was the best vote I ever gave; that I had supported the public interest, and cleared my conscience in giving it, instead of gratifying the private ambition of a man."[16]

Crockett gutted out the rest of the first legislative session, working as hard as he could on a myriad of proposed legislation and making more friends as well as enemies, such as James K. Polk, who pushed for the sale of public lands to finance universities.[17] Crockett opposed Polk on this issue, firmly believing that universities were the realms of the upper classes and that subsidizing land-grant institutions did not help the poor and the squatters in his ten-county district. To Crockett and others like him from the backcountry, formal education was not nearly as important as the experience a man could garner from everyday life on the frontier.

Without fail, Crockett always took up for the settlers; he believed they suffered at the hands of land speculators. This was duly noted in the Nashville newspapers in September 1824, when Crockett attempted to stop a proposed land practice that was damaging to the hardworking occupants of land controlled by speculators and greedy owners. This measure called for selling off large tracts of vacant state lands for cash, a move that meant Crockett's poor constituents would be priced out of contention. He believed that he, and others like him who had the courage and fortitude to seek out and open new lands for their families, had just as many rights as, if not more rights than, outsiders who wanted to buy large acreages.

Crockett demanded that squatters be given a fair opportunity to purchase the land. He openly condemned the speculators and accused them of "pretending to be great friends to the people in saving their land" when they actually "had gone up one side of the creek and down another, like a *coon*, and pretended to grant the poor people great favors in securing them occupant claims—they gave them a credit of a year and promised to take cows, horses, &c., in payment. But when the year came around, the notes were in the hands of others; the people were sued, cows and horses not being sufficient to pay for securing it." Crockett compared these warrants to "counterfeit bank notes in the hands of the person who obtained them, and die [*sic*] on their hands."[18]

When, on October 22, 1824, the final session came to a close an exhausted Crockett was ready to go home. He was tired of squabbling over land rights, endless committee meetings, and boardinghouse food. His state political career had come to an end. But his national political career was just beginning. As wearisome as some of the proceedings might have been in Murfreesboro, Crockett surmised that maybe the place he could go and get more accomplished for the poor people he represented was in Washington, D.C. Just three days after the close of the final session, he circulated a letter to his constituents reporting on his activities on their behalf in the state legislature. After giving a summary of his accomplishments, he made a request:

Fellow Citizens of the Ninth Congressional District—

I now avail myself of the privilege common to every freeman, of offering myself as a candidate for a seat in the next Congress of the United States. It is not my design at this time to go into a detail of any of the subjects which may be expected to engage the attention of the next Congress, not to discuss any of the public measures of the country—sufficient time will intervene between now and the period of election, to see and converse with many of you—all I will now undertake to say is, that I feel as much interest in your welfare, and if elected, will bestow as much labor in promoting your interest as any other,

> I am, very respectfully, your obedient servant,
> David Crockett
> Nashville, 25th October, 1824

It was a bold move, but perhaps not so surprising for someone courageous enough to battle a bear with a knife or wade through icy river water to fetch a keg of gunpowder. Crockett believed he had a good chance of defeating his opponent—the incumbent congressman Adam Alexander. Crockett recalled that Alexander's congressional vote on the tariff law of 1824 increased the already high rates and "gave a mighty heap of dissatisfaction to his people."[19] Crockett's friends told him that Alexander was vulnerable and that, despite his wealth and connections, he could be beaten. They were wrong. Crockett may have been well liked by many people, but the congressional district he wished to represent covered eighteen counties, which meant Crockett would have to cover much territory. He simply could not afford the travel required to reach areas where he was not as well known, let alone come up with funds to buy those tobacco twists and drams of whiskey that had won him votes in the past. He stumped as much as he could afford and hoped for the best. In the end, Crockett's down-home affectation and charm was no match for a well-funded incumbent whose powerful allies waged a newspaper campaign against Crockett that kept him on the defensive during the spring and into the long, hot summer of 1825, a time of sparse rain, soaring temperatures, and wildfires throughout both hemispheres, particularly in America.

Even Crockett's presumed ace in the hole—Alexander's support of a controversial tariff law—turned sour when the price of cotton skyrocketed. Alexander credited this rise on the tariff law and predicted it would raise the price of everything else they made to sell. "I might as well have sung *salms* [*sic*] over a dead horse, as to try to make people believe otherwise," offered Crockett, "for they knowed their cotton had raised, sure enough, and if the colonel hadn't done it, they didn't know what had."[20]

The election of August 1825 proved closer than anticipated. The margin was just 267 votes. Alexander polled 2,866 votes to Crockett's 2,599.[21] He took the defeat hard but he was not done for—not in the least. He headed to his place on the Obion. There he could make new plans. He could head out into the canebrakes and lick his wounds.

TWENTY-SIX

BIG TIME

ONLY WEEKS AFTER the disappointing election loss, a resilient Crockett already was regaining his confidence. He was back on his land, which, due to expansion, was no longer in Carroll County but newly formed Gibson County.[1] Betsy and the children were a comfort, and so was the news of September 24, 1825: For service rendered in the War of 1812, Crockett would be issued a Military Land Grant for twenty acres in Lawrence County, his former home and place of enlistment.[2] Sale of this new property would bring some welcome income. Not surprisingly, what Crockett needed the most was money—as much as it would take to pay off campaign debts and an impressive stack of other past-due bills.

Financially cornered at thirty-eight years old, Crockett tapped into another natural resource, the forest itself. His plan called for felling timber to be made into pipe staves that would be loaded into vessels and floated down the Mississippi River to New Orleans.[3] From his travels as a state legislator, Crockett was aware that the manufacture of barrels was a huge industry. Cooperages stayed busy trying to keep up with the great demand for barrels, casks, and kegs. Practically every commodity and product had to be shipped and stored in wooden containers, including milled flour, turpentine, nails, dried meats, gunpowder, molasses, sugar, coffee, shoes, lobster, paints, pickles, rice, maple syrup, and even money. In Tennessee and neighboring Kentucky, barrels were in constant demand to hold the rivers of sipping whiskey that poured from commercial distilleries and moonshine camps.

During his hunts, Crockett sometimes encountered the rugged men whose livings were made on the rivers. They had stories about New Orleans, a major southern market and port, where heaps of rough staves shipped down the Mississippi cluttered the waterfront. Many of the staves were exported abroad and assembled into barrels while local coopers snapped up the rest.

Crockett found a likely place for his new enterprise on Obion Lake, just south of Reelfoot Lake, close to the Mississippi and about twenty-five miles due west of his abode.[4] He rounded up a small crew of hired hands to assist him—promising them wages after the staves were delivered—and they went to work setting up a camp. They gathered timber for staves and for the two large flatboats needed to transport the finished staves downriver. Drawing on some of the boat building techniques he observed years before while visiting relatives in Fentress County, Crockett had some notion about the kind of flatboats he wanted, and he assigned a few helpers to that task. He dispatched the rest of the crew to bring in the wood.

The area around the lake was still cloaked with large stands of timber, including oak, gum, poplar, hickory, and maple. In years to come, as more sawmills sprang up, many of these trees would be gone. White oak was the wood of choice for the coopers who turned out sturdy whiskey barrels, and, consequently, these were some of the first trees cut down. Near the lake, many of the ancient cypress trees—another prized wood—also were taken. All the felled timber was hauled back to camp by horse and oxen teams. After milling, the lumber was cut into narrow strips, or staves, that would be used to form part of the sides of barrels.

Crockett faithfully supervised the stave-making operation for a time, but eventually the call of the hunt was too tempting. He rationalized that although the workers did not expect to get paid until they reached New Orleans, he had promised to provide all their meals. "I worked on with my hands till the bears got fat, and then I turned out to hunting, to lay in a supply of meat,"[5] Crockett wrote. This memorable series of bear hunts stretched through the rest of 1825 and well into the spring of 1826. By his count, Crockett killed 105 bears, including 47 in a one-month period.

During that winter and spring, Crockett occasionally broke away from his hunting companions to check on the hired hands busily turning out staves and supply them with fresh meat. In the early spring of 1826, the hunting winding down, Crockett was pleased to find that in his absence both boats had been completed and were fully loaded with more than 30,000 barrel staves. Anxious to pocket a hefty profit in New Orleans and pay his workers, Crockett ordered the flatboats pushed off, and soon enough they were moving down the Obion River to the Mississippi.

Both of the boats were unwieldy craft built of rough lumber and intended only to get as far as New Orleans, where they would be disassembled and the lumber sold for scrap. From there Crockett and the crew, with money in their purses, would take a riverboat back to Tennessee.

The short trip on the Obion went well enough, but once they entered the broad and powerful Mississippi, it became apparent that none of the crew possessed the navigational skills to make the long journey ahead. Crockett had never before attempted to navigate such a great river. "I found all my hands were bad scar[r]ed, and in fact I believe I was scar[r]ed a little worse of any; for I had never been down the river, and I soon discovered that my pilot was as ignorant of the business as myself,"[6] Crockett lamented.

The boats, top-heavy from all the staves, turned sideways and drifted out of control. Crockett ordered the men to lash the rafts together, but that only made a bad situation worse. They could no longer maneuver the boats nor land them. As night fell, crewmen on passing boats and people with lanterns on the riverbank shouted advice but nothing seemed to work.

"Our boats were so heavy that we couldn't take them much any way, except the way they wanted to go, and just the way the current would carry them," Crockett explained. "At last we quit trying to land, and concluded just to go ahead as well as we could, for we found we couldn't do any better."[7]

Sometime during the long night, Crockett went below in the cabin to rest and think about "how much better bear-hunting was on hard land, than floating along on the water." He was still below deck when, just as the town of Memphis appeared on a distant bluff, the boats, still lashed together, crashed into a sawyer, a huge raft of drift timber lodged in the river bottom and pointed upstream. The impact separated the boats, and the lead barge was pulled under, while the second craft nosed beneath it, with Crockett still below the deck. He scrambled around, looking for a way to escape as water rushed into the cabin. The only exit he could find was a window, too small for him to crawl through.

"I began to think that I was in a worse box than ever," recalled Crockett. "But I put my arms through and hollered as loud as I could roar, as the boat I was in hadn't yet quite filled with water up to my head, and the hands who were next to the raft, seeing my arms out, and hearing me holler, seized them, and began to pull."

Finally, just as the boat was about to go under, the men jerked Crockett free, ripping off his clothes and a fair amount of his skin in the process. "I was, however, well pleased to get out in any way, even without shirt or hide." All hands leaped to safety on a pile of driftwood, where they spent the rest of the night, cold, hungry, half naked, but alive. Not a man had been lost. "While I was setting there, in the night, floating about on the drift, I felt happier and better off than I ever had in my life before, for I had just made such a marvelous escape,"[8] rejoiced the ever optimistic Crockett.

At just about sunrise, the bedraggled crew hailed a passing boat headed for Memphis, where spectators lining the bluff greeted them. In the cheering crowd was Marcus Brutus Winchester, a gentleman ten years younger than Crockett, and the eldest son of General James Winchester.[9] Marcus had left school at age sixteen to fight alongside his father in the War of 1812, where they both were captured by the British at the Battle of River Basin and sent to prison in Quebec. In 1819, General Winchester was one of the founders of Memphis along with some others, including Andrew Jackson and John C. McLemore, one of Crockett's chief creditors.[10] The elder Winchester, a great lover of history, named the city Memphis after the ancient Egyptian city on the Nile.

In the spring of 1819, Marcus came to Memphis on a flatboat, but his craft dodged the sawyers and snags. With financial help from his father, he opened the town's first store, a fashionable place of business on Front Street, just south of Jackson Street, where he erected one of the finest houses in town.[11] When he and Crockett met in 1826, Marcus was on the verge of becoming the newly incorporated city's first mayor and was said to be "the most graceful, courtly, elegant gentleman that ever appeared upon Main Street."[12]

At first glance, it seemed that young Winchester and Crockett had so little in common that any sort of friendship was highly unlikely. Besides the great disparity in lifestyle, upbringing, and personal wealth, the Winchesters were Jacksonians and had no use for anyone who did not fully support Old Hickory. But Marcus Winchester was his own man and, despite his many civic duties and business accomplishments, possessed a definite streak of rebel. In 1823 he had thrown caution to the wind and wed Amarante Loiselle, brilliant and educated in France, and reputed to be one of the most beautiful women in the South. She was one-sixteenth black, which was why the wedding took place in her hometown of New Orleans, where mixed-race marriages were legal. Eventually being wed to "a woman of color" would prove Winchester's undoing in Memphis. Yet even when the nasty racial slurs began after he served as mayor, Winchester remained steadfast with his beloved wife, even if it meant his certain ruin.[13]

On the calamitous morning in 1826, Winchester, seeing Crockett's distressful situation, ran to his nearby dry goods store and returned with trousers for him. Later he brought Crockett and the rest of the crew to the store and provided them with completely new outfits, hats, and shoes. Then they went to the Winchester residence, where the lovely

Amarante welcomed their guests with as fine a meal as they had ever eaten. Crockett regaled his hosts with some of his best stories, and later, at a tavern, he and his crew were toasted for having survived their ordeal on the river.[14]

A few days later, Crockett and one of his crew booked passage on a steamboat—the first that Crockett had ever boarded—and went down-river as far as Natchez, the town of antebellum mansions perched on the river bluffs, in the hope that they might discover some of the 30,000 staves. The search proved fruitless.[15] Crockett went back to Memphis and spent a bit more time with his new friend Marcus Winchester. The two men discussed Crockett's future and what might lie ahead. When Crockett left Memphis on a boat headed upriver to his home, Winchester gave him some money. It was not charity, nor did he feel sorry for his new backwoods friend. The money was meant as encouragement for Crockett to take another risk: a second run for U.S. Congress, for which Winchester pledged his support.

"The Victory Is Ours"

Crockett finally reached the Obion River and made his way to his home in Gibson County in the late spring of 1826. It had been almost nine months since he had seen his wife or spoken with his children. True to form, as soon as he got back he turned right around and left again—this time for another crack at the bears. They had come out of hibernation, and Crockett wanted to add to his tally. He was out another month and took down 47 more, bringing the total to 105 bears killed over the seven-month-long season.[1]

"It is in the bear hunt that he is most himself,"[2] wrote Richard Slotkin in *Regeneration through Violence*, the first of his trilogy on the mythology of the American West. "In the bear hunt the forces opposing him, keeping him from his desires, become tangible. They can be met in direct, open combat and vanquished. . . . The source of Crockett's satisfaction with politics lies in his association of vote-getting and hunting. . . . They are quantifiable indicators of the degree of his prowess, symbols of great deeds of skill."

It is doubtful if Elizabeth Crockett ever figured out just what kept her wayward husband always on the move and away from home. She and the children played no real role in Crockett's world. In fact, his wives and offspring were not prominently featured in his autobiography. Instead they almost became "conquests of a hunt, as do bearskins, votes, and a powerful reputation in the community."[3] Elizabeth had to know that neither she nor the land could ever hold her husband. For that reason, she was far from pleased when he announced that he was going to try another run for Congress, for these were not times when all wives accompanied their political husbands to Washington.

On September 16, 1826, it became official—Crockett once again offered himself as a candidate for a seat in the U.S. Congress. "I have again been induced to submit my pretensions to a generous, high minded and magnanimous people,"[4] Crockett wrote to voters on that date. "I am opposed to the Administration of this man from the Yankee states, called John Q. Adams; I am opposed to the conduct of the Kentucky orator, H. Clay [Henry Clay]; I am greatly opposed to our present Representative's vote on the Tariff." In closing, Crockett made one more promise. "I will not set [sic] silently, and permit the interest of my District to be neglected, while I have got a tongue to speak and a head to direct it. . . . I am the rich-man's safe-guard, and poor man's friend."

Crockett opened his campaign in the spring of 1827. He realized that running against an incumbent opponent was always difficult, but he felt he could best Colonel Adam Rankin Alexander, despite having lost to him in the previous election. This time, Crockett had the much-needed backing of a solid financial benefactor. Crockett put his trust in Major Marcus Winchester; Memphis, on the western edge of the sprawling Ninth Congressional District, was the second largest congressional district in the nation, with more than 22,000 voters.[5] Since their first encounter, following the riverboat accident, Crockett and Winchester had become even better acquainted, and Winchester was impressed with Crockett's grit and style. He lent the campaign $250, endorsed Crockett, and talked him up to friends and associates throughout the region.[6]

"We frequently met at different places," Crockett wrote of Winchester, "and as he thought I needed, he would occasionally hand me a little more cash; so I was able to buy a little of 'the *creature*,' to put my friends in a good humour, as well as the other gentlemen."[7]

Besides Crockett and Alexander, a third candidate entered the race—the politically ambitious William Arnold. He was a veteran of the War of 1812 and a prominent attorney from Jackson who had been elected major general of the Tennessee Militia in 1826.[8] Crockett, however, remained undaunted, even though he faced two high-profile opponents with illustrious military records. He figured that he had a military and political record all his own and that in the long run it would be more appealing to the general populace.

During the campaign, a sharp decline in the price of cotton hurt Alexander, whose past support of the tariff law came back to hurt him, just as Crockett had long predicted. Both Arnold and Alexander also helped Crockett's cause by largely ignoring him and focusing on each other. At one campaign stop, Gen. Arnold spoke and directed his remarks at Alexander as if Crockett were not even there. After a time, a large flock of noisy guinea fowls happened upon the scene and made such a clatter that the flustered Arnold had to stop talking until the birds could be driven away.[9] Crockett recalled,

> I let him finish his speech, and then walking up to him, said aloud, "Well, colonel, you are the first man I ever saw that understood the language of fowls." I told him that he had not had the politeness to name me in his speech, and that when my little friends, the guinea-fowls, had come up and began to holler "Crockett, Crockett, Crockett," he had been ungenerous enough to stop, and drive *them* all away. This raised a universal shout among the people for me, and the general seemed mighty bad plagued. But he got more plagued than this at the polls in August.[10]

That was exactly the folksy style that the crowds found so appealing. Crockett had become a seasoned campaigner who spoke the language of the voters. All of his speeches sounded much like the auto biography that he and Thomas Chilton would pen just a few years later, peppered with country expressions and his own peculiar brand of idioms and phrases. He was affable and did not seem to take himself too seriously. All of it worked in his favor. Crockett defeated both his opponents by a substantial margin. Arnold had 2,417 votes, Alexander received 3,646, and Crockett polled 5,868 votes, giving him a plurality of 2,222 votes.[11]

David Crockett, "the gentleman from the cane," most comfortable, it seemed, hunting bears, appeared to be as strange a congressman-elect as there ever would be in American history. Some people, in fact, who recalled the seemingly impossible occurrence in 1811 when the great earthquake caused the Mississippi to run backward, were even more shocked by the news of Crockett's election. Crockett himself may even have been surprised, though it might have been another instance of feigned modesty when, years after the election, he told a friend that "he never knew why the people of his district elected him to Congress, as it was a matter he knew precious little about at the time and had no idea what he would be called on to do when he arrived in Washington."[12]

Early nineteenth-century pundits scratched their heads and wondered what had happened. The answer appeared clear. What had happened was that from the ranks of eligible voters, a huge number of white men—many encouraged by wives still almost a century away from being permitted to cast votes—turned out for Crockett. His vote count more than doubled the number of votes he had received just two years before, and, even more impressive, more than 12,000 voters cast ballots on election day, twice the number who voted in 1825. At least half of them supported Crockett.[13] That is what made the difference—those hardscrabble farmers, squatters, stave makers, coon hunters, militia privates, storekeepers, tavern owners, and so many more. In their minds, and espousing early progressive sentiment, they were sending one of their own to Congress. At last they would have their own champion—and one without landholdings and aristocratic pretensions—fighting on their behalf. Crockett defined what it meant to be a populist—an advocate for the rights and interests of ordinary people. Flushed with victory in the autumn of 1827, Crockett felt invincible.

Just a few weeks after the election, Crockett surprised and delighted Elizabeth with a trip to her family home in North Carolina. His eldest son, twenty-year-old John Wesley, accompanied them. Their first stop was Nashville, a future state capital known as the "Athens of the South," where a meeting was arranged with John Patton Erwin, a rising attorney and the son of Colonel Andrew Erwin and Jane Patton, from Elizabeth's family in North Carolina. Not only did young Erwin have family ties to the Crocketts, he also was closely linked to noted statesman Henry Clay (serving as secretary of state under President John Quincy Adams), an intellectual who spoke seven languages fluently, drafted the Monroe Doctrine, and was an ardent foe of slavery. Erwin was the husband of Anne Brown Clay, the daughter of the Kentuckian who had become a force to be reckoned with in Congress and on five occasions tried but failed to become U.S. president.[14]

Erwin was puzzled by the newly elected congressman's visit, for although his voting record did not always show it, Crockett still backed Old Hickory. The animosity between Clay and Jackson had only grown following the controversial 1824 presidential race, when Clay played a pivotal role in vanquishing candidate Jackson and sending his opponent, John Quincy Adams, to the White House. It was about then that Jackson began referring to Clay as the "Judas of the West."[15] Considering that Clay and Jackson so despised each other, a meeting between Crockett and Clay's son-in-law might have been viewed as absolute betrayal by the Jackson camp. On the other hand, an ardent Jackson supporter asking for an introduction to Jackson's chief nemesis may have aroused Erwin's suspicions.

It turned out that Erwin had nothing to fear. Crockett explained that when he got to Congress he planned "to pursue his own course," but he also looked forward to receiving wise counsel from proven political veterans such as the Honorable Henry Clay, a revered Kentucky lawyer first elected to the U.S. Senate in 1806. In a letter sent to Clay shortly after the visit, Erwin gave a rather blunt assessment of Crockett. "He is not only illiterate but he is rough & uncouth, talks much & loudly, and is by far, more to his proper place, when hunting a Bear, in a Cane Break, than he will be in the Capital."[16] But beyond the obvious and somewhat contrived frontier image, Erwin also offered a telling appraisal of Crockett's strengths. "He is independent and fearless & has a popularity at home that is unaccountable," Erwin wrote. "He is the only man that I know in Tennessee that could openly oppose Genl. Jackson in his District & be elected to Congress."

From Nashville, the Crocketts moved on to eastern Tennessee and visited friends and family in the country where Crockett was raised. One of the stops was at the home of lifelong friend James Blackburn. Others came there as well, and Crockett told them old stories from the past and some of his best tales about the bear hunts, his escapade on the river, and the recent election. Many years later, John L. Jacobs, then in his eightieth year, recalled the day Crockett spent at Blackburn's place.[17] Jacobs was just a boy and had seen Crockett when he stopped to give Jacobs's widowed mother the dollar he had borrowed from her husband.

"James Blackburn had a corn-shucking in my neighborhood," remembered Jacobs.

> There were many hands around the heap. We saw a fine gentleman riding toward the house. He alighted and went into the house, and made himself known, passed the usual compliments, then came down to the men around the heap of corn, gave a general shaking of hands with all the citizens, then turned up the cuffs of his fine broadcloth and went to shucking corn with the other hands. He worked on till dinner was announced, then ate his dinner and left for his home. That was the last sight I ever had

of this wonderful man. I shall give you a description of Davy Crockett: He was about 6 feet high, weighed two hundred pounds, had no surplus flesh, broad shouldered, stood erect, was a man of great physical strength, of fine appearance, his cheeks mantled with a rosy hue, eyes vivacious, and in form, had no superior.[18]

The day after they left Blackburn's home and returned to the road to North Carolina, Crockett experienced what was probably a recurrence of his malaria, which he described as "billes feaver" (bilious fever).[19] Despite feeling poorly, he managed to finish the ride with Elizabeth and John Wesley. As soon as they arrived at her parents' home in Swannanoa, South Carolina, Crockett was put to bed and a doctor summoned. The physician turned to a standard remedy of the time and bled the patient, which weakened him even more and forced him to stay bedridden for several weeks.

By November 6, Crockett had regained enough strength to witness a duel between his friend Sam Carson and Dr. Robert Brank Vance.[20] Both men were from influential families in western North Carolina, and they had been pitted against each other in heated political races. Carson had defeated Vance for a seat in Congress in 1825, and Vance had tried again and failed in 1827. Near the close of that heated campaign, Vance made serious accusations about the Carson family's loyalty, even claiming that Carson's father had been a cowardly Tory during the Revolutionary War. More insults flew, and soon a duel was arranged, as was the custom among southern gentlemen who felt their honor and reputation had been tarnished.

Crockett thought dueling was ridiculous, but he was loyal to his friends, and it was said that he even drilled Carson in pistol practice. Crockett also was in the small party that rode with Carson and his second to the dueling ground across the state line at Saluda Gap, in South Carolina, where dueling was still legal.[21] There the frail Crockett watched as Carson and Vance marched off their aces, turned, and fired their pistols. Vance was struck mortally wounded and fell at first fire. He died at midnight. Before the smoke from the dueling pistols lifted, Crockett—somewhat revived by a burst of adrenaline—was on his horse riding off to spread the news. One of Carson's daughters later wrote that "he rode his horse almost to death, beat his hat to pieces & came dashing up yelling 'The Victory is Ours.' "[22]

Due to his prolonged recovery, Crockett did not have time to accompany his wife and son back to the family home in far western Tennessee. He would have to press on to Washington City in order to attend the December 3 opening of Congress. Elizabeth and John Wesley wished David well on his new adventure, and they departed the Patton home, taking with them three young slaves, parting gifts from her father.[23]

After some more bloodletting, Crockett also took his leave. He was sorry that he had not been well enough to enjoy shooting matches with his father-in-law at the "Target Tree," a large oak near the Patton home where they blazed away at targets. Crockett, still racked with pain and fever, climbed on his horse and rode off. The newly reelected Sam Carson and his colleague Lewis Williams, a ten-year veteran of Congress, accompanied him. It was a grueling journey for a sick man, but Crockett's companions kept him occupied with stories about what he could expect and what he should avoid in Washington City.

At last they arrived. Crockett and the others were directed to a neighborhood not far from Capitol Hill, where there were plenty of hotels and boardinghouses and an array of busy taverns. One of the popular choices on Pennsylvania Avenue was the McKeown Hotel, remembered as the place where "The Star-Spangled Banner" was first sung in 1814. Many visitors, including American Indian delegations from the far West, preferred the St. Charles Hotel. One of the city's most prestigious hostelries was Brown's Indian Queen Hotel. Each evening, Jesse Brown—"the Prince of Landlords"—presided over a table offering decanters of whiskey and brandy free to all guests. Some of the wealthier politicos could afford the sixteen-dollar-a-night hotel rates, but many congressman chose the more reasonably priced boarding houses, known as "messes."

Crockett took a room at Mrs. Ball's rooming house on Pennsylvania Avenue, located across the street from the Indian Queen. Here he would share meals and accommodations with several other congressmen from Virginia, Alabama, North Carolina, and Connecticut. Three members of the Kentucky delegation boarded at Mrs. Ball's, including the honorable Thomas Chilton, a representative who would come to play a key role in Crockett's future. Soon enough he would meet his fellow boarders, mostly all fellow members of Congress from across the land.

CROCKETT AT THE ALAMO.

When I war at the battle of the Alamo, whar the creturs thought to catch us like a weazel asleep, I heated my gun red hot in firing so quick, and thar war no need in pulling a trigger, and drawin a lead, for the gun went off nat'ral and kilt a Mexican sojer every time. Arter my ammunition war gone, I swept down twelve of 'em with one sweep of my musket. It war the best job that kill-devil ever did. I think it war a duty to clear the country of setch varmint's as much as foxes and wolves and crocodiles. Arter that battle, I counted about fifty that had killdevil's mark on 'em, f r I knowed every bullet-hole that cum from them balls of killdevils. Luke Wing took off scalps enough to make his wife a Sunday petticoat with the hair hangin' down, and she said it was the warmest Sunday petticoat she ever had on. I never fout so hard before but wonst, and that war when thar war a feller running agin me for Kongress, and I dared out all that voted for him. That time I put seventeen eyes into my pocket; but at the Alamo, I might have took a smart chance of eyes if I had wanted to do it; but thar eyes war so far in the head, it war not wo th my trouble to dig 'em out; so I let 'em lay and rot on the field; but I took a bundle of scalps and sent 'em home to Mrs. Crockett, to sew 'em together and make a patchwork ed-quilt of 'em.

Almanac illustration with text.
(Photograph by Dorothy Sloan, Dorothy Sloan Rare Books)

PART IV

TWENTY-EIGHT

MAN WITHOUT A PARTY

ROCKETT WAS STAGE CENTER beneath a shining light. After yeoman political performances in Tennessee—where he honed and perfected his craft—the homespun forty-year-old found himself in the best theater of all: the nation's capital. Here all sorts of forces and influences, such as a curious national press, a bevy of hack writers, and a gaggle of self-serving partisan politicians, waited in the wings. All of them recognized the unrefined backwoodsman's raw magnetism and potential as a kind of political prop and populist mouthpiece. They saw that Crockett's antics, eccentricities, and colorful style would propel him to national and eventually international acclaim and ridicule. Dealing with such attention required a willing participant with a healthy ego able to fend off critics and detractors. At the same time, it also meant that Crockett had to put up with some manipulation and allow his public image and persona to be molded and choreographed.

When he first arrived in Washington City to take his seat in the Twentieth Congress, many of his colleagues found that Crockett certainly possessed a natural charm but also often exhibited rather unconventional behavior. His conversations and speeches were peppered with his folksy and sometimes clever idioms and expressions, many of which seemed peculiar to others who came from the larger urban areas of the country. While it was true that Crockett had his share of quirks, many of his so-called eccentricities were blown out of proportion and exaggerated by political enemies both in the press and political arena. Contrary to many written accounts and most of the Crockett film portrayals, he did not go to Congress wearing a hunting shirt and coonskin hat, but turned out in the standard high collared coat, dress shirt, vest, and cravat of the time.

"I remember David Crockett well and always with pleasure," recounted William L. Foster, whose father, Senator Ephraim H. Foster, had been a friend and associate. "He was very often a guest of my father, always a pleasant, courteous, and interesting man, who, though uneducated in books, was a man of fine instincts and intellect. . . . I never saw him attired in a garb that could be regarded as differing from that worn by a gentleman of his day—never in coonskin cap or hunting shirt."[1]

No matter the wardrobe he chose, the robust backwoodsman in gentleman's clothes puzzled his detractors and skeptics. Some of them seriously questioned if he had the intellect to survive the cutthroat world of Washington. They believed Tennessee would have been better served by having Crockett back at Reelfoot Lake.[2]

As it turned out, the question was not so much whether Crockett was ready for Washington but whether Washington was ready for Crockett. It is true that, during his three terms in the U.S. Congress, Crockett failed to get a single piece of legislation passed, even his beloved land bill for poor settlers and squatters. However, he emerged as a national celebrity, and served as an unwitting voice of and living symbol for a concept that, until nine years after Crockett's death in 1836, did not have an official name—Manifest Destiny.

Influential magazine editor John L. O'Sullivan coined the name for this disputed political philosophy in an 1845 editorial when he wrote of "the right of our manifest destiny to over spread and to possess the whole of the continent which Providence has given us. . . . This is our high destiny, and in nature's eternal, inevitable decree of cause and effect we must accomplish it."[3] Manifest Destiny became a rallying cry throughout the nation for all of those who ardently believed that it was the exclusive right of the white population of America to invade, occupy, and settle all the land reaching westward across the continent to the Pacific shore. As cultural critic and historian Richard Slotkin noted, "men like Davy Crockett became national heroes by defining national aspiration in terms of so many bears destroyed, so much land preempted, so many trees hacked down, so many Indians and Mexicans dead in the dust."[4]

Yet at the same time, Crockett also symbolized the poor and downtrodden whom he had always stood up for throughout his life. He was not afraid to buck the system or oppose authority, including those at the top of the chain of command. In fact, it was Crockett's inability to compromise that resulted in such a dismal showing when it came to getting his own pieces of legislation passed in Congress and enacted into law. His Scots-Irish stubbornness, frontier pride, and a tendency to speak directly, even if it came out as an insult, did not serve him well and often resulted in loss of votes and support in congressional committees and on the floor of Congress. Still, numerous hardworking settlers in his home district never lost faith in Crockett, and found their man in Washington endearing.

"Crockett emerged as a symbol of the dawning 'Age of the Common Man,'" wrote Paul Hutton. "His generation, the first to face the future without the guidance of the Republic's Founding Fathers, looked to the frontier for the regenerative values once associated with the revolutionary generation. Westerners like Crockett were the flag bearers of a 'Manifest Destiny' reaffirming that this new generation was the master of both the environment and its own future. The rise of the West—along with men like Jackson, Clay, Sam Houston, and Crockett—represented the triumph of American democracy and a final rejection of decadent European values of class and aristocracy."[5]

Crockett had little notion that he was symbolic of anything when he first took up residence in Washington, although his confidence in himself increased daily as he became more comfortable with his new surroundings. Early in his first term, while still recovering from recurrent malaria, he dashed off a letter to his friend James Blackburn in Tennessee. After giving Blackburn a medical update, Crockett wrote, "I think I am getting along very well with the great men of this nation[,] much better than I expected."[6] It did not take long before Crockett's opinion changed and much of his optimism disappeared.

"There's too much talk," he complained after just a short time in Congress. "Many men seem to be proud they can say so much about nothing. Their tongues keep working, whether they've any grist to grind or not. Then there are some in Congress who do nothing to earn their pay but listen day after day. But considering the speeches, I think they earn every penny, amounting to eight whole dollars a day—provided they don't go to sleep. It's harder than splitting gum logs in August, though, to stay awake."[7]

Crockett found that in the halls of Congress a genial disposition and quick wit could get him only so far. His vast repertoire of frontier yarns served him well when on the campaign stump but did not have the same impact or import in Washington. He never learned how to compromise. His fiercely independent spirit and belief that he was obligated to vote his conscience even if it was contrary to his own party took a heavy toll.

Crockett's stubbornness even extended to his own political party, much to the annoyance of the Democratic leadership. To win the passage of his land bill, he needed all the help he could muster, especially from the rest of the Tennessee delegation and from the supporters of Andrew Jackson, poised to become the next president of the United States. Even before he publicly broke from the Jackson crowd, Crockett took issue with key Jackson supporters and anyone else unwilling to fully support squatters' rights in the western lands. This stance put Crockett squarely at odds with the wealthy planters and land speculators who financially supported Jackson.[8] When Crockett's break with Jackson and the others became known in 1830, Congressman James K. Polk, later to become President Polk, sniffed: "I have no other feelings towards Col. Crockett than those of pity for his folly."[9]

Throughout 1828 and into 1829, however, Crockett tried to maintain a relationship with everyone he could in order to push his land legislation. That definitely still included Old Hickory, who finally defeated his nemesis John Quincy Adams in the bitterly contested presidential election of 1828 and was sworn into office the following March. Jackson's campaign had positioned the often-arrogant Tennessean as a self-made man of the people and the first president to be born in a log cabin. Adams, on the other hand, was characterized as an aloof aristocrat who, much like his father, lacked the political savvy required to garner support for any of his pet programs.

Although Crockett's political life consumed much of his time and energy during this period, he also had issues to face back in Tennessee. He wrestled with a substantial debt, and also tried placating Elizabeth, who was tired of her husband's continued inability to keep the family solvent. She blamed much of Crockett's troubles on his penchant for drink, lack of any business sense, and failure to maintain any semblance of a spiritual life.

While Crockett had to endure Elizabeth's personal assaults at home, he also had to suffer an onslaught of scurrilous stories and fabrications about his character, concocted by political enemies who smelled blood. Finally, on November 25, 1828, about a week before Jackson's victory at the polls, Crockett reached his breaking point and struck back. On that date, the *National Banner and the Nashville Whig* published an embarrassing description of Crockett's crude behavior at a dinner hosted by President Adams almost a year earlier, on November 27, 1827, to welcome new members of Congress to the capital.[10] The planted newspaper stories presented Crockett as a complete bumpkin who sipped from the finger bowls and accused a waiter of stealing his dinner when the man was simply clearing the table for the next course. "I then filled my plate with bacon and greens," Crockett was alleged to have said. "And whenever I looked up or down the table, I held on to my plate with my left hand" so no one else would take it away.[11]

President Adams's meticulously kept diary indicates that no such behavior occurred on that date. Adams noted that he received Congressman Lewis Williams of North Carolina, accompanied by "Crocket [*sic*] a new member from Tennessee." In other notations about the occasion Adams wrote that "Colonel Crockett was very diverting at our dinner," which more than likely meant the freshman legislator told some of his better frontier tales.[12]

Humiliated by the guffaws in Washington circles, Crockett was upset when some of his constituents posed questions about his outlandish behavior at a presidential event. To counter the published stories, he contacted two highly respected congressmen who also were in attendance and asked them to write letters refuting such blatant lies. On January 4, just a day after they received Crockett's request, Congressman James Clark, of Kentucky, and Congressman Gulian Crommelin Verplanck, of New York, responded with letters supporting Crockett.

"I was at the same dinner, and know that the statement is destitute of every thing like truth," wrote Clark, who had filled the congressional seat vacated by Henry Clay's elevation to secretary of state and was an early organizer of the Whig Party in Kentucky. "I sat opposite to you at the table, and held occasional conversation with you, and observed nothing in your behavior but was marked with the strictest priority."[13] Verplanck, not only a veteran political figure but a respected man of letters, wrote in his letter of support to Crockett, "Your behavior there was, I thought, perfectly becoming and proper; and I do not recollect or believe that you said or did anything resembling the newspaper account." Verplanck was a skilled writer of satire and a member of the "Knickerbocker group," along with Washington Irving, William Cullen Bryant, and James Kirke Paulding, an author and public official who would soon become intimately involved with Crockett's life.[14]

The letters of denial eventually were printed in various newspapers, including the *Jackson Gazette*, but as Crockett geared up for a reelection campaign for another two-year term, yet another story, written by someone using the pen name Dennis Brulgrudery, described Crockett's politicking style as a mixture of flattery, drunkenness, venality, and dishonesty.[15]

In early 1829, while forced to defend his reputation and counter personal attacks, Crockett composed one of the more difficult letters he would ever have to write. It was scrawled to his brother-in-law George Patton in Buncombe County, North Carolina.[16] In the long epistle

Crockett spoke of the tragic news "of the death of our poor little niece Rebecca Ann Burgin." The little girl had been killed in a horrible accident at Crockett's farm in Tennessee while playing near the ox-driven grain mill that had been built several months earlier. "She was with my children . . . walking round after the oxen and stopped opposite one of the outside posts and caught her head against the post and mashed it all to peaces [sic]. Poor little creature never knew what hurt her. I thought almost as much of her as one of my own."

In the same letter, Crockett also explained that he was attempting to alter the course of his life by giving up spirits and that he intended to imbibe nothing stronger than cider. "I trust that god will give me fortitude in my undertaking," he wrote. "I have never made a pretention [sic] to religion in my life before. I have run a long race tho I trust that I was called in good time. I have been reproved many times for my wickedness by my dear wife who I am certain will be no little astonished when she gets information of my determination."[17]

In March 1829, just after he watched the swearing-in of Andrew Jackson as the seventh president of the United States, along with Vice President John C. Calhoun of South Carolina, Crockett launched his own campaign for reelection to the Twenty-first Congress of the House of Representatives. When newspaper smears accused him of every sin imaginable, including adultery, drunkenness, and gambling, Crockett replied with humor and sarcasm. "They accuse me of adultery! It's a lie. I never ran away with any man's wife that wasn't willing . . . they accuse me of gambling! It's a lie; I always plank the cash . . . and, they accuse me of being a drunkard! It's a d—d lie, for whisky can't make me drunk."[18]

Although Crockett's chief opponent was once again Colonel Adam Alexander, he remained quietly confident of victory throughout the reelection campaign. He may not have been able to get his land bill through Congress, but it was not for any lack of trying. He knew that effort would be in the voters' minds when they went to the polls, and he was correct.

In the August election Crockett was rewarded with another term in Congress. Alexander gathered 3,641 votes and two minor candidates pooled a total of 168 votes. Crockett received 6,773 votes for a plurality of 3,132 votes.[19]

While he basked in another clear victory over Alexander, Crockett had to wonder exactly who was most responsible for all the defamatory stories and ugly accusations that had been heaped on him both before and during the campaign. He had his suspicions that the responsible parties were not only the Whigs but also some Jacksonian Democrats. As the new decade came around, Crockett realized that he had become a man without a party.

TWENTY-NINE

TRAILS OF TEARS

WITH THE BEGINNING of the 1830s, time was running out not only politically but physically as well for David Crockett. He had reached his midforties, then viewed by some as the beginning of old age. Taking into consideration his vigorous lifestyle, the privations he had endured, and his many near-encounters with death, Crockett remained in fairly good physical shape. There was the occasional flare-up from the malaria and some old wounds that ached, but for the most part Crockett was fit.

With a growing number of legislative critics, Crockett realized that his physical stamina and mental alertness were essential to gaining passage of the Tennessee land bill and for his own political survival. Detractors from all camps were angry that, when it came to support of the measures they sponsored, Crockett left no room for compromise.

Early in his second term, Crockett became a leading opponent against any further appropriations for the United States Military Academy at West Point, New York. He firmly believed that the academy—founded in 1802—was an inherently elitist institution "managed for the benefit of the noble and wealthy of the country." Crockett's negative feelings about the academy no doubt resulted from some of the treatment he had received during the Creek War, including his superior officer's failure to act on his scouting report until it was corroborated by another commissioned officer. Crockett felt so strongly about this matter that he even proposed the abolishment of the academy.[1]

In speaking at length on behalf of his proposed resolution, Crockett stressed: "A man could fight the battles of his country, and lead his country's armies, without being educated at West Point."[2] He also pointed out that Andrew Jackson and several other past military heroes had not attended the academy and yet became effective leaders. "Gentlemen were not up to the task of commanding soldiers," said Crockett. They were "too delicate, and could not rough it in the army because they were too differently raised."[3] Crockett's proposal was quickly tabled and soon quietly died, but not before alienating him even more with other legislators from all political persuasions.

On February 24, 1830, just a day before Crockett offered his resolution concerning the abolition of West Point, another important proposal was introduced in Congress—President Andrew Jackson's Indian Removal Act. The passage and enactment of this legislation would be remembered as one of the darkest moments in the nation's history.

Crockett's Indian philosophy differed substantially from Andrew Jackson's and from that of his diehard supporters, who pushed his controversial legislation through both houses of Congress. The legislation gave Jackson the power to negotiate treaties with the Indian tribes living east of the Mississippi. Under these treaties, the tribes were to give up all their lands in exchange for lands to the west. The Indians most affected were the southeastern tribes—Cherokee, Chickasaw, Choctaw, Creek, and eventually the Seminole. They were all too familiar with Sharp Knife and his paternalistic view of Indians from long before he became president. Some of them had fought against him and others had battled alongside him as allies. All of them knew that Jackson considered them an "ill-fated race."[4]

Yet Jackson's betrayal of his former allies and his fierce advocacy of removal amounted to one of the most appalling periods in this nation's relationship with American Indians. "If I had known that Jackson would drive us from our homes, I would have killed him at Horseshoe,"[5] said Tsunu Iahunski, a Cherokee veteran of the Creek War who fought on Jackson's side. Tsunu Iahunski was originally named Gulkalaski and had become acquainted with Andrew Jackson years before the bloody clash against the Creeks at Horseshoe Bend. He was the Cherokee known for having saved Jackson's life during the battle by slaying a Creek warrior who had Jackson at his mercy. When the Indian Removal Act was being considered, Cherokee Chief John Ross sent Gulkalaski to Washington to appeal to Jackson and ask him to reconsider uprooting tribal people from their ancestral homeland. After he heard Gulkalaski's plea, Jackson reportedly snapped at him, "Sir, your audience is ended, there is nothing I can do for you." After that, Gulkalaski became known as Tsunu Iahunski, or "One who tries, but fails."[6]

In an effort to maintain their tribal independence, the southeastern tribes, especially the Cherokees and Creeks, adopted many of the elements of the white world. This meant abandoning the old ways— the traditions and customs that the whites frowned on and considered pagan and offensive. Many of the prosperous mixed-bloods accepted the whites' religion and lifestyle. They dressed like whites, ate the same type of food, started a plantation culture that included the keeping of black slaves to work the fields. Part of the rationale was tribal survival, with the hope that the whites would leave them alone if they became more like them. In the long run none of it mattered. Jackson and his troops eventually moved the tribes westward, sometimes at the point of bayonets down several "Trails of Tears" to Indian Territory, present-day Oklahoma, where they were referred to as the "Five Civilized Tribes," a pejorative term still used by many.[7]

"Andrew Jackson has been saddled with a considerable portion of the blame for this monstrous deed," Robert V. Remini, one of Jackson's biographers, wrote of the Removal Act.

> He makes an easy mark. But the criticism is unfair if it distorts
> the role he actually played. His objective was not the destruction
> of Indian life and culture. Quite the contrary. He believed the

removal was the Indian's only salvation against certain extinction.
. . . Yet he practiced a subtle kind of coercion. He told the tribes
he would abandon them to the mercy of the states if they did
not agree to migrate west.[8]

Jackson's own words serve as the best evidence of how he felt about
Indian people and their tribal lands. In a message delivered to Congress
in late 1830, several months after the Removal Act became the law of the
land, Jackson spoke of his hope that relocation to a distant land would
help the tribes "cast off their savage habits and become an interesting,
civilized and Christian community."[9] He went on to say:

> Toward the aborigines of the country no one can indulge a more
> friendly feeling than myself, or would go further in attempting
> to reclaim them from their wandering habits and make them a
> happy, prosperous people. . . . To save him from this alternative,
> or perhaps utter annihilation, the General Government kindly
> offers him a new home, and proposes to pay the whole expense
> of his removal and settlement. . . . May we not hope, therefore,
> that all good citizens, and none more zealously than those
> who think the Indians oppressed by subjection to the laws of
> the States, will unite in attempting to open the eyes of those
> children of the forest to their true condition, and by a speedy
> removal to relieve them from all the evils, real or imaginary,
> present or prospective, with which they may be supposed to be
> threatened.[10]

Although some historians tried to present a balanced picture of Jackson's role in Indian Removal, it is clear that Jackson had no real concern
whatsoever for the Indians—"the children of the forest"—whose lives
he disrupted. To this day there remain traditional Cherokee and Creek
people in Oklahoma who refuse to handle or even touch twenty-dollar
bills, which since 1929 have been imprinted with the image of Andrew
Jackson. These Indian people find commemorating Jackson's presidency

on legal tender an insult to the memory of ancestors who died along "the trail where they cried." Some equate having Jackson's picture on the money to printing Adolf Hitler's face on the bills. Through the years, there have been petitions calling for the U.S. Treasury Department to remove Jackson from the twenty-dollar bill. One of the candidates suggested as a suitable replacement is John Ross, the much-revered chief who led the Cherokee Nation during the horrors of Indian removal.[11]

David Crockett, however, is still remembered by many Indian people in Oklahoma as one of the few white men in government who had the courage to stand up to Jackson and vote against his Indian Removal Act.[12] Crockett may not have been the most vociferous opponent of Jackson's removal legislation, but he was the lone member of the entire Tennessee congressional delegation to vote against the bill on May 24, 1830, when it passed by the narrow margin of 102 to 97.[13] Cherokee Chief John Ross wrote Crockett a letter of thanks for his courageous stance. It was a brave act and, some have said, a politically naive vote. Crockett stood his ground against all of his colleagues, his president, and, as he well knew at the time, the vast majority of the citizens he represented. It took little time for the news to reach voters in West Tennessee that the man they had put in office, primarily to help turn old tribal land into farms for squatters and settlers, had betrayed them.

In the final pages of his 1834 autobiography, Crockett wrote about casting his vote against Indian Removal, which he described as an "infamous" measure. "I opposed it from the purest motives in the world," wrote Crockett.

> Several of my colleagues got around me, and told me how well they loved me, and that I was ruining myself. They said this was a favourite measure of the president, and I ought to go for it. I told them I believed it was a wicked, unjust measure, and that I should go against it, let the cost to myself be what it might; that I was willing to go with General Jackson in every thing that I believed was honest and right; but further from this, I wouldn't go for him, or any other man in the whole creation;

that I would sooner be honestly and politically d—nd, than hypocritically immortalized. . . . I voted against this Indian bill, and my conscience yet tells me that I gave a good honest vote, and one that I believe will not make me ashamed in the day of judgment.[14]

Despite Crockett's explanation, some historians have taken exception with this account. They claim that, while Crockett may have had some empathy for the Indians and their plight, his opposition to the legislation was mostly driven by his growing relationship with the eastern Whigs and his mounting hatred of Jackson.

"Some have cast doubts as to the sincerity of David's efforts on behalf of native Americans citing his eagerness to fight in the Creek War in 1813," points out historian Joe Swann. "But when one reads the Creek War section of the *Narrative* it is not difficult to see that David saw the insanity of war and the cruelty of men charged with its prosecution. He knew his stand was contrary to the feelings of his constituents back home but David was very bull-headed and felt he was morally right."[15]

Other historians, including James Atkins Shackford, contended that Crockett never delivered a speech protesting the Indian Removal Act during debate on the floor of Congress. Whether or not Crockett actually delivered the speech, a report was published in 1830 showing that his prepared remarks about the measure were entered in the records of the House of Representatives, some five days before passage of the bill.[16] This document, written in third person, stressed that Crockett "would never let party govern him in a question of this great consequence." It goes on to explain that Crockett had "many objections to the bill—some of them of a very serious character. One was, that he did not like to put half a million of money into the hands of the Executive, to be used in a manner which nobody could foresee, and which Congress was not to control. Another objection was, he did not wish to depart from the role which had been observed towards the Indian nations from the foundation of the government. He considered the present application as the last alternative for these poor remnants of a once powerful people. Their only chance of aid was at the hands of Congress. Should its members turn a deaf ear to their cries, misery must be their fate. That was his candid opinion."[17]

Crockett also said that he considered the removal measure "oppression with a vengeance," and he found that intolerable. His speech against the Indian Removal Act also was published in the *Jackson Gazette* twice in June 1830. In February 1831, he issued a sixteen-page letter to the voters in his congressional district in which he shared his views on several key issues of the day.[18] Included in the letter are several pointed complaints about the performance of President Jackson, such as "my heart bleeds when I reflect on his cruelty to the poor Indians. I never expected it of him."

By that time Crockett had long abandoned the Jackson ranks and his own congressional delegation. His stand against the Jackson and Polk forces on Indian Removal and the Tennessee vacant land issue would prove costly. Crockett must have seen the proverbial writing on the wall even before he returned home and launched his reelection campaign in the spring of 1831. The break with the popular Old Hickory did not play well on the western frontier of Tennessee, nor did all the time Crockett was spending with Yankee Whigs.

"I found the storm had raised against me sure enough," Crockett wrote of his 1831 homecoming between sessions of Congress, "and it was echoed from side to side, and from end to end in my district, that I had turned against Jackson. This was considered the unpardonable sin. I was hunted down like a wild varment [*sic*], and in this hunt every little newspaper in the district, and every little pin-hook lawyer was engaged. Indeed, they were ready to print any and every thing that the ingenuity of man could invent against me."[19]

Crockett's enemies were even more determined to see his defeat. His opponent, handpicked by Jackson and the Democratic leadership, was William Fitzgerald, a thirty-four-year-old lawyer and judge from Dresden, the seat of Weakley County, and a loyal and prominent Jacksonian. From the start of the campaign, it was apparent that Crockett faced not only Fitzgerald but also the entire Jackson machine, including Martin Van Buren, a former U.S. senator and governor of New York who became Jackson's secretary of state and then replaced John C. Calhoun as vice president in Jackson's second term of office from 1833 to 1837. Crockett had always looked at Van Buren with a jaundiced eye and usually called him "the little Red Fox," or "the Magician," two of the nicknames ascribed to the urbane and squat little man who also was an adept and clever political operator.[20] Crockett believed Van Buren manipulated Jackson and was mainly interested in advancing his own career and agenda. Even before his break with Jackson was complete, Crockett wrote, "I am still a Jackson man, but General Jackson is not; he has become a Van Buren man."[21]

The campaign of 1831 was ugly from start to finish. Jackson wanted Crockett out of office and said so many times. In an April 23, 1831, letter to his friend Samuel Jackson Hayes, the president wrote: "I trust, for the honor of the state, your Congressional District will not disgrace themselves longer by sending that profligate man Crockett back to Congress."[22]

With Jackson's backing and the support of Polk's political machine, Fitzgerald made great inroads into Crockett's base of voter support in the district. Editorial coverage seemed to favor Fitzgerald. The *Jackson Gazette*, at one time politically neutral, not only threw its support to Fitzgerald but also published many smear stories about Crockett filled with the recurring lurid accusations of his supposed rampant gambling and drinking escapades. In endorsing Fitzgerald, the newspaper first took a swipe at Crockett. "He can't 'whip his weight in wild cats,' nor 'leap the Mississippi,' nor 'mount a rainbow and slide off into eternity and back at pleasure' . . . but this we believe, that Mr. Fitzgerald will make a better legislator; that he will far excel Col. Crockett upon the floor of Congress, as the Col. does him in the character of a *mountebank*," the popular word at the time for a charlatan or trickster.

One of the Fitzgerald camp's favorite dirty tricks was to spread word of where Crockett was going to appear but not inform Crockett. Then, when he failed to show up, Fitzgerald or one of his backers would speak to the crowd and tell them that Crockett was afraid to appear.[23]

Finally, over the long summer of 1831, Crockett became so frustrated by the barrage of lies that he made a fateful mistake. He stopped relying on his good humor to win votes and instead allowed his anger to take over, putting out the word that if Fitzgerald made any more false charges he would receive a good country thrashing.[24] On a scorching July afternoon at a joint appearance in Paris, Tennessee, Fitzgerald was scheduled to speak before Crockett, who was present with a large number of his partisans. Fitzgerald was well aware of Crockett's threat, and when he rose to address the large crowd, he placed an object wrapped in a handkerchief on the table. Fitzgerald began his remarks by explaining that all the charges made against Crockett were true, and that he was going to repeat them despite Crockett's threat of violence. He began his stock stump speech, and when he reached the part where he heaped insults on his opponent, Crockett, as promised, rose from his place in the audience and began advancing on Fitzgerald. When Crockett was just a few feet from him, Fitzgerald reached down and pulled a pistol from the handkerchief, leveled it at Crockett's chest, and warned that if he took one more step forward it would be his last. Fitzgerald's action was so sudden and unexpected that a surprised Crockett stopped. He briefly hesitated and turned around and retreated into the crowd. Word of the incident at Paris became the chief topic of discussion throughout the district. It did more to damage Crockett's reputation than all the outlandish newspaper stories, chicanery, and other ploys combined.

It was hardly a surprise that Crockett was defeated in the August 1831 election. According to official returns, Fitzgerald received 8,534 votes to Crockett's 7,948. Despite Crockett winning the majority in seventeen of the eighteen counties of his district, Madison County voters—and the *Jackson Gazette*—put Fitzgerald over the top, with 1,214 votes to just 429 for Crockett. It was close enough for Crockett to contest it, but the 586 margin of votes held.[25]

Only a few days after his defeat, Crockett declared in a letter, "I would rather be beaton [*sic*] and be a man than be elected and be a little puppy dog."[26] Crockett's other consolation in defeat was the gift of time. He would be able to get out of debt, or at least try. He could hunt bears, see about family needs, and mend the broken political fences on the home front with the voters upset about his support of the Cherokees. And, most of all, there would be time to watch the Crockett legend expand.

—— **THIRTY** ——

LION OF THE WEST

AFTER SAILING INTO the harbor at Newport, Rhode Island, in May of 1831, Alexis de Tocqueville, the renowned French historian and political scientist, began his tour of the United States to both study the prison system and observe American democracy in action. During nine months of traveling from the East Coast to the Mississippi River, Tocqueville filled fourteen notebooks with his observations and interview notes from more than two hundred Americans he met along the way, and his recollections are particularly germane to this story.

"Europeans think a lot about the wild, open spaces of America, but the Americans themselves hardly give them a thought," Tocqueville wrote in *Democracy in America*. "The wonders of inanimate nature leave them cold, and, one may almost say, they do not see the marvelous forests surrounding them until they fall beneath the ax. The American people see themselves marching through wildernesses, drying up marshes, diverting rivers, peopling the wilds, and subduing nature."[1]

Tocqueville's visit came at a time of great upheaval and change in America's political system, with the birth of the Democratic Party under Jackson's leadership and the rise of the anti-Jackson Whigs. The young nobleman, from an aristocratic family that had managed to survive the French Revolution, marveled at "the constant agitation of parties," and the necessity for party candidates to "haunt the taverns, drink and argue with the mob" in order to attract votes. The lack of a hierarchical social order, so different from Europe, particularly impressed the more patrician Frenchman. When he entered the House of Representatives in Washington City, the effete Tocqueville was "struck by the vulgar demeanor of that great assembly." He observed, "One can often look in vain for a single famous man. Almost all the members are obscure people whose names form no picture in one's mind. They are mostly village lawyers, tradesmen, or even men of the lower classes. In a country where education is spread almost universally, it is said that the people's representatives do not always know how to write correctly."[2]

One of the more curious specimens Tocqueville encountered was one of those Americans marching across the wilds—Monsieur David Crockett of Tennessee. Unfortunately, Crockett was no longer in Congress at the time of Tocqueville's visit to that august body in Washington, or the Parisian would have beheld someone most memorable. It is not unlikely, given the fact that he never mentioned him, that the two men ever met, but once Tocqueville got to Tennessee, it is evident that he heard plenty about Crockett. Tocqueville's daily diary notes about the "gent from the cane" were both succinct and telling, and describe something that would never have happened in France. "Two years ago the inhabitants of this district of which Memphis is the capital sent to the House of Representatives in Congress an individual named David Crockett, who had received no education, could read only with difficulty, had no property, no fixed dwelling, but spent his time hunting, selling his game for a living, and spending his whole life in the woods."[3]

Tocqueville's description of Crockett was not far off target. In late 1831, following his loss to William Fitzgerald in the congressional election, Crockett's political and personal prospects appeared to be slim to none. After so many years of being absent and generally derelict in his duties as both husband and father, Crockett realized that his marriage was in a shambles and his relationship with much of his family strained.

Back in the spring of 1830, as he prepared to break from the Jacksonians, political obligations had prevented him from attending the marriage of his son William to Clorinda Boyett, followed just four days later by the nuptials of his eldest daughter, Margaret (Polly), to Wiley Flowers.[4] A growing circle of Whig cronies, especially Thomas Chilton, the Kentucky congressman who lived in Crockett's Washington boardinghouse, received more of his time and attention than Elizabeth and their children.

Earlier in 1831, Crockett had been sued yet again by one of his creditors. As a result of the legal action, he sold his house and twenty-five acres of property in Weakley County to his stepson, George Patton, who needed a place of his own after marrying Rhoda Ann McWhorter.[5] Crockett pocketed $100 in the transaction and then a few months later sold Patton a ten-year-old "Negro girl named Adaline" for $300, to pay off another past-due debt. Just below his signature on the deed and the bill of sale for the slave girl, Crockett wrote, "Be allways sure you are right then Go, ahead."[6] This marked the first-known written record of Crockett's famous credo, which would become closely linked with his name in the last years of his life and well beyond.

Soon after his election loss, Crockett was forced to "go ahead" and sell off the rest of his property to cover campaign debts and living expenses. He then leased a twenty-acre tract of heavily forested land adjoining the low grounds of the South Fork of the Obion. Before he signed the six-year contract, Crockett promised Dr. Calvin Jones, the wealthy physician who owned the Carroll County land, that he would make improvements by clearing for crop fields; building a cabin, smoke house, and stables; digging a well; and setting out some fruit trees.[7]

Elizabeth, Crockett's wife, had reached her limit. She could no longer tolerate Crockett's behavior—all the hunting, excessive drinking, and his chronic pattern of abandoning his family. The ebullient public person contradicted the reckless personal one. She packed up and moved with those children still at home to Gibson County to reside with Patton kinfolk. "She had endured enough of Crockett," wrote William C. Davis, in *Three Roads to the Alamo*. "Relations with David remained amicable but distant. Perhaps it seemed fitting. His constituents had abandoned him, and now so had his wife."[8]

Elizabeth briefly returned to Buncombe County, North Carolina, to visit other family members, including her father, Robert Patton, now a widower. When she returned to Tennessee, her father decided to go back with her and take up residence on some of the land he still owned there. Shortly after arriving, the prosperous yeoman farmer purchased another 1,200 acres and distributed the land among his five daughters and sons-in-law living in the area.[9] Described as "a sturdy Presbyterian" and a "fond and beneficent parent," Patton only lived in Tennessee for about a year; he died on November 11, 1832, and was buried on a bluff overlooking the Obion River.[10] The elder Patton maintained his fondness of Crockett, despite the conflict between his son-in-law and daughter. Crockett always addressed Patton as "Father," and it was no surprise that both Crockett and George Patton, a son of the deceased, were named as executors of Robert's last will and testament drafted just prior to his death.[11]

Throughout 1832, Crockett lived a solitary life at the cabin he built on the leased land, dabbled a bit in farming, and took to the canebrakes and thickets as often as possible, his hounds the uncomplaining companions his wife could no longer be. Occasionally visitors and family stopped for a visit, and he made a few forays out in the district and further just to stay connected to political friends and allies.

Guided solely by his natural instincts, Crockett had become, in the words of Shakespeare, the wise fool. From his failures, he learned not to fear the contempt and derision of others but to mock his enemies as well as himself. He recognized that, in many instances, the untutored could penetrate to more profound truths and insights than those burdened with learning and convention. Crockett embodied the Shakespearean truth, "The fool doth think he is wise, but the wise man knows himself to be a fool."[12]

Ironically, while Crockett contemplated his future and continued, almost single-handedly, to reduce the black bear population in West

Tennessee, his star was rising higher and higher back east. Tantalized by the many newspaper accounts, most of them outrageous and exaggerated tales planted by political opponents and seldom denied by Crockett, the press and the public, as if he had become a broadsheet celebrity, clamored for more. Crockett was clearly missed. His rapidly growing audience of fans and followers hungered for his return to the limelight of Jacksonian society. There was a steady buzz about Crockett from the plush Indian Queen Hotel in Washington City, where lobbyists treated lawmakers to lavish meals, to the phalanx of steamboats flanking the docks on the tawny Mississippi at St. Louis.

One newspaper, lamenting Crockett's absence from Congress, labeled him "an object of universal notoriety" and went on to report that "to return to the capitol without having seen Col. Crockett, betrayed a total destitution of curiosity and a perfect insensibility to the Lions of the West."[13] Prior to the last election, a man in the galleries of Congress who had heard the Tennessean speak from the floor flatly stated, "Crockett was then the lion of Washington. I was fascinated with him." Others who knew Crockett believed, however, that perhaps "Sly Fox of the West" would have been a more appropriate moniker.

The American public had no knowledge of the private Crockett and his lifelong struggle to rise above his station and remain debt free. They saw only the Crockett that appealed to them—the new kind of American who embodied the most attractive qualities of the literary heroes created by James Fennimore Cooper and Sir Walter Scott.

Crockett's growing fame was further demonstrated on April 25, 1831, when a farce in two acts, written by James Kirke Paulding and entitled *The Lion of the West, or a Trip to Washington*, opened at the Park Theater in New York, the largest city in the nation and America's theatrical capital.[14] Within moments of the opening-night performance, it became apparent that the drama's peculiar hero, Colonel Nimrod Wildfire—decked out in buckskin clothes, deerskin shoes, and an outlandish wildcat-skin hat—was none other than David Crockett, the original gentleman from the cane.

"Colonel Wildfire . . . [is] an extremely racy representation of Western blood, a perfect non-pareil, half steamboat, half alligator, and etc.," read an early newspaper review.

> [He] possesses many original traits which never before have appeared on stage. The amusing extravagances and strange features of character which have grown up in the western states are perhaps unique in the world itself. . . . Of the play itself . . . we cannot speak too highly of it. Possessing all of the peculiar points, wit, sarcasm and brilliancy of Paulding, it shows him in a quite pleasing light—that of a successful delineator of native manners and indigenous character. There are materials enough in this wide country to construct a school of comedy peculiarly our own. Why not collect them? Mr. Paulding has set an example worthy of being followed up.[15]

A native of the state of New York, Paulding was a prolific and talented writer of mainly satirical plays and novels. His confidant, early collaborator, and brother-in-law was Washington Irving, another highly acclaimed early American writer and the author of such enduring tales as "Rip Van Winkle" and "The Legend of Sleepy Hollow."[16] Both men were associated with the Knickerbockers, a group of authors who, by 1832, ruled the literary community in New York City. Included in their ranks were James Fenimore Cooper, Fitz-Greene Halleck, and William Cullen Bryant. Another well-known Knickerbocker, and a possible source of Paulding's interest in Crockett as a lead character, was Gulian Crommelin Verplanck. He was the New York congressman who had written a letter of support for Crockett in the wake of trumped-up stories about his behavior at a dinner with President John Quincy Adams, who by 1831 had been elected to Congress.[17]

Paulding had written *The Lion of the West* in 1830 for a competition sponsored by James Henry Hackett, a noted actor who put up a cash prize for a new and original American comedy. Hackett, considered one of the finest Shakespearean comedians of his day, coveted a leading role for himself and was delighted when he learned that his friend Paulding was gathering material based on the experiences of frontiersmen. Paulding wrote the portrait painter John Wesley Jarvis, asking him for some "sketches, short stories, and incidents of Kentucky or Tennessee manners, and especially some of their peculiar phrases and comparisons." He also suggested that Jarvis "add or *invent*, a few ludicrous Scenes of Col. Crockett at Washington."[18]

Not surprisingly, Paulding's play was the one Hackett selected for production. Months before *Lion* premiered, word got out that Hackett's portrayal of Nimrod (a synonym for hunter) Wildfire was a caricature of Crockett loosely based on episodes from his colorful life.[19] Paulding and Hackett, most likely fearful of legal action, emphatically denied any connection between Wildfire and Crockett. On December 15, 1830, Crockett himself received a note from Paulding reassuring him that there was absolutely no intentional use of Crockett's image and life experiences in the comedy. At first Crockett accepted Paulding's denial as the truth. "I thank you . . . for your civility in assuring me that you had no reference to my peculiarities," Crockett wrote to Paulding on December 22. "The frankness of your letter induces me to say a declaration from you to that effect was not necessary to convince me that you were incapable of wounding the feelings of a strainger [*sic*] and unlettered man who had never injured you."[20]

However, when the play opened in New York in late 1831and audiences saw Hackett in full frontier regalia and heard him utter his first words, the Crockett influence was unmistakable. "My name is Nimrod Wildfire—half horse, half alligator and a touch of the airthquake—that's got the prettiest sister, fastest horse, and ugliest dog in the District, and can out-run, outjump, throw down, drag out, and whip any man in all Kaintuck."[21]

Throughout the drama Wildfire spouted a stream of backwoods witticisms, such as "You might as well try to scull a potash kettle up the falls of Niagara with a crowbar for an oar," or the insensitive boast that he was "primed for anything from a possum hunt to a nigger funeral," reflecting the racist language of the day. Newspaper articles about Crockett may have inspired much of the play's language, but many of the frontier epithets were straight from the pen of Paulding and not from the tongue of Crockett. Some of the news stories were of dubious origin, such as one published in late 1828 that called Crockett "one of the most eccentric and amusing members of Congress," and said that his family coat of arms included a rifle, a butcher's knife, and a tomahawk.[22] The article went on to tell of Crockett's boast that he could whip any man in the House of Representatives and also "could wade the Mississippi, carry a steamboat on his back and whip his weight in wild cats."

What is certain is that the national mythologizing of Crockett had already begun, even in his lifetime, making it difficult to separate what Crockett actually said from what others made up about him. The Paulding play was replete with backwoods lingo and bastardized words that, over time, several sources erroneously attributed to Crockett. He did, in fact, use much of the slang, idioms, and sayings of the time in his daily lexicon and various writings, but he did not coin the more colorful words uttered by Nimrod Wildfire, such as *catawampus*, *jubus*, *tetotaciously exflunctified*, *gullywhumping*, *flutterbation*, and the popular *ripsnorter*, which probably originated in 1840, four years after Crockett's death.[23] But it was *sockdolager*, a word that meant the ultimate or decisive, as in a knockout punch, that became most associated with Crockett as a result of its usage in the Paulding play. While preparing for a duel, Wildfire in speaking of his opponent brags, "He'll come off as badly as a feller I once hit with a sledge hammer lick over the head—a real sogdolloger [*sic*]. He disappeared altogether; all they could ever find of him was a little grease spot in one corner."

Interestingly, the term sockdolager was widely used for many years, including by Mark Twain, who, as a young Samuel Clemens, was taken with frontier stories. Twain was influenced by reading Crockett's 1834 autobiography as well as the fictionalized accounts of the buckskin hero in the many Crockett almanacs that appeared for more than twenty years after his death. In fact, sockdolager actually appears in Twain's classic work *The Adventures of Huckleberry Finn*.

Like Twain, Abraham Lincoln was yet another historical figure who fell under the spell of the mythical Crockett, incorporating his style of self-effacing humor into the fabric of his political life. Lincoln admired Crockett, a man, like himself, who grew up in poverty and became a national icon. Both Crockett and Lincoln also had gregarious personalities and a penchant for telling humorous stories, though Lincoln had a brooding, introspective side that Crockett, a more unselfconscious sort, could not have appreciated. Ironically, the humorous word sockdolager figured in one of the most tragic moments in American history. On April 14, 1865, during a performance of *Our American Cousin* at Ford's Theatre, in Washington, D.C., John Wilkes Booth was poised outside the box where Lincoln, his wife, and their guests sat watching the action below. A veteran thespian who knew the play well, Booth waited for the line to be spoken that always got the most laughs: "Well, I guess I know enough to turn you inside out, old gal—you sockdologizing old man-trap."[24] As the audience roared in delight, Booth stepped inside the box and fired his small pistol.

Thirty-two years before the first presidential assassination, when Lincoln was a young Whig politician, Crockett had his own memorable moment in another Washington, D.C., theater. On the evening of December 21, 1833, at a benefit performance of *The Lion of the West* staged at the Washington Theater, Crockett, who had returned to the capital, was escorted to a special reserved seat in the front row, stage center.[25] The capacity audience cheered and hollered in recognition. Then the curtain slowly rose and James Hackett sprang onto the stage, dressed in the leather leggings and wildcat-skin hat of Colonel Nimrod Wildfire. He walked to the edge of the stage and ceremoniously bowed to the smiling Crockett, who, in turn, rose from his seat and returned the bow to Hackett. The crowd responded with a volley of thunderous applause. All the while, the actor portraying the legend and the real man continued to bow and smile.

THIRTY-ONE

BEAR-BIT LION

T HE *LION OF THE WEST* became the inspiration for and the cornerstone of future writings about Crockett. This satirical spoof sparked a seemingly endless series of unauthorized biographies and ghostwritten books attributed to him.

In his role as Nimrod Wildfire, James Hackett enjoyed great success and garnered brilliant reviews and the praise of adoring audiences. Noted a New York critic in late 1831, "At the fall of the curtain there was one universal and continuous call kept up for Mr. Hackett, who promptly answered it [and] returned thanks for 'the indulgence the public had uniformly extended, not only to himself in the [im]personation, but to the inexperienced attempts of our native dramatists in drawing characters indigenous to this country.' "[1] Hackett thus came to absorb much of the heartfelt attention that the defeated Crockett now enjoyed.

In 1833 Hackett took the revised show—retitled *A Kentuckian's Trip to New York in 1815*—to London's fashionable West End, introducing the indomitable Nimrod Wildfire to audiences at the Royal Opera House in Covent Garden. Crockett's reputation had reached across "the big pond," as Wildfire called the Atlantic Ocean, creating an image of the American West that would spread throughout the continent.[2] Even when British critics unfamiliar with American frontier culture failed to understand the simple storyline and audiences were puzzled by the American dialect, Hackett consistently won praise for his portrayal of the lead character's tough sensibility that the refined British specifically associated with their former colony. Hackett also was the party most responsible for establishing the coonskin cap as Crockett's headgear. As Crockett scholar Paul Hutton pointed out: "No authentic contemporary portrait or written account identifies such a crown upon the 'King of the Wild Frontier's' regal head before 1835. The first drawing of Crockett in a fur cap (it is a wildcat skin) graces the cover of *Davy Crockett's 1837 Almanack*, and it is a copy of a drawing of Hackett as Nimrod Wildfire that was used to publicize the play."[3]

Paulding continued to churn out more literary works, reaching the zenith of his fame as a popular American writer in the 1830s. Besides his writing, Paulding also held various governmental positions and went on to serve as the secretary of the navy under President Martin Van Buren from 1838 to 1841.[4] With a change in administration, Paulding, though effectively forgotten today, returned to his literary pursuits at his farm near Hyde Park, New York, where he died in 1860, leaving behind a bounty of writing including *The Lion of the West*, the most-often performed play on the American stage before a dramatization of *Uncle Tom's Cabin* premiered in 1852.

By the time Crockett finally saw the play and had his memorable face-to-face session with Wildfire in December 1833, his life had rebounded somewhat. He remained estranged from Elizabeth and constantly scrambled for money, but the notoriety generated about him from the play continued to sweep the country. As one writer, mindful of Crockett's favorite activity, put it, "he surfaced refreshed but famished, like a bear rousing from hibernation."[5] While Crockett accepted the realities of misfortune, violence, and even death, he focused on the present and embraced the collection of possibilities that life offered. As a variation of a later adage put it: "Some days you eat the bar, some days the bar eats you."[6] It was a fatalistic view that Crockett would have appreciated.

At the beginning of 1833, a book sparked in part by the Paulding drama and entitled *The Life and Adventures of Colonel David Crockett of West Tennessee* was published in Cincinnati. Later in the year, after a few changes were made in the text, the book was reissued in New York and London as the *Sketches and Eccentricities of Colonel David Crockett of West Tennessee*. For many years the anonymous author was reputed to be a Virginia novelist, James Strange French. Although French always denied writing the book, its authorship was ascribed to him based on the opinion of the illustrious Edgar Allan Poe, who, in his early literary career, was best known as a scathing critic rather than as a writer of fiction and poetry.[7] As critic for the *Southern Literary Messenger* in 1836, three years after *Sketches* appeared, Poe wrote a piece about French's recently published two-volume novel, *Elkswatawa; or, The Prophet of the West*. Featured in the novel was the "Crockettrean character," Poe wrote, named "Earthquake," an obvious allusion to the "land of the shakes." Poe mentioned in passing that French also had written the *Sketches* book about Crockett.

"This novel [*Elkswatawa*] is written by Mr. James S. French of Jerusalem, Virginia—the author, we believe of 'Eccentricities of David Crockett,' a book of which we know nothing beyond the fact of its publication."[8] From that point forward, French was most often cited as the author of *Sketches*. In 1956, however, over a century later, James Shackford's Crockett biography made the claim that, although French had the copyright for *Sketches* and received royalties, he did not write the book. According to Shackford, the author was Matthew St. Clair Clarke, a staunch Whig who—due to his political affiliation—had lost his post as clerk of the House of Representatives under Jackson.[9]

"If Clarke was the author, why did he copyright the book in the name of another?" That was Shackford's rhetorical question. "The answer is evident," he wrote. "The volume was composed as part of an effort to re-elect David Crockett to Congress as an anti-Jacksonian and supporter of the United States Bank, and to increase his usefulness through a multiplication of his fame."[10]

Clarke knew Crockett from his first days in Congress, and the two became friends. Like most others, Clarke was known to enjoy listening to Crockett's yarns about hunting and life in the backwoods. The two men traveled together at various times when Crockett visited back east, and Clarke may have visited Crockett in west Tennessee. "The country which it falls my lot most particularly to describe, is the western district of Tennessee; and of that, to me, that most interesting spot, was Col. Crockett's residence," the author writes in the introduction to *Sketches*. "There, far retired from the bustle of the world, he lives, and chews, for amusement, the cud of his political life. He has settled himself over the grave of an earthquake, which often reminds him of the circumstance by moving itself as if tired of confinement. The wild face of the country—the wide chasms—the new formed lakes, together with its great loneliness, render it interesting in the extreme to the traveler."[11]

The book was immensely popular and sold well, but anyone who read it and had also seen the stage drama *Lion of the West* would have recognized the curious similarity in language and choice of story content. In creating dialogue for the book, lines from the play were directly pirated from Nimrod Wildfire and put into Crockett's mouth, as if now the stage creation provided the source for biography. In many instances the phrasing was altered but the intent retained. For example, in *Lion of the West*, Wildfire boasts: "I'm half horse, half alligator, a touch of the airth-quake, with a sprinklin' of the steamboat! If I an't I wish I might be shot! Heigh! Wake snakes, June bugs are coming." The book version read: "I am that same David Crockett, fresh from the backwoods, half-horse, half-alligator, a little touched with the snapping turtle; can wade the Mississippi, leap the Ohio, ride upon a streak of lightning, and slip without a scratch down a honey locust; can whip my weight in wild cats,—and if any gentleman pleases, for a ten dollar bill, he may throw in a panther,—hug a bear too close for comfort, and eat any man opposed to Jackson."[12]

In general the book is overwritten, in stylized prose filled with clichés and odd characterizations. Several chapters consist of folk tales written in a thick Dutch accent, a popular form of storytelling on the frontier. There is little of substance about Crockett as a man but mostly a series of tales and anecdotes that bolstered, as it did in the later style of action-hero comics, the image of a mythical frontier character. The writing played to the masses of disenfranchised whites who craved stories about feats of great strength, stalking wild beasts, and killing Indians. "Davy Crockett was famous for tales of his hunting, fighting, and joking," one writer pointed out. "No one bothered to invent similar high-flown stories about Congressman Crockett."[13]

While appealing to the masses, the book met a mixed reception elsewhere, particularly among the highbrow classes who considered Crockett nothing more than a bumptious court jester and buffoon. Typical of these detractors was the critique of *Sketches* that appeared in the *New England* magazine:

> The gentleman who is the subject of these Sketches, was not much known beyond the circle of his neighbors and fellow-hunters, till, a few years ago, when, by one of those strange and erratic concurrences of circumstances, which sometimes happen in the political system, he was found in one of the seats of the House of Representatives of the United States. . . . The writer of these Sketches has, creditably to himself, withheld his name, and, in that respect, we cannot but think he was more careful of his own reputation than he has been of that of his illustrious subject, or that of the multitude of counselors of which the subject is so useful and ornamental a member.[14]

Although Crockett claimed to have been irate and embarrassed by an unauthorized biography, he recognized the tremendous impact the book had in expanding his name recognition with the public, elevating his stature on the national political scene—albeit not always in the most flattering manner. Still, it deeply bothered Crockett, given his impecunious circumstances, that he never enjoyed any financial reward from the book and that not one cent of royalties was offered to him. Crockett determined that his pocket and reputation would be better off if he were to pen his own book. After all, there was no one was more qualified to tell the story of a man's life than the man who lived it. Before any book could be written, however, other business more immediate had to be addressed.

Out in the canebrakes Crockett continued to hear the siren call of Washington City. An election for the Twenty-third Congress loomed in August 1833, and Crockett had a hankering to get back his seat from William Fitzgerald. By then he took nothing for granted when it came to politics. He fully understood that the reelection of Andrew Jackson to a second term in 1832 would make it that much more difficult to unseat the incumbent Fitzgerald. Crockett would need all the help his friends in the Whig Party could muster on his behalf.

During the campaign, he made an effort to keep his sense of humor and build rapport with the voters, but without coming off as the buffoon his critics and enemies portrayed him to be. The Jacksonian camp tried to help Fitzgerald by gerrymandering his congressional district in such a way that it would work against Crockett. They also published a vitriolic tract, *The Book of Chronicles*, filled with attacks on Crockett and his political motives written in biblical language. The author of the *Chronicles* was Adam R. Huntsman, a Tennessee attorney and rising star in Jackson's fledgling Democratic Party, who had lost a leg in the Creek Indian War. It was replaced by a wooden leg.[15]

"I had Mr. Fitzgerald, it is true, for my open competitor," Crockett wrote, "but he was helped along by all his little lawyers again, headed by old Black Hawk, as he is sometimes called (alias) Adam Huntsman, with all his talents for writing '*Chronicles*,' and such like foolish stuff. . . . But one good thing was, and I must record it, the papers in the district were now beginning to say 'fair play a little,' and they would publish on both sides of the question."[16]

The results of the election in August 1833 were close, but Crockett surprisingly managed a victory. "The contest was a warm one, and the battle well-fought," explained Crockett, "but I gained the day, and the Jackson horse was left a little behind."[17] In fact, the Jacksonian machine was left a total of 173 votes behind, according to official election returns, with Fitzgerald polling 3,812 votes to Crockett's 3,985.

Crockett's victory, given his popular celebrity, got the attention of the nation, particularly the leaders of the Whig Party. Crockett was now considered electable and, with the exception of Andrew Jackson, probably the most popular man in Tennessee, if not the nation. The influential *Niles' Weekly Register*, a pro-Whig national journal published in Baltimore, came out with a glowing tribute to Congressman Crockett. It read, in part:

> A great deal has been said in the newspapers concerning Col. Crockett, who has been again elected a member of congress from Tennessee. It was the misfortune of the colonel to have received no school education in his youth, and since to have had but little opportunity to retrieve that defect; but he is a man of a strong mind, and of great goodness of heart. The manner of his remarks are so peculiar that they excite much attention, and are repeated because of their originality; but there is a soundness, or point, in some of them which shows the exercise of a well disciplined judgment—and we think it not easy for an unprejudiced man to communicate with the colonel without feeling that he is honest.[18]

Out in west Tennessee, Crockett readied himself for a triumphal return to the nation's capital. As he had done in the past when facing debt, he again treated human beings like the livestock he took to market. In his capacity as the executor of the Robert Patton estate, it is recorded that he sold an eighteen-year-old slave, Sofia, to his friend Lindsey Tinkle for $525. He also sold two slave boys, Aldolphus and Samuel, to his stepson George Patton for $480 and $372, respectively, as well as a husband and wife, Daniel and Delila, together for $660.[19] The infusion of cash paid off some bills and also provided Crockett with some cash until his congressional pay resumed.

His bag packed and the hounds entrusted to his sons, Crockett once more headed east to Washington City, arriving at Mrs. Ball's Boarding House well before the December 2 opening of Congress. Crockett had new people to meet, old friends to greet, and some scores to settle. He also had a book that needed to be written.

THIRTY-TWO

GO AHEAD

WITH HIS CONFIDENCE RESTORED, his seat in Congress reclaimed, Crockett was more than ready to leave behind the makeshift cabin, where he lived alone on a piece of hardscrabble leased land, and join his Whig allies while ensconced at Mary Ball's comfortable boardinghouse on Pennsylvania Avenue. His two-year absence from Washington City had made him grow fonder of the drama and excitement of the national political scene; the capital even in these early days pulsed with an energy not to be found in Tennessee and addictive to those who experienced it.

True to the familiar motto customarily ascribed to him—"Be always sure you are right, then go ahead"—Crockett behaved, in effect, like a lead hound plunging into the cane. When the Twenty-third Congress convened, on December 2, 1833, Crockett was ready for action. He openly condemned Jackson, whom the Whigs now referred to as "King Andrew the First," for his assault on the Bank of the United States and opposition to renewal of the bank's charter. Jackson had been wary of banks since he was a young man in the 1790s and had lost a sizable amount of money in a bank investment. He believed the Second Bank of the United States, chartered in 1816 just five years after the First

Bank of the United States lost its charter, was nothing but a monopoly and that its president, Nicholas Biddle, was guilty of corrupt lending practices. While Congress was out of session, Jackson not only vetoed the bank charter but also removed all government funds and deposited them in privately owned state financial institutions that became known as "pet banks." Crockett favored keeping the government's money in the Second United States Bank, and believed that Jackson was acting out of personal spite. A loan that Crockett had received in the past had been forgiven by Biddle, an action that endeared him and the institution to Crockett.[1] Besides joining the other lawmakers battling Jackson on the banking issue, Crockett also introduced proposals concerning his Tennessee Land Bill. Apparently he labored under the false belief that all of his newfound notoriety would somehow ensure passage of the land legislation that had previously eluded him. "My land Bill is among the first Bills reported to the house and I have but little doubt of its passage during the present Session,"[2] Crockett boasted in a letter to one of his constituents. It would never come to pass.

Another dream, however, would soon be realized. By December 1833, Crockett was hard at work on his autobiography. At last he would have a book of his own done that would clear up some of the misconceptions caused by the earlier works about his life. It also would bring in money and earn him increased recognition among the press and the public. After watching others profit from his life and adventures, Crockett figured that—as one of his many chroniclers later put it—"he might as well taste the pie he had helped bake."[3]

To accomplish this daunting task, Crockett knew he would need a great deal of help. He turned to his friend Thomas Chilton, the Kentucky lawyer who also had first entered the House of Representatives in 1827. Like Crockett, Chilton had served two terms, was voted out of office, and had just been reelected as an Anti-Jacksonian.[4] Chilton and Crockett not only shared a room at the boardinghouse but they also "sang out of the same hymnal" when it came to their political views, particularly a mutual disillusionment with Jackson and an extreme dislike of his heir apparent, Vice President Martin Van Buren, a native of Kinderhook, New York, who grew up speaking Dutch as his first language. Over the years, Chilton had helped Crockett write legislative documents, speeches, and circular letters for constituents, so he seemed the obvious choice for collaborator on the autobiography.

"I am ingaged [*sic*] in writing a history of my life and I have Completed one hundred and ten pages and I have Mr. Chlton [*sic*] to correct it as I write it,"[5] Crockett wrote to his son John Wesley, on January 10, 1834. He also explained that publishing houses in New York and Philadelphia had expressed some interest in the book and that he expected it would "contain about two hundred pages and will fully meet all expectations." Crockett went on to tell John Wesley that he would likely tour the eastern states to promote and sell the book once it was published. "I intend never to go home until I am able to pay all my debts and I think I have a good prospect at present and I will do the best I can," Crockett wrote.

In much of his correspondence to friends, Crockett urged them to tell their local booksellers about the autobiography, which, he promised, would be "just like myself, a plain and singular production." This mission statement was repeated in the book itself: "I want the world to understand my true history, and how I worked along to rise from a canebrake to my present station in life."[6]

The writing went relatively fast, taking just about two months, with Crockett dictating his thoughts and memories to Chilton in the comfort of their room. In developing the text, the two turned to a variety of sources for inspiration and as models to follow. One of these was *The Autobiography of Benjamin Franklin*, the traditional title given for the unfinished record of Franklin's life, which he wrote with considerable humor and wit in the final decades of his life, between 1771 and 1790.

First published in France in 1791, Franklin's work appeared two years later in an English edition. It was said to have been the first secular biography printed in the United States and served as the model for many more authors to follow. According to popular legend, a well-thumbed copy was among Crockett's possessions when he made his trek from Tennessee to the Mexican state of Texas in late 1835.[7]

Like Franklin, Crockett avoided discussing any of his serious fail-ings. Other similarities linked the two men, superficial and substantive, including the fact that both were known to wear fur caps—Franklin to delight and charm his many admirers in France, Crockett to prop up his colorful frontiersman image. Franklin portrayed himself as home-spun but shrewd, with plenty of horse sense. He also was one of the first American writers to make a case for the notion that a lack of for-mal education was actually beneficial. This was a game plan from which Crockett planned not to stray.

"Both were self-made men," Joe Reilly, of Drexel University, explained during a presentation about the two men in 2007.

> They volunteered for glory and fame. They had political and economic goals they chose to pursue. To establish and maintain their public image they manipulated the contemporary media by publishing an Autobiography. Ben Franklin published *Poor Richard's Almanac* for 25 years. He became wealthy from it. Davy Crockett was the supposed author of an almanac series for 20 years. He had no financial interest in them and never profited from it except for notoriety. He was an early example of others profiting from a celebrity.[8]

Another literary work that influenced Crockett was an English translation of Ovid's *Metamorphoses*, which had been published in 1774 in Ireland. The University of Tennessee's 2003 acquisition of this copy of the *Metamorphoses*—bearing an authenticated Crockett signature and with a complete provenance—provided some additional insight into both the historic and the mythical Crockett.[9]

One of the most influential works in the Western literary canon, this epic narrative poem in which Ovid tells of the creation and history of the world through the legends of the gods, and their transformation of humans into nonhuman forms, has inspired great writers from Chaucer to Shakespeare to Joyce. This particular copy of the Ovid classic came to the attention of the University of Tennessee in late March 2003, when

Aaron Purcell, a special collections archivist, randomly scanned eBay. com. The online listing that drew Purcell's attention provided a detailed provenance of the book—published by John Exshaw, the edition had been issued by a family of prominent printers and booksellers on Dame Street, in Dublin.[10] Along with other information about the book, the seller included a digital image from the endpages. When he examined it, Purcell was stunned. He could not believe what he saw on the computer screen—David Crockett's distinctive autograph, scrawled in ink.

"The online description had a very strong scan of Crockett's signature," according to Purcell, who quickly compared the computer version to archival documents signed by Crockett.[11] If, as Purcell thought, the autograph was genuine, he had "unearthed an almost too-good-to-be-true find: a book that had once belonged to Tennessee's backwoods hero, Davy Crockett."

After several weeks, the book finally arrived. Following careful examination, it was determined that the Crockett signature inside was authentic, making the book an invaluable addition not only to the rare book collection but to American history. The text of the accompanying affidavit from the seller, Erby Madrese Markham, a woman then in her nineties, revealed even more about the book and Crockett. Markham explained that when Crockett gave the book to her great-uncle, Thomas Owen, a friend of Thomas Chilton, he advised, "If he could read this book he could whip any bear." Crockett and Chilton told Thomas that they read the book to get a better understanding of myths and fables as they prepared to write the *Narrative*.

"The news that Special Collections had acquired a book owned by Davy Crockett that carried his signature was truly a signal event," declared Crockett scholar Michael A. Lofaro in a university library publication. "Like many a frontiersman, Crockett was never renowned as a reader, and a book that he owned and signed at the rear as testimony to the fact that he had read it could lend true insight into the man and perhaps into the works that he himself authored or encouraged."[12] Lofaro added:

We are left with the tantalizing proposition that Crockett's reading of this compendium of myths may have had a significant impact on the evolution of the narratives that essentially define his legendary status through tall tales. While only further study can prove or disprove this hypothesis, it is also well to note that *Metamorphoses* does translate from the Latin as *transformations* and that the first line of Ovid's text reads "my intention is to tell of bodies changed to different forms."[13]

The book's importance to Crockett is significant, and it is important to realize that the work had been available since the mid-1700s, when lexicographer Nathan Bailey translated the original Latin text into English, primarily for use in school classrooms. This meant that Crockett—who certainly did not master Latin but, contrary to some accounts was not an illiterate backwoods bumpkin—could have read much of the book, including the main introduction, the story summaries, the various notes, and a final explanation of the history and mythology of each of the fables. Moreover, besides Crockett's signature on page 392, Thomas Owen, the man to whom the book was given, signed the same page, with the date 1832.

Another critical detail contained in the book's affidavit of provenance is the mention of Thomas Chilton, friend of both Crockett and Owen, the man who received the book from Crockett as a gift. Certainly much credit for the Crockett autobiography was due Tom Chilton, who had an ear for his friend's vast repertoire of stories laced with idioms and phrases. Chilton also proved quite helpful in negotiating a contract for the 211-page book, which was officially completed on January 28, 1834.[14]

On February 3, the manuscript was shipped to the publisher selected by Chilton and Crockett—E. L. Carey and A. Hart in Philadelphia, a then venerable house with a solid reputation for publishing such well-known authors as Henry Wadsworth Longfellow.[15] In the cover letter to the publisher, which was, like the manuscript, in Chilton's handwriting and dictated by Crockett, the coauthors cavalierly mentioned that they had no time to have the manuscript copied, so they shipped the only copy. "It has been hastily passed over for correction, and some small words may have been omitted," Crockett wrote. "If so you will supply them. It needs no corrections of *spelling* or *grammar*, as I make no literary pretensions."[16] The lone copy of the manuscript arrived safely in Philadelphia, and the publishers immediately distributed a broadside with the announcement:

> It may interest the friend of this genuine Son of the West to learn, that he has lately completed, with his own hand, a narrative of his life and adventures, and that the work will be shortly published by Messrs. Carey & Hart, of Philadelphia. The work bears this excellent and characteristic motto by the author:

> *I leave this rule for others, when I'm dead:*
> *Be always sure you're right—THEN GO AHEAD!*

Three weeks later, Crockett again wrote Carey and Hart, expressing how anxious he was to see bound books, and instructing the publisher to split the royalties between himself and Chilton, although he stressed that this arrangement had to remain confidential.[17] Only a month later, the results were in and everyone was pleased. The book, as they say, was a runaway success. The first editions of *A Narrative of the Life of David Crockett, of the State of Tennessee,* had sold out and the presses busily cranked out more. Within a few months the book went into a sixth printing, which, at fifty cents per copy wholesale, made Carey and Hart a profit and began to pay royalties to the two authors as well. Some sources estimated that at least 10,000 copies sold that first year, which computed to at least $2,000 for Crockett. While not a fortune, that sum would have at least whittled down some of his enormous personal debt. The book also was a great source of pride for Crockett, and he devoted much of his time to promoting it and urging others to buy as many copies as possible, no doubt appeasing his publisher.

Crockett's vivid and compelling descriptions of bear hunting and his account of his role in the Creek War are sometimes inaccurate or embellished. Yet, despite deviation from fact, much of the *Narrative* is supported by independent accounts. Ultimately, the book remains an important record of a time and place in American history when the fledgling nation was defining itself.

In the preface of the *Narrative* dated February 1, 1834, Crockett heaps much criticism on the author of *Sketches*. He also explains that in his book he has "endeavored to give the reader a plain, honest, homespun account of my state in life, and some few of the difficulties which have attended me along its journey, down to this time." Much like Crockett, the *Narrative* remains a paradox. It serves as a fairly reliable source, despite embellishments, for both the mythical and the authentic man. It also captures much of Crockett's personality, down-to-earth charm, and wit, while providing insights into the brutality of frontier life and the cutthroat world of politics. Embedded with backwoods idioms and seasoned with Crockett's own dialect, proverbs, and humorous misspellings, the *Narrative* endures as a historical and political document. It is also a genuine American work, in the tradition of the writings of Ben Franklin and Mark Twain, though perhaps not as literary. Most of all, the autobiography gives the reader the voice of David Crockett—loud, clear, and unforgettable.

Throughout the spring of 1834, adoring fans gathered around Crockett wherever he went. They wanted to shake his hand or get his autograph on the title page of his book or a scrap of paper. He was glad to accommodate them and made it a point to tell his well-wishers that his book was the only true and honest account of his life and times. In one copy presented for signing, he wrote, "I David Crockett of Tennessee do certify that this Book was written by my self and the only genuine history of my life that ever has been written."[18]

As proud as Crockett was of his best-selling autobiography, there were others who were equally pleased with the book's tremendous success. The leadership of the Whig Party had become thoroughly persuaded that they had found the ideal remedy needed to rid the nation of King Andrew Jackson. All that remained was for them to convince Crockett.

THIRTY-THREE

JUST A MATTER
OF TIME

B Y THE SPRING OF 1834, Crockett was a best-selling author, congressman, and raconteur extraordinaire. Despite a failed personal life, he seemed as content as he had ever been. He had reached what Renaissance writer Michel de Montaigne described as the precise age of retirement for warriors.[1]

Nonetheless, over the next two years he would participate in two journeys that were more than eventful and would forever alter his legacy. Before he left on his first trip, Crockett spent some time in Washington with his old Tennessee friend Sam Houston. Both men had been early protégés of Old Hickory, and they remained on amicable terms even though Houston was still loyal to Jackson.

Houston, the hero of Horseshoe Bend, had himself enjoyed some success in politics but had been out of the mainstream since the spring of 1829, when his eleven-week marriage to nineteen-year-old Eliza Allen proved unworkable and suddenly ended. The emotionally depleted Houston had then abruptly resigned as the governor of Tennessee.[2] He had journeyed across the Mississippi to Indian Territory, present-day Oklahoma, and lived with the Cherokees, who had, long before, adopted him and named him the Raven. There he married Diana Rogers, a mixed-blood Cherokee from a powerful family. Together they ran Wigwam Neosho, a trading post near Cantonment Gibson, the farthest military outpost in the United States, commonly called Fort Gibson but also known as the "Hell Hole of the Southwest."[3]

Soldiers posted there called it the "Graveyard of the Army," and spent their off-duty time playing cards, racing horses, drinking, and carousing with loose women. The Wigwam was located right on the Texas Road, and all kinds of travelers—rough traders, zealous missionaries, and passing settlers—stopped to have a look at the "late governor of Tennessee."[4] If they were lucky, he was sober, for Houston swilled great quantities of the Monongahela whiskey, cognac, and rum he illegally traded. Much to his embarrassment, Houston became known by a new name—Oo-tse-tee Ar-dee-tah-skee, Big Drunk. The name was not even Cherokee but Osage, an obvious way of denying the white man his Cherokee identity.[5]

During a brief period of sobriety in 1832, Houston returned to Washington and stayed at the Indian Queen Hotel while tending to some business on behalf of the Cherokee. While staying there, he took offense when he spied a less than flattering reference to him in a newspaper story. The comments were attributed to William Stanberry, an anti-Jacksonian representative from Ohio. Houston—described as being as "mad as a fighting cock"—vowed vengeance.[6] That came several days later, when a still fuming Houston happened upon Stanberry strolling along Pennsylvania Avenue. Houston accosted him with a hickory cane that had been cut from a tree at Jackson's Hermitage. He savagely beat the Ohio lawmaker, who managed to pull a pistol and press it against his attacker's chest; but the weapon misfired. This enraged Houston even more, and the caning intensified until a limp Stanberry was left bloody and bruised. News of the altercation quickly spread in the rough-and-tumble political maelstrom of the 1830s, and President Jackson quipped that he wished "there were a dozen Houstons to beat and cudgel the members of Congress."[7]

Houston, however, was soon arrested and brought before the House of Representatives, charged with contempt of Congress. Francis Scott Key, the esteemed composer of "The Star-Spangled Banner," was secured as his defense counsel, and Jackson footed the bill for a new suit of clothes for Houston, who usually wore colorful Cherokee dress or a rough buckskin coat.[8] After four days of speeches and debate—which included Houston quoting the Apostle Paul and Shakespeare—and despite James K. Polk's effort to defeat the measure, the House voted 106 to 89 for conviction. Houston received what was considered a slap-on-the-wrist reprimand and told to go and sin no more, at least when carrying a hickory stick. Junius Brutus Booth, the nation's foremost Shakespearean actor and the father of a trio of famous stage performers, including future presidential assassin John Wilkes Booth, was in the gallery when Houston spoke. Afterward, as applause thundered through the crowded chamber in support of Houston, the elder Booth rushed to his side and embraced him, exclaiming, "Houston, take my laurels!"[9]

Two years later, in April of 1834, when Crockett and Houston—over a few horns—met in Washington, they more than likely recalled the famous caning incident, as well as other incidents from their past. By 1834 Houston had ended his self-imposed exile among the Cherokees in Indian Territory and made his first sorties south of the border, in the Mexican state of Texas, where he had begun acquiring property for himself and some of Jackson's allies. He was back in Washington City on one of his periodic lobbying trips. Everywhere he went he spread the word of the disgruntled Anglo colonists in Mexico preparing to stage an uprising and wrest away *Tejas* and make it their own. During their time together, Houston told Crockett many of the stories about Texas that convinced him to go see it for himself eighteen months later.

"I do think within one year that it [Texas] will be a Sovereign State and acting in all things as such," Houston wrote on April 24, 1834, to James Prentiss, a New York land speculator who in 1830 founded one of the first of two land companies to speculate in Texas. "Within three years I think it will be separated from the Mexican Confederacy, and will remain so forever. . . . Texas, will be bound to look to herself, and to do for herself—this present year, must produce events, important to her future destiny. . . . The course that I may pursue, you must rely upon it, shall be for the true interests of Texas."[10]

Later that day, after Houston wrote to Prentiss about the untapped potential of Texas, he somehow managed to convince Crockett to come along with him to meet a young woman who was then apparently the toast of European capitals and the talk of Washington City. That afternoon the two Tennesseans paid a social call on Octavia Claudia Walton, the consummate Southern belle who, at the time, was considered the most vivacious and talented hostess in America. She was the paternal granddaughter of George Walton, a signer of the Declaration of Independence, and the daughter of George Walton Jr., a territorial governor of Florida.[11] Besides impeccable English, she spoke seven languages, including Seminole, and could sing, dance, and play the guitar and piano. As an adolescent she had charmed Lafayette with her French conversation, and after Edgar Allan Poe met her in Baltimore, he was inspired to write "Octavia," a poem of unrequited love.[12] During her travels around the globe she was received by Queen Victoria and Pope Pius IX, presented to Napoleon III, and dined with Robert and Elizabeth Browning. Some of her admirers included U.S. presidents and Edwin Booth, Washington Irving, and Henry Wadsworth Longfellow.[13]

If there was any truth to the story that Houston was attempting to court Walton, it is a loss that no record has been found of the visit between them. It is known that both men signed Octavia's autograph book, but Crockett did not relate any details in his autobiography, and if Houston had an amorous interest in the young woman he failed to forge any meaningful relationship. "I take great pleasure in recording my name in Miss Octavia Walton's Album as a testimonial of my respects for her Success through life and I hope she may enjoy the happiness and pleasures of the world agreeable to her expectation as all Ladys of her sterling worth, merits,"[14] Crockett scrawled in the book. Walton took the album with her in 1835, when her family relocated to Mobile, Alabama. George Walton Jr. later served as mayor of Mobile and his daughter met and married Dr. Henry S. Le Vert, an esteemed French physician.[15]

On April 25, following their visit with Octavia Walton, both Crockett and Houston took their leave of Washington City. After spending several days together, Crockett undoubtedly was impressed with Houston's prolific stories of the immense opportunity that waited in the vastness of Texas, where game was plentiful, the weather tolerable, and land could be had at little cost. All that remained was to wrest it away from the Mexicans, who had abolished slavery and placed many restrictions on the Anglo colonists who left the United States to become Mexican citizens. Later that day Houston struck for the Southwest, all the while, as he wrote to a friend, "making plans for the liberation of Texas."[16]

When Crockett left Washington, Congress was still in session. With Houston's seductive talk of Texas still resonating, Crockett faced the first of his back-to-back trips. He plunged into a three-week book promotional tour of several major eastern cities—Baltimore, Philadelphia, New York, Newport, Boston, Lowell, Providence, and Camden. During the whirlwind journey, he would travel for the first time on a sailing vessel and also enjoy his first ride on a train. He would be courted by political allies, both toasted and skewered by the press, talk himself hoarse at banquets, and wear out his hand signing autographs. From the start he had to have known that his tour would not go unnoticed by anyone, especially his political enemies. It was an error in judgment for which Crockett would pay dearly.

The Whigs carefully choreographed every stop along the way. Although the name "Whig" had been in use for at least two years, it was formally adopted as the official name of the party just eleven days before the start of Crockett's tour.[17] Whig leaders fully expected Crockett to attract even more disenfranchised voters to their ranks from the anti-Jackson forces, including former members of the National Republican Party who supported states' rights, Democrats who disagreed with Jackson over the Second Bank of the United States, northern industrialists, and southern planters.

Several months before the book tour, a delegation of Whigs from Mississippi had asked Crockett if he would consider running for president of the United States. They wished to offer his name as a candidate in 1836.[18] The Mississippians told Crockett they wanted a candidate as popular as Jackson in the west to offset the anticipated Democratic contender, Martin Van Buren of New York. They promised "to go the whole hog" for Crockett.

"You speak in the strongest possible terms of my fitness for the office of President of the United States, and a discharge of its duties," Crockett wrote in response to the Whig offer. "In this you may be right, as I suspect there is likely something in me that I have never yet found out. I don't hardly think, though, that it goes far enough for the Presidency, though I suppose I could do as the 'Government' has done—make up a whole raft of Cabinet Ministers, and get along after a manner. . . . It is the way with all great men, never to seek or decline office. If you think you can run me in as President, just go a-head. I had a little rather not; but you talk so pretty, that I cannot refuse. If I am elected, I shall just seize the old monster party by the horns, and sling him right slap into the deepest place in the great big Atlantic sea."[19]

Besides their mutual hatred of Jackson and his inner circle, the Whigs and Crockett shared few other interests. Still, the party leadership believed that the best alternative to Jackson and his probable successor, Martin Van Buren, was, indeed, Crockett. While he may have been guided by a different set of interests and philosophies than the mercantile-oriented Whig Party, Crockett also saw his Whig alliance as a chance to finally get his land bill passed in Congress. As others have said, Crockett may have been politically naive, but he was not a fool simply seeking public praise and acting as a Whig puppet. He wanted to sell books and make some money.

Everywhere Crockett went on the tour, there were large and adoring crowds of well-wishers. Many of these admirers were drawn by Crockett's colorful personality, others invited by local Whig Party officials. From the first night of the tour, spent at Barnum's Hotel in Baltimore, where a dinner was held in Crockett's honor, his official hosts were Whig friends. They made up a large part of the crowd when he delivered a speech beneath the imposing white marble statue of George Washington perched atop a 160-foot column at Mount Vernon Place. The same was true the next morning when a large delegation of Whigs escorted him to a waiting steamer that took him across Chesapeake Bay. Crockett then boarded a train to Delaware City and cruised up the Delaware River to Philadelphia. In the City of Brotherly Love, he drew larger crowds than even the two-headed kitten on display in a nearby hotel lobby, where the creature was predicted to "turn out a first rate mouser."[20]

The Whigs in Philadelphia definitely knew how to host a shindig worthy of a possible presidential contender. Just days before Crockett's arrival, the party sponsored what was called a "Jubilee in honor of the triumph of the Whigs of New York in defense of the Constitution and laws."[21] The gala event was held at Powelton, Col. John Hare Powel's country estate, situated on the west bank of the Schuylkill River near the city waterworks. It was a grand affair carefully planned by a committee of 100 faithful Whigs, who wisely arranged for a moratorium on tolls for the day at the bridges. Stores and factories were closed throughout the city, and as a result more than 60,000 celebrants showed up at the jubilee. Refreshment stands scattered all around the grounds were stocked with barrels of ale and cider, 500 hams, 1,000 beef tongues, and great servings of cheese and bread.[22]

Some Philadelphia Whigs were still nursing hangovers by the time Crockett arrived. He was met at the wharf by a throng and then whisked in a fancy carriage drawn by four bays to his quarters at the United States Hotel, undoubtedly chosen because it stood just across Chestnut Street from the United States Bank, which had earned the ire of Old Hickory and his followers.

"The Colonel is a 'wig,' " quipped a newspaper reporter, describing Crockett's arrival and his attendance at the popular minstrel show *Jim Crow*.

He has declared himself if so briefly and emphatically. . . . He was received and followed by a great number of enthusiastic admirers, who roared and shouted with much energy and fervor. When [Crockett] arrived at his hotel, the koon-killer in imitation of Henry Clay, came out upon the portico, bowed graciously, and smiled encouragingly upon the devoted multitude. He did not speak, but there was that in his eye which promised that the colonel would go ahead, and accordingly, after dispatching with western energy, several cups of tea, he proceeded without a sign of trepidation to the Walnut Street theatre to see *Jim Crow*. The house was full and peal after peal of applause greeted the city's guest. Jim Crow bowed to Crockett, and Crockett bowed to Crow.[23]

Jim Crow featured Thomas "Daddy" Rice, the most admired black-face comedian of the day. During his stay, Crockett also was given special tours of the U.S. Mint, the waterworks, the Navy Hospital, and the insane asylum. He gave his stock anti-Jackson speech at several stops, but one of his more rousing addresses was delivered at the newly opened Philadelphia Stock Exchange. A crowd of men in high top hats pushed and shoved for the best vantage point in order to see the famous frontiersman. Crockett rose to give his address and the roar diminished. When he spoke the entire assembly fell silent, each of them eager to hear every word.

"Seven months ago this was the most flourishing country in the world," Crockett told them.

Look at it now; and what do you see? You behold your commerce suspended your laborers wandering about for employment; your mechanics starving; and above all you see the best currency in the world deranged; And gentlemen, what is all this for? To gratify the will of a superannuated old man; a man whose popularity, like the lightning of heaven, blasts and withers all that comes within its influence! His leading object, in all the mischief he has done, has been to destroy the best monied institution on earth. But, gentlemen, will you submit to this experiment?[24]

The response was a great cry of "Never! Never!" Everyone present knew that Crockett was, of course, referring to President Jackson. "It is clear that he is fishing for the Presidency," one newspaper reported.

After meeting with his publishers about more print runs of the autobiography, Crockett departed Philadelphia for New Jersey and New York City, where his Whig handlers afforded him a royal welcome at the train station before escorting him to his plush accommodations at the American Hotel. Crockett's activities ranged from taking in a ribald burlesque show and delivering a speech at the New York Stock Exchange to dining with famed humorist and writer Seba Smith, the creator of Major Jack Downing, a fictional Crockett-like character. After a quick tour of Gotham's notorious Five Points slum—a Sixth Ward haven for Van Buren supporters and the most squalid neighborhood in the city— Crockett cracked that he "would rather risque [sic] myself in an Indian fight than venture among those creatures after night."[25]

Crockett was fascinated by what he witnessed at Peale's Museum of Curiosities and Freaks. He was mesmerized by the performance of a ventriloquist who also was an accomplished magician who made money disappear and then reappear—a feat that Crockett pointed out was best accomplished by Old Hickory.[26] All of the eclectic collection of exhibits—most of which eventually ended up in the hands of showman P. T. Barnum—were on display for Crockett's inspection. He had seen nothing like it ever before: copies of the works of Leonardo da Vinci and other old masters, collections of snuff boxes, medals, whales' teeth, and Seneca Indians in traditional regalia. One of the featured freaks was a five-year-old-girl who weighed 250 pounds, the kind of display of human curiosities typical of the era. The menagerie also included a rhinoceros, a two-headed calf with six legs, and an assortment of live rattlesnakes, tigers, and, much to Crockett's delight, bears.[27] The curators breathed collective sighs of relief when assured that their famous guest was not armed.

Helen Chapman, a seventeen-year-old girl, also at the museum that afternoon, described her impression of Crockett in a letter to her mother:

> I have seen a great man. No less of one than Col. Crockett. I . . .
> sat close by him so I had a good opportunity of observing his
> physiognomy. . . . he is wholly different from what I thought
> him. Tall in stature and large in frame, but quite thin, with black

hair combed straight over his forehead, parted from the middle and his shirt collar turned negligently back over his coat. He has rather an indolent and careless appearance and looks not like a "go ahead" man.[28]

The rest of the tour became a blur for Crockett. He was ferried across the Hudson River to show off his marksmanship in a shooting match in Jersey City, and then took a steamship to Boston, by way of Newport and Providence, where large crowds waved and cheered. At one of the dinners in Boston, attended by 100 young Whigs, he tasted champagne for the first time and commented that it was like "supping [sic] fog out of speaking trumpets," and a far cry from Tennessee sipping whiskey.[29] Crockett declined an invitation to visit nearby Cambridge, fearful that the folks at Harvard University might try to give him an honorary degree. At Lowell, Massachusetts, a burgeoning New England labor city where the Industrial Revolution had already begun, a textile tycoon showed Crockett through his busy mill and presented him with a handsome woolen suit.

At tour's end, he retraced his journey through Boston to New York and Philadelphia. The only hitch occurred during a brief speech stop in Camden, New Jersey, where a clever pickpocket victimized Crockett and some of his escorts. As usual, he was able to turn the incident into a political joke by speculating that the thief had to have been a Jackson man.[30]

On May 13, Crockett returned to Washington City and collapsed in his feather bed at the boardinghouse. The euphoria of his book tour was soon to wear off. All the adoring crowds and the compliments of self-serving Whigs had no currency in Congress. If anything, the attention was deemed inappropriate, with jealousy and political apprehension the underlying factors.

THIRTY-FOUR

GONE TO TEXAS

W HILE ON THE BOOK TOUR, as well as during his tenure in Congress, Crockett commissioned portrait artists to capture his likeness. Not a particularly vain man, Crockett certainly did not wish to be remembered as yet another dandified politician clad in a suit and high-collar shirt with a cravat around his neck. That was the Crockett portrayed in Chester Harding's oil painting executed in Boston during the Whig book tour.[1] Crockett's family liked that depiction as well as a half-length full-size portrait by Rembrandt Peale, brother of Rubens Peale, who started the museum of oddities that Crockett had visited in New York.[2] Between 1833 and 1834, he sat for at least six portraits by five different artists. While Crockett was satisfied with the portraits, including the one he lost when he accidentally left it behind on a steamboat, he still hoped for a look that better suited how he actually saw himself in his role as the classic hunter hero.

As soon as he returned to Washington in mid-May 1834, and before the extended session of Congress officially closed six weeks later, Crockett sat for a portrait by artist John Gadsby Chapman.[3] It was while Chapman worked on an artistic study of Crockett's head to be used for the next election campaign that the artist and his subject came up with the idea of a full-length portrait of Crockett getting ready to do what he did best—go bear hunting.

Other artists who had painted Crockett portrayed him, in his own words, as "a sort of cross between a clean-shirted Member of Congress and a Methodist Preacher."[4] Crockett had another idea. "If you could catch me on bear-hunt in a 'harricane' with hunting tools and gear, and a team of dogs, you might have a picture better worth looking at," Crockett told Chapman. The artist wisely heeded the advice and decided to render a likeness of his subject in hunting garb, rejecting the standard Washington politician dress. The result was a full-length, life-size portrait of Crockett clad in a well-worn linsey-woolsey hunting shirt, buckskin leggings, and moccasins.

"I admitted, that I would be delighted to try it, but it would have to be a large picture and, as I never saw a harricane, or bear hunt, I should be obliged to give him a great deal more bother to explain all about them, and to show me what to do,"[5] Chapman later wrote.

Besides scouring the city of Washington for the appropriate costume, Chapman had to secure several props, including a butcher knife and a hatchet to make the Crockett painting as authentic-looking as possible. Finding a rifle "to conform to his [Crockett's] fastidious ideas of perfection proved difficult," according to Chapman. Finally, "an old sportsman on the Potomac" provided a rifle, and although the barrel was a few inches shorter than Crockett preferred for bear hunts, he was generally pleased.[6] Crockett and Chapman even paid a Sunday afternoon courtesy call on the owner at his home in nearby Alexandria, Virginia. The visit was so cordial that Crockett invited the gentleman to "come out to Tennessee for a riproarious bar-hunt." In return, Crockett left with gifts from his host, including a powder horn, a bullet pouch, and a bit of old leather, which he used to fashion a hatchet sheath.

"A grand old fellow," Crockett exclaimed to Chapman as they walked back to their hotels. "A grand old fellow that! When I'm President, I'll be shot if I don't put him into the War Department, he uttered prematurely."[7]

With all the accoutrements of the hunt in place, Chapman then looked for some hounds to add to the painting in order to lend even greater authenticity to the scene. Chapman suggested using his own dog, which he described as "a general sporting animal, of a highly valued breed. With remarkable record for scent, intelligence, courage and endurance—besides being thoroughly trained for service as a model."[8]

Crockett would have none of it. He believed thoroughbred dogs lacked the traits needed for best coping with a bear. "There's plenty of first-rate fellows to be found about the country carts any market day," said Crockett. "Come with me tomorrow and I'll show you. It does my eyes good to look at some of them, and think what a team of beauties they would be—with their tails chopped off—in a roll-and-tumble tussle with a big bear."[9]

Some stray hounds were found and the portrait completed. Chapman selected a lively pose struck by Crockett one afternoon when he walked into the studio and "gave a shout that raised the whole neighborhood."[10] The striking oil on canvas depicted Crockett standing among three mongrel hounds, his left arm crooked to hold his rifle, his right arm raised and grasping his broad-brimmed felt hunting hat as he waves the dogs on to the hunt. The portrait was one of Crockett's favorites.[11]

Over the course of six weeks, while working on the large likeness of Crockett on the hunt, Chapman developed a warm friendship with the colorful congressman and later put his thoughts and impressions to paper. Although it is brief, the nine-page reminiscence offers great insight into the true character of Crockett at that stage in his life.

"During the progressive intimacy that grew out of familiar intercourse with Col. Crockett, while engaged upon his portrait, he rarely, if ever, exhibited either in conversation or manner, attributes of coarseness of character that prevailing popular opinion very unjustly assigned to him," Chapman wrote.

> I cannot recall to mind an instance of his indulgence in gasconade or profanity. There was an earnestness of truth in his narrations of events, and circumstances of his adventuresome life, that made it obvious: while the heroic type of his grand physical

development, equal to any emergency of achievement—his clear unfaltering eye, and with all gentle and sympathetic play of features, telegraphing, as it were, directly from a true heart, overflowing with kind feeling and impulse, irresistibly dispelled suspicion of insincerity and braggartism. . . . The ease and readiness with which Crockett adapted himself to circumstances of personal position and intercourse were remarkable, at times even masterly. He would seem to catch, in the first moment of introduction, the tone and characteristics of a new acquaintance and as well to comprehend, and rarely failed in agreeably confirming preentertained opinions in reference to himself.[12]

Chapman liked recounting an incident that occurred when he was exhibiting his copies of old masters and original sketches at Mrs. Ball's Boarding House on Pennsylvania Avenue. While taking a break, the artist was fully engrossed with one of Crockett's many high adventure stories when there was a rap on his door. It was a sightseeing guide escorting two gentlemen on a tour of Washington City. They were hopeful that they could gaze upon the famed frontiersmen-turned-politician and steal a few moments of his time. Much to Chapman's surprise, Crockett welcomed them with a "comical air of resignation, at the same time putting on his hat, and throwing one leg over the arm of his chair, and greeting them with cordial extension of hand, but not rising."[13] He urged his guests to take seats and make themselves at home while the guide nervously made formal introductions of his "distinguished friends," stressing that they had come to the capital expressly to pay their respects to Crockett.

"A lively conversation was very soon improvised," Chapman wrote.

The colonel told several of his best stories—"hoped the gentlemen would have a safe and pleasant journey home, and find all right when they got there" adding "his best regards to the ladies of their families." Evidentially highly gratified with their visit, with a cordial hand shaking all around, they took their leave. As the door closed the Colonel shook himself out of dramatic pose, replaced his hat upon the table, and, as it were, thinking aloud, murmured, "Well—they came to see a bar, and they've seen one—hope they like the performance—it did not cost them any thing any how. Let's go take a horn!"[14]

Chapman's studio became a place of refuge for Crockett. During the six weeks that he went back and forth for sittings, he used Chapman as a sounding board and father confessor who had no political axe to grind, no favors to ask, and was always ready to listen. One morning when Crockett appeared for a scheduled sitting before going to the Capitol, Chapman immediately noticed "a marked change in his manner and general bearing, his step less firm and his carriage less erect and defiant."[15] He saw a crumpled letter in Crockett's hand and what he later described as a subdued expression on his face that had never been there before. Chapman asked if he had received some bad news, and Crockett told him that the letter was from his eldest son, John Wesley,[16] in Tennessee, who spoke of his own religious conversion, and chastised his father for his public behavior, and his rank failure to tend to the family needs. "Thinks he's off to Paradise on a streak of lightning," Crockett told Chapman, adding that the scolding "Pitches into me, pretty considerable."

It was clear to Chapman that Crockett's "thoughts and sympathies had been abruptly and touchingly recalled from present surroundings to home and heart memories. . . . The awkwardness of his efforts to resume his usual dash of manner was painful to witness."[17] No amount of public reverie or public adulation, it was clear, could fully detach Crockett from the family he had abandoned, both financially and emotionally.

When he was with Chapman, however, Crockett could be himself. There he had no need to "shake out" of the dramatic pose he often struck when dealing with his doting fans or his foes. Chapman recalled the afternoon he happened upon Crockett at the foot of the great descent to Pennsylvania Avenue looking "very much fagged" and not at all his usual jovial self. He told Crockett how tired he looked, as if he had just delivered a long speech to the House of Representatives. Crockett exclaimed, "Long speech to thunder, there's plenty of 'em up there for that sort of nonsense, without my making a fool of myself, at public expense. I can stand good nonsense—rather like it—but such nonsense as they are digging at up yonder, it's no use trying to—I'm going home."[18]

By "going home," Crockett meant that he was going back to his quarters at the nearby boardinghouse, not back to his estranged family in Tennessee. Yet even as he trudged down the avenue, forces were hard at work to ensure he would indeed go home to those canebrakes where his detractors thought he belonged and should forever remain.

Everyone in Congress, including Crockett's Whig friends, noticed a change in him after the book tour. Many historians and biographers agree that going on the tour with Congress still in session was possibly the greatest political blunder Crockett ever committed. They maintain it gave his enemies in the Jackson camp plenty of fodder to use against him. All that had to be done was to point out that, as a duly elected representative of the people, Crockett missed important votes, floor debates, and other congressional business while he traipsed around the country having a high time with his Whig pals. Although he would not be the last American politician to evade his legislative duties, his constituents in Tennessee felt they had been taken advantage of. The man supposed to be looking out for their interests was busy peddling books and speaking out against America's laudable commander-in-chief, a Tennessee man himself. It was a point well made, and when Crockett offered feeble excuses for his absence by blaming it on illness, it only compounded the severity of the situation.[19] Everyone in the country, let alone Washington City, had been reading about Crockett's junket for weeks.

Crockett's frustration was evident in his verbal assaults on Jackson, Van Buren, and their followers, as they became more caustic and breached all sense of decorum, even for the already raucous House of Representatives. There were several instances in the chamber when the sound of the gavel rang out like a rifle shot as the Speaker of the House tried to bring the out-of-control Crockett to order. The sergeant-at-arms and his underlings stood at the ready and legislators pushed their brass spittoons beneath their desks in case a scuffle erupted in the aisles between feuding members, especially the demonstrative gentleman from the cane.

The book tour had clearly diminished his political effectiveness. Crockett was fully aware that his entire political future hinged on the passage of his land legislation, and he knew the chances of that ever happening receded with each passing day. To say that Crockett was distraught would have been an understatement. His hatred of Jackson grew to uncontrollable excess, and he eagerly let those feelings be known to his colleagues in Washington and to his constituents.[20] The spectacle suggested a man out of control, as events moved increasingly into public view.

In Tennessee, concerned voters began to make inquiries about the land bill. Crockett had no real answers. Any pleasant memories of the recent tour had evaporated. He felt trapped and more and more alone. "I now look forward toward our adjournment with as much interest as ever did a poor convict in the penitentiary to see his last day come,"[21] he wrote. "We have done but one act, and that is that the will of Andrew, the first king, is to be the law of the land. He has tools and slaves enough in Congress to sustain him in anything he may wish to effect. . . . I thank God I am not one of them. I do consider him a greater tyrant than Cromwell, Caesar or Bonaparte . . ."

In the end, Crockett did not even stay for the rest of the session but bolted the day before the official close. He did not head out west to Tennessee but instead boarded a stagecoach bound for Baltimore and then on to Philadelphia. There he was to meet with his publishers, accept some promised gifts, and deliver a July Fourth speech at Independence Hall along with Senator Daniel Webster and some other resolute Whigs. The anti-Jacksonians, while politically smart enough to figure that Crockett had no real chance of ever becoming president, still considered him a useful weapon to unleash at staged events and political rallies.

Reaching Philadelphia on June 30, Crockett was again escorted to the United States Hotel on Chestnut Street and given the sort of pampered treatment a prized gladiator received before entering the arena.

On the evening of July 1 at a special ceremony near the old state house, he was given a special custom-made rifle that had been promised to him during his earlier book tour by the young Whigs of Philadelphia. J. M. Sanderson, the renowned local gunsmith the Whigs had commissioned to create the weapon, presented it to Crockett, along with a silver tomahawk inscribed with the words "Go Ahead Crockett," a butcher knife, a shot pouch, and an ornate gilded liquor canteen shaped like a bound book and filled with first-rate sipping whiskey. There also was a powder horn with silver mounts inscribed "Tho. H. Benton to David Crockett 1832."[22] The inscription was curious, since by 1832 Crockett was a known Jackson enemy and Tom Benton, despite earlier differences, was one of Jackson's staunchest supporters. Soon the room broke out in laughter when it became known that it was a bogus inscription etched by some of Crockett's Whig friends as a political prank.

The richly ornamented rifle was a treasure to behold. The inscription in gold read: "Presented by the Young Men of Philadelphia to Hon. David Crockett of Tennessee." On the stock, a silver plate depicted an alligator with its open jaws, a deer, and a possum. Sanderson also inlaid a gilded arrow into the barrel near the muzzle, and the words "Go Ahead" were etched near the front sight. Crockett was visibly moved with the gifts, especially the rifle. He vowed to use it in defense of his country and to hand it down to his sons for the same purpose. As was the common custom of most hunters of the time, Crockett gave all his rifles names. The well-used rifle he had been using for many years was called "Betsey," his favorite moniker for guns, and so he told the crowd that this newest weapon in his arsenal would be called "Pretty Betsey."[23]

The following day Crockett and Sanderson traveled just across the Delaware River to nearby Camden, New Jersey, and spent part of the day test-firing the weapon. Crockett was pleased with the gun and told those with him that it operated every bit as well as it looked. "I shot tolerable well, and was satisfied that when we became better acquainted, the fault would be mine if the varmints did not suffer,"[24] he wrote.

Back in Philadelphia for Independence Day, Crockett was in fine form, mingling with Daniel Webster and other Whig luminaries. He delivered his standard speech attacking Old Hickory and received thunderous applause. Crockett departed a couple of days later, after acquiring an elegant pitcher imported from China for his wife Elizabeth (Betsy) and meeting gunpowder manufacturer E. I. du Pont, a director on the board of the Second Bank of the United States, who gave him a dozen canisters of powder for the new "Pretty Betsey" in his life.[25]

After a circuitous journey mostly by train and steamboat, and several stops in Virginia, Ohio, Indiana, and Kentucky, Crockett finally set foot nearly three weeks later in Tennessee on July 22 at the Mills Point boat landing, where his son William waited with a wagon to make the thirty-five-mile trip home.[26] Family members, especially those who had seen the comings and goings of Crockett for so many years, provided a lukewarm reception, and no sooner had he unpacked than he was forced to face what had become the constant round of legal actions over promissory notes past due. Sales of his autobiography had yielded some relief, but Crockett's poor fiscal judgment and lack of money management skills trumped any easing of his financial miseries.

In this aspect of his life, Crockett had become his father, the debt-ridden John Crockett who had eventually followed his son and other family members to the land of the shakes, where he died in September of 1834.[27] Just as had happened in the case of his father-in-law's passing, David was named the administrator of his father's estate, which not surprisingly amounted to very little. Prior to leaving that fall of 1834 to return for the next session of Congress, Crockett had to borrow even more money just to make the trip.

Besides his financial problems, Crockett was aware that he would face strong opposition in the approaching congressional elections in August of 1835. Word on the streets of Washington City and in the hills and canebrakes of Tennessee was that one of Crockett's main political enemies, Adam R. Huntsman, was ready to do battle for the Twelfth Congressional seat. Nicknamed "Old Black Hawk" by Crockett and a lawyer by trade, Huntsman, after having lost a leg in the Creek War in 1813, had gone on to become a powerful figure in the fledgling Democratic Party in Tennessee. He was a close friend of Andrew Jackson and

James K. Polk, and was reputed to be a forceful campaigner, practical joker, and excellent speaker.[28]

"Adam Huntsman is out in opposition to David Crockett for Congress, in the district represented by the Colonel," announced a front-page blurb in the Gettysburg *Adams Sentinel* of November 24, 1834. "We take it the Colonel will care very little about such a 'varment as that are.' He will 'chaw him up in a flash.' "[29]

However, before he could concentrate on another political campaign, Crockett once more had to get his finances in order. His publishers denied him any further cash advances, so he schemed with another of his boardinghouse friends, Pennsylvania Congressman William Clark, to write yet another book—this time a work based on the event-packed Crockett tour of the eastern cities. After a good deal of cajoling, Crockett was able to convince Carey and Hart to publish such a book and Clark to write it. The agreement with Clark was for Crockett to provide him with a collection of newspaper accounts, speeches given on the tour, and any other odd notes and documents that could be organized and cobbled together to form a book.

Yet at the expense of his congressional duties, including efforts to pass his notorious land bill, Crockett spent almost all of his time working on the book. Throughout his years spent in Congress, his top priority had been to make sure that the land of western Tennessee was made available and affordable to the settlers who had tamed it. Still unrealized, that unattainable dream seemed further jeopardized because of the financial exigencies of turning out another book.

Laboring under the unrealistic hope that it would be published by January 1835, Crockett quickly fulfilled his part of the agreement. He was rewarded with some advance money from the publisher, but Clark, his aging and ailing co-conspirator, fell ill, and the book did not hit stores until March. It was issued with a title suggested by Crockett—*An Account of Col. Crockett's Tour to the North and Down East in the Year of Our Lord One Thousand Eight Hundred and Thirty Four.* The lengthy title caused some to speculate unkindly that Crockett must have been paid by the word.

Even before the book was released, Crockett, realizing that publishing could pay him more handsomely than politics, had come up with yet another idea for his publishers. He proposed writing a satirical biography of Martin Van Buren. Carey and Hart were skeptical. They feared that Crockett would turn out a libelous attack that would put them in court facing slander charges. Crockett persisted. His hatred for Van Buren was equal to or greater than his hatred for Jackson. In a letter to Charles Schultz, of Cincinnati, penned on Christmas Day 1834, Crockett stated, "I have almost given up the ship as lost."[30] He went on to write that if Van Buren were elected as the next president, Crockett's only alternative would be to leave the United States, "for I never will live under his kingdom." He then added that he would "go to the wildes [*sic*] of Texas," where living under Mexican rule would be "a Paradise to what this will be."

After much hand wringing, Crockett's Philadelphia publishers released the Van Buren book in June of 1835, although without listing the firm's name on the title page. The biography was given a less than catchy title, *The Life of Martin Van Buren, Hair-apparent to the "Government," and the Appointed Successor of General Jackson*. Most sources theorize that the misspelling of the word *Heir* as *Hair* was an intentional mistake to give the book a bit of backwoods flavor or was meant to ridicule Van Buren's famously smooth and hairless pate.[31] The book, as scurrilous as everyone thought it would be, was attributed to Crockett, but any contribution he actually made was minimal at best, since it was once again ghostwritten, penned this time by Augustin Smith Clayton, a jurist who represented Georgia in Congress from 1832 to 1835.[32]

By the time the vitriolic biography appeared, the question of Van Buren becoming the Democratic candidate for president was purely academic. In May 1835, at the second national convention of the Democratic Party in Baltimore, Van Buren had become the unanimous choice of the delegates and was nominated.[33] Crockett continued to hold out hope that he could still be defeated in the general election, but he finally admitted that he was not the man to do it. By then the Whigs agreed. They concluded that Crockett had served his purpose and outlived his usefulness. Crockett had sensed their waning support for some time, and it was not a surprise when he joined the majority of the Tennessee delegation in signing a letter asking Tennessee senator Hugh Lawson White to run as the Whig candidate in the next presidential election.[34] White, the son of General James White, the founder of Knoxville, had been Jackson's friend and succeeded him to the U.S. Senate in 1825. Since then, however, he had been twice reelected, but not without becoming disillusioned with Jackson and the charges that Old Hickory had overstepped his authority. White also felt slighted when Jackson asked Van Buren to be his running mate and then made it obvious that he wanted the Yankee dandy from New York to become the next president.

Crockett, in an election battle of his own, knew that unless he kept his seat in the House of Representatives there would be no chance for him ever to run again for the presidency. His book schemes, travel junkets, and congressional floor antics had taken a toll on his credibility among the voters. To add to his miseries, he had once again come home without having passed the Tennessee Vacant Land Bill.

Huntsman proved to be a vigorous campaigner, with no lack of barbs to fling at Crockett. Many people saw Huntsman's peg leg as a symbol of his courage and service to the nation as an Indian fighter. On at least one occasion during the campaign, Crockett found a way to turn his opponent's wooden limb to his own advantage. The incident in question occurred during the heat of the campaign battle, when both candidates traveled the circuit together making stump speeches along the way. Often they stayed under the same roof, as was the case on this evening when they were quartered at the home of a prosperous farmer who happened to have a comely daughter. In the wee hours, after everyone was asleep, Crockett crept out of bed, took a wooden chair, and rattled the knob of the door of the young woman's room. She woke up screaming, and Crockett put one foot on the rung of the chair and used it like a crutch to hobble back to his own bed. The farmer mistook the sound for the tapping of Huntsman's wooden leg and, aware of the politician's penchant for beautiful women, burst into his quarters and demanded an explanation. Crockett acted as peacemaker and intervened. He calmed down the farmer but not before getting his vote and a promise that he would tell everyone about the lecherous one-legged Huntsman.

If the farmer kept his word and voted for Crockett in the August election, it was not enough. It turned out to be a close race, but in the end Crockett picked up 4,400 votes compared to 4,652 cast for Huntsman.[35]

Defeat did not come easily to Crockett. As was the case in past losses, he was bitter and angry. "I have no doubt that I was Completely Raskeled out of my election," Crockett wrote to his publishers on August 11, just five days after the voting. "I will be rewarded for letting my tongue Speake what my hart thinks. . . . I have Suffered my Self to be politically Sacrafised to Save my Country from ruin and disgrace and if I am never again elected I will have the gratification to know that I have done my duty."[36]

Many newspapers took Crockett to task. The colorful frontiersman always made good copy, no matter if he was portrayed as a superhero or, as the *Arkansas Gazette* now called him, that "buffoon, Davy Crockett." When his forty-ninth birthday came around on August 17, there was not much to celebrate. On August 31, the editors of the *Charleston Courier* offered their assessment:

Col. Davy Crockett, hitherto regarded as the Nimerod [*sic*] of the West, has been beaten for Congress by a Mr. Huntsman. The Colonel has lately suffered himself to be made a lion, or some other wild beast, tamed, if not caged, for public shew [*sic*]—and it is no wonder that he should have yielded to the prowess of a Huntsman, when again let loose in his native wilds. We fear that "Go ahead" will no longer be either the Colonel's motto or destiny.[37]

The newspaper was wrong, for "Go ahead" was exactly what Crockett had in mind. Soundly defeated in Washington and in his home state, he looked now for solace elsewhere, having heard for a long time stories about the opportunities that waited in Texas. He had repeatedly declared that he would head to Texas and live under Mexican rule if Van Buren ever became president. Crockett decided he could not wait for that election.

During this period of the 1830s and for several years to come, it was not uncommon to see the letters *G. T. T.* painted or carved on the doorways of cabins in Tennessee and other parts of the country, especially the South. It was a sure sign that the occupants had picked up and were, as they said, "*Gone to Texas.*" The slogan was first seen in print in 1825, and had become a popular expression for those people who had committed crimes or owed money or just did not want to be found.[38] When bill collectors went looking for defaulters and found an empty house, they realized those they sought had absconded and had gone to Texas. It became common that when a grand jury returned indictments but the sheriff had no luck bringing in the accused, he would report back that they had gone to Texas. When a banker rifled the vaults of his institution and made a successful getaway, he, too, was gone to Texas.

And when a man had a broken marriage, lost his job, but hoped to start fresh as a land agent on the Mexican frontier, he, too, was gone to Texas.

THIRTY-FIVE

TIME OF THE COMET

Bᴇ LATE AUTUMN OF 1835, near the end of Jackson's second term as president, Crockett had "gone to Texas." In this land of turmoil and revolt he soon joined other historical refugees destined to become larger-than-life legends, thanks to the hyperbole of the press and biased historians. These mythmakers surgically removed any flaws and foibles, rationalized motivations, and justified deeds. In so doing, they created not only a plethora of heroic figures but also one of the most iconic symbols of gallantry and independence in America—the Alamo.

Crockett had never heard of the Alamo and certainly had no thought of taking part in any revolt against Mexico when, on October 31, 1835, he composed a letter to George Patton, his brother-in-law in Swannanoa, North Carolina. "I am on the eve of Starting to the Texes . . . we will go through Arkinsaw and I want to explore the Texes well before I return."[1]

At the time of Crockett's departure for Texas, he and Elizabeth still lived apart, but he had hoped that, if the trip panned out and he found some suitable land, she would be willing to try a fresh start. At a going-away frolic attended by family and friends, there was pit-roasted barbecue, dancing, logrolling and shooting contests, and plenty of storytelling. It was said that Crockett was in fine spirits, took several horns of whiskey, and played the fiddle.[2]

Crockett set out on this scouting trip with a trio of traveling companions—nephew William Patton, brother-in-law Abner Burgin, and Lindsey Tinkle, the neighbor who had bought one of the slave girls Crockett had sold from the Patton estate. The four men packed their horses much as they would have done in preparation for a long bear hunt. They took salted meat, bedrolls, and a full compliment of weapons and ammunition. No doubt Crockett slipped some gunpowder into his saddlebag and shooting pouch. Contrary to popular belief, he did not take Pretty Betsey, the fancy weapon presented to him by the Whigs in Philadelphia, but opted for just plain Betsey, his well-used long gun.[3]

On the morning of November 1, the four men mounted up, Crockett astride a large chestnut horse with a white star on its forehead. People later recalled that his spirits were high. He was in his hunting clothes, riding with men he liked, and ahead waited the promise of adventure and opportunity.

Like many others making the same journey at the time, Crockett understood what he faced once he crossed the Red River and left the United States. He had to have been aware that, in the weeks before he departed, the animosity had increased between the government of Mexico and the American settlers, called Texians, in the Mexican state of Coahuila y Tejas. The white colonists were becoming increasingly tired of living under Mexican rule, and they headed for war with hopes of forming their own separate republic. Many of these Anglos were illegal immigrants and did not abide by Mexican law. All citizens were required to join the Catholic Church, accept the language and laws of the governing country, and, by the late 1820s, observe the ban on the enslavement of human beings.

To the Anglos' way of thinking, slaves were too important to give up, particularly for the wealthier southerners who were accustomed to the plantation system style of farming. "The discussion of slavery in the West begins in Texas, the heart of the region's slave regime," writes Quintard Taylor Jr., African American history scholar. "Slaveholders unapologetically proclaimed both the agricultural need for black labor and their right to own their fellow human beings."[4]

Slavery had been a volatile issue in Texas ever since the early 1820s, when Stephen Fuller Austin convinced the Mexican government, which had just won its independence from Spain, that Anglo settlers would provide a buffer on the northern frontier between the settlements to the south and the raiding Comanches. The original three hundred families that Austin led to what was promised as the land of milk and honey soon multiplied. Prospects of free land lured thousands of whites across the Sabine and Red rivers. By 1823 at least 3,000 U.S. citizens had entered Texas illegally, along with 700 legitimate settlers.[5] About the same time, the Austin Colony had established an unofficial capital at San Felipe de Austin, on the west bank of the Brazos River. Two years earlier, Austin was already expressing concern over what he perceived would become a major problem with the Mexican government and the colonists.

"The principal difficulty is slavery, this they will not admit—as the law is all slaves are to be free in ten years, but I am trying to have it amended so as to make them slaves for life and their children free at 21 years—but do not think I shall succeed in this point, and that the law will pass as it is now, that the slaves introduced by the settlers shall be free after 10 years,"[6] Austin wrote in a dispatch from Mexico City in 1822.

Only five years later, the Austin Colony's political and social hub of San Felipe was "still in swaddling clothes" when Noah Smithwick arrived. The feisty nineteen-year-old had a "strong aversion to tearing up God's earth," so took up blacksmithing instead of farming.[7] Smithwick left behind one of the most accurate memoirs of the first Anglo settlement in Texas. He described pioneer doctors who devoted most of their practice to "dressing wounds and holding inquests," running hounds after feral hogs in the river bottoms, trying to stay clear of a certain lawyer "who had a penchant for dueling," and a poet whose verse so disturbed some San Felipeans that they gave him a "new suit of tar and feathers" and ran him out of town.[8] The offending verse from the unnamed bard that resulted in his "poetical flight" read:

The United States, as we understand,
Took sick and did vomit the dregs of the land.
Her murderers, bankrupts and rogues you may see,
All congregated in San Felipe.

More importantly, Smithwick also wrote of the colonists' true motives for moving into the province and their decision to take the land away from Mexico. According to Smithwick, many of his fellow settlers were social outcasts and deadbeat exiles from the Mississippi Valley and across the southern states eager to acquire cheap land or get a new lease on life. "Faulty statutes in the United states sent many a man to Texas," he wrote.[9]

Smithwick also described wealthy landowners who established cotton plantations and imported large numbers of slaves. "Over on the Brazos . . . a planter from South Carolina . . . had over 100 slaves, with which force he set to work clearing ground and planting cotton and corn. He hired two men to kill game to feed them on, and the mustangs [wild horses] being the largest and easiest to kill . . . the negroes lived on horse meat till corn came in."[10]

Slavery was indeed an important issue in the Texas war of rebellion, just as it would be a decade later in the Mexican-American War. Yet because slavery is antithetical to hero worship, often the subject has been noticeably absent in discussions of early Texas settlement by Anglo immigrants. The fact remains that by the late 1820s Mexico had a politically active and strong abolitionist movement. In 1829 a new Mexican constitution prohibited slavery, which so outraged the big landowners and speculators in Texas that a provision was drafted that permitted slavery under certain conditions. That was soon rescinded and a new policy put into place. It allowed all slaves currently residing in Texas to remain but banned the importation of additional slaves. It also decreed that children born to slaves in the territory would be free. At the same time, the Mexican government passed a law blocking any further American immigration into Texas. By 1830 there were more than 20,000 settlers and 2,000 slaves living in Texas, making Anglos more numerous than Mexicans.

The flood of immigrants was overwhelming, and brought even more problems. Many of the new arrivals disregarded the laws, refused to pay customs fees, and took part in illegal smuggling activities. This provoked a great outcry from Mexican newspapers and political leaders fearful that the white colonists would attempt a revolution. During a speech to a secret session of the Mexican congress in 1830, one political leader warned: "Mexicans! Watch closely, for you know all too well the Anglo-Saxon greed for territory. We have generously granted land to these Nordics; they have made their homes with us, but their hearts are with their native land. We are continually in civil wars and revolutions; we are weak, and know it—and they know it also. They may conspire with the United States to take Texas from us. From this time, be on your guard!"[11]

The situation only worsened for the Mexican government. By 1835, the population had ballooned to 35,000, including 3,000 black slaves. All of this changed the very nature of the province. Most of the new-comers spoke only English, pretended to practice Catholicism, and "true to their manly Southern roots, kept slaves at a time when the peculiar institution had been abandoned by the rest of Mexico."[12]

That August, as Crockett was reeling from his election loss in Tennessee, Austin continued to press for not only a continuation of slavery but also for independence from Mexico. In a letter to his cousin, Mary Austin Holley, he wrote:

> The situation of Texas is daily becoming more and more interesting, so much so that I doubt whether the Government of the United States or that of Mexico can much longer look on with indifference, or inaction. It is very evident that Texas should be effectually, and fully, *Americanized*,—that is—settled by a population that will harmonize with their neighbors on the *East*, in language, political principles, common origin, sympathy, and even interest. *Texas must be a slave country. It is no longer a*

matter of doubt. The interest of Louisiana requires that it should be. A population of fanatical abolitionists in Texas would have a very dangerous and pernicious influence on the overgrown slave population of that state. Texas must and ought to become an outwork on the west, as Alabama and Florida are on the east, to defend the key of the western world—the mouths of the Mississippi. Being fully Americanized under the Mexican flag would be the same thing in effect and ultimate result as coming under the United States flag. A gentle breeze shakes off a ripe peach. Can it be supposed that the violent political convulsions of Mexico will not shake off Texas as soon as it is ripe enough to fall? All that is now wanting is a great immigration of good and efficient families this fall and winter. Should we get such an immigration, especially from the Western States—all is done; the peach will be ripe.[13]

The mostly southern-born white settlers of Texas were on a collision course with the Mexican government. The two sides could no longer avoid the slavery issue. Mexico now fully supported equality for its entire population, while many of the white immigrants wanted Texas to become an empire for slavery.

Gen. Antonio López de Santa Anna y Pérez de Lebrón, president of Mexico and commander of the Mexican army, puzzled as to why a province in his republic still allowed slaves, asked: "Shall we permit those wretches to moan in chains any longer in a country whose kind laws protect the liberty of man without distinction of cast or color?"[14] Santa Anna posed the rhetorical question in early 1836, just as Crockett was making his way to Texas.

Crockett himself was not opposed to slavery, having bought and sold slaves over the years, though never on a large scale. But he was not so passionate about slavery that he went to Texas to take part in a revolt. He was more interested in shooting the bison on the Texas prairie than killing "yaller niggers," as Mexicans were sometimes called.[15] Crockett's only concern with the war that raged between transplanted Americans and the forces of Gen. Santa Anna was whether its outcome would help him get some land sooner rather than later. Shortly after he lost his last congressional race in August of 1835, he explained in a letter that one of his main reasons for leaving the United States was to get away from Jackson and Van Buren until they were no longer in power. "I do believe Santa Ana's [sic] kingdom [Mexico] will be a paradise, compared with this, in a few years,"[16] he wrote.

His decision to go to Texas, then, was not impulsive. Texas promised Crockett a fresh start and new opportunities for homesteading as well as politicking.[17]

A desire for land and not heroism was on Crockett's mind as he and his companions made their way south. The quartet of riders made stops at several towns, including Jackson and Bolivar, and along the way picked up others who wanted to go to Texas. As many as thirty riders had joined Crockett's entourage by the time they finally rode into Memphis on November 10. Most of them would stay in Memphis or drop out along the journey through Arkansas and across the Mexican border into Texas.

While spending a few days in Memphis, Crockett looked up old friends such as Mayor Marcus Winchester, the well-known business and political figure who had invested money and energy in his earlier political campaigns. The river town, with its many pleasurable distractions, had always proved inviting to Crockett. Much time also was spent enjoying horns of drink with citizens and comrades at the Union Hotel, Hart's Saloon, and Neil McCool's establishment. It was at this time that Crockett made his famous declaration to the Tennessee voters: "Since you have chosen to elect a man with a timber toe to succeed me, you may all go to hell and I will go to Texas."[18] Most likely he repeated the statement many times as he traveled southward to the U.S.-Mexico border.

From Memphis, Crockett and his followers were ferried across the Mississippi and into Arkansas. They reached the territorial capital of Little Rock in the late afternoon of November 12. "A rare treat," declared the *Gazette*, one of the city's daily newspapers.

Among the distinguished characters who have honored our City with their presence within the last week, was no less a personage than Col. DAVID CROCKETT—better known as DAVY CROCKETT—the *reel critter* himself—who arrived on Thursday evening last, with some 6 or 8 followers. . . . The news of his arrival rapidly spread, and we believe within bounds, when we say, that hundreds flocked to see the wonderful man, who, it is said, can whip his weight in wild-cats, or grin the largest panther out of a tree.[19]

While in Little Rock, Crockett visited a popular tavern, was entertained by a puppet show, and bagged a deer he hung up and butchered behind the Jefferies Hotel. At one point, he showed off his skill with Betsey at a shooting match where it was said he struck the center of the bull's eye with both his first and second shots. Later a large group of anti-Jacksonians toasted Crockett at a banquet held in his honor at the hotel. He obliged them by lambasting the president and vice president. Crockett also had high praise for Arkansas and told the overflow crowd: "If I could rest anywhere it would be in Arkansas, where the men are the real half-horse, half-alligator breed such as grow nowhere else on the face of the universal earth but just around the backbone of North America."[20]

But Crockett was not ready to rest and soon departed Little Rock with his followers bound for Texas. Many others were making the same journey. "The *Texas fever* is beginning to develope [*sic*] itself in Little Rock," reported a Virginia newspaper. "Four young men, who have caught the patriotic flame, took their departure from our city . . . to gather laurels on the plains of Texas."[21] Large bands of heavily armed men rode down the old military road that had been used to herd the displaced Choctaws to the western lands of Indian Territory. At the crossroads town of Washington, Arkansas, they paused to refresh and then continued on the Southwest Trail winding its way to the border crossings on the Red River.

Crockett may have traversed at least a short stretch of southern Indian Territory, and then near Lost Prairie, Arkansas, he finally crossed the meandering Red River to the Mexican side. He entered in the far northeast corner of Texas at the Jonesboro Crossing.[22] While in the area, a settler named Isaac Jones encountered Crockett, who bolstered his dwindling finances by swapping his old watch and thirty dollars in cash for Crockett's fancy engraved timepiece given to him by the citizens of Philadelphia in 1834.[23]

Crockett apparently liked what he found in the Red River country of northeast Texas. He spent his first night in Texas at the home of John Stiles, a Kentucky native, who helped guide Crockett to the home of Capt. William Becknell, the famed "Father of the Santa Fe Trade," the route from Franklin, Missouri, to the ancient capital of New Mexico that came to be called the Santa Fe Trail.[24] Becknell opened the popular trade route in 1821, lived as a fur trapper for a short period, and returned to Franklin in 1825. Ten years later he led a party of Missourians to Texas and had only recently finished building his cabin when Crockett and his party showed up for a visit.

The Becknell homestead was about eight miles from Clarksville, founded by James Clark, an early white settler. Clark's wife, Isabella Hadden Hopkins Hanks Clark, was the widow of John Hanks, who— according to local legend—was a relative of Nancy Hanks, mother of Abraham Lincoln.[25] When Isabella, 31, learned of Crockett's plans to go hunting, she immediately saddled a horse and rode off to warn him of a band of Comanche raiders in the area. She "struck the trail of David Crockett and by following the trodden grass trailed him" and his party to the Becknell place on the prairie west of Clarksville. The young woman and Becknell strongly suggested that Crockett and his men "turn south down the Choctaw trail and strike the Spanish trail into San Antonio at Nacogdoches, thus avoiding these wild tribes who were then on the war-path west of here," wrote Pat Clark, the grandson of James and Isabella.

> David Crockett, being a great hunter, was prevailed upon by Capt. Becknall [sic] to stop for a few days and rest his horses; and the party went on a hunt in the country west of here. Old Uncle Henry Stout . . . himself being a great hunter and one

of the most remarkable guides on any frontier, went with Mr. Crockett out for one hundred miles or more with the hope they might strike the famous herds of buffalo, which Mr. Crockett was extremely anxious to do. While out hunting they were riding through some skirts of timber with grass and weeds in the ravines often coming up to the saddle skirts of the horses. There were no roads or bridle paths anywhere. They suddenly rode into droves of bees nesting in the grass. Evidently the City of Honey Grove got its name from this circumstance and David Crockett afterwards referred to that place as Honey Grove.[26]

The prairies, clumps of blackjack trees, fertile soil, and streams lined with cottonwoods appealed to Crockett, and he later wrote in a letter to family in Tennessee that he found this land to be "the garden spot of the world."[27] There also was an abundance of game, and Crockett enjoyed hunting so much that he was hesitant to leave and explore any further. He stayed on for a while longer and even failed to show up on time for a Christmas rendezvous with other members of his party. Soon rumors began circulating that the great bear hunter and marksman had run afoul of some warring Indians. By early 1836 stories of Crockett's death began appearing in eastern newspapers.

"A letter was read to-day by a member of Congress from Brownsville, Tennessee, in which it was stated that intelligence had been received there of the death of Col. David Crockett, in Texas, soon after his arrival in that country,"[28] reported the *New Bedford Mercury*, on February 26, 1836.

When it was learned that he was hunting and had not been scalped by Kickapoos or Comanches, Crockett came in for some barbs. Those who were following his journey presumed that he wanted to get into the heart of Texas to take part in the fight against the Mexican government. "You may have heard that David Crockett set out for this country with a company of men to join the army," wrote Edward Warren, of Bangor, Maine, during an 1836 Texas visit. "He has forgotten or waved [*sic*] his original intention & stopped some 80 to 100 miles to the north of this place to hunt Buffalo for the winter! For a long time, it was feared that he & his party had been destroyed by the tribes of wild Indians through which he intended to pass. But, at last, it is ascertained that he is at his favorite amusement."[29]

Finally, in early January of 1836, Crockett and his original three companions reined up their horses in Nacogdoches, the oldest town in Texas. He was reluctant to leave the good hunting grounds, but he had also heard stories about the successes of Sam Houston, his old Tennessee friend; Stephen Austin; and other land agents, or *empresarios*, who had established land agencies and were on their way to becoming wealthy men. Crockett believed that, at last, he could gain his own fortune, and in a place where he could hunt almost every day of the year. As one author noted, Crockett was "in a state of euphoria."[30]

Throughout Crockett's long ride from Tennessee to Texas, Halley's Comet, the most famous of all the celestial nomads, was clearly visible, just as it is every seventy-six years or so. Across the land people were in awe when they spied the object slowly making its way through the night sky.[31] For centuries people believed a comet appeared as a harbinger of chaos and disaster. Comets were to be feared. One medieval pope even excommunicated Halley's Comet and declared it an "instrument of the devil."

The appearance of Halley's Comet in 1835–1836 was blamed for catastrophes around the world, including a horrific fire in New York City that raged for several days and nights, the massacre of 280 people in Africa by Zulu warriors, and wars that erupted across Latin America. The Seminole Indians in Florida saw in the comet's long tail a sign of the tragedy that soon descended on them as they lost their homes and were exiled to Indian Territory.

Among many Americans, especially Anglo Texans, Halley's Comet signaled the impending fall of the Alamo. But for the Tejanos—the people of Mexican blood living in Texas—the comet was a portent of the Mexican army's defeat at San Jacinto.

Halley's Comet was rediscovered in August 1835, about the time of Crockett's defeat for another term in Congress. It was visible for an extended period and could still be seen long enough for enterprising promoters to issue *The Comet Almanack for 1836*. It sold well but not nearly as well as the *Davy Crockett Almanack* of that year with a cover illustration of Crockett wading the Mississippi River on a pair of stilts. Stories made the rounds, in newspapers and future almanacs, claiming that Crockett and his nemesis Andrew Jackson had forged a truce and that Old Hickory had commissioned Crockett to scale the Alleghenies and wring the tail off the comet before it could char the earth.[32] By the time the comet finally vanished in May 1836, not to be seen again until 1910, the ashes of the Alamo, the last battle of Crockett's life, were long cold and scattered.

THIRTY-SIX

EL ALAMO

WHEN THE CROCKETT ENTOURAGE rode into Nacogdoches on January 5, 1836, they were warmly greeted with a cannon salute, and that evening they were feted at a great banquet. Crockett had taken his time in getting to the old Spanish town, where many volunteers were gathering and some of the revolutionary leaders were plotting the overthrow of the Mexican government. The local citizens, of course, assumed Crockett's sole purpose in coming to Texas was to join in the battle. Mindful of a future in politics and not wishing to disappoint, Crockett responded with one of his robust and colorful speeches.

"I am told, gentlemen," Crockett said to his hosts,

that when a stranger like myself arrives among you, the first inquiry is, what brought him here. To satisfy your curiosity at once as to myself, I will tell you all about it. I was, for some years, a member of Congress. In my last canvass, I told the people of my district that if they saw fit to reelect me, I would serve them as faithfully as I had done before. But, if not, they might go to hell, and I would go to Texas. I was beaten, gentlemen, and here I am.[1]

The well-used "hell or Texas" phrase was a proven crowd pleaser and worked every time. Crockett beamed as everyone present at the banquet erupted in loud cheers. "We'll go to the city of Mexico and shake Santa Anna as a coon dog would a possum," one newspaper reported the "old bear hunter" shouted back. "The roar of applause was like a thunder-burst."[2]

Like other volunteers gathering in Nacogdoches, Crockett had to take the oath of allegiance and become a citizen if he was ever going to run for office in Texas and own land. The date that Crockett took the oath is not known but it is certain that he did appear before Judge John Forbes and swear his allegiance to the provisional government of Texas.[3] His young nephew William Patton took the oath as well, but the other two original members of the Crockett party from Tennessee—Abner Burgin and Lindsey Tinkle—apparently had second thoughts about staying in Texas. They bid Crockett and Patton farewell and returned home to the land of the shakes.[4]

Before he raised his hand and swore the oath, Crockett examined the document and took exception with the requirement to uphold "any future government." Most likely thinking of Andrew Jackson, Santa Anna, or both, Crockett expressed his fears of a dictatorship and urged Judge Forbes to insert the word "republican" just before the word "government."[5] The judge obliged and quickly scribbled in the additional word. Crockett took the oath and joined other volunteers who enlisted for a period of six months in the Voluntary Auxiliary Corps of the Texian Army.

> I do solemnly swear that I will bear true allegiance to the Provisional Government of Texas, or any future republican Government that hereafter may be declared, and that I will serve her honestly and faithfully against all her enemies and opposers whatsoever, and observe and obey the orders of the Governor of Texas, the orders and decrees of the present and future authorities and the orders of the officers appointed over

me according to the rules and regulations for the government of
Texas. So help me God.[6]

Crockett was told that, in exchange for his service as a mercenary
for the Texians, he would receive a huge allotment of more than 4,000
acres of land and become eligible to hold elective office in the future.
This prospect became even more certain on January 9, when Crockett and some followers rode into the town of San Augustine, about
thirty-five miles from Nacogdoches. The citizens of San Augustine
also greeted Crockett with a cannon salute and the women of the
town laid out a sumptuous feast to mark his visit. Crockett stayed
at the home of Shelby Corzine, an Alabama native and veteran of
the Battle of Horseshoe Bend in 1814.[7] Besides reminiscing about
the Creek War, the two veterans discussed the upheaval in Texas and
a role for Crockett in Texas politics. A delegation of San Augustine
civic leaders also approached their famous guest about the possibility of him representing their community in the forthcoming constitutional convention. Crockett was not quite ready to tackle such a
job, and there was not enough time to get his name on the ballot for
the March 1 convention. He wisely demurred, ingenuously telling
the town fathers that he had come to Texas to fight and not run for
office. He left the door open, however, when he went on to say that
he would "rather be a member of the Convention than of the Senate
of the United States."[8]

While still in San Augustine, Crockett began drafting a letter to
his daughter Margaret and her husband, Wiley Flowers, in Tennessee.
Penned less than two months before his death, it is Crockett's last known
surviving correspondence.[9]

9 January 1836
Saint Augusteen, Texas

Mr. Wiley Flowers,
Crockett P.O.
Gibson County, Tennessee.

My dear Sone & daughter,

This is the first time I have had the opportunity to write to
you with convenience I am now blessed with excellent health
and am in high spirits although I have had many difficultys to
encounter I have got through safe and have been received by
every body with the open arm of friendship I am hailed with
a hardy welcome to this country a dinner and a party of Ladys
have honored me with an invitation to participate with them
both in Nacogdoches and this place the cannon was fired here
on my arrival and I must say as to what I have seen of Texas it is
the garden spot of the world the best land and the best prospect
for health I have ever saw is here and I do believe it is a fortune
to any man to come here there is a world of country to settle it
is not required here to pay down on your League of Land every
man is entitled to his head right of 400-428 [4,428] acres they
may make the money to pay for it off the land

I expect in all probability to settle on the Bodark or Choctaw
Bayou of Red River that I have found no doubt the richest
country in the world good Land and plenty of timber and the
best springs and good mill streams good range clear water and
ever appearance of good health and game plenty It is in the pass
where the Buffalo passes from north to south and back twice a
year and bees and honey plenty

I have a great hope of getting the agency to settle that
country and I would be glad to see every friend I have settle
there It would be a fortune to them all I have taken the oath of

the Government and have enrolled my name as a volunteer for six months and will set out for the Rio Grand in a few days with the volunteers from the United States all volunteers is entitled to a vote for a member of the convention or to be voted for and I have but little doubt of being elected a member to form a constitution for this Province

I am rejoiced at my fate I had rather be in my present situation than to be elected to a seat in Congress for life I am in hopes of making a fortune for my self and family as bad has been my prospects

I have not wrote to William but have requested John to direct him what to do I hope you show him this letter and also your brother John as it is not convenient at this time for me to write to them

I hope you will do the best you can and I will; do the same do not be uneasy about me for I am with friends

I must close with great respects your affectionate Father Farewell

David Crockett

Crockett's final letter very clearly spells out his objectives. His own words leave little doubt that he saw Texas as a place to make the fortune that had always eluded him and at the same time reemerge on the national political scene.

By January 13, four days after having written the letter, Crockett had returned to Nacogdoches, and, had they not yet departed, may have given the letter to Burgin and Tinkle to take back to Tennessee. William Patton, Crockett's loyal nephew, either remained in Nacogdoches due to illness or, even more likely, accompanied Crockett to the Alamo, but left there before the final siege began.[10]

Only three days later, on January 16, 1836, Crockett rode out of Nacogdoches and headed southwest among a gang of recruits dubbed the Tennessee Mounted Volunteers—a misnomer, since only a few of them hailed from the Volunteer State. Captain William B. Harrison, a young man from Ohio, was made company commander, and Crockett took his own place as a common private, although he clearly commanded much respect and influence due to his celebrity, age, and personality.[11]

This final Crockett ride across Texas has been described as having "the air of a political campaign."[12] In a way, that was precisely what it was—an audition for the rebels of Texas and a chance for Crockett to meet potential voters and inspect more land that could one day be added to his holdings. He made time to hunt and show off his marksmanship as the riders meandered toward the Trinity River and beyond to Washington-on-the-Brazos, a supply center and, as of December, Gen. Houston's headquarters and the concentration point for volunteers and mercenaries. Houston was not present when Crockett and his party arrived. Squabbling factions had split the Texian force into two distinct camps. Simply put, there were those who followed the unconventional Sam Houston, who had come to Texas with strong ties to Andrew Jackson, and on the other side there were the powerful forces involved with establishing a provisional government that leaned toward a conservative Whig philosophy. This group was diametrically opposed to Houston and Jackson and had their own ideas about how Texas should be governed.

Originally, Crockett had thought he would be going all the way to the Rio Grande to help in the Texian cause. Once he got to Washington-on-the-Brazos, however, he seems to have changed his focus. His eyes turned to San Antonio de Bexar, where many of the anti-Jackson forces had gathered. They were fully prepared to defend the city and make their stand at the Alamo despite the orders of Houston to destroy the old mission and depart as soon as possible. The senior ranking men at the Alamo were not keen on Houston and wanted him replaced as commander in chief. When it came to choosing between the two sides, Crockett—despite his friendship with Houston—allowed his hatred of Jackson to cloud his better judgment. Crockett went to San Antonio.

After several days in Washington-on-the Brazos, Crockett and the other riders were San Antonio–bound. They took their leave and ferried across the Brazos River below its confluence with the Navasota River. As they headed west, the riders encountered the Swisher family at a settlement that came to be called Gay Hill.

"At the time I saw Colonel Crockett, I judged him to be about forty years old [Crockett was forty-nine],"[13] recalled John Swisher many years later. At the time, Swisher—a Tennessee native who moved to Texas with his family in 1833—was only seventeen years old, and although he was nine years shy when guessing Crockett's age, his physical description appeared to be accurate in every detail. "He was stout and muscular, about six feet in height, and weighing 180 to 200 pounds," Swisher wrote in his memoirs.

> He was of a florid complexion, with intelligent gray eyes. He had small side whiskers, inclining to sandy. His countenance, although firm and determined, wore a pleasant and genial expression. Although his early education had been neglected, he had acquired such a polish from his contact with good society that few men could eclipse him in conversation. He was fond of talking and had an ease and grace about him which, added to his strong natural sense and the fund of anecdotes that he had gathered, rendered him irresistible.[14]

Swisher—who would go on to serve as the youngest Texian at the Battle of San Jacinto—was skilled with a rifle, and when he lugged home a freshly killed deer, Crockett praised the youngster and challenged him to a friendly shooting match, which ended in a draw when Crockett handicapped himself to give the young man a chance. The "young hunter," as Crockett called Swisher, was so thrilled that he declared he "would not have changed places with the president himself." Crockett enjoyed his stay of several days with the Swisher family and each night entertained them with his growing arsenal of stories. "He conversed about himself in the most unaffected manner without the slightest attempt to display any genius or smartness," Swisher recalled. "He told us a great many anecdotes, many of which were common place and amounted to nothing within themselves, but his inimitable way of telling them would convulse us in laughter."[15]

The laughter spread to San Antonio de Bexar when Crockett and about a dozen companions rode into town beneath a cold drizzle during the second week of February. Crockett's presence boosted the spirits of the Alamo defenders. He spoke to the citizen soldiers and townsfolk in one of San Antonio's plazas: "Fellow citizens, I am among you. I have come to your country, though not I hope, through any selfish motive whatever. I have come to aid you all that I can in your noble cause. I shall identify myself with your interest, and all the honor that I desire is that of defending, as a high private, in common with my fellow-citizens, the liberties of our common country."[16]

On the evening of February 10, Crockett received a warm reception from other volunteers—a ragamuffin band of Anglo and Hispanic rebels—who had heard that the Lion of the West was coming to join them. But the lighthearted mood at the celebratory fandango soon faded as the celebrants learned that Gen. Santa Anna was bearing down on San Antonio. Santa Anna—known as the "Napoleon of the West"[17]—led a sizable force made up of Mexican army regulars, Mayan Indians who spoke no Spanish, and raw conscripts.

For the next several days, the volunteers and mercenaries stepped up their preparations for the coming confrontation with the Mexican army. While they stocked the Alamo with rations, water, and ammunition, Crockett did his best to keep everyone entertained with his litany of backwoods yarns and jokes. On February 22, with the Mexican force within striking distance, another fandango was held to celebrate George Washington's birthday and also out of defiance in the face of what was expected to be a horrific fight. The following day, the garrison of about two hundred Texians barricaded themselves inside the Alamo just before Santa Anna and his troops marched into town. There would be no quarter—only the promise of death. The siege was on.

Crockett was undoubtedly the most famous person to take part in the thirteen-day siege at the Alamo. Sharing the limelight with him were

James Bowie and William Travis. This Alamo trio has often been portrayed as romanticized heroes. In truth, they were—like all humans—flawed and no more or less heroic than any of those from either side who took part in the siege and storming of the Alamo. Bowie had become famous in many circles because of the trademark knife he used with much proficiency in bloody duels and altercations. He did not himself make the knife; rather, his brother Rezin commissioned it for him. Some years earlier, the Bowie brothers partnered with Jean Lafitte, the notorious privateer who supplied mercenaries for Andrew Jackson at the Battle of New Orleans. The Bowies helped Lafitte traffic the many slaves he smuggled into Galveston Island and sold to plantation owners.

Beside making a fortune as a dealer in human cargo and subverting the ban on the slave trade, Bowie—like Stephen Austin—also became a land speculator. He sold fraudulent claims in Arkansas Territory, masterminded a series of property swindles in Louisiana, and speculated in Texas land. Bowie saw that there was an immense profit to be made in Texas real estate. He learned Spanish, joined the Catholic Church, became a Mexican citizen, and married into one of San Antonio's prominent Tejano families. When his wife and two children died during a cholera epidemic, Bowie went into an alcoholic depression that lasted until his death in a sickbed at the Alamo, where he served as commander of volunteer soldiers.

William Barrett Travis, commander of the regular army troops defending the old mission fortress, was an attorney by trade. He knew Bowie from San Felipe, where he served as the knife fighter's counsel. A South Carolina native, Travis—like many others—came to Texas to escape bad debts and avoid going to prison. After abandoning his pregnant wife and young son in Alabama, he entered Texas illegally and immediately became involved in the slave trade.[18] He settled in San Felipe de Austin in 1831, obtained some land from Stephen Austin, and established his law practice. He enjoyed the company of women, was known to devour Sir Walter Scott novels, and divorced his wife in 1836 when she showed up to save their marriage.[19] Although he neglected to pay off the debts left behind in Alabama, Travis soon began acquiring land and slaves, including a young black man known only as Joe.[20] He would stay with his white master all the way to the end at the Alamo, where his life was spared because he was a slave. Travis was one of the first to die at the final Alamo assault, of a bullet to the brain. He was twenty-six years old.

Then there was Crockett—the real-life Nimrod Wildfire and Lion of the West. What transpired at the Alamo was pure theater and an ideal venue for Crockett, who was center stage. His participation in the quintessential event in Texas history was all part of a drama that had been playing out for the almost half-century that he had lived, and the final scene took place at the Alamo. The curtain calls, however, have never ceased for the Davy Crockett of imagination. The Alamo is what most people think of when they hear his name. Other than the ubiquitous raccoon cap only worn in later years for the benefit of his adoring fans, it is the Alamo that most evokes the image of Crockett.

Accounts of Crockett's activities during the siege include reports of his effort to bolster morale among the men with stories and playing lively jigs on a borrowed fiddle. It was said that Crockett and a Scotsman named John McGregor, who brought his bagpipes to the fight, amused the garrison, and perhaps even the surrounding Mexican troops, with their musical interludes in between skirmishes and repulsed assaults.[21]

The storming and seizing of the Alamo was inevitable, coming as it did after nearly two weeks of steady bombardment. On the night of March 5, the Mexican guns went silent. In the cold early morning darkness of the following day, the Mexican soldiers advanced. This time, despite great casualties, they were not turned away. They came in great waves and penetrated the walls and defenses. The battle lasted less than an hour. Every defender of the Alamo was killed. Only Travis's slave and the wife and infant of one of the slain defenders survived.

Almost immediately the "last stand" at the Alamo was compared to the resolve of the Spartans facing the Persian army at the Battle of Thermopylae. A newspaper editorial published just eighteen days after the fall of the Alamo read:

That event, so lamentable, and yet so glorious to Texas, is of such deep interest and excites so much our feelings that we shall never cease to celebrate it, and regret that we are not acquainted with the names of all those who fell in that fort, that we might publish them, and thus consecrate to future ages the memory of our heroes who perished at the *Thermopylae of Texas.*[22]

The press and the public dissected the lives and deaths of the principal players, including Crockett. Even his estranged wife, Elizabeth, and his family back in Tennessee could not grasp the fact that this seemingly invulnerable frontiersman was dead. He had fooled death too many times in the past. Not until several months after the fall of the Alamo did Elizabeth know for sure that her husband would never again walk through the cabin door. She was convinced when a parcel was delivered to her home. Inside was Crockett's watch, the one he sold for thirty dollars to help with costs during his trek to Texas. There was also a letter to Elizabeth from Isaac Jones, the man who had purchased the timepiece.

> The object of this letter, is to beg that you will accept the watch . . . as it has his name engraved on the surface, it will no doubt be the more acceptable to you. With his open frankness, his natural honesty of expression, his perfect want of concealment, I could not but be very much pleased. And with a hope that it might be an accommodation to him, I was gratified at the exchange, as it gave me a *keepsake* which would often remind me of an honest man, a good citizen and a pioneer in the cause of liberty, amongst his suffering brethren in Texas.[23]

Elizabeth was grateful, for she and Crockett's kinfolk had no one to bury. Just hours after the fall of the Alamo, the bodies of approximately 183 defenders were laid in layers on a large pile of wood and dry branches and the pyre was set ablaze.[24] Left with many unanswered questions, the family went ahead, just as Crockett would have done. Robert Patton Crockett, the oldest son from Elizabeth's first marriage, went to

Texas in 1838 and joined the new republic's army. John Wesley Crockett went to the U.S. Congress in 1837 and served two terms, representing his father's former district. He was able to push through the passage of a land bill similar to the measure Crockett had long championed. By 1854, Elizabeth was finally granted the "league of land" promised to Crockett as his share for serving as a Texas soldier. She and some of the family moved to Texas and built a good cabin. Elizabeth wore black every day until her own death, in 1860.[25] She died never knowing for sure how her husband had been killed on the morning of March 6, 1836, at the Alamo.

Indeed, no one knows with any certainty how David Crockett died. His death has been obscured by legend, with accounts and theories of his death including scenarios both implausible and ludicrous. The two adult survivors, Travis's slave Joe and Susannah Wilkerson Dickinson, had managed to stay hidden during the battle. Both of them independently claimed that, after the fighting stopped, they saw Crockett lying dead and mutilated with the corpses of Mexican soldiers all around him. Neither of them saw or knew how or when Crockett was killed. Nonetheless, the popular press and dime novelists used these accounts to perpetuate the Crockett myth.[26]

One popular theory was that Crockett died while swinging old Betsey over his head. Some claimed that Crockett donned a disguise and snuck away from the Alamo like a sniveling coward. Still others believed Crockett was among a gang of fifty or more defenders who tried to escape the doomed mission only to be cut down by Mexican cavalry. Stories appeared claiming that reports of Crockett's death were false. An Ohio newspaper stated that Crockett was discovered alive among a stack of Texians executed by the Mexican troops and was taken to a private residence, where his wounds were dressed and he was making a successful recovery: "He had received a severe gash with a tomahawk on the upper part of his forehead, a ball in his leg, and another through one of his thighs, besides several other minor wounds."[27] In 1840, four years after the battle, a Texas newspaper published an account of William C. White, who maintained that he had seen "with his own eyes in the mines of Gendelejera [Guadalajara], in Mexico our own immortal CROCKETT, and heard from his own lips an account of his escape from the massacre at the Alamo."[28] As late as 1893, the *New York Times* reported that San Antonio policemen saw Col. Crockett at the Alamo after it had been converted into a subpolice station. The bold headline read, DAVY CROCKETT'S "GHOST." According to the report, on rainy, dismal nights Crockett and "the spirits of those who lost their lives within . . . hold a levee in the upper rooms of the structure." Especially troubling were the loud sounds that sounded like dancing and an apparition in the place where Crockett lost his life.[29]

Gen. Sam Houston spelled out what may be the most likely scenario soon after the fall of the Alamo. In a dispatch sent March 11 to Col. James Fannin, Houston broke the news of the deaths of all of the defenders and stated, "After the fort was carried seven men surrendered, and called for Santa Anna, and for quarter. They were murdered by his order."[30] Although Houston did not mention Crockett by name, his letter adds credence to the persistent rumor that at least seven individuals were taken captive and summarily executed. Another reference to prisoners being executed appeared in 1837, when Ramón Martínez Caro, Santa Anna's secretary, wrote that Gen. Manuel Fernández Castrillón had discovered five men hiding inside the Alamo after it had been taken by Mexican troops. Instead of immediately killing them, the general ordered the captives taken before Santa Anna, who reprimanded Castrillón for disobeying his command to give no quarter and take no prisoners. Santa Anna then turned his back while soldiers killed the prisoners. "We all witnessed this outrage which humanity condemns but which was committed as described," wrote Martínez Caro. "This is a cruel truth, but I cannot omit it."

Almost 140 years after the fact, the strongest source of proof of Crockett's death emerged. In 1975, the memoir of a Mexican army officer serving under Santa Anna at the Alamo, which had come to light in Mexico in 1955, at the height of the Disney-inspired Crockett television series, was first translated into English. The 680-page diary, written by José Enrique de la Peña, supported the claims that Crockett was one of seven survivors captured by Mexican soldiers and executed by order of General Santa Anna:

> Some seven men survived the general carnage and, under the protection of General Castrillón, they were brought before Santa Anna. Among them was one of great stature, well proportioned, with regular features, in whose face was the imprint of adversity, but in whom one also noticed a degree of resignation and nobility that did him honor. He was the naturalist David Crockett, well known in North America for his unusual adventures, who had undertaken to explore the country and who, finding himself in Bejar at the very moment of surprise, had taken refuge in the Alamo, fearing that his status as a foreigner might not be respected. Santa Anna answered Castrillón's intervention in Crockett's behalf with a gesture of indignation and, addressing himself to the sappers, the troops closest to him, ordered his execution. The commanders and officers were outraged at this action and did not support the order, hoping that once the fury of the moment had blown over these men would be spared; but several officers who were around the president and who, perhaps, had not been present during the danger, became noteworthy by an infamous deed, surpassing the soldiers in cruelty. They thrust themselves forward, in order to flatter their commander, and with swords in hand, fell upon these unfortunate, defenseless men just as a tiger leaps upon his prey. Though tortured before they were killed, these unfortunates died without complaining and without humiliating themselves before their torturers.[31]

Publication of the Peña narrative in the United States set off an avalanche of controversy in Texas and beyond. The many staunch defenders of the popular and romanticized image of the Alamo and Crockett were livid and not only challenged the diary but insisted it was a forgery. A rush of articles and books either defending the historic document or attacking it followed. Despite careful expert examination of the narrative and the declaration of a University of Texas forgery professional that the memoir appeared to be authentic, many skeptics were still unconvinced.[32] They could not accept Peña's explanation of Crockett's death and continued to refer to it as the most famous unsolved homicide in history.

For the many scholars and Crockett researchers every bit as devoted to the historic figure as those in love with the myth, the overwhelming evidence supports the Peña narrative. And in the end, does it truly matter how Crockett died? Is his death less noteworthy or dramatic? As longtime Crockett scholar Paul Hutton notes:

> He died as he had lived, boldly facing his opponents with unflinching determination to be sure he was right—and then go ahead! That he did not fall at the height of battle, ringed by the men he had slain with his clubbed rifle and knife, is of no consequence. Such a death would have been out of character with his life. He was no warrior chieftain—no combination of Beowulf and Roland—but was rather a pioneer turned politician who came to symbolize western egalitarianism and unbridled opportunity.[33]

To those who claim that God made Texas, one may say that, figuratively, Crockett invented Texas. His blood and the blood of all who died with him transformed the Alamo into an American cultural icon, affecting economic and political conditions in Texas and beyond. The oft-used battle cry "Remember the Alamo!"—employed just weeks later by Sam Houston to inspire his force when they captured General Santa Anna and defeated the Mexican army at San Jacinto—still reverberates through history and culture. For many Anglo Texans and others, those three words conjure images of patriotic heroes, unabashed sacrifice, and love of liberty.

The Alamo remains the most instantly recognized battle in American history, with the possible exception of Gettysburg. It has been said that not until the Battle of the Little Big Horn and the death of George Armstrong Custer forty years after the Alamo would Americans have a more vainglorious event to rally around. Texans also used the Alamo and the revolt against Mexico to establish a republic and, later, a state that they believed unique and more special than any other. In 1845, when the Republic of Texas gave up its sovereignty to become the biggest state in the Union, it did so with the caveat—depending on whose interpretation of the Texas Constitution is followed—that it could secede at any time and split into five separate entities, thus creating four new states.[34] The strong belief among many Texans was that their independence— their Lone Star status—had been bought and paid for at the Alamo.

Crockett's death sums up the single most important aspect of his brief stay in Texas. His contribution to the Lone Star State resulted not so much from how he lived but how he died. His impact on Texas derives precisely from his death in that battered Spanish mission. In death he turned into an even more marketable commodity than he had been in life, and the Alamo eventually would become the state's biggest tourist attraction and one of the most popular historic sites in the nation.

Crockett's death helped fuel the flames of rebellion against Mexico and also made him a celebrated martyr for the cause. This contributed to the creation of the prideful, sometimes bellicose, stereotypical image of swaggering, boastful Texans bursting with superlatives and pride when describing the land they love. Crockett's demise also helped turn the Alamo into the "Cradle of Texas Liberty" and a monument to Anglo westward expansion that became known as Manifest Destiny.

There was the David Crockett of historical fact, and there is the Davy Crockett of our collective imagination. The first was a man who led a most interesting and colorful life. The other is the American myth, featuring Crockett as a symbolic figure with superhuman powers; in this version, Crockett is frequently used by others to promote their own interests. Both Crockett and the Alamo remain ensnared in clouds of myth.

In the end, Crockett was a uniquely American character and a formidable hero in his own right. He should not be judged by his death but rather by his life—including the good and the bad and the shades of gray. Consider him as a legend and a hero, but always bear in mind that he was a man willing to take a risk. That was what he symbolized and that is how he should be remembered.

ACKNOWLEDGMENTS

Writing a book is ultimately a solitary act. But the process of getting to the point of the actual writing and all that transpires after a manuscript is completed is far from solitary. This book—my sixteenth—was no exception. It took many people besides me to get the job done. Each of them was important, many were essential, and a few of them were so invaluable that without them this book would never have been written.

Two people who absolutely fit in that last category are Suzanne Fitzgerald Wallis and Joseph A. Swann. That is why I dedicated the book to them. This gesture is but a small token of my appreciation to both of them.

Suzanne is my life partner, best friend, lover, and chief collaborator. Her wisdom, diligence, and encouragement are largely responsible for this book as well as for all the others I have written and those yet to come. Suzanne, with assistance from our quirky feline muse, Sophie, is there for me every day whether I deserve it or not.

Joe Swann not only acted as a tireless guide and excellent source of knowledge about all things Crockett but also unselfishly shared his entire unpublished manuscript detailing Crockett's many years spent in Tennessee. The voice and vision of Joe Swann echoes throughout much of this book. Joe showed me places and led me to people that I would not have found on my own. He and his lovely wife, Rebecca, the epitome of a gracious Tennessean, nourished my mind and body at their comfortable home. I will never forget their hospitality and kindness.

Another person who figured prominently in the development of this book is James Fitzgerald. Jim is my literary agent and also happens to be one my wife's trio of Irish brothers. Jim and I have known each other for more than forty years. At times we also have been known to battle like a pair of boar bears, but I always know that ultimately I can count on Jim, one of the savviest individuals in the strange and sometimes turbulent world of publishing.

As they have done in the past with my other books they have published, the entire editorial, design, marketing, and promotional team at W. W. Norton is once more to be commended for helping make this book a reality. Robert Weil, my esteemed editor, was at the helm of this effort and was there for me every single step of the way. Throughout my career as an author I have been fortunate to encounter some topflight editors. All of them play second fiddle to Bob Weil. He is bar none the most diligent, driven, and dedicated editor drawing breath today. I defy anyone to tell me otherwise. Likewise, Bob's hardworking assistants—in the case of this book, Lucas Wittmann and Phil Marino—never let me down. Both of these young men have learned well from Bob, a proven mentor whose long line of editorial assistants from over the years have gone on to much success in publishing.

During the long research and writing process, I also was fortunate to have happened upon other knowledgeable and helpful sons and daughters of Tennessee. Much like Joe and Becky Swann, these people opened their hearts and homes to me and made the development of this book much more enjoyable. Two Tennesseans at the top of this list are Jere Ellis and Jim Claborn. Jere took care of me in West Tennessee, and Jim was one of my primary guides in East Tennessee. Both men deserve medals on their chests for their assistance.

Jere resides at Blue Cut near Tiptonville, Tennessee, not far from one of David Crockett's favorite hunting sites at Reelfoot Lake. Beside staying active in his community and taking the time to show authors the secret places and hidden corners of Crockett's former stomping grounds, Jere maintains the Eagle Tree Gallery, where his vast inventory of museum-quality Southwestern Indian art, crafts, and artifacts attracts people from all over the country. Unquestionably, this book would not have been the same without the assistance and input I received from Jere. Thank you, my friend, for your graciousness and guidance, and also a special thanks for introducing me to Boyette's, a dining oasis since 1921 that consistently turns out catfish, hush puppies, and coleslaw to die for.

Jim Claborn, who hails from Talbott, a small community near Morristown, Tennessee, the site of the Crockett Tavern Museum, was recommended to me when I sought out people with a passion for history to show me the ropes in "Crockett Country" of eastern Tennessee. Jim is an accomplished historian and teacher, but most of all he is a masterful storyteller. Together with another excellent teacher and historian, Bill Henderson, Jim coauthored *Hamblen County, Tennessee: A Pictorial History*, and he often portrays Crockett in full costume for a variety of audiences. His guidance and infusion of information and knowledge was of great help to me. Thanks, my friend.

I was fortunate to have a pair of capable and resourceful researchers helping me every step of the way. In Knoxville, Tennessee, the research assignment went to Kevin Pettiford, a fine journalist and freelance writer, who prowled and probed archives, libraries, and museums in my behalf. Kevin never came up empty-handed, and I appreciate not only his consistency and hard work but his ability to go over and beyond when it came to finding those elusive morsels of the past that often remain undiscovered.

On the home front, I was fortunate to have the research assistance of William "Trey" Stewart, a native Tulsan who started his work with me just prior to his senior year at Middlebury College in Vermont. Trey is also a self-starter, who required very little direction once a task was assigned to him. A dedicated student of American history and a fine developing writer, Trey is also a sturdy rugby player, which helps explain the tenacity and dogged persistence he demonstrated in all of his fine work for me. Also, special thanks to Anne Payne, a good friend and neighbor who put in untold hours helping Suzanne gather photographs, images, and permissions for the book.

Speaking of support at home while laboring over Mister Crockett, our dear friends Sue and Steve Gerkin as always were there every minute along the way to offer moral support and encouragement. Many thanks to you, Tex and Spud. I am very grateful for our friendship.

Before writing one word of this book, I conferred with Paul Andrew Hutton, a distinguished professor of history at the University of New Mexico and the former president of Western Writers of America and executive director of the Western History Association. Like me, Paul has an affinity for Henry McCarty, aka Billy the Kid, as well as for David Crockett. In fact, Paul has been laboring on his own book about Crockett for many years. I am so grateful to him for encouraging me to proceed with my book and also for providing me with several contacts who proved to be important sources and fonts of information about Crockett and his times.

Others who merit mention and my profound thanks include Sally A. Baker, site director, Crockett Tavern Museum, Morristown, Tennessee; Cherel Bolin Henderson, director, and Lisa Oakley, curator of education, East Tennessee Historical Society, Knoxville; Steve Cotham, manager, C. M. McClung Historical Collection, Knox County Public Library, Knoxville, Tennessee; Robert D. Jarnagin, Dandridge, Tennessee; Lura B. Hinchey, director, and Ernie Hodges and Bobby Shands, volunteers, Jefferson County Archives, Dandridge, Tennessee; Strawberry Luck, Tennessee State Museum, Nashville, Tennessee; Nick Wyman, Research Services, Special Collections Library, University of Tennessee, Knoxville; Joe Bone, manager, Last Home of Davy Crockett Museum, Rutherford, Tennessee; Joy Bland, historian, Direct Descendants and Kin of David Crockett; Tennessee State Library and Archives, Nashville; Michael A. Lofaro, professor of American studies and American literature, University of Tennessee, Knoxville; William B. Eigelsbach, Reference Services, University of Tennessee Special Collections Library, Hoskins Library, Knoxville; National Society of Colonial Dames of America in the State of Tennessee; Gert Petersen and the Franklin County Historical Society, Winchester, Tennessee; State of Tennessee Department of Education, Nashville; Lawrence County (Tennessee) Historical Society; The Mid-West Tennessee Genealogical Society, Jackson, Tennessee; Tennessee

Historical Commission, Nashville; Lake County (Tennessee) Historical Society; Joe and Bernadine Widdifield, Panther Springs, Tennessee.

Thanks also to Aaron D. Purcell, associate professor and director of Special Collections and University Libraries, Virginia Tech University, Blacksburg; Daughters of the Republic of Texas Library at the Alamo, San Antonio; Berkeley County Historical Society, Martinsburg, West Virginia; Gowen Research Foundation, Lubbock, Texas; Alabama Department of History and Archives, Montgomery; Andrew Burstein, Louisiana State University, Baton Rouge; Dr. Joe Reilly, Drexel University, Philadelphia, Pennsylvania; the San Jacinto Museum, Houston, Texas; Birmingham Public Library Cartographic Collection, Birmingham, Alabama; Craig Remington, Department of Geography, University of Alabama, Tuscaloosa; Rick Watson, Harry Ransom Humanities Research Center, University of Texas at Austin; Linda Stone, curator, Woolaroc Museum, Bartlesville, Oklahoma; Aryn Glazer, Prints and Photographs Collection, Dolph Briscoe Center of American History, University of Texas at Austin; Oklahoma State Senate Historical Preservations Fund, Inc., Oklahoma City; Dorothy Sloan and Shelby Smith, Dorothy Sloan Rare Books, Austin, Texas; Print Collection, Miriam and Ira D. Wallach Division of Art, Prints and Photographs, The New York Public Library; G. W. Blunt White Library at Mystic Seaport Museum, Mystic, Connecticut; Ronald McCoy, Tulsa, Oklahoma; Emily Priddy, Tulsa, Oklahoma; Linda Priddy, Herrin, Illinois; Robert McCubbin, Santa Fe, New Mexico; Larry Yadon, Tulsa, Oklahoma; Danny and Barbara Moon, Hickman, Kentucky; and Phillipe Garmy, Stillwater, Oklahoma.

NOTES

ONE • "KILT HIM A B'AR"

1 Lyrics by Tom Blackburn, music by George Bruns, copyright 1954, Wonderland Music Co.

2 David Crockett, *A Narrative of the Life of David Crockett of the State of Tennessee* (Philadelphia: E. L. Carey and A. Hart, 1834), 190.

3 Ibid., 190–91. Some sources contend that Crockett's story about climbing a tree and sliding down to stay warm was pure invention—one of his exaggerated yarns later picked up and reprinted in almanacs and newspapers. Others disagree and believe the story has the ring of truth.

4 Ibid.

5 Ibid., 194.

6 J. H. Grime, *Recollections of a Long Life* (Lebanon, TN: 1930), 8. Rev. John Harvey Grime, a prominent Baptist preacher and religious leader throughout the South, recalled that as a boy in Tennessee he had a hunting dog named after Davy Crockett and another he named Jolar after Crockett's favorite dog.

TWO • BORN ON A RIVERBANK IN FRANKLIN

1 No records of David Crockett's birth exist. In all probability, August 17, 1786, is correct. It has always been the accepted date of birth.

2 Kathryn E. Jones, *Crockett Cousins* (Graham, TX: K. E. Jones, 1984; 2nd printing, rev. ed., 1986), 21–24.

3 From Joy Bland e-mail to the author, April 8, 2009.

4 Joy Bland, "Genealogical Discovery," *Go Ahead: Newsletter of the Direct Descendants and Kin of David Crockett* 25, no. 1, August 2008, 3.

5 Ibid.

6 Ibid.

7 Robert L. Geiser, *The Illusion of Caring* (Boston: Beacon Press, 1973), 148.

8 This quote is attributed to Mary Boykin Chestnut, the daughter of a South Carolina governor and the wife of James Chestnut Jr., the son of one of antebellum South Carolina's largest landowners.

9 Crockett, *Narrative*, 16.

10 James Atkins Shackford, *David Crockett: The Man and the Legend*, edited by John B. Shackford (Chapel Hill: University of North Carolina Press, 1956), 7.

11 Curtis Carroll Davis, "A Legend at Full-Length: Mr. Chapman Paints Colonel Crockett—and Tells About It," *Proceedings of the American Antiquarian Society* (Worcester, MA: American Antiquarian Society, April 1960), 170. Crockett made this statement to artist John Gadsby Chapman in 1834 while sitting for his portrait in Chapman's studio in Washington, D.C.

12 David Dobson, *Directory of Scots in the Carolinas, 1680–1830* (Baltimore: Genealogical Printing Company, 2002), 52. The name Crockett may have come from the ancient Norse word *krok-r*, meaning crook, hook, or bend and probably the root of the old English word *crock*.

13 Joseph A. Swann, "The Early Life & Times of David Crockett, 1786–1812," unpublished manuscript.

14 Ibid.

15 Ibid.

16 Ibid. Lowland Scots were an interesting mixture of Celts, Romans, Scandinavians, Germans, English, Irish, and Scots. The region of southern Scotland and northern England was an age-old border battleground where lawlessness had become a way of life. Residents of this contested landscape raided back and forth across the border from before the time of the Romans in the first century AD. This lawlessness and fighting escalated by the seventeenth century, creating an environment of strife and disorder, which effectively undermined any kind of sustained economic opportunity. During the sixteenth and seventeenth centuries the British government confiscated a great deal of Catholic-owned property and enacted penal laws restricting land ownership exclusively to Protestants.

17 Ibid. Over three or four generations, the Scots succeeded in developing the Ulster-Londonderry area that had been torn apart by war and poverty into a thriving industrial region. By the middle of the seventeenth century the county of Ulster was almost totally populated by Scots-Irish. The marshes and bogs had been drained, and fertile lands were planted with a new crop—the potato—brought by Sir Walter Raleigh from the American Indians and soon a staple in the Irish diet. At the same time, the manufacture of woolen and linen products flourished until the English manufacturers tired of Scots in Ulster shipping goods to the American colonies. This resulted in the implementation of harsh trade restrictions, including a ban of the exportation of Irish wool products to anywhere in the world except England and Wales. The mostly English landlords of Ulster also employed a policy referred to as rack-renting, which doubled or even tripled the property rent. The word "rack" became a term of protest, evoking the medieval torture device, to denote excessive rents.

18 Ibid.

THREE • THE CROCKETTS ARRIVE

1 Crockett, *Narrative*, 14.
2 Ibid., n. 3.
3 Jim Webb, *Born Fighting: How the Scots-Irish Shaped America* (New York: Broadway Books, 2004), 133.
4 Swann, "The Early Life & Times."
5 Ibid.
6 Webb, *Born Fighting*, 118. Although the term Scotch-Irish is commonly used in the United States, the author points out that in other countries, especially Scotland, it is considered rude to refer to a person as being Scotch. He explains that Scotch is a whiskey and that Scots are people whose roots go back to Scotland.
7 Swann, "Early Life & Times."
8 Jones, *Crockett Cousins*, 4. Located on the Potomac River, separating Virginia and Maryland, the ferry was established in 1744 and was named for Evan Watkins, the ferry owner who resided at his nearby home and farm, Maidstone-on-the-Potomac, a site well known to the Crocketts and other early Scots-Irish.
9 Ibid., 4. Frederick County, VA, Court Records, Order Bk. 2, 456.
10 Ibid., 4–5. It also has been suggested that Elizabeth may have been somehow related to a William Patterson who was mentioned in several deeds involving the Crocketts, and may account for the name Patterson bestowed on one of their grandsons.
11 Swann, "Early Life & Times."
12 Jones, *Crockett Cousins*, 4. Throughout the early 1770s, the names of David the elder and other family members appeared on legal documents and records in Tryon County and later when it became Lincoln County. These records include various Crocketts serving as witnesses for property deeds, codicils to wills, and mortgages. On at least two occasions David and his eldest son, William, served together as jurors, including on a January 1775 criminal trial in which the jury panel ruled in favor of the defendant and found Thomas Espey, a Tryon County justice of the peace, not guilty of a charge of extortion.
13 Robert Morgan, *Boone: A Biography* (Chapel Hill: Algonquin, 2007), 20.
14 Jones, *Crockett Cousins*, 39.
15 Swann, "Early Life & Times."
16 Crockett, *Narrative*, 14.

FOUR • OVER THE MOUNTAIN

1 Jones, *Crockett Cousins*, 6.
2 John R. Finger, *Tennessee Frontiers, Three Regions in Transition* (Bloomington and Indianapolis: Indiana University Press, 2001), 39–41.

3 Ibid., 39.

4 Wayne C. Moore, "Paths of Migration," *First Families of Tennessee: A Register of Early Settlers and Their Present-Day Descendants* (Knoxville: East Tennessee Historical Society, 2000), 30.

5 J. G. M. Ramsey, *The Annals of Tennessee* (Charleston, SC: Walkers & Jones, 1853; reprinted in 1967 for the East Tennessee Historical Society, Knoxville; reprinted in 1999 by Overmountain Press), 94.

6 Ibid., 96.

7 John Trotwood Moore and Austin P. Foster, *Tennessee, The Volunteer State* (Nashville and Chicago: S. J. Clarke, 1923), v.

8 Jones, *Crockett Cousins*, 2, 6.

9 Wilma Dykeman, *Tennessee, A History* (New York: W. W. Norton & Company, 1984), 43–44.

10 Ibid.

11 Jones, *Crockett Cousins*, 3, 6. The document signed by two David Crocketts was called the Washington County Petition. It provides additional proof that the David Crockett who is the subject of this book had an uncle named David Crockett Jr.

12 Crockett, *Narrative*, 15.

13 James Mooney, *Myths of the Cherokee and Sacred Formulas of the Cherokees* (Nashville: Charles and Randy Elder-Booksellers Publishers, reproduced 1982, originally published by the Bureau of American Ethnology in 1891 and 1900), 55.

14 Crockett, *Narrative*, 15–16.

15 Shackford, *David Crockett: The Man and the Legend*, 4–5.

16 Swann, "Early Life & Times."

17 Crockett, *Narrative*, 16.

18 Jones, *Crockett Cousins*, 101.

19 Swann, "Early Life & Times."

20 James Collins, *Autobiography of a Revolutionary Soldier*, edited by John M. Roberts (Clinton, LA: Feliciana Democrat, 1859; reprinted New York: Arno Press, 1979), 22.

FIVE • ON THE NOLICHUCKY

1 Fred Brown, *Marking Time: East Tennessee Historical Markers and the Stories Behind Them* (Knoxville: University of Tennessee Press, 2005), 112. Rev. Samuel Doak, a Presbyterian minister and a major influence on the Tennessee frontier, came up with the cry for liberty in 1780 after delivering a sermon to the Overmountain Men preparing for the King's Mountain battle. Doak urged them to fight with "the sword of the Lord and of Gideon," and the Scots-Irish Presbyterians before him responded as one: "The sword of the Lord and of our Gideons."

2   Wayne C. Moore, "Paths of Migration," 39.

3   Ibid.

4   Harriette Simpson Arnow, *Seedtime on the Cumberland* (Lexington: University of Kentucky Press, 1983), 195. As the author points out, women listening from behind fort walls often mistook the battle whoops of their own returning menfolk, bearing fresh scalps, for those of Indians.

5   Crockett, *Narrative*, 14–15. Except for the *Roster of Soldiers from North Carolina in the American Revolution* listing John Crockett as a member of the Lincoln County militia, no detailed record of his service record has been found. There is, however, a record provided for John's brother Robert, who filed for a pension in 1833 based on his service during the Revolution. It shows Robert serving in various militia posts for several weeks or months at a time from June 1776 until 1781, when he was discharged. Since Robert and John were from the same family and were close in age, their military service records might be similar.

6   Court Records of Washington County, Virginia—Minutes, vol. 1, 39, August 1778.

7   Jones, *Crockett Cousins*, 6–7.

8   Court Records of Washington, County, Virginia, 54.

9   Ibid.

10 Shackford, *David Crockett: The Man and the Legend*, 5.

11 Austin P. Foster, *Counties of Tennessee, A Reference of Historical and Statistical Facts for Each of Tennessee's Counties* (Nashville: Department of Education, State of Tennessee, 1923. Reprinted by The Overmountain Press, 1998), 14. The county was named in honor of General Nathanael Greene, the Rhode Islander who played a key role in the American victories against the British in the South.

12 Ramsey, *Annals of Tennessee*, 121. The Crockett cabin was located near the confluence of the Big Limestone and the Nolichucky within a large plot of land known as Brown's Purchase, after Jacob Brown, an itinerant merchant from South Carolina, who had purchased it from the Cherokees with a load of trade goods.

13 Shackford, *David Crockett: The Man and the Legend*, 5.

14 Ibid., 6.

15 Ibid., 33, 34, 431, n. 17, n. 19.

16 Swann, "Early Life & Times."

17 Arnow, *Seedtime*, 194. Known as "Little John" by the Indians he fought, Sevier, of French Huguenot descent, also was called "the handsomest man in Tennessee."

18 Ramsey, *Annals of Tennessee*, 386–87.

19 Ibid. Greene County became a bastion of support for the State of Franklin— one of the great political experiments on the eighteenth-century frontier—and

the capital was established at Greeneville, founded in the early 1780s. John Crockett took an active part in meetings and signed various documents and petitions pertaining to the State of Franklin.

20 Swann, "Early Life & Times."

21 Ramsey, *Annals of Tennessee*, 517–18.

22 Ibid.

23 Ibid., 659.

24 Crockett, *Narrative*, 18–20.

25 Stanley J. Folmsbee, *A Narrative of the Life of David Crockett of the State of Tennessee* by David Crockett, A Facsimile Edition with an Introduction and Annotations by James A. Shackford and Stanley J. Folmsbee (Knoxville: University of Tennessee Press, 1973), 19.

26 Swann, "Early Life & Times."

SIX • A BOY'S LEARNING

1 Swann, "Early Life & Times." Greene County Deed Book, vol. 3, 320, November 27, 1792, John Crockett from St of NC 197 acres Stogdons Fork, Lick Creek, Grant #1243.

2 Alice Daniel, *Log Cabins of the Smokies* (Gatlinburg, TN: Great Smoky Mountains Natural History Association, 2000), 3.

3 Crockett, *Narrative*, 20.

4 Fred Brown, "The Stoneciphers," *Knoxville News-Sentinel*, September 22, 1996. The Stonecipher family had come to America from Germany by way of Rotterdam in the mid-1700s. They were hired by the governor of Virginia to cut stone for buildings in the expanding Tidewater lands and in 1777 the family moved to the new frontier that would become Tennessee.

5 Ibid.

6 Crockett, *Narrative*, 21.

7 Brown, "Stoneciphers."

8 Ibid.

9 Crockett, *Narrative*, 21.

10 Brown, "Stoneciphers." Absalom and Sarah Stonecipher raised ten children. When Absalom died at the age of eighty-two in 1851, he had outlived David Crockett by fifteen years.

11 Kay K. Moss, *Southern Folk Medicine, 1750–1820* (Columbia: University of South Carolina Press, 1999), 2, 27.

12 Ibid., 8. For example, Dr. Benjamin Rush, a signer of the Declaration of Independence and a renowned Philadelphia physician, knew enough to counsel his aspiring students to seek out practitioners of domestic medicine. "When you go abroad always take a memorandum book and whenever you hear an old woman say such and such herbs are good, or that a compound makes a good

medicine or ointment, put it down, for, gentlemen, you may need it." Before his death in 1813, Rush was professor of the practice of medicine at the University of Pennsylvania, America's preeminent medical school at the time.

13 Swann, "Early Life & Times."

14 Michal Strutin, *Gristmills of the Smokies* (Gatlinburg, TN: Great Smoky Mountains National History Association, 2000), 3.

15 Ibid., 7.

16 A millstone believed to have been removed from the site of the Crockett gristmill destroyed in the 1794 flood was eventually donated to the Crockett Tavern Museum in Morristown, TN, where it can still be seen.

17 Crockett, *Narrative*, 21.

18 From the Crockett Tavern and Pioneer Museum files. Swann, "Early Life & Times.

19 Jones, *Crockett Cousins*, 39: Grant of 300 acres in Jefferson County, TN, to John Crockett, April 14, 1792. Estle P. Muncy, *People and Places of Jefferson County* (Rogersville, TN: East Tennessee Printing Co., 1994), 3, 5–8. Formed by Territorial Governor William Blount in 1792 and bounded by the French Broad and Holston rivers, the county was named for Thomas Jefferson. The following year Dandridge, established in honor of Martha Dandridge Custis Washington, the wife of President Washington, was named the county seat. Mossy Creek, named for the profusion of long, vividly green moss fronds waving in the currents of the stream, was first settled in the 1780s. The community retained its name for almost 120 years, until 1901, when it became Jefferson City

20 William Douglas Henderson and Jimmy W. Claborn, *Hamblen County: A Pictorial History* (Virginia Beach, VA: Donning Company, 1995), 85.

21 Crockett, *Narrative*, 22.

22 Shackford, *David Crockett: The Man and the Legend*, 7.

SEVEN • COMING OF AGE

1 Warren Moore, *Mountain Voices: A Legacy of the Blue Ridge and Great Smokies* (Chester, CT: Globe Pequot Press, 1988), 39.

2 Shackford, *David Crockett: The Man and the Legend*, 7.

3 Henderson and Claborn, *Hamblen County*, 85. A development of private residences was built on the 1,952-foot-high Crockett Ridge starting in the early 2000s.

4 Crockett, *Narrative*, 22.

5 June 14, 1797, Bent Creek Day Book, May 1796–June 5, 1800.

6 Crockett, *Narrative*, 22–23.

7 Wallace L. McKeehan, Sons of DeWeitt Colony Texas, 1997–2006, The Sylar Family, www.tamu.edu/ccbn/mckstorysylarframe.htm. His family surname means "ropemaker" in German. It was spelled a variety of ways in Amer-

ica, including Sylar, Seiler, Silor, and Siler, the spelling used by David's new employer. In 1793, Siler married fourteen-year-old Jane Hartley, and they established themselves near the home of her father, Peter Hartley, in Rockbridge County, VA.

8 Ibid. The famed Natural Bridge formed an arch that was sacred to Indian tribes and one of the wonders of the new world for European visitors during the eighteenth and nineteenth centuries.

9 Crockett, *Narrative*, 23.

10 Ibid., 23–24.

11 Ibid., 24.

12 Ibid., 24–25.

13 Ibid., 25–26.

14 Ibid., 29.

15 Ibid., 29–30.

16 Ibid., 30.

17 Ibid., 32.

18 Ann K. Blomquist, ed., *Cheek's Cross Roads, Tennessee Store Journal, 1802–1807* (Baltimore: Gateway Press, 2001), ix.

EIGHT • THE ODYSSEY

1 Swann, "Early Life & Times."

2 Extracted from files of the Berkeley County Historical Society, Martinsburg, West Virginia.

3 Crockett, *Narrative*, 32.

4 Ibid., 33.

5 Ibid.

6 Ibid., 34.

7 Ibid., 35.

8 Ibid. Perhaps the horses pulling the wagon did see a ghost, as Crockett humorously suggested. Elliott City, MD, formerly named Elliott's Mill, has been called the most haunted small town in the state and one of the most haunted spots on the eastern seaboard.

9 Ibid., 36–37.

10 Ibid., 37.

11 Ibid., 38.

12 Ibid., 39.

13 Ibid., 39–40.

14 James Strefhan Johnson III, "The Evolution of an American Small Town," master's thesis, Massachusetts Institute of Technology, June 2004, 18. A warrant was issued for Boone's arrest, but by then he had moved on. To this day the document is intact at the courthouse.

15 Shackford, *David Crockett: The Man and the Legend*, 10.
16 Ibid.
17 Crockett, *Narrative*, 40.
18 Ibid., 40–41.
19 Ibid., 41.
20 Ibid., 42.
21 Ibid.
22 Ibid., 42–43.

NINE • RISE ABOVE

1 Swann, "Early Life & Times."
2 Lareine Warden Clayton, *Stories of Early Inns and Taverns of the East Tennessee Country* (Nashville: National Society of the Colonial Dames of America in the State of Tennessee, 1995), 85. The costliest spirit at the time was wine, at ten cents for a half pint, the same price as a full dinner.
3 Crockett, *Narrative*, 45.
4 Ibid.
5 Swann, "Early Life & Times."
6 Ibid.
7 Ibid.
8 John and Margaret Thornbrough Canaday Family, www.freepages.family.roots web.ancestry.com/~mygerman. In later years, Lost Creek Meeting became a station on the Underground Railroad, helping runaway slaves find freedom.
9 Swann, "Early Life & Times."
10 Ibid.
11 Crockett, *Narrative*, 46.
12 Ibid., 46–47.
13 Ibid., 47.
14 Swann, "Early Life & Times."
15 Ibid.
16 Bent Creek Baptists Church Minutes, Saturday, February 4, 1803. The baptism took place on Samuel Riggs's property.

TEN • LOVESICK

1 Crockett, *Narrative*, 47.
2 Swann, "Early Life & Times."
3 Crockett, *Narrative*, 47–48.
4 Ibid., 48.
5 Ibid., 48–49.
6 Ibid., 49.

7 Ibid.

8 Crockett and Thomas Chilton, a friend and colleague in the U.S. Congress, read Ovid's classic work as they prepared to write the Crockett autobiography.

9 Ibid. Records show that the Elders lived along Lick Creek, in Greene County, at the same time as David and his family.

10. Swann, "Early Life & Times," quoting an 1893 article by Alexander Hynds in the *Louisville Courier Journal*.

11 Crockett, *Narrative*, 50.

12 Randell Jones, *In the Footsteps of Davy Crockett* (Winston-Salem, NC: John F. Blair, 2006), 21–22.

13 Jefferson County Marriage Records Book 1, Entry Number 526, Jefferson County Courthouse, Dandridge, TN. The Crockett-Elder license at the Jefferson County courthouse is a copy. The original document was mistakenly discarded during a housecleaning of the archives, and eventually ended up in the possession of a private party in Tampa, FL. When it surfaced at a broadcast of *Antiques Roadshow*, an appraiser from Christie's in New York said the document's historical significance was immeasurable.

14 Crockett, *Narrative*, 53.

15 Ibid., 53–54.

16 Ibid., 54.

ELEVEN • POLLY

1 Crockett, *Narrative*, 54.

2 Ibid., 55.

3 Shackford, *David Crockett: The Man and the Legend*, 13.

4 Crockett, *Narrative*, 57. In Crockett's day virtually all people of German extraction were simply described as *Dutch*, as in Pennsylvania Dutch.

5 Crockett, *Narrative*, 57.

6 Ibid., 58.

7 Ibid., 58–59.

8 Robert E. Corlew, *Tennessee: A Short History* (Knoxville: University of Tennessee Press, 1981), 111–12.

9 Crockett, *Narrative*, 58.

10 Swann, "Early Life & Times."

11 Crockett, *Narrative*, 59. Plaguy, also plaguey, meaning irritating or bothersome.

12 Ibid., 59–60.

13 Shackford, *David Crockett: The Man and the Legend*, 14. Crockett described Billy Finley as being "clever," at that time a word meaning *friendly* or *sociable*.

14 Crockett, *Narrative*, 61.

15 Ibid., 62.

16 Ibid., 63.

17 Ibid., 64.

18 Crockett's first rifle, owned by noted Crockett historian Joseph Swann, has been in his family's possession for several generations. The rifle is on public display at the Museum of East Tennessee History in Knoxville. See "Crockett's First Rifle," photograph and story.

19 Ibid.

20 *Jefferson County Marriage and Bond Book, 1792–1840*, Marriage Bond, "David Crockett to Polly Finley," August 12, 1806, Jefferson County Courthouse, Dandridge, Tennessee.

21 Ibid.

22 Joseph Swann, "The Wedding of David Crockett and Polly Finley," *Go Ahead: Newsletter of the Direct Descendants and Kin of David Crockett* 23, no. 2 (December 2006), 2–4.

23 Ibid., 3.

TWELVE • FINLEY'S GAP

1 Crockett, *Narrative*, 67.

2 Ibid.

3 Swann, "Early Life & Times." Swann, whose own family settled in the area early on, states that an Indian trader named Isaac Thomas guided several of the men from the expedition who later settled on lands they had traversed. Swann believes it is possible that John Crockett was among the soldiers who followed the route down Long Creek to its source on the south side of Bays Mountain and over the mountain near Finley's Gap to the Dumplin Creek valley, which followed on to the southwest.

4 Muncy, *People and Places of Jefferson County*, 183.

5 Ibid., 200.

6 J. L. Caton, "Davy Crockett and Polly Finley in Jefferson County," March 1, 1958, transcription of unpublished memoir of George Cox, Crockett File, Jefferson County Historical Archives, Jefferson County Courthouse, Dandridge, TN.

7 Ibid.

8 Crockett, *Narrative*, 68.

9 Joseph A. Swann, "The History of David Crockett's First Rifle," unpublished paper.

10 Swann, "Early Life & Times."

11 Crockett, *Narrative*, 68.

12 Written account of John L. Jacobs, Cullasaja, Macon County, NC, November 22, 1884, Tennessee State Library and Archives, Nashville.

13 Hugh Talmadge Lefler, ed., *A New Voyage to Carolina by John Lawson* (Chapel Hill: University of North Carolina Press, 1967), 116. Originally published in

London in 1709, Lawson's journal was the first popular American travel book, an international best seller, and an important source document for colonial natural history. The origin of the bearskin as ceremonial headwear dates to the early 1700s, when several British regiments adopted sixteen-inch-high bearskin hats.

14 Arnow, *Seedtime*, 398.
15 Ibid.
16 Ibid.
17 Information obtained by Joseph Swann gleaned from the Quarles Family files of Reverend Reuell Prichett, former Jefferson County (TN) historian.
18 Crockett, *Narrative*, 68.
19 Joseph A. Swann, Transcript Copies of Circuit Court File 1808–1835, Jefferson County Archives, Jefferson County Courthouse, Dandridge, TN.
20 *Heritage Jefferson County* (Dandridge: The Bicentennial Committee of Jefferson County, TN, 1976), 4.
21 Ibid., 4–5.
22 Swann, Transcript Copies. Only a few years later, Trimble would allow a young Sam Houston—future political hero of Tennessee and Texas—to spend six months reading for the law in Trimble's office before Houston established his own law office in Lebanon, TN.
23 Ibid.
24 Ibid.

THIRTEEN • KENTUCK

1 Written account of John L. Jacobs.
2 Ibid.
3 Ibid.
4 Crockett, *Narrative*, 68. Lincoln County was created in 1808 and named after Revolutionary War hero General Benjamin Lincoln. In 1806, the Cherokees and Chickasaws ceded the land comprising the new county to the United States, and settlers began arriving immediately to get their share of the fertile soil.
5 From *Surveyors Entry Book C, Surveyors District II*, Entry No. 3944, 414, Tennessee State Archives. "Surveyed. David Crockett . . . enters 5 acres of land in Lincoln County and on the head waters of the East fork of Mulberry Creek a North Branch of the Elk River. Beginning at a Beech marked D.C. Standing about 60 or 70 yards north eastwardly."
6 Crockett, *Narrative*, 69.
7 The Gowen Papers, Gowen Research Foundation, Lubbock, TX, http://freepages.geneaology.roots.web.com/-gowenrf.
8 Ibid.

9 John S. C. Abbott, *David Crockett: His Life and Adventures* (New York: Dodd & Mead, 1875), 86.

10 Ibid.

11 Crockett, *Narrative*, 69.

12 William C. Davis, *Three Roads to the Alamo* (New York: HarperCollins, 1998), 25.

13 Jones, *In the Footsteps of Davy Crockett*, 42.

14 Ibid.

15 Gert Petersen, *David Crockett, The Volunteer Rifleman: An Account of His Life, while a Resident of Franklin County, 1812–1817* (Winchester, TN: Franklin County Historical Society, 2007), 11–13. Archard Hatchett (1782–1852) and his son, James L. Hatchett (1838–1904), were laid to rest in the Hatchett Cemetery on the family farm, according to the Cemetery Records of Franklin County, Tennessee, as compiled by the Franklin County Historical Society, Winchester, TN.

16 Ramsey, *Annals of Tennessee*, 94.

17 Russell Family Files, Kraus-Everette Genealogy, www.larkcom.us/ancestry/main/.

18 Bean Family Files, Kraus-Everette Genealogy, www.larkcom.us/ancestry/main/.

19 Ibid.

20 Robert V. Remini, *Andrew Jackson and the Course of American Empire, 1767–1821* (New York: Harper & Row, 1977), 115.

21 Ibid.

22 Ibid.

23 Franklin County, TN, Files, Tennessee Historical Commission; Tennessee Historical Society, Nashville, TN; Franklin County Historical Society, Winchester, TN.

24 Bean Family Files, Kraus-Everette Genealogy.

FOURTEEN • "REMEMBER FORT MIMS"

1 John S. Bowman, general ed., *The World Almanac of the American West* (New York: World Almanac/Pharos Books, 1986), 88. President Madison proclaimed a state of war between the United States and Britain on June 19, 1812. He had received the support of the House of Representatives (79–49) on June 4 and of the Senate (19–13) on June 18. Madison and Congress were unaware that on June 16 the British agreed to suspend orders authorizing British ships stopping American vessels.

2 Paul S. Boyer, ed., *The Oxford Companion to United States History* (New York: Oxford University Press, 2001), 814.

3 Ibid.

4 Tom Kanon, "Brief History of Tennessee in the War of 1812" (Nashville: Ten-

nessee State Library and Archives, 2008), www.tennessee.gov/tsla/history/
military/tn1812.h.

5 Crockett, *Narrative*, 71.

6 Finger, *Tennessee Frontiers*, 232.

7 Remini, *Andrew Jackson and the Course of American Empire*, 188.

8 Ibid.

9 Ibid.

10 David Stewart and Ray Knox, *The Earthquake That Never Went Away* (Marble
Hill, MO: Gutenberg-Richter Publications, 1993), 17.

11 Ibid., 21. The largest quake occurred on February 7, 1812. It is considered to
be one of the largest quakes not only in the United States but in the world.
This is the quake that caused the Mississippi to run backward. The retro-
grade motion of the river lasted only a few hours, but the resulting waterfalls
remained for two or three days.

12 Norma Hayes Bagnall, *On Shaky Ground: The New Madrid Earthquakes of
1811–1812* (Columbia: University of Missouri Press, 1996), 41, 49, 50.

13 Russell H. Caldwell, *Reelfoot Lake Remembered* (Union City, TN: Caldwell's
Office Outfitters, Inc., 2005), 24.

14 Lake County Tennessee Historical Society, *History and Families, Lake County
Tennessee, 1870–1992* (Paducah, KY: Turner Publishing, 1993), 14.

15 Remini, *Andrew Jackson and the Course of American Empire*, 188.

16 Buddy Levy, *American Legend: The Real-Life Adventures of David Crockett* (New
York: Berkley Books, 2005), 38–39.

17 Ibid.

18 Richard Boyd Hauck, *Davy Crockett: A Handbook* (Lincoln: University of
Nebraska Press, 1982), 19.

19 H. W. Brands, *Andrew Jackson: His Life and Times* (New York: Anchor Books,
2006), 192.

20 Ibid., 194.

21 Ibid., 195.

22 Ibid.

FIFTEEN • "WE SHOT THEM LIKE DOGS"

1 Crockett, *Narrative*, 73.

2 Arthur M. Schlesinger Jr., general ed., *The Almanac of American History* (New
York: Bramhall House, 1986), 197.

3 Crockett, *Narrative*, 71–72.

4 Ibid.

5 Ibid., 73.

6 Petersen, *David Crockett, The Volunteer Rifleman*, 14.

7 Ibid.

8   From "Regimental Histories of Tennessee Military Units During the War of 1812," prepared by Tom Kanon, Tennessee State Library and Archives, Nashville, Tennessee.

9   *Family Histories: Franklin County Tennessee, 1807–1996* (Winchester, TN: Franklin County Historical Society, 1996), 14.

10   Remini, *Andrew Jackson and the Course of American Empire*, 191.

11   Webb, *Born Fighting*, 188.

12   Brands, *Andrew Jackson: His Life and Times*, 188–90.

13   Ibid., 196.

14   Crockett, *Narrative*, 75.

15   Ibid.

16   Crockett, *Narrative*, 82.

17   James Parton, *The Life of Andrew Jackson, in Three Volumes* (New York: Mason Brothers, 1860), vol. 1, 427–29. The journalist James Parton wrote this book less than fifteen years after Andrew Jackson's death. It is considered the first scholarly biography of the seventh president, although Parton said that even after years of study, instead of discovering the real Jackson, he found only an enigma.

18   Crockett, *Narrative*, 85–86.

19   Petersen, *David Crockett, The Volunteer Rifleman*, 18.

20   Ibid., 19.

SIXTEEN • RIDING WITH SHARP KNIFE

1   Petersen, *David Crockett, The Volunteer Rifleman*, 20.

2   House of Strother Newsletter, February 1991, vol. 3, no. 1, 10.

3   Petersen, *David Crockett, The Volunteer Rifleman*, 20.

4   Benson John Lossing, *The Pictorial Field-Book of the War of 1812* (New York: Harper & Brothers, 1868), 764.

5   Petersen, *David Crockett, The Volunteer Rifleman*, 20.

6   Crockett, *Narrative*, 92.

7   Ibid., 92–93.

8   Ibid., 93.

9   Andrew Burstein, *The Passions of Andrew Jackson* (New York: Alfred A. Knopf, 2003), 93.

10   Remini, *Andrew Jackson and the Course of American Empire*, 227, 383–84.

11   Petersen, *David Crockett, The Volunteer Rifleman*, 22.

12   Lossing, *Pictorial Field-Book*, 766. According to Lossing, Jackson shared in his soldier's privations and also ate acorns to sustain life.

13   Crockett, *Narrative*, 93.

14   Shackford, *David Crockett: The Man and the Legend*, 27.

15   Brands, *Andrew Jackson: His Life and Times*, 212.

16   Petersen, *David Crockett, The Volunteer Rifleman*, 24.

SEVENTEEN • "ROOT HOG OR DIE"

1 A. J. Langguth, *Union 1812: The Americans Who Fought the Second War of Independence* (New York: Simon & Schuster, 2006), 284.
2 Ibid., 284–85.
3 Ibid., 285.
4 Finger, *Tennessee Frontiers*, 234.
5 Ibid.
6 Remini, *Andrew Jackson and the Course of American Empire*, 216–17.
7 Ibid., 217.
8 Petersen, *David Crockett, The Volunteer Rifleman*, 32.
9 Remini, *Andrew Jackson and the Course of the American Empire*, 219.
10 Ibid., 226.
11 Ibid., 231.
12 Finger, *Tennessee Frontiers*, 235.
13 Ibid.
14 Remini, *Andrew Jackson and the Course of American Empire*, 21.
15 Ibid., 232–33.
16 Crockett, *Narrative*, 101.
17 Ibid.
18 Petersen, 33.
19 Ibid.
20 Crockett, *Narrative*, 102.
21 Ibid.
22 Ibid., 103.
23 Petersen, *David Crockett, The Volunteer Rifleman*, 35, 37.
24 Crockett, *Narrative*, 106.
25 Ibid., 107.
26 Ibid., 109–10.
27 Ibid., 115.
28 Several sources and dictionaries credit Crockett with having introduced this idiomatic expression in his published autobiography in 1834. It was used in many parts of the country well prior to that date.
29 Crockett, *Narrative*, 120.
30 Ibid., 122.

EIGHTEEN • CABIN FEVER

1 Crockett, *Narrative*, 123.
2 Ibid.
3 Ibid., 123–24.

4 Petersen, *David Crockett, The Volunteer Rifleman*, 43.

5 Crockett, *Narrative*, 124–25.

6 Walter J. Daly, M.D., "The 'Slows,' The Torment of Milk Sickness on the Midwest Frontier," *Indiana Magazine of History* 102 (March 2006): 29.

7 Ibid., 30–31.

8 Ibid., 34. One of the most characteristic symptoms of the sickness was an offensive odor to the patient's breath, often so strong that it could be detected on entering a frontier cabin.

9 Crockett, *Narrative*, 125.

10 Ibid., 125–26.

11 Jones, *Crockett Cousins*, 24.

12 Crockett, *Narrative*, 126.

13 Shackford, *David Crockett: The Man and the Legend*, 34.

14 Old Buncombe County Genealogical Society, *Old Buncombe County Heritage Book,* vol. 2 (Winston-Salem, NC: Hunter Publishing Co., 1981), 289.

15 Crockett, *Narrative*, 126.

16 Ibid., 127.

17 Petersen, *David Crockett, The Volunteer Rifleman*, 47.

18 Ibid.

NINETEEN • A TINCTURE OF LUCK

1 Crockett, *Narrative*, 118–20.

2 Van Zandt County Genealogical Society, Canton, TX, www.txgenweb3.org/txvanzandt/vzgs.htm.

3 Franklin County, TN, Will Book, 1808–1847, Folder 036 A, Franklin County Courthouse Annex, Winchester, TN. Frances T. Ingmire, *Franklin County, Tennessee, Abstracted Wills, 1808–1875* (St. Louis: Frances Terry Ingmire, 1984), 27–28. David signed the document, but his brother John was unlettered and left his mark. Besides the Crocketts, a local man named John W. Holder was the third witness to the signing of the Van Zandt last will and testament. Jacob Van Zandt Sr. died January 6, 1818. One of his grandsons and the son of Jacob Jr., Crockett's hunting mate, was Isaac Van Zandt, born in Franklin County in 1812. He went on to become an important political leader in the Republic of Texas, died of yellow fever while campaigning for governor in 1847, and had a Texas county named in his honor. Another descendant—Townes Van Zandt—became one of the premier Texas musicians during the 1970s and 1980s. Townes died at his Tennessee home of either a heart attack or a blood clot following hip surgery on New Year's Day 1997, the same date that his idol, Hank Williams, died of a heart attack in 1953.

4 Crockett, *Narrative*, 127.

5 Ibid., 127–28. Tuscaloosa, AL, Tuscaloosa County, Alabama Department of

History & Archives, Montgomery, AL, www.archives.state.al.us/counties/tus
caloo.html. Incorporated in 1819, just one day after Alabama became a state,
Tuscaloosa served as the state capital from 1826 until 1846.

6 Ibid.

7 Crockett, *Narrative*, 128.

8 Sonia Shah, "Resurgentmalaria.com," www.resurgentmalaria.com/americas,
2006. This Web site, hosted by investigative journalist Sonia Shah, provides
history, background, new technology, and other information about the disease.

9 Crockett, *Narrative*, 129.

10 Ibid.

11 Ibid., 130.

12 Ibid.

13 Ibid., 131–32.

14 Ibid., 132.

TWENTY • "ITCHY FOOTED"

1 Jones, *Crockett Cousins*, 23.

2 Brands, *Andrew Jackson: His Life and Times*, 314–15.

3 Remini, *Andrew Jackson and the Course of American Empire*, 329.

4 Wilma Mankiller and Michael Wallis, *Mankiller: A Chief and Her People* (New
York: St. Martin's Press, 1993), 86.

5 Remini, *Andrew Jackson and the Course of American Empire*, 330.

6 Ibid.

7 Ibid., 331.

8 Crockett, *Narrative*, 132–33.

9 Shackford and Folmsbee, Facsimile Edition, 132, n. 17.

10 Jones, *Crockett Cousins*, 70. The will of Robert Crockett was written on September 8, 1834, and probated on March 2, 1836. Will Book C, 196, Cumberland County, KY.

11 Samuel K. Cowan, *Sergeant York and His People* (New York: Grosset & Dunlap, 1922), 24–25.

12 Conrad "Coonrod" Pile Files, http//homepages.rootsweb.ancestry.com/~bp
2000/fentress/pile_c.htm.

13 Ibid.

14 Ibid. Coonrod Pile and his wife, Mary Pile, were interned in the Wolf River
Cemetery at Pall Mall. Nearby their graves lie the remains of the famous great-
great-grandson, Sergeant Alvin C. York.

15 Alvin C. York, *Sergeant York: His Own Life Story and War Diary* (New York:
Doubleday & Doran, 1928), March 1918 entry.

16 The Gowen Papers, Gowen Research Foundation, Lubbock, TX, http://free
pages.geneaology.roots.web.com/~gowenrf.

TWENTY-ONE • "NATURAL BORN SENSE"

1 Bobby Alford, *History of Lawrence County, Tennessee* (n.p., the author, 1994), 21.
2 Petersen, *David Crockett, The Volunteer Rifleman*, 49. According to Petersen, Crockett became a member of the Shoal Creek Corporation in April 1817.
3 Lawrence County Historical Society, *Lawrence County, Tennessee, Pictorial History* (Paducah, KY: Turner Publishing, 1994), 14.
4 Alford, *History of Lawrence County, Tennessee*, 21.
5 Ibid., 27.
6 Ibid., 17. Jackson began work on the Military Road in the autumn of 1816, and the new route was completed in 1820. It was 516 miles in length, a reduction of more than 220 miles from the route of the Natchez Trace. In 1822, mail service from Nashville to New Orleans was transferred to the new road, effectively replacing the Natchez Trace as the major north-south highway.
7 Ibid., 18. Foster, *Counties of Tennessee*, 82. Murfreesboro remained the state capital until 1826, when the capital moved yet again to Nashville, thirty-five miles to the north.
8 Alford, *History of Lawrence County, Tennessee*, 28–29. On September 20, 1823, a petition containing the names of 220 citizens of Lawrence County was sent to the state legislature stating that the chosen location for Lawrenceburg was suitable.
9 Ibid., 28.
10 Crockett, *Narrative*, 133.
11 Ibid., 133–34.
12 Shackford, *David Crockett: The Man and the Legend*, 38.
13 Crockett, *Narrative*, 135. By the early 1820s, when Crockett held state and federal elective office, he had read some law. A law book that Crockett reportedly gave a friend in 1828 ended up on display at the Alamo.
14 Alford, *History of Lawrence County, Tennessee*, 24.
15 Crockett, *Narrative*, 137.
16 Alford, *History of Lawrence County, Tennessee*, 25.
17 Crockett, *Narrative*, 138.
18 Ibid.
19 Jones, *Crockett Cousins*, 23.

TWENTY-TWO • GENTLEMAN FROM THE CANE

1 Shackford, *David Crockett: The Man and the Legend*, 41.
2 Joseph C. Guild, *Old Times in Tennessee* (Nashville: Tavel, Eastman & Howell, 1878), 322–24. Judge Jo Guild, as he was best known, was a Crockett contemporary, a veteran of the Seminole War, and a well-known Tennessee lawyer.

3 Ibid., 138–45. Irvine's commission was dated February 17, 1820.

4 Alford, *History of Lawrence County, Tennessee*, 31.

5 Crockett, *Narrative*, 144.

6 Levy, *American Legend*, 87.

7 MemphisHistory.com, www.memphishistory.org/Beginnings/FoundersandPio neers/JohnCMclemore/tabid/112/Default.aspx. One of the founders of Memphis, McLemore was touted as a potential gubernatorial or senatorial candidate, but he never ran for office. He lost much of his wealth when the LaGrange and Memphis Rail Road failed and the financial panic in 1837 further reduced his holdings. In an effort to accumulate another fortune, he joined the California gold rush in 1849. He remained in California twelve years, returning to Memphis before his death in 1864.

8 Shackford, *David Crockett: The Man and the Legend*, 43.

9 Crockett, *Narrative*, 138.

10 Davis, *Three Roads to the Alamo*, 70.

11 Crockett, *Narrative*, 140.

12 Ibid.

13 Ibid., 141–42.

14 Jones, *Crockett Cousins*, 24. Matilda, Crockett's youngest child, would live longer than any of her siblings. She survived three husbands and died in Gibson County, TN, on July 6, 1890, a month before her sixty-ninth birthday.

15 Crockett, *Narrative*, 143.

16 Ibid. In his autobiography, Crockett wrote that when they met, Polk was a member of the state legislature. Crockett was confused. Polk was still clerk of the state senate and would not become a legislator until the next term. Beginning in 1825, Polk was elected to his seven terms in the U.S. Congress; thus he was a fellow representative of Crockett's during all of Crockett's state legislative and congressional years.

17 Shackford, *David Crockett: The Man and the Legend*, 47.

18 Ibid., 52.

19 Levy, *American Legend*, 95–96.

TWENTY-THREE • LAND OF THE SHAKES

1 Crockett, *Narrative*, 144.

2 Shackford, *David Crockett: The Man and the Legend*, 50.

3 Levy, *American Legend*, 97.

4 Edward S. Ellis, *The Life of Colonel David Crockett*, reprinted from the 1884 edition (Honolulu: University Press of the Pacific, 1984), 58–59.

5 Ibid., 145.

6 Ibid.

7 Crockett, *Narrative*, 144–45.

8 Guy S. Miles, "David Crockett Evolves, 1821–1824," *American Quarterly* 8, no. 1 (Spring 1956): 53. In a footnote in his seven-page essay, Miles, described as "a Tennessee hunter and Professor of English at Morehead State College," praised the soon to be published work of Professor James Atkins Shackford, noting that "it is badly needed as a corrective to too much surmising on the key figure." The University of North Carolina Press published Shackford's work, *David Crockett: The Man and the Legend,* later that year.

9 Shackford, *David Crockett: The Man and the Legend,* 53.

10 Jonathan K. T. Smith, *The Land Holdings of Colonel David Crockett in West Tennessee* (Jackson, TN: Mid-West Tennessee Genealogical Society, 2003), 11.

11 Ibid.

12 Crockett, *Narrative,* 147.

13 "A Sportsmen's Paradise," *New York Times,* January 11, 1891.

14 Ibid.

15 Crockett, *Narrative,* 148.

16 Ibid., 149–50.

17 Ibid., 151.

18 Ibid., 152–53.

19 Ibid., 154.

20 Smith, *Land Holdings,* 12.

TWENTY-FOUR • IN THE EYE OF A "HARRICANE"

1 Shackford, *David Crockett: The Man and the Legend,* 56.

2 Ibid. Mansil Crisp was born in North Carolina in 1764 and lived in South Carolina from the 1790s to the early 1800s, when he moved to Tennessee. He died in 1850.

3 Jones, *In the Footsteps of Davy Crockett,* 34.

4 Shackford, *David Crockett: The Man and the Legend,* 57–58.

5 Herbert L. Harper, ed., *Houston and Crockett: Heroes of Tennessee and Texas: An Anthology* (Nashville: Tennessee Historical Commission, 1986), 147.

6 Shackford, *David Crockett: The Man and the Legend,* 58. Crockett quotes from the *Nashville Whig,* August 14, 1822.

7 John Patton Erwin, a native of North Carolina and member of the Whig Party, served as mayor of Nashville in 1821–1822 and again in 1834–1835.

8 Carroll County (TN) Deed Book A, 29–30.

9 Crockett, *Narrative,* 155.

10 Foster, *Counties of Tennessee,* 102.

11 Carroll County (TN) Court Minutes, 1821–1826, vol. 1, 20.

12 First Families Old Buncombe (FFOB), Patton Family records, www.obcgs.com/patton.htm.

13 Jones, *Crockett Cousins,* 45.

14 Hauck, *Davy Crockett: A Handbook*, 34–35.

15 Crockett, *Narrative*, 155.

16 Ibid., 155–56.

17 Ibid.

18 Ibid.

19 Ibid., 161.

20 Crockett, *Narrative*, 162–63.

21 Ibid., 163–64.

22 Ibid., 164–65.

TWENTY-FIVE • A FOOL FOR LUCK

1 Foster, *Counties of Tennessee*, 115–16. Madison County was created on November 7, 1821, from the Western District, and the first courthouse was completed in Jackson in September 1822.

2 Crockett, *Narrative*, 166.

3 Ibid., 166–67.

4 Ibid., 167.

5 Remini, *Andrew Jackson and the Course of American Empire*, 63, 160. William Butler married Martha Hays, the daughter of Rachel Jackson's sister.

6 Crockett, *Narrative*, 167–68.

7 Ibid., 167.

8 Shackford, *David Crockett: The Man and the Legend*, 64.

9 Ibid.

10 Ibid., 66.

11 Ibid.

12 Jones, *In the Footsteps of Davy Crockett*, 34–36.

13 Ibid., 35–36.

14 Hauck, *Davy Crockett: A Handbook*, 38.

15 Shackford, *David Crockett: The Man and the Legend*, 67.

16 Crockett, *Narrative*, 171.

17 Levy, *American Legend*, 120.

18 *National Banner and Nashville Whig*, September 27, 1824.

19 Crockett, *Narrative*, 172.

20 Ibid., 173.

21 Levy, *American Legend*, 124.

TWENTY-SIX • BIG TIME

1 Jones, *In the Footsteps of Davy Crockett*, 37.

2 Gert Petersen, *A Chronology of the Life of David Crockett*, unpublished, 2001, 25.

3 Shackford, *David Crockett: The Man and the Legend*, 74.

4 Ibid.

5 Crockett, *Narrative*, 174.

6 Crockett, *Narrative*, 195.

7 Ibid., 196.

8 Ibid., 198–99.

9 Petersen, *Chronology*, 26.

10 *History of Shelby County, Tennessee* (Nashville: Goodspeed Publishing Co., 1886–1887), 865–67.

11 Ibid.

12 Michael Lollar, "First Memphis Mayor Receives a Grave Injustice," *Memphis Commercial Appeal*, commercialappeal.com, May 26, 2009.

13 Ibid. Amarante Winchester was ostracized by Memphis society, and Winchester's career declined. Eventually city aldermen passed an ordinance forbidding anyone of mixed race from owning property or living within the city limits. This caused the Winchesters to move to a farm outside of Memphis. They remained married until her death in 1840. Two years later, Winchester married a nineteen-year-old widow. Later he was elected to the state legislature. He died in 1856.

14 Levy, *American Legend*, 132.

15 Ibid., 133.

TWENTY-SEVEN • "THE VICTORY IS OURS"

1 Jones, *In the Footsteps of Davy Crockett*, 78.

2 Richard Slotkin, *Regeneration Through Violence: The Mythology of the American Frontier, 1600–1860* (Norman: University of Oklahoma Press, 2000), 414–15.

3 Ibid., 415.

4 *Jackson Gazette*, Jackson, TN, Circular Letter "To the Republican Voters of the 9th Congressional District of the State of Tennessee," David Crockett, Gibson County, September 16, 1826.

5 Davis, *Three Roads to the Alamo* (New York: HarperCollins, 1999), 119–20. Shackford, *David Crockett: The Man and the Legend*, 82. By 1830 only a congressional district in Illinois had more voters than the Ninth District.

6 Shackford, *David Crockett: The Man and the Legend*, 82.

7 Crockett, *Narrative*, 201–2.

8 Shackford, *David Crockett: The Man and the Legend*, 81–82.

9 Crockett, *Narrative*, 204.

10 Ibid.

11 Mark Derr, *The Frontiersman: The Real Life and Many Legends of Davy Crockett* (New York: William Morrow and Company, 1993), 143.

12 Davis, *Three Roads to the Alamo*, 123.

13 Ibid., 122–23.

14 Ibid., 124. Anne Brown Clay was born in Lexington, KY, on April 15, 1807, the daughter of Henry Clay and Lucretia Hart. Anne married James Patton Erwin on October 21, 1823, in Fayette County, KY. She died of blood poisoning shortly after childbirth, in November 1835.

15 Christopher Marquis, "Andrew Jackson: Winner and Loser in 1824," *American History* 43, no. 1 (April 2008): 57.

16 Davis, 124–25.

17 Written account of John L. Jacobs.

18 Ibid.

19 Shackford, *David Crockett: The Man and the Legend*, 84.

20 Levy, *American Legend*, 142.

21 Z. T. Fulmore, *The History and Geography of Texas as Told in County Names* (Austin: E. L. Steck, 1915), 105–6. Carson was elected to Congress in 1827, 1829, and 1831. Once a trusted friend of Andrew Jackson, he became estranged from Sharp Knife and was defeated in the campaign of 1833. Carson lived for a time in Texas, where a county was named for him, and he died in Hot Springs, AR, in 1840.

22 Shackford, *David Crockett: The Man and the Legend*, 86.

23 Levy, *American Legend*, 142.

TWENTY-EIGHT • MAN WITHOUT A PARTY

1 Shackford, *David Crockett: The Man and the Legend*, 283–84. William L. Foster's father, Ephraim H. Foster, served two terms as a U.S. senator from Tennessee. He had been Andrew Jackson's personal secretary during the Creek and New Orleans campaigns but fell out with Jackson over fiscal policies and became an early leader in the Whig Party.

2 *History and Families of Lake County, Tennessee, 1870–1992*, 14. Historical records show that Crockett made camp beneath the towering cypress trees on Bluebank Bayou in the land of the shakes during the early 1830s.

3 Excerpted from John L. O'Sullivan, "Annexation," *United States Magazine and Democratic Review* 17 (July 1845): 5–10, from David J. Voelker, www.history tools.org, 2004.

4 Slotkin, *Regeneration Through Violence*, 5.

5 Paul Andrew Hutton, "Mr. Crockett Goes to Washington," *American History* 35, no. 1 (April 2000): 26. Dr. Hutton teaches history at the University of New Mexico and has devoted many years to Crockett research.

6 Swann, "Early Life & Times." Crockett's letter to James Blackburn is dated February 28, 1828.

7 Walter Blair, "Six Davy Crocketts," *Southwest Review* 25 (July 1940): 452–53.

Although some other sources have questioned the authenticity of this quote, it sounds like vintage Crockett.

8 Paul Hutton, Introduction, *Narrative*, xxi.

9 Blair, "Six Davy Crocketts," 110–11.

10 Davis, *Three Roads to the Alamo*, 126. John Quincy Adams Diary 37, November 11, 1825–June 24, 1828, 349.

11 Abbott, *David Crockett: His Life and Adventures*, 260–63.

12 Adams, Diary 37, 349.

13 Congressman James Clark letter, *Jackson (TN) Gazette*, February 14, 1829.

14 Congressman Gulian C. Verplanck letter, *Jackson (TN) Gazette*, February 14, 1829.

15 Dennis Brulgrudery, pseudonym, letter, *Jackson (TN) Gazette*, March 7, 1829.

16 David Crockett letter to George Patton, January 27, 1829, transcript provided by Joe N. Bone, manager-curator, Crockett Cabin-Museum, Rutherford, TN.

17 Ibid.

18 *Missouri Republican*, August 15, 1829.

19 Levy, *American Legend*, 161.

TWENTY-NINE • TRAILS OF TEARS

1 Levy, *American Legend*, 163.

2 Shackford, *David Crockett: The Man and the Legend*, 114.

3 Levy, *American Legend*, 163–64.

4 Burstein, *Passions of Andrew Jackson*, 185.

5 Mankiller and Wallis, *Mankiller*, 88.

6 Ibid.

7 Ibid., 79.

8 Remini, *Andrew Jackson and the Course of American Empire, 1767–1821*, 264.

9 President Andrew Jackson's Case for the Removal Act, First Annual Message to Congress, December 8, 1830.

10 Ibid.

11 Based on the author's personal observations and associations with many members of the Cherokee Nation, including several principal chiefs, as well as tribal activists and scholars of Cherokee cultural history. Besides completely shunning twenty-dollar bills, some Oklahoma Indians have been known to ink large X's across Jackson's face.

12 Martin Luther King Jr. also has been suggested as a replacement for Jackson on the twenty-dollar bill.

13 Levy, *American Legend*, 168.

14 Crockett, *Narrative*, 205–6.

15 Swann, "Early Life & Times."

16 Walter Blair, *David Crockett: Legendary Frontier Hero* (Springfield, IL: Lincoln-Herndon Press, 1955, rev. ed. 1986), 181–87.

　　From *Speeches on the Passage of the Bill for the Removal of the Indians, Delivered in the Congress of the United States, April and May, 1830* (Boston: Perkins and Marvin, 1830; New York: Jonathan Leavitt, 1830).

17 Ibid.

18 Shackford, *David Crockett: The Man and the Legend*, 116–17, 129. Levy, *American Legend*, 174–75.

19 Crockett, *Narrative*, 206–7.

20 Levy, *American Legend*, 173.

21 Shackford, *David Crockett: The Man and the Legend*, 112.

22 Davis, *Three Roads to the Alamo*, 181–82.

23 Ibid., 207–8.

24 Shackford, *David Crockett: The Man and the Legend*, 132.

25 Davis, *Three Roads to the Alamo*, 186.

26 Shackford, *David Crockett: The Man and the Legend*, 133.

THIRTY • LION OF THE WEST

1 Alexis de Tocqueville, *Democracy in America*, trans. George Lawrence, ed. J. P. Mayer (New York: Harper & Row, 1966), 485.

2 Ibid., 200.

3 Alexis de Tocqueville, Journal Entry, Memphis, Tennessee, December 20, 1831, 267, www.tocqueville.org/tn.hmm.

4 Jones, *Crockett Cousins*, 23. William Finley Crockett wed Clorinda Boyett on March 18, 1830, and Margaret Finley Crockett wed Wiley Flowers on March 22, 1830. Both weddings took place in Gibson County, TN.

5 Smith, *Land Holdings*, 42–43. Some authors, including Shackford, have confused the two George Pattons. The George Patton who purchased Crockett's 25-acre tract in 1831 was his stepson and not his brother-in-law, the other George Patton, who resided in Buncombe County, North Carolina.

6 Shackford, *David Crockett: The Man and the Legend*, 136.

7 Ibid., 133.

8 Davis, *Three Roads to the Alamo*, 310.

9 Jones, *Crockett Cousins*, 45.

10 Smith, *Land Holdings*, 44.

11 Ibid.

12 William Shakespeare, *As You Like It*, The New Folger Library of Shakespeare (New York: Simon & Schuster, 2004), act 5, scene 1.

13 M. J. Heale, "The Role of the Frontier in Jacksonian Politics: David Crockett and the Myth of the Self-Made Man," *Western History Quarterly* 4 (October 1973): 406.

14 Levy, *American Legend*, 182.

15 Vera M. Jiji, ed., *A Sourcebook of Interdisciplinary Materials in American Drama: J. K. Paulding, The Lion of the West* (Brooklyn: Produced by the Program for Culture at Play: Multimedia Studies in American Drama, Humanities Institute, Brooklyn College, 1983), 10–11. The review appeared in the *Morning Courier and New York Enquirer*, April 27, 1831.

16 Andrew Burstein, *The Original Knickerbocker: The Life of Washington Irving* (New York: Basic Books, 2007), 10–11. In 1793, when Washington Irving was ten years old, his brother William married Julia Paulding, the older sister of James Kirke Paulding. According to Burstein, Paulding is noteworthy for being the first outside the Irving clan to be considered a confidant, and, as important, the one who introduced Washington Irving to Sleepy Hollow.

17 Ibid., 246. Others belonged to the Knickerbockers, but the five listed were the most remarkable.

18 Davis, *Three Roads to the Alamo*, 171–72. John Wesley Jarvis was born in England and was the nephew of John Wesley, founder of Methodism. Jarvis painted the portraits of many well-known American figures, including Andrew Jackson, Henry Clay, and James Fenimore Cooper. He was known for his flamboyant dress and manner during his prime years, but his work declined and he died in poverty in New York in 1840.

19 The word *nimrod*, which means hunter, was taken from Nimrod, the name of the mighty hunter and king, and Noah's great-grandson in the Old Testament.

20 William I. Paulding, *Literary Life of James K. Paulding* (New York: Charles Scribner's Sons, 1867), 218–19. William I. Paulding was the son of James Kirke Paulding.

21 Ibid.

22 *Adams Sentinel*, Gettysburg, PA, December 17, 1828.

23 Jiji, *Sourcebook*, 27.

24 Jay Winik, *April 1865: The Month That Saved America* (New York: HarperCollins, 2001), 233.

25 Hauck, *Davy Crockett: A Handbook*, 47.

THIRTY-ONE • BEAR-BIT LION

1 Jiji, *Sourcebook*, 11. Quoting *Morning Courier & New York Enquirer*, November 24, 1831.

2 Ibid. Shackford, *David Crockett: The Man and the Legend*, 256.

3 Hutton, Introduction, *Narrative*, xix.

4 Information provided by Department of the Navy, Naval Historical Center, Washington Navy Yard, Washington, D.C. President Martin Van Buren appointed James K. Paulding the eleventh secretary of the navy. He served from July 1, 1838, to March of 1841. Among other governmental positions he

held were those of secretary to the Board of Navy Commissioners from 1815 to 1823 and naval agent from 1824 to 1838.

5 Levy, *American Legend*, 184.

6 The etymology of the old adage "bit by the bear" is uncertain, but the phrase possibly served as one of the sources for a classic line uttered by actor Sam Elliott in the 1998 dark comedy film *The Big Lebowski*, produced by Ethan and Joel Coen. In his role as "The Stranger," Elliot said: "A fella wiser than myself once said, 'Sometimes you eat the bar, and sometimes, the bar, well, he eats you.' "

7 Shackford, *David Crockett: The Man and the Legend*, 262. The *Southern Literary Messenger* was published in Richmond, VA, from 1834 until 1864. Publisher Thomas Willis White hired Edgar Allan Poe in 1835 as a staff writer and critic. Poe, who usually did not use his middle name during this period, lasted only a month before he was fired for excessive drinking. He was soon rehired and for a time served as the editor of the journal. Poe published thirty-seven reviews of American and foreign books and periodicals while working for the *Messenger*. He left in 1837 but continued to contribute articles and reviews until his death in 1849.

8 Ibid.

9 Ibid., 262–63.

10 Ibid., 263.

11 Matthew St. Clair Clarke (probable author), *Sketches and Eccentricities of Colonel David Crockett of West Tennessee* (New York: J. & J. Harper, 1833). Reprint of *Life and Adventures of Colonel David Crockett of West Tennessee* (Cincinnati, 1833), 20.

12 Ibid., 164.

13 James T. Pearce, "Folk Tales of the Southern Poor-White, 1820–1860," *Journal of American Folklore* 63, no. 250 (October–December 1950), 398.

14 *The New England Magazine* 5, no. 6 (1833), 513–14. The magazine was launched in Boston in 1831 and ceased publication in 1835. *American Monthly Magazine* was its successor.

15 Shackford, *David Crockett: The Man and the Legend*, 139–41.

16 Crockett, *Narrative*, 210.

17 Ibid.

18 H. Niles, *Niles' Weekly Register*, Baltimore, MD, September 7, 1833. Archivists contend that this publication was an early precursor to modern news magazines.

19 Shackford, *David Crockett: The Man and the Legend*, 144.

THIRTY-TWO • GO AHEAD

1 Hauck, *Davy Crockett: A Handbook*, 70–71.

2 Shackford, *David Crockett: The Man and the Legend*, 147.

3 Levy, *American Legend*, 192.

4 Ibid. Thomas Chilton was born in 1798 near Lancaster, KY, a son of Reverend Thomas John Chilton and Margaret Bledsoe. One week before his seventeenth birthday, he married and started study for ordination as a Baptist minister. At the same time, he studied for the bar, and he eventually established a legal practice before entering politics. In 1835, Chilton had tired of politics and resumed the practice of law as well as his Baptist ministry. During a revival meeting in Alabama, he converted to Christianity his maternal cousin, Robert Emmett Bledsoe Baylor, who went on to become an ordained Baptist minister and in 1845 cofounded Baylor University in Texas. Chilton pastored churches in Alabama and Texas, where he died in 1854. The town of Chilton, TX, was named for his son, Lysias B. Chilton, and a grandson, Horace Chilton, became the first native-born Texan to serve in the U.S. Senate from Texas.

5 Shackford, *David Crockett: The Man and the Legend*, 148.

6 Crockett, *Narrative*, 172.

7 Joseph A. Swann, Presentation to the East Tennessee Historical Society, Knoxville, February 12, 2003.

8 Joe Reilly, PhD, Presentation to the International Psychohistorical Association, Fordham University, New York, June 7, 2007.

9 Aaron D. Purcell and Michael A. Lofaro, "The Davy Crockett Experience, Now Online! Part I: Born on a Mountain, Bought on EBay," University of Tennessee, *The Library Development Review*, 2002–2003, 6.

10 Ovid's *Metamorphoses* (Dublin: J. Exshaw, 1774), in fifteen books: with the notes of John Minellius, and others, in English.

11 From Aaron Purcell e-mail to the author, March 27, 2009. Aaron D. Purcell, PhD, currently serves as director of Special Collections and associate professor at the University Libraries at Virginia Tech, Blacksburg, VA. Michael A. Lofaro, PhD, professor of American studies and American literature, University of Tennessee, Knoxville.

12 Purcell and Lofaro, "The Davy Crockett Experience, Now Online!" 7.

13 Michael A. Lofaro, "Part II: Davy And Ovid?" *Library Development Review* (University of Tennessee), 2002–2003, 7.

14 Shackford, *David Crockett: The Man and the Legend*, 265.

15 Ibid., 265–66.

16 Ibid., 266.

17 Ibid., 267–68.

18 Davis, *Three Roads to the Alamo*, 331.

THIRTY-THREE • JUST A MATTER OF TIME

1 Michel de Montaigne, "Of Age," *Essays of Michel de Montaigne*, translated by Charles Cotton, edited by William Carew Hazlitt, 1877, www.fullbooks.com/The-Essays-of-Montaigne-VB.html.

2 James L. Haley, *Sam Houston* (Norman: University of Oklahoma Press, 2002),

50–52. Houston had just turned forty-six when he wed the teenaged Eliza Allen at her family's home, Allenwood, on January 22, 1829. The marriage was doomed before it started. Apparently the young woman had never loved Houston. She loved a suitor her family disapproved of, and it was for this reason that they insisted she marry Houston.

3 Jack Gregory and Rennard Strickland, *Sam Houston with the Cherokees, 1829–1833* (Norman and London: University of Oklahoma Press, 1967), 36, 44–45. Diana Rogers was the daughter of Captain John "Hell-Fire-Jack" Rogers, a wealthy Scottish trader who had been a Tory captain in the American Revolution, had fought at the Battle of Horseshoe Bend, and later directed the Cherokee emigration to Arkansas. Diana's uncles were Chief John Jolly and Chief Tallantusky. Her brothers operated profitable trading establishments and saltworks, and her sisters married wealthy Cherokee merchants. She was related to Sequoyah, whose alphabet had made him one of the most important figures in the Cherokee Nation.

4 Ibid., 44–46.

5 Haley, *Sam Houston*, 74–75.

6 Ibid., 81.

7 Bill Porterfield, "Sam Houston, Warts and All," *Texas Monthly*, July 1973, www.texasmonthly.com/1873-07-01/feature6.php.

8 Haley, *Sam Houston*, 82.

9 Ibid., 84. Booth was born in England in 1796 and named for Marcus Junius Brutus, one of the main assassins of Julius Caesar. Booth was the father of John Wilkes, Edwin, and Brutus Booth Jr. He enjoyed a thirty-year acting career that brought him critical acclaim throughout the nation. In his later years, Booth suffered from a combination of acute alcoholism and insanity. His health steadily declined, and he became known as "Crazy Booth, the mad tragedian." In 1852, following a tour of California, performing with sons Edwin and Junius Brutus Jr., the elder Booth drank impure river water while on a steamboat and died after enduring five days of fever.

10 Ibid., 85.

11 From *Catalogue of the Centennial Exhibition Commemorating the Founding of the Mount Vernon Ladies' Association of the Union, 1853–1953*, Mount Vernon, VA: 1953. In her later years, Madame Le Vert worked tirelessly on behalf of the "Save Mount Vernon" movement. She also authored *Souvenirs of Travel*, a record of her two journeys through Europe in the 1850s.

12 Poe probably wrote "To Octavia" in 1827.

> When wit, and wine, and friends have met
> And laughter crowns the festive hour
> In vain I struggle to forget
> Still does my heart confess thy power
> And fondly turn to thee!
> But Octavia, do not strive to rob

My heart of all that soothes its pain
The mournful hope that every throb
Will make it break for thee!

13 Alabama Women's Hall of Fame, Octavia Walton Le Vert (1811–1877), www
   .awhf.org/levert.html.

14 Shackford, *David Crockett: The Man and the Legend*, 308, n. 24.

15 Alabama Women's Hall of Fame, http://famousamericans.net/octaviawalton
   levert/. Octavia and her husband had five children, several of whom died as
   children. During the Civil War, she remained in Mobile and welcomed both
   Union and Confederate soldiers to the family home. Public opinion turned
   against her, and she was denounced as a "Yankee spy." By the close of the war,
   her husband was dead and most of their money gone. She traveled and gave
   public readings until her death in 1877.

16 Haley, *Sam Houston*, 101.

17 Arthur M. Schlesinger Jr., gen. ed., *The Almanac of American History* (New
   York: Bramhall House, 1986), 229.

18 *The Gettysburg Star & Republican Banner*, Gettysburg, PA, March 11, 1834.

19 Ibid. Crockett's letter of response to the Mississippi Whigs was written in
   Washington City and dated February 24, 1834.

20 *Working Man's Advocate*, New York, May 3, 1834.

21 Joseph Jackson, *Market Street Philadelphia: The Most Historic Highway in
   America, Its Merchants and Its Story*. Originally published as a series of articles
   in the *Public Ledger* in 1914 and 1915, it was republished by the newspaper in
   book form in 1918, 193.

22 Leon S. Rosenthal, *A History of Philadelphia's University City* (Philadelphia:
   West Philadelphia Corporation, 1963), http://uchs.net/Rosenthal/rosen thal-
   tofc.html.

23 *The Mail*, Hagerstown, MD, May 9, 1834.

24 *Working Man's Advocate*, New York, May 3, 1834.

25 William Groneman III, *David Crockett: Hero of the Common Man* (New York:
   Forge Books, Tom Doherty Associates, 2005), 117.

26 Levy, *American Legend*, 205.

27 Ibid. Irving Wallace, *The Fabulous Showman: The Life and Times of P. T. Barnum* (New York: Alfred A. Knopf, 1959), 69–70.

28 Davis, *Three Roads to the Alamo* (New York: HarperCollins, 1999), 390–91.

29 Groneman, *David Crockett: Hero of the Common Man*, 118.

30 Ibid., 120.

THIRTY-FOUR • GONE TO TEXAS

1 From information provided by the Tennessee State Museum, Nashville, from
  July 2001 exhibition titled *A Brush with History: Paintings from the National
  Portrait Gallery*. Chester Harding (1792–1866) is the only artist known to

have painted a portrait of Daniel Boone from life. Boone sat for the portrait near his Missouri home just a few months before his death in 1820. When Crockett sat for his portrait in Boston during the 1834 book tour, Harding was considered the city's most popular painter.

2 Shackford, *David Crockett: The Man and the Legend*, 289. In appendix 4 of his book, Shackford devotes ten pages (pp. 281–91) to discussing the various Crockett portraits.

3 John Gadsby Chapman (1808–1889) was born in Alexandria, VA, and named for his maternal grandfather John Gadsby, a well-known tavern keeper. He displayed an interest in art early on and received encouragement from several established painters. Besides his formal training, he traveled abroad and in Italy copied the works of the old masters. James Fenimore Cooper commissioned Chapman to copy Guido Reni's work *Aurora*, and Chapman also accompanied Samuel F. B. Morse, inventor of the telegraph, on two sketching trips in Italy. Chapman returned to the United States in 1831, married, and had three children. He contributed illustrations to some of the works of James Kirke Paulding, creator of *The Lion of the West*. Chapman and his family moved to Italy and resided there for many years. Chapman visited the United States briefly after his wife died and returned for good in 1884. He spent his last five years living in Brooklyn.

4 Grime, *Recollections*, 165.

5 Davis, "A Legend at Full-Length," 165.

6 Ibid., 166.

7 Ibid., 167.

8 Ibid.

9 Ibid.

10 Ibid., 168.

11 Ibid., 159, 168. Crockett biographer James A. Shackford claimed that Crockett's eldest son, John Wesley Crockett, did not consider Chapman's portrait to be the best likeness of his father. Chapman, in his nine-page handwritten reminiscence of Crockett and the portrait, states, "From its beginning to completion, Colonel Crockett's interest in the execution of the picture never abated, and it received his unqualified approval in every aspect."

12 Ibid., 171–72.

13 Ibid., 172.

14 Ibid., 173.

15 Ibid., 171.

16 John Wesley Crockett (1807–1852) studied law, was admitted to the bar, and established a law practice in Paris, TN. He held numerous local and state offices before being elected as a Whig to the Twenty-fifth and Twenty-sixth Congresses, serving the same district his famous father had represented earlier. John Wesley served in Congress from 1837 to 1841 and was next elected to

be the attorney general for the ninth district of Tennessee, and served from 1841 to 1843. In 1843 he moved to New Orleans and became a commission merchant as well as a newspaper editor. He returned to Tennessee in 1852 and died there that same year. He was buried in Paris, TN.

17   Davis, "A Legend at Full-Length," 171.

18   Ibid., 173.

19   Shackford, *David Crockett: The Man and the Legend*, 164.

20   Ibid., 163, 166.

21   Ibid., 167.

22   Ibid., 167–68; 309, n. 19. James C. Kelly and Frederick S. Voss, *Davy Crockett: Gentleman from the Cane*, An Exhibition Commemorating Crockett's Life and Legend on the 200th Anniversary of His Birth, Published by the National Portrait Gallery, Smithsonian Institution, City of Washington, and the Tennessee State Museum, Nashville, 1986, 28–29.

23   Shackford, *David Crockett: The Man and the Legend*, 309, n. 19.

24   Jones, *In the Footsteps of Davy Crockett*, 181.

25   Shackford, *David Crockett: The Man and the Legend*, 169.

26   Ibid., 170.

27   Levy, *American Legend*, 216.

28   Adam R. Huntsman Biographic Sketch, Adam Huntsman Papers, 1835–1848, Tennessee State Library and Archives, Nashville, TN. The collection is made up almost entirely of correspondence written by Huntsman to his friends and political allies. Most of the letters were written to James K. Polk, then governor of Tennessee. In these letters Huntsman has written entirely of politics, the progress of his party, and the campaigns of the candidates. Many of the letters refer to Crockett, defeated by Huntsman in 1835. The majority of the letters were written from Jackson, TN, where Huntsman resided.

29   *Adams Sentinel* 9, no. 6 (November 26, 1834).

30   Crockett letter to Charles Schultz, December 25, 1834, Gilder-Lehrman Collection, Pierpont Morgan Library, New York.

31   Jones, *In the Footsteps of Davy Crockett*, 178.

32   Ibid., 178–79. Shackford, *David Crockett: The Man and the Legend*, 119.

33   Jones, *In the Footsteps of Davy Crockett*, 201.

34   Davis, *Three Roads to the Alamo*, 399.

35   Levy, *American Legend*, 227.

36   Crockett letter to Carey and Hart, August 11, 1835, Crocket Vertical File, Maryland Historical Society.

37   *Charleston Courier*, August 31, 1835.

38   *National Gazette and Literary Register*, Philadelphia, PA, December 29, 1825. "There are now four vacancies in the senate of Missouri; that the legislature convenes in January next, and the acting Governor has failed to issue writs of election. . . . Col. McGuire has resigned, Mr. Carr has removed from the State,

Mr. Brown is at Santa Fe, in the service of the General Government, and Col. Palmer is said to have taken French leave and *gone to Texas.*" The term *French leave* is used to describe someone who evades creditors.

THIRTY-FIVE • TIME OF THE COMET

1 Shackford, *David Crockett: The Man and the Legend,* 210.

2 Davis, *Three Roads to the Alamo,* 408.

3 Jones, *In the Footsteps of Davy Crockett,* 187.

4 Quintard Taylor, *In Search of the Racial Frontier* (New York: W. W. Norton & Company, 1998), 54.

5 Ibid., 39.

6 Stephen F. Austin correspondence to Edward Lovelace (or Josiah Bell), City of Mexico, November 22, 1822. Correspondence Regarding Slavery in Texas, Sons of DeWitt Colony, Texas, www.tamu.edu/ccbn/dewitt/dewitt.htm, Wallace L. McKeehan, ed.

7 Noah Smithwick, *The Evolution of a State or Recollections of Old Texas Days* (Austin: Gammel Book Company, 1900), online edition, Southwestern Classics On-Line/Lone Star Junction, 1997, www.oldcardboard.com/lsj/olbooks/smithwic/otd.htm. Noah Smithwick was born in Martin County, North Carolina, on January 1, 1808. Smithwick moved with his family to Tennessee in 1814 and then drifted with the tide of emigration to Texas in 1827. He was a keen observer of many events during the evolution of Texas, and his lurid anecdotes were first published in book form in 1900. Texas historian J. Frank Dobie considered Smithwick's work the "best of all books dealing with life in early Texas." The Noah Smithwick Papers, 1835–1922, are located at The Center for American History, The University of Texas at Austin.

8 Ibid.

9 Ibid.

10 Ibid.

11 T. R. Fehrenbach, *Lone Star: A History of Texas and Texans* (New York: Collier Books, 1980), 152.

12 Terry Corps, *Historical Dictionary of the Jacksonian Era and Manifest Destiny* (Lanham, MD: Scarecrow Press, 2006), 306–7.

13 Eugene C. Baker, "Stephen F. Austin and the Independence of Texas," *Southwestern Historical Quarterly Online* 13, no. 4 (1933): 271, www.tsha.utexas.edu /publications/journals/shq/online/v013n4/article_1.html. Mary Phelps Austin Holley, born in Connecticut in 1784, was a first cousin to Stephen F. Austin. Her brother, Henry Austin, and his family had gone to Texas to join the Austin Colony, and Mary was a frequent visitor. Both her father and her husband, Horace Holley, a Unitarian minister, died of yellow fever, as did Mary, in 1846.

14 Taylor, *In Search of the Racial Frontier,* 41.

15 David J. Weber, ed., *Foreigners in Their Native Land: Historical Roots of the Mexican Americans* (Albuquerque: University of New Mexico Press, 1973), 152.

16 The University of Tennessee Special Collections Library, MS 1225, David Crockett letter "To the Editors" [Gales & Seaton], Weakley County, TN, August 10, 1835.

17 Hauck, *Davy Crockett: A Handbook*, 47.

18 Shackford, *David Crockett: The Man and the Legend*, 212.

19 *The Gazettte*, Little Rock, AR, November 17, 1835.

20 *Time* magazine, "Just Around the Backbone of North America," October 7, 1957, www.time.com/time/magazine/article/0,9171,809942,00.html.

21 *Richmond Enquirer* 32, no. 63, December 10, 1935.

22 Jones, *In the Footsteps of Davy Crockett*, 194–95. Jonesboro was established by ferryman Henry Jones in 1815 and became a major hub as both the farthest navigable point upstream on the Red River and a terminus for Trammel's Trace.

23 Shackford, *David Crockett: The Man and the Legend*, 213–14.

24 Pat B. Clark, *The History of Clarksville and Old Red River County* (Dallas: Mathis, Van Nort & Co., 1937), 14–15.

25 Ibid., xiv.

26 Ibid., 12.

27 Shackford, *David Crockett: The Man and the Legend*, 216.

28 *New-Bedford Mercury* 29, no. 34, February 26, 1836.

29 Jones, *In the Footsteps of Davy Crockett*, 199.

30 Levy, *American Legend*, 245.

31 Davis, *Three Roads to the Alamo*, 409.

32 Hutton, Introduction, *Narrative*, xxv.

THIRTY-SIX • EL ALAMO

1 *Arkansas Gazette*, May 10, 1836. This account of the Nacogdoches banquet speech was published more than two months after the fall of the Alamo. Various versions of the speech also appeared in several other newspapers of the day.

2 Jones, *In the Footsteps of Davy Crockett*, 204, quoting *Niles' Weekly Register*, April 9, 1836.

3 Shackford, *David Crockett: The Man and the Legend*, 218–19.

4 Ibid., 216.

5 Ibid., 217–18. John Forbes, *The Handbook of Texas Online*, www.tsha.utexas .edu/handbook/online/view/FF/ff08.html. Forbes was born in Cork, Ireland, in 1797 and immigrated to the United States in 1817. He settled in Cincinnati, OH, and in 1834 moved with his family to Nacogdoches, where he became chairman of the Committee of Vigilance and Public Safety. He was

elected first judge of Nacogdoches Municipality on November 26, 1835, and administered the oath of allegiance to many army recruits, including Crockett, as they passed through Nacogdoches. He went on to become aide-de-camp to Sam Houston and served during the campaigns at Anahuac and San Jacinto. It was said that he acquired Santa Anna's sword. In 1856 he became mayor of Nacogdoches, and he died there in 1880.

6 John H. Jenkins, ed., *Papers of the Texas Revolution*, vol. 4 (Austin: Presidial Press, 1973), 13–14.

7 Davis, *Three Roads to the Alamo*, 414. Corzine came to Texas from Alabama in 1835 and settled near San Augustine. In October 1836 he was elected senator to the First Congress of the Republic of Texas, but he resigned two months later to become judge of the First Judicial District. Corzine died in San Augustine in 1839.

8 Ibid.

9 Copy of original Crockett letter and accompanying transcript from Sally Baker, Crockett Tavern Museum Archives, Morristown, TN.

10 Rod Timanus, *On the Crockett Trail* (Union City, TN: Pioneer Press, 1999), 41. *Handbook of Texas Online*, s.v. "Patton, William Hester," www.tshaonline .org/handbook/online/articles/PP/fpa54.html. Helen Widener, "Republic of Texas—Freedom Fighter—William Patton," *Irving Rambler*, August 2, 2007, 11. At one point there were two William Pattons reported at the Alamo, but neither of them was there on March 6 when the old mission was stormed. The older one was William Hester Patton, a Kentuckian who had commanded a company of Texian insurgents at the siege of Bexar from December 5 through December 10, 1835. This Patton became the aide-de-camp to General Houston. After the Battle of San Jacinto, he was given custody of Santa Anna and accompanied him to Washington, D.C., prior to the Mexican leader's release and subsequent return to Mexico. Patton went on to serve in the Second Congress of the Republic of Texas and was murdered by bandits at his home on the San Antonio River in 1842. The other Patton—Crockett's nephew—may have been sent from the Alamo bearing a message. If so, he thus was spared the fate of the others who perished there. On March 17 his name appeared on the muster rolls of Captain Henry Teal's company of regulars, an outfit that fought at San Jacinto. Although he was due a sizable parcel of land for his military service, Patton probably left Texas soon after his discharge.

11 Hutton, Introduction, *Narrative*, xxix–xxx.

12 H. W. Brands, *Lone Star Nation* (New York: Anchor Books, 2004), 349–50.

13 John M. Swisher, *The Swisher Memoirs*, edited by Rena Maverick Green (San Antonio: Sigmund Press, 1932), 18–19.

14 Ibid.

15 Ibid.

16 Paul Robert Walker, *Remember the Alamo: Texians, Tejanos, and Mexicans Tell Their Stories* (Washington, DC: National Geographic Society, 2007), 34.

17 Michael Wallis and Suzanne Fitzgerald Wallis, *Songdog Diary: 66 Stories From the Road* (Tulsa: Council Oak Publishing, 1996), 146–49. After March 6, 1836, Santa Anna was also called the "Butcher of the Alamo," depending on the side of the border. "His Serene Highness," the moniker Santa Anna preferred, had a love-hate relationship with the Mexican citizens he governed off and on for many years. "If I were God," he once said, "I would wish to be more." He survived a few expulsions, coup attempts, and exiles, as well as battles against the United States and France. The dictator, who had lost a leg to a French cannonball at Veracruz in 1838, died alone, in poverty and mostly forgotten, on June 21, 1876.

18 Davis, *Three Roads to the Alamo*, 204–6.

19 James L. Haley, *Texas: From Frontier to Spindletop* (New York: St. Martin's Press, 1991), 29.

20 Davis, *Three Roads to the Alamo*, 282–83.

21 Amelia Williams, "A Critical Study of the Siege of the Alamo and of the Personnel of Its Defenders," *Southwestern Historical Quarterly* 32, no. 4 (1934): 237. John McGregor was born in Scotland in 1808 and emigrated to Texas in the early 1830s. When Sam Houston put out the call for volunteers, McGregor left his farm, armed with a shotgun and his bagpipes, and rode west to San Antonio, where he became known as the "Piper of the Alamo."

22 Editorial in the *Telegraph and Register*, published at San Felipe de Austin (vol. 1, no. 24), Thursday, March 24, 1836.

23 Shackford, *David Crockett: The Man and the Legend*, 214.

24 Walker, *Remember the Alamo*, 54–55.

25 Levy, *American Legend*, 285–86.

26 Hauck, *Davy Crockett: A Handbook*, 50–51.

27 Marshall J. Doke Jr., "A New Davy Crockett Story," *Heritage* 4 (2007): 29.

28 *Brazoria Courier*, Brazoria, TX, March 31, 1840.

29 *New York Times*, May 18, 1893.

30 Davis, *Three Roads to the Alamo*, 568.

31 A Guide to the José Enrique de la Peña Collection, 1835–1840, 1857, Center for American History, University of Texas at Austin. The bulk of the collection consists of Peña's personal papers, which provide an eyewitness account of the Mexican army's campaign to suppress the Texas Revolution. The personal papers fall into two sections: a field diary of 109 pages and an extended memoir of 400 pages based upon the diary. Peña wrote the memoir by verifying happenings he recorded in his field diary and by adding information based on his fellow officers' reports.

32 "Controversial Alamo Memoir Appears Authentic, Says UT Austin Forgery

Expert," University of Texas at Austin, Office of Public Affairs, May 4, 2000. Following several weeks of evaluation, a University of Texas forgery expert said that he found the memoir's paper consistent with the materials of the period, and watermarks in the diary paper match watermarks in the paper used by the Mexican army at the time. He further declared the narrative to be genuine and said he saw "no signs that the memoir had been tampered with."

33 Hutton, Introduction, *Narrative*, xxxv–xxxvii.

34 The Texas Constitutions of 1836 or 1876 and the U.S. Constitution do not provide explicit provisions for the state's right of secession. Proponents of Texas secession, however, point out that Article 1, Section 1, of the Texas Constitution adopted in 1876 states that "Texas is a free and independent state, subject only to the Constitution of the United States," and makes no mention of the state's being subject to either the U.S. President or U.S. Congress. They also note that the Texas Constitution states, "All political power is inherent in the people . . . they have at all times the inalienable right to alter their government in such manner as they might think proper." In 2009, Texas Governor Rick Perry, as part of a reelection campaign, suggested secession as an alternative that Texas might want to pursue. "There's a lot of different scenarios," Perry said at that time. "We've got a great union. There's absolutely no reason to dissolve it. But if Washington continues to thumb their nose at the American people, you know, who knows what might come out of that. But Texas is a very unique place, and we're a pretty independent lot to boot." The Texas Constitution does clearly spell out an option to divide itself into five separate entities. The Ordinance of Annexation, passed on July 4, 1836, by the Texas Convention, reads: "New States of convenient size not exceeding four in number, in addition to said State of Texas and having sufficient population, may, hereafter by the consent of said State, be formed out of territory thereof, which shall be entitled to admission under the provisions of the Federal Constitution . . ."

BIBLIOGRAPHY

PRIVATE COLLECTIONS

Dorothy Sloan Collection, Dorothy Sloan Rare Books, Austin, Texas
Emily Priddy Collection, Tulsa, Oklahoma
Joseph A. Swann Collection, Maryville, Tennessee
Ron McCoy Collection, Tulsa, Oklahoma

ARCHIVES, MUSEUMS, LIBRARIES, AND HISTORICAL SOCIETIES

Berkeley County Historical Society, Martinsburg, WV
Birmingham Public Library Cartographic Collection, Department of Geography,
    University of Alabama, Tuscaloosa, AL
Buffalo and Erie County Historical Society Archives, Buffalo, NY
Calvin M. McClung Historical Collection, Knoxville, TN
Crockett Tavern Museum, Morristown, TN
Daughters of the Republic of Texas Library at the Alamo, San Antonio, TX
Dolph Briscoe Center for American History, University of Texas at Austin, Austin,
    TX
Drexel University Archives, Philadelphia, PA
East Tennessee Historical Society, Knoxville, TN
East Tennessee History Center, Knoxville, TN
Franklin County, TN, Files, Tennessee Historical Commission
Franklin County Historical Society, Winchester, TN
Gilder-Lehrman Collection, Pierpont Morgan Library, New York, NY
Gowen Papers, Gowen Research Foundation, Lubbock, TX
Great Smoky Mountains Heritage Center, Townsend, TN
G. W. Blunt White Library at Mystic Seaport Museum, Mystic, CT
Harry Ransom Humanities Research Center, University of Texas at Austin, Austin,
    TX
Jefferson County Archives, Dandridge, TN
Library of Congress, Manuscript Division, Washington, D.C.
Mountain Heritage Center and the Hunter Library Special Collections, Western
    Carolina University, Cullowhee, NC

National Archives and Records Administration, Washington, D.C.

Newberry Library, Chicago, IL

New York Public Library, New York, NY

Rosenberg Library, Galveston, TX

San Jacinto Museum, Houston, TX

Tennessee Historical Society, Nashville, TN

Tennessee State Library and Archives, Nashville, TN

Tennessee State Museum, Nashville, TN

University of Tennessee Special Collections Library, Hoskins Library, Knoxville, TN

University of Texas at Austin, Office of Public Affairs

Van Zandt County Genealogical Society, Canton, TX

Woolaroc Museum, Bartlesville, OK

BOOKS

Abbott, John S. C. *David Crockett: His Life and Adventures.* New York: Dodd, Mead, 1874.

Aderman, Ralph M., ed. *The Letters of James Kirke Paulding.* Madison: University of Wisconsin Press, 1962.

Alderman, Pat. *The Overmountain Men.* Johnson City, TN: Overmountain Press, 1970.

Alford, Bobby. *History of Lawrence County, Tennessee.* Published privately by the author, 1994.

Arnow, Harriette Simpson. *Seedtime on the Cumberland.* Lexington: University of Kentucky Press, 1983.

Bagnall, Norma Hayes. *On Shaky Ground: The New Madrid Earthquakes of 1811–1812.* Columbia: University of Missouri Press, 1996.

Beebe, B. F., and James Ralph Johnson. *American Bears.* New York: David McKay Company, 1965.

Benson, John. *The Pictorial Field-Book of the War of 1812.* New York: Harper & Brothers, 1868.

Blair, Walter. *David Crockett: Legendary Frontier Hero.* Rev. ed. Springfield, IL: Lincoln-Herndon Press, 1986.

Blomquist, Ann K., ed. *Cheek's Cross Roads, Tennessee Store Journal, 1802–1807.* Baltimore: Gateway Press, 2001.

Botkin, Benjamin A., ed. *A Treasury of American Folklore.* New York: Crown, 1944.

Bowman, John S., general ed. *The World Almanac of the American West.* New York: World Almanac/Pharos Books, 1986.

Boyer, Paul S., ed. *The Oxford Companion to United States History.* New York: Oxford University Press, 2001.

Brands, H. W. *Lone Star Nation*. New York: Anchor Books, 2004.

———. *Andrew Jackson: His Life and Times*. New York: Anchor Books, 2006.

Brown, Fred. *Marking Time: East Tennessee Historical Markers and the Stories Behind Them*. Knoxville: University of Tennessee Press, 2005.

Brunner, Bernd. *Bears: A Brief History*. New Haven, CT: Yale University Press, 2007.

Burke, James Wakefield. *David Crockett: The Man Behind the Myth*. Austin: Eakin Press, 1984.

Burstein, Andrew. *The Passions of Andrew Jackson*. New York: Alfred A. Knopf, 2003.

———. *The Original Knickerbocker: The Life of Washington Irving*. New York: Basic Books, 2007.

Caldwell, Russell H. *Reelfoot Lake Remembered*. Union City, TN: Caldwell's Office Outfitters, 2005.

Campbell, Randolph B. *Gone to Texas: A History of the Lone Star State*. New York: Oxford University Press, 2003.

Chemerka, William R. *The Davy Crockett Almanac and Book of Lists*. Austin: Eakin Press, 2000.

Clark, Pat B. *The History of Clarksville and Old Red River County*. Dallas: Mathis, Van Nort & Co., 1937.

Clarke, Matthew St. Clair (probable author). *Sketches and Eccentricities of Colonel David Crockett of West Tennessee*. New York: J. & J. Harper, 1833.

Clayton, Lareine Warden. *Stories of Early Inns and Taverns of the East Tennessee Country*. Nashville: National Society of the Colonial Dames of America in the State of Tennessee, 1995.

Clifton, Juanita, as told to Lou Harshaw. *Reelfoot and the New Madrid Quake*. Asheville, NC: Victor Publishing Company, 1980.

Cobia, Manley F. Jr. *Journey into the Land of Trials*. Franklin, TN: Hillsboro Press, Providence Publishing Corp., 2003.

Collins, James. *Autobiography of a Revolutionary Soldier*. John M. Roberts, ed. Clinton, LA: Feliciana Democrat, 1859; reprinted New York: Arno Press, 1979.

Corlew, Robert E. *Tennessee: A Short History*. Knoxville: University of Tennessee Press, 1981.

Corps, Terry. *Historical Dictionary of the Jacksonian Era and Manifest Destiny*. Lanham, MD: Scarecrow Press, 2006.

Cowan, Samuel K. *Sergeant York and His People*. New York: Grosset & Dunlap, 1922.

Crackel, Theodore J., ed. *The Papers of George Washington*. Charlottesville: University of Virginia Press, 2007.

Crockett, David. *A Narrative of the Life of David Crockett of the State of Tennessee*. Philadelphia: E. L. Carey and A. Hart, 1834.

Dameron, J. David. *King's Mountain: The Defeat of the Loyalists, October 7, 1780*. Cambridge, MA: Da Capo Press, 2003.

Daniel, Alice. *Log Cabins of the Smokies.* Gatlinburg, TN: Great Smoky Mountains Natural History Association, 2000.

Davis, William C. *Three Roads to the Alamo: The Lives and Fortunes of David Crockett, James Bowie, and William Barret Travis.* New York: HarperCollins, 1998.

———. *Lone Star Rising: The Revolutionary Birth of the Texas Republic.* New York: Free Press, 2004.

———. *The Pirates Lafitte: The Treacherous World of the Corsairs of the Gulf.* New York: Harcourt, 2005.

Derr, Mark. *The Frontiersman: The Real Life and Many Legends of Davy Crockett.* New York: William Morrow and Company, 1993.

Dobson, David. *Directory of Scots in the Carolinas, 1680–1830.* Baltimore: Genealogical Printing Company, 2002.

Dorson, Richard M. *American Folklore.* Chicago: University of Chicago Press, 1959.

Dykeman, Wilma. *The French Broad.* New York: Henry Holt and Company, 1955.

———. *Tennessee, A History.* New York: W. W. Norton & Company, 1984.

East, Ben. *Bears.* New York: Crown, 1977.

Ellis, Edward S. *The Life of Colonel David Crockett.* Philadelphia: Porter and Coates, 1884.

Family Histories: Franklin County, Tennessee, 1807–1996. Winchester, TN: Franklin County Historical Society, 1996.

Fehrenbach, T. R. *Lone Star: A History of Texas and Texans.* New York: Collier Books, 1980.

Feldman, Jay. *When the Mississippi Ran Backwards: Empire, Intrigue, Murder, and the New Madrid Earthquakes.* New York: Free Press, 2005.

Finger, John R. *Tennessee Frontiers: Three Regions in Transition.* Bloomington & Indianapolis: Indiana University Press, 2001.

Fischer, David Hackett. *Albion's Seed: Four British Folkways in America.* New York: Oxford University Press, 1989.

Folmsbee, Stanley J. *A Narrative of the Life of David Crockett of the State of Tennessee* by David Crockett, A Facsimile Edition with an Introduction and Annotations by James A. Shackford and Stanley J. Folmsbee. Knoxville: University of Tennessee Press, 1973.

Foster, Austin P. *Counties of Tennessee, A Reference of Historical and Statistical Facts for Each of Tennessee's Counties.* Nashville: Department of Education, State of Tennessee, 1923. Reprinted by The Overmountain Press, 1998.

French, Janie Stewart, and Zella Armstrong. *The Crockett Family and Connecting Lines.* Bristol, TN: King Printing Co., 1928.

Fulmore, Z. T. *The History and Geography of Texas as Told in County Names.* Austin: E. L. Steck, 1915.

Garland, Hamlin, ed. *The Autobiography of David Crockett.* New York: Charles Scribner's Sons, 1923.

Geiser, Robert L. *The Illusion of Caring.* Boston: Beacon Press, 1973.

Gregory, Jack, and Rennard Strickland. *Sam Houston with the Cherokees, 1829–1833*. Norman: University of Oklahoma Press, 1967.

Grime, J. H. *Recollections of a Long Life*. Lebanon, TN: Self-published,1930.

Groneman, William, III. *Death of a Legend: The Myth and Mystery Surrounding the Death of Davy Crockett*. Plano, TX: Republic of Texas Press, 1999.

———. *David Crockett: Hero of the Common Man*. New York: Forge Books, Tom Doherty Associates, 2005.

Guild, Joseph C. *Old Times in Tennessee*. Nashville: Tavel, Eastman & Howell, 1878.

Haley, James L. *Texas: From Frontier to Spindletop*. New York: St. Martin's Press, 1991.

———. *Sam Houston*. Norman: University of Oklahoma Press, 2002.

Hardin, Stephen. *Texian Iliad: A Military History of the Texas Revolution*. Austin: University of Texas Press, 1994.

Harper, Herbert L., ed. *Houston and Crockett: Heroes of Tennessee and Texas: An Anthology*. Nashville: Tennessee Historical Commission, 1986.

Hauck, Richard Boyd. *Davy Crockett: A Handbook*. Lincoln: University of Nebraska Press, 1982.

Henderson, William Douglas, and Jimmy W. Claborn. *Hamblen County: A Pictorial History*. Virginia Beach, VA: Donning Company, 1995.

History of Shelby County, Tennessee. Nashville: Goodspeed Publishing Co., 1886–1887.

Hoig, Stan. *Jesse Chisholm: Ambassador of the Plains*. Niwot, CO: University Press of Colorado, 1991.

Holbrook, Stewart H. *Davy Crockett: From the Backwoods of Tennessee to the Alamo*. New York: Random House, 1955.

Hough, Emerson. *The Way to the West, and the Lives of Three Early Americans: Boone—Crockett—Carson*. Indianapolis: Bobbs-Merrill, 1903.

Howe, Daniel Walker. *What Hath God Wrought*. New York: Oxford University Press, 2007.

Hutton, Paul. Introduction. *A Narrative of the Life of David Crockett of the State of Tennessee*. Lincoln: University of Nebraska Press, 1987; reprinted from the 1834 edition published by E. L. Carey and A. Hart, Philadelphia.

Ingmire, Frances T. *Franklin County, Tennessee, Abstracted Wills, 1808–1875*. St. Louis: Frances Terry Ingmire, 1984.

James, Marquis. *The Raven: The Life Story of Sam Houston*. Grosset & Dunlap, 1929.

Jenkins, John H., ed. *Papers of the Texas Revolution*. Austin: Presidial Press, 1973.

Jiji, Vera M., ed. *A Sourcebook of Interdisciplinary Materials in American Drama: J. K. Paulding, The Lion of the West*. Brooklyn: Produced by the Program for Culture at Play: Multimedia Studies in American Drama, Humanities Institute, Brooklyn College, 1983.

Johnson, Michael L. *Hunger for the Wild: America's Obsession with the Untamed West*. Lawrence: University Press of Kansas, 2007.

Jones, Kathryn E. *Crockett Cousins*. Graham, TX: K. E. Jones, 1984, 2nd printing, rev. ed., 1986.

Jones, Randell. *In the Footsteps of Davy Crockett*. Winston-Salem, NC: John F. Blair, 2006.

Kelley, Paul. *Historic Fort Loudon*. Vonore, TN: Fort Loudon Association, 1958.

Kennedy, Roger G. *Rediscovering America*. Boston: Houghton Mifflin, 1990.

Kephart, Horace. *Our Southern Highlanders*. Knoxville: University of Tennessee Press, 1976.

Kilgore, Dan. *How Did Davy Die?* College Station: Texas A&M University Press, 1978.

Lake County Tennessee Historical Society. *History and Families, Lake County Tennessee, 1870–1992*. Paducah, KY: Turner Publishing, 1993.

Langguth, A. J. *Union 1812: The Americans Who Fought the Second War of Independence*. New York: Simon & Schuster, 2006.

Lawrence County Historical Society. *Lawrence County, Tennessee, Pictorial History*. Paducah, KY: Turner Publishing, 1994.

Lefler, Hugh Talmadge, ed. *A New Voyage to Carolina by John Lawson*. Chapel Hill: University of North Carolina Press, 1967.

Levy, Buddy. *American Legend: The Real-Life Adventures of Davy Crockett*. New York: Berkley Books, 2005.

Lofaro, Michael A. *Davy Crockett: The Man, the Legend, the Legacy*. Knoxville: University of Tennessee Press, 1985.

Lofaro, Michael A., and Joe Cummings, eds. *Crockett at Two Hundred: New Perspectives on the Man and the Myth*. Knoxville: University of Tennessee Press, 1989.

Lord, Walter. *A Time to Stand*. New York: Harper & Row, 1961.

Lossing, Benson John. *The Pictorial Field-Book of the War of 1812*. New York: Harper & Brothers, 1868.

Mankiller, Wilma, and Michael Wallis. *Mankiller: A Chief and Her People*. New York: St. Martin's Press, 1993.

McCutcheon, Marc. *The Writer's Guide to Everyday Life in the 1800s*. Cincinnati: Writer's Digest Books, 1993.

Mooney, James. *Myths of the Cherokee and Sacred Formulas of the Cherokees*. From the 19th and 7th Annual Reports, Bureau of American Ethnology. Reprint. Nashville: Elder Booksellers, 1982. Reproduced 1982, originally published by the Bureau of American Ethnology in 1891 and 1900.

Moore, John Trotwood, and Austin P. Foster. *Tennessee, The Volunteer State*. Nashville and Chicago: S. J. Clarke, 1923.

Moore, Warren. *Mountain Voices: A Legacy of the Blue Ridge and Great Smokies*. Chester, CT: Globe Pequot Press, 1988.

Moore, Wayne C. "Paths of Migration." In *First Families of Tennessee: A Register of Early Settlers and Their Present-Day Descendants*. Knoxville: East Tennessee Historical Society, 2000.

Morgan, Robert. *Boone: A Biography*. Chapel Hill: Algonquin, 2007.

Moss, Kay K. *Southern Folk Medicine, 1750–1820*. Columbia: University of South Carolina Press, 1999.

Muncy, Estle P. *People and Places of Jefferson County*. Rogersville, TN: East Tennessee Printing Co., 1994.

Myers, John. *The Alamo*. Lincoln: University of Nebraska Press, 1948.

Nabokov, Peter. *Native American Testimony: A Chronicle of Indian-White Relations from Prophecy to the Present, 1492–1992*. New York: Viking Penguin, 1991.

Old Buncombe County Genealogical Society. *Old Buncombe County Heritage Book*. Volume 2. Winston-Salem, NC: Hunter Publishing Co., 1981.

Ovid. *Metamorphoses*. Dublin: John Exshaw. With the notes of John Minellias, and others, in English: with a prose version of the author by Nathan Bailey. 1774.

Parrington, Vernon Louis. *Main Currents in American Thought*. New York: Harcourt, Brace, 1927.

Parton, James. *The Life of Andrew Jackson*. In three volumes. Vol. 1. New York: Mason Brothers, 1860.

Paulding, William I. *Literary Life of James K. Paulding*. New York: Charles Scribner's Sons, 1867.

Peña, José Enrique de la. *With Santa Anna in Texas: A Personal Narrative of the Revolution*. Translated and edited by Carmen Perry. College Station: Texas A&M University Press, 1975.

Petersen, Gert. *David Crockett, The Volunteer Rifleman: An Account of His Life, while a Resident of Franklin County, 1812–1817*. Winchester, TN: Franklin County Historical Society, 2007.

Phelan, James Jr. *History of Tennessee: The Making of a State*. Boston and New York: Houghton, Mifflin, 1888.

Ramsey, J. G. M. *The Annals of Tennessee*. Charleston, SC: Walkers & Jones, 1853. Reprinted 1967 for the East Tennessee Historical Society, Knoxville; reprinted 1999 by Overmountain Press.

Raphael, Ray. *A People's History of the American Revolution*. New York: New Press, 2001.

Remini, Robert V. *Andrew Jackson and the Course of American Empire, 1767–1821*. New York: Harper & Row, 1977.

———. *The Battle of New Orleans*. New York: Penguin, 1999.

Ritchie, Robert C., and Paul Andrew Hutton, eds. *Frontier and Region*. San Marino, CA: Huntington Library Press, 1997.

Roosevelt, Theodore. *Hunting the Grizzly and Other Sketches*. New York: G. P. Putnam & Sons, 1902.

Rourke, Constance. *American Humor: A Study of the National Character.* New York: Harcourt, Brace and Co., 1931.

———. *Davy Crockett.* New York: Harcourt, Brace and Co., 1934.

Rubin, Joan Shelley. *Constance Rourke and American Culture.* Chapel Hill: University of North Carolina Press, 1980.

Schlesinger, Arthur M., Jr., gen. ed. *The Almanac of American History.* New York: Bramhall House, 1986.

Schullery, Paul. *The Bear Hunter's Century: Profiles from the Golden Age of Bear Hunting.* New York: Dodd, Mead & Company, 1989.

Seigenthaler, John. *James K. Polk.* New York: Times Books, 2004.

Shackford, James Atkins. *David Crockett: The Man and the Legend.* Edited by John B. Shackford. Chapel Hill: University of North Carolina Press, 1956.

Slotkin, Richard. *Regeneration Through Violence: The Mythology of the American Frontier, 1600–1860.* Middletown, CT: Wesleyan University Press, 1973. Reprinted by University of Oklahoma Press, 2000.

Smith, Henry Nash. *Virgin Land: The American West as Symbol and Myth.* Cambridge, MA: Harvard University Press, 1978.

Smith, Jonathan K. T. *The Land Holdings of Colonel David Crockett in West Tennessee.* Jackson, TN: Mid-West Tennessee Genealogical Society, 2003.

Speeches on the Passage of the Bill for the Removal of the Indians, Delivered in the Congress of the United States, April and May, 1830. Boston: Perkins and Marvin, 1830; New York: Jonathan Leavitt, 1830.

Sprague, William C. *Davy Crockett.* New York: Macmillan, 1915.

Stewart, David, and Ray Knox. *The Earthquake That Never Went Away.* Marble Hill, MO: Gutenberg-Richter Publications, 1993.

Strutin, Michal. *Gristmills of the Smokies.* Gatlinburg, TN: Great Smoky Mountains Natural History Association, 2000.

Swisher, John M. *The Swisher Memoirs.* Edited by Rena Maverick Green. San Antonio: Sigmund Press, 1932.

Taylor, Quintard. *In Search of the Racial Frontier.* New York: W. W. Norton & Company, 1998.

Thompson, Ernest T. *The Fabulous David Crockett, His Life and Times in Gibson County.* Rutherford, TN: David Crockett Memorial Association, 1956.

Timanus, Rod. *On the Crockett Trail.* Union City, TN: Pioneer Press, 1999.

Tocqueville, Alexis de. *Journey to America.* Translated by George Lawrence. Edited by J. P. Mayer. London: Faber and Faber, 1959.

———. *Democracy in America.* Translated by George Lawrence. Edited by J. P. Mayer. New York: Harper & Row, 1966.

Tryon, Warren S., ed. *A Mirror for Americans: Life and Manners in the United States 1790–1870 as Recorded by American Travelers.* Chicago: University of Chicago Press, 1952.

Tunis, Edwin. *Frontier Living*. Cleveland and New York: World Publishing Company, 1961.

Walker, Paul Robert. *Remember the Alamo: Texians, Tejanos, and Mexicans Tell Their Stories*. Washington, DC: National Geographic Society, 2007.

Wallace, Irving. *The Fabulous Showman: The Life and Times of P. T. Barnum*. New York: Alfred A. Knopf, 1959.

Wallis, Michael, and Suzanne Fitzgerald Wallis. *Songdog Diary: 66 Stories from the Road*. Tulsa: Council Oak Publishing, 1996.

Webb, Jim. *Born Fighting: How the Scots-Irish Shaped America*. New York: Broadway Books, 2004.

Weber, David J., ed. *Foreigners in Their Native Land: Historical Roots of the Mexican Americans*. Albuquerque: University of New Mexico Press, 1973.

————. *The Mexican Frontier, 1821–1846*. Albuquerque: University of New Mexico Press, 1982.

Winik, Jay. *April 1865: The Month That Saved America*. New York: HarperCollins, 2001.

Woodward, Grace Steele. *The Cherokees*. Norman: University of Oklahoma Press, 1963.

York, Alvin C. *Sergeant York: His Own Life Story and War Diary*. New York: Doubleday & Doran, 1928.

PERIODICALS, NEWSPAPERS, AND JOURNALS

Adams Sentinel, Gettysburg, PA, December 17, 1828.

Adams Sentinel, vol. 9, no. 6, Gettysburg, PA, November 26, 1834.

Arkansas Gazette, Little Rock, AR, May 10,1836.

"The Bear Hunter." *Time*, January 4, 1960.

Bent Creek Baptists Church Minutes, Saturday, February 4, 1803.

Blair, Walter. "Six Davy Crocketts." *Southwest Review* 25, July 1940.

Bland, Joy. "Genealogical Discovery." *Go Ahead: Newsletter of the Direct Descendants and Kin of David Crockett*, 25, no. 1, August 2008.

Brazoria Courier, Brazoria, TX, March 31, 1840.

Brown, Fred. "The Stoneciphers," *Knoxville News-Sentinel*, September 22, 1996.

Catalogue of the Centennial Exhibition Commemorating the Founding of the Mount Vernon Ladies' Association of the Union, 1853–1953, Mount Vernon, VA: 1953.

Charleston Courier, August 31, 1835.

Daly, Walter J., M.D. "The 'Slows,' The Torment of Milk Sickness on the Midwest Frontier." *Indiana Magazine of History* 102 (March 2006). Bloomington: Trustees of Indiana University, 2006.

David Crockett letter to George Patton, January 27, 1829. Transcript provided by Joe N. Bone, manager-curator, Crockett Cabin-Museum, Rutherford, TN.

Davis, Curtis Carroll. "A Legend at Full-Length: Mr. Chapman Paints Colonel Crockett—and Tells About It." *Proceedings of the American Antiquarian Society.* Worcester, MA: American Antiquarian Society, April 1960.

Doke, Marshall J., Jr. "A New Davy Crockett Story." *Heritage* 4 (2007). Austin: Texas Historical Foundation.

The Gazette, Little Rock, AR, November 17, 1835.

The Gettysburg Star & Republican Banner, Gettysburg, PA, March 11, 1834.

A Guide to the José Enrique de la Peña Collection, 1835–1840, 1857, Center for American History, University of Texas at Austin.

Heale, M. J. "The Role of the Frontier in Jacksonian Politics: David Crockett and the Myth of the Self-Made Man." *Western History Quarterly* 4 (October 1973).

Henderson, Cherel B., ed. *Tennessee Ancestors* 17, no. 3. Knoxville: East Tennessee Historical Society, December 2001.

Hutton, Paul Andrew. "Mr. Crockett Goes to Washington." *American History* 35, no. 1 (April 2000). Leesburg, VA: Primedia History Group.

Jackson Gazette, Jackson, TN. Circular Letter "To the Republican Voters of the 9th Congressional District of the State of Tennessee," David Crockett, Gibson County, September 16, 1826; February 14, 1829; March 7, 1829.

Jacobs, John L. Cullasaja, Macon County, NC, November 22, 1884, Tennessee State Library and Archives, Nashville.

Kelly, James C., and Frederick S. Voss. *Davy Crockett: Gentleman from the Cane.* An Exhibition Commemorating Crockett's Life and Legend on the 200th Anniversary of His Birth. Published by the National Portrait Gallery, Smithsonian Institution, City of Washington, and the Tennessee State Museum, Nashville, 1986.

Kinzer, Stephen. "A Worry for Germany: Resurgent Nationalism." *New York Times*, July 27, 1991.

Lofaro, Michael A. "Part II: Davy and Ovid?" University of Tennessee, *Library Development Review*, 2002–2003.

The Mail, Hagerstown, MD, May 9, 1834.

Marquis, Christopher. "Andrew Jackson: Winner and Loser in 1824." *American History* 43, no. 1 (April 2008).

Miles, Guy S. "David Crockett Evolves, 1821–1824," *American Quarterly* 8, no. 1 (Spring 1956).

Missouri Republican, August 15, 1829.

Morning Courier and New York Enquirer, April 27, 1831; November 24, 1831.

Nashville Whig, August 14, 1822.

The Natchez Ariel, Natchez, MS, October 19, 1827.

National Banner and Nashville Whig, September 27, 1824.

National Gazette and Literary Register, Philadelphia, PA, December 29, 1825.

The New-Bedford Mercury, vol. 29, no. 34, New Bedford, MA, February 26, 1836.

The New England Magazine 5 (6), Boston: J. T. and E. Buckingham, December 1833.

New York Times, May 18, 1893.

Niles' Weekly Register, Baltimore, MD, September 7, 1833.

Pearce, James T. "Folk Tales of the Southern Poor-White, 1820–1860." *Journal of American Folklore* 63, no. 250 (October–December 1950).

Purcell, Aaron D., and Michael A Lofaro. "The Davy Crockett Experience, Now Online!" University of Tennessee, *Library Development Review*, 2002–2003.

"Regimental Histories of Tennessee Military Units During the War of 1812." Prepared by Tom Kanon. Tennessee State Library and Archives, Nashville, TN.

Richmond Enquirer, vol. 32, no. 63, Richmond, VA, December 10, 1935.

Spong, John, senior ed. Davy Crockett entry, "The 30 Most Stylish Texans of All Time." *Texas Monthly*, March 2009.

"A Sportsmen's Paradise," *New York Times*, January 11, 1891.

Swann, Joseph A. "The Wedding of David Crockett and Polly Finley." *Go Ahead: Newsletter of the Direct Descendants and Kin of David Crockett* 23, no. 2, December 2006.

Telegraph and Register, published at San Felipe de Austin. Vol. 1, no. 24, March 24, 1836.

The United States Magazine and Democratic Review 17, July 1845.

University of Tennessee Special Collections Library. MS 1225, David Crockett letter "To the Editors" (Gales & Seaton), Weakley County, TN, August 10, 1835.

Widener, Helen. "Republic of Texas—Freedom Fighter—William Patton." *Irving Rambler*, Irving, TX, August 2, 2007.

Williams, Amelia. "A Critical Study of the Siege of the Alamo and of the Personnel of Its Defenders." *Southwestern Historical Quarterly* 32, no. 4, 1934, Austin: Texas State Historical Association.

Working Man's Advocate, New York, May 3, 1834.

ELECTRONIC DOCUMENTS AND SOURCES

Adams, John Quincy. Diary 37, November 11, 1825–June 24, 1828. *The Diaries of John Quincy Adams: A Digital Collection*. Boston, MA: Massachusetts Historical Society, 2009, www.masshist.org/jqadiaries.

Alabama Women's Hall of Fame, http://famousamericans.net/octaviawaltonlevert/.

Alabama Women's Hall of Fame, Octavia Walton Le Vert (1811–1877), www.awhf.org/levert.html.

Alamo Images, Changing Perceptions of a Texas Experience, A Humanities Exhibition, Texas Humanities Resource Center in collaboration with DeGolyer Library, Southern Methodist University, Dallas, TX, www.humanities-interactive.org/texas/alamo/.

Austin, Stephen F. Correspondence to Edward Lovelace (or Josiah Bell), City of Mexico, November 22, 1822. Correspondence Regarding Slavery in Texas, Sons of DeWitt Colony Texas, www.tamu.edu/ccbn/dewitt/dewitt.htm, Wallace L. McKeehan, ed.

Baker, Eugene C. "Stephen F. Austin and the Independence of Texas." *Southwestern Historical Quarterly Online*, 13, no. 4 (1930): 271, www.tsha.utexas.edu/publi cations/journals/shq/online/v013n4/article_1.html.

Bean Family Files, Kraus-Everette Genealogy, www.larkcom.us/ancestry/main/.

Brinkley, Douglas. "The Great Bear Hunt." *Expedition Journal*, May 5, 2001, www .nationalgeographic.com, National Geographic Society, 2004.

Brune, Herman W. "Legend, Lore, & Legacy: Ben Lilly." *Texas Parks and Wildlife Magazine*, 2005, www.tpwmagazine.com/archieve/2003/jan/legend.

John and Margaret Thornbrough Canaday Family, www.freepages.family.rootsweb .ancestry.com/~mygerman.

Correspondence Regarding Slavery in Texas, Sons of DeWitt Colony, Texas, www .tamu.edu/ccbn/dewitt/dewitt.htm, Wallace L. McKeehan, ed.

First Families Old Buncombe (FFOB), Patton Family records, www.obcgs.com/ patton.htm.

Forbes, John. *The Handbook of Texas Online*, www.tsha.utexas.edu/handbook/ online/view/FF/ff08.html.

The Gowen Papers, Gowen Research Foundation, Lubbock, TX, http://freepages .geneaology.roots.web.com/-gowenrf.

Handbook of Texas Online, s.v. "Patton, William Hester," www.tshaonline.org/ handbook/online/articles/PP/fpa54.html.

Hardin, Rozella. "Legendary Mountain Men Live on in Local Folklore." *Eliza- bethton Star*, Elizabethton, TN, September 6, 2000, www.starhq.com/contact/ departments/.

Kanon, Tom. "Brief History of Tennessee in the War of 1812." Nashville: Tennes- see State Library and Archives, 2008, www.tennessee.gov/tsla/history/military/ tn1812.h.

Lollar, Michael. "First Memphis Mayor Receives a Grave Injustice." *Memphis Com- mercial Appeal*, May 26, 2009, www.commercialappeal.com.

McKeehan, Wallace L. Sons of DeWitt Colony, Texas, 1997–2006. The Sylar Fam- ily, www.tamu.edu/ccbn/mckstorysylarframe.htm.

Memphis History.com, www.memphishistory.org/Beginnings/Foundersand Pio- neers/JohnCMclemore/tabid/112/Default.aspx.

Montaigne, Michel de. "Of Age." *Essays of Michel de Montaigne*. Translated by Charles Cotton. Edited by William Carew Hazlitt, 1877, www.fullbooks.com/ The-Essays-of-Montaigne-VB.html.

Conrad "Coonrod" Pile Files, http://homepages.rootsweb.ancestry.com/~bp2000/ fentress/pile_c.htm.

Porterfield, Bill. "Sam Houston, Warts and All." *Texas Monthly*, July 1973, www .texasmonthly.com/1873-07-01/feature6.php.

Rosenthal, Leon S. *A History of Philadelphia's University City.* Philadelphia: West Philadelphia Corporation, 1963, http://uchs.net/Rosenthal/rosenthaltofc.html.

Russell Family Files, Kraus-Everette Genealogy, www.larkcom.us/ancestry/main/.

Shah, Sonia. "Resurgentmalaria.com," www.resurgentmalaria.com/americas, 2006.

Smithwick, Noah. *The Evolution of a State or Recollections of Old Texas Days.* Austin: Gammel Book Company, 1900. Online edition, Southwestern Classics On-Line/ Lone Star Junction, 1997, www.oldcardboard.com/lsj/olbooks/smithwic/otd.htm.

The Tennessee Encyclopedia of History and Culture. Knoxville: University of Tennessee Press, 2002, Online Edition.

Time magazine. "Just Around the Backbone of North America," October 7, 1957, www.time.com/time/magazine/article/0,9171,809942,oo.html.

Tocqueville, Alexis de. Journal Entry, Memphis, TN, December 20, 1831, www .tocqueville.org/tn.htm.

Tuscaloosa, Alabama, Tuscaloosa County, Alabama Department of History and Archives, Montgomery, AL, www.archives.state.al.us/counties/tuscaloo.html.

Van Zandt County Genealogical Society, Canton, TX, www.txgenweb3.org/tx vanzandt/vzgs.htm.

Voelker, David J. www.historytools.org, 2004.

Waller, Preston Lynn, PhD. "Celebrities versus Heroes: A Case Study Using Characters from the Alamo Legend and its Cinematic Interpretation." McLennan Community College, Waco, TX, www.mclennan.edu/faculty/waller/alamo.htm.

Washington, George. *The Papers of George Washington, Digital Edition.* Edited by Theodore J. Crackel. Charlottesville: University of Virginia Press, 2007.

GOVERNMENT DOCUMENTS

Carroll County (TN) Deed Book A, 29–30.

Carroll County (TN) Court Minutes, 1821–26, vol. 1, 50.

Court Records of Washington County, Virginia—Minutes. Vol. 1, 39. August 1778.

Department of the Navy. Naval Historical Center, Washington Navy Yard, Washington, D.C.

Franklin County, TN, Will Book, 1808–1847. Folder 036 A. Franklin County Courthouse Annex, Winchester, TN.

Frederick County (VA) Court Records. Order Bk. 2, 456.

Greene County (NC) Deed Book. Vol. 3, 320, November 27, 1792, John Crockett from St of NC 197 acres Stogdons Fork, Lick Creek, Grant #1243.

Jefferson County Marriage Records Book 1. Entry Number 526. Jefferson County Courthouse, Dandridge, TN.

Jefferson County Marriage and Bond Book, 1792–1840. Marriage Bond, "David Crockett to Polly Finley," August 12, 1806. Jefferson County Courthouse, Dandridge, TN.

Surveyors Entry Book C, Surveyors District II, Entry No. 3944, 414. Tennessee State Archives.

Transcript Copies of Circuit Court File 1808–1835. Jefferson County Archives, Jefferson County Courthouse, Dandridge, TN.

UNPUBLISHED WORKS

Caton, J. L. "Davy Crockett and Polly Finley in Jefferson County." March 1, 1958. Transcription of unpublished memoir of George Cox. Crockett File, Jefferson County Historical Archives, Jefferson County Courthouse, Dandridge, TN.

Johnson, James Strefhan, III. "The Evolution of an American Small Town," Masters of Science in Architecture thesis, Massachusetts Institute of Technology, June 2004.

Peterson, Gert. *A Chronology of the Life of David Crockett.* Unpublished manuscript, 2001.

Reilly, Joe, PhD. Presentation to the International Psychohistorical Association, Fordham University, New York, June 7, 2007.

Swann, Joseph A. "The Early Life & Times of David Crockett, 1786–1812." Unpublished manuscript.

———. "The History of David Crockett's First Rifle." Unpublished paper.

———. Presentation to the East Tennessee Historical Society, Knoxville, February 12, 2003.

INDEX

Page numbers in *italics* refer to illustrations.
Page numbers beginning with 313 refer to endnotes.

ABOUT THE AUTHOR

A best-selling author and award-winning reporter, Michael Wallis is a historian and biographer of the American West who has gained national prominence for a body of work beginning in 1988 with *Oil Man*, his biography of Frank Phillips.

His fifteen other books include *Route 66: The Mother Road*, credited with sparking the resurgence of interest in the highway, as well as *The Real Wild West: The 101 Ranch and the Creation of the American West*, *Mankiller: A Chief and Her People*, *Way Down Yonder in the Indian Nation: Writings from America's Heartland*, *Pretty Boy: The Life and Times of Charles Arthur Floyd*, and *Billy the Kid: The Endless Ride*. His work has appeared in hundreds of national and international magazines and newspapers, including *Time, Life, People, Smithsonian, The New Yorker*, and the *New York Times*.

Wallis has won many prestigious awards and honors. They include the Will Rogers Spirit Award, the Western Heritage Award from the National Cowboy & Western Heritage Museum, the Oklahoma Book Award from the Oklahoma Center for the Book, and the Best Western Nonfiction Award from the Western Writers of America.

He was inducted into the Writers Hall of Fame of America and the Oklahoma Professional Writers Hall of Fame, and was the first inductee into the Oklahoma Route 66 Hall of Fame. He received the Arrell Gibson Lifetime Achievement Award from the Oklahoma Center for the Book, as well as the Lynn Riggs Award and the first John Steinbeck Award.

A charismatic speaker who has lectured extensively throughout the United States, Wallis was featured as the voice of the Sheriff in *Cars*, an animated feature film from Pixar Studios.

Wallis and his wife, Suzanne Fitzgerald Wallis, make their home in Tulsa, Oklahoma.